In Media Res

THE GRIOT PROJECT BOOK SERIES

Editor:
Carmen Gillespie, Bucknell University

The Griot is a central figure in many West African cultures. Historically, the Griot held many functions, including as a community historian, cultural critic, indigenous artist, and collective spokesperson. Borrowing from this rich tradition, the Bucknell University Griot Institute for Africana Studies and the Griot Project Book Series define the Griot as a metaphor for the academic and creative interdisciplinary exploration of the arts, literatures, and cultures of African America, Africa, and the African diaspora.

The publications of the Griot Project Series consist of scholarly monographs and creative works devoted to the interdisciplinary exploration of the aesthetic, artistic and cultural products and intellectual currents of historical and contemporary African America and of the African diaspora using narrative as a thematic and theoretical framework for the selection and execution of its projects. The series will be edited by the Director of the Bucknell University Griot Insitute, Carmen Gillespie, and considers potential publications in Africana studies from a wide range of disciplines.

The series aims to produce three books during each three-year period, beginning with the year 2011. Each book will be approximately 100–300 manuscript pages in length and will generally have a minimum 500-book print run. The audience for the books produced by the Griot Project Series will be academics, artists, and will include a lay audience, as well. We ask potential authors to submit for consideration works that have expansive and inclusive appeal and significance.

Titles in the series

James Braxton Peterson, ed. *In Media Res: Race, Identity, and Pop Culture in the Twenty-First Century*

Myron Hardy, *Catastrophic Bliss*

Carmen Gillespie, ed. *The Clearing: Forty Years With Toni Morrison, 1970–2010*

In Media Res

Race, Identity, and Pop Culture in the Twenty-First Century

Edited by James Braxton Peterson

BUCKNELL UNIVERSITY PRESS
Lewisburg

Published by Bucknell University Press
Copublished by The Rowman & Littlefield Publishing Group, Inc.
4501 Forbes Boulevard, Suite 200, Lanham, Maryland 20706
www.rowman.com

Unit A, Whitacre Mews, 26-34 Stannary Street, London SE11 4AB

Copyright © 2014 by Rowman & Littlefield for edited collections

All rights reserved. No part of this book may be reproduced in any form or by any electronic or mechanical means, including information storage and retrieval systems, without written permission from the publisher, except by a reviewer who may quote passages in a review.

British Library Cataloguing in Publication Information Available

Library of Congress Cataloging-in-Publication Data Available

Cloth: 978-1-61148-649-0
Electronic: 978-1-61148-650-6

∞™ The paper used in this publication meets the minimum requirements of American National Standard for Information Sciences—Permanence of Paper for Printed Library Materials, ANSI/NISO Z39.48-1992.

Printed in the United States of America

This book is dedicated to my Mom

Barbara Josephine Delaney-Green Peterson

Thank you for bringing me into this world *in medias res*

Contents

List of Illustrations ix

Acknowledgments xi

Introduction: Into the Midst of Things 1
James Braxton Peterson

Part I: Head Matter: The Mind and the Mask 9

1 An Empire State of Mind 11
Imani Perry

2 Consolidating a Hip Hop Nation: Revisiting the Videotaped Police Beating of Rodney King, Twenty Years Later 21
Tanji Gilliam

3 Head on Straight, Mask on Crooked: MF DOOM and the Trope of the Mask 35
Nicholas James

4 Superhero Aesthetics in Hip Hop Culture 49
Will Boone

Part II: Visual Matter — 71

5 I Have a Meme: Photography, Interactive Memory, and Digital Commemorations of the March on Washington — 73
Paul M. Farber

6 How Deep? Skin Deep? A Case Study on Shameful National Orientations — 87
Emily Churilla

7 Faggoty/White/Uniform: Gays in the Military and *A Few Good Men* — 101
Scott St. Pierre

Part III: Global Flows — 117

8 Selected Poems — 119
Suheir Hammad

9 The Communal Womb in Haile Gerima's *Sankofa* — 125
Belinda Monique Waller-Peterson

10 South Asian Hip Hop Wannabes and the Chavs Who Love Them: The Blackening of British Culture in Gautam Malkani's *Londonstani* — 143
Delores B. Phillips

11 "A True and Faithful Account of Mr. Ota Benga the Pygmy, written by M. Berman, Zookeeper," — 169
Adam Mansbach

Part IV: Culture of Personality — 179

12 Richard Pryor's Pain: From Stand-Up Comedy to Hollywood Film — 181
Sean Springer

13 You Are Now Tuned Into the . . . Greatest: Jay-Z and the Spectacle of the Cool — 201
Wilfredo Gomez

14 Disassembling the "Matrix of Domination": Janelle Monae's Transformative Vision — 215
Carrie Walker

15 "Dreams of the Drum": A Keynote Address — 239
Michael Eric Dyson

Bibliography — 251

Index — 273

About the Contributors — 287

List of Illustrations

3.1	"Born Like This Again," Computer Image, art by John Jennings	34
4.1	"Super G," Computer Image, art by John Jennings	48
5.1	"I Have a Meme," Computer Image, art by John Jennings	72
11.1	"Almost Native," Computer Image, art by John Jennings	168
12.1	"Tears of a Clown," Computer Image, art by John Jennings	180
14.1	"Metropolis Reduxxed," Computer Image, art by John Jennings	214

Acknowledgments

A collection of this size and scope requires a genuine communal effort to bring it to fruition. And in fact, *In Media Res* relies on the collective efforts of multiple academic and artistic communities. First and foremost I would like to acknowledge and thank all of the contributors to this volume. You can read about them all in the contributors section but please note that in addition to writing these pieces—that is, dealing with my editorial nagging for some time now—each of the contributors to this volume have also presented their work, shared their research, and/or artistry with university students and scholars at the University of Pennsylvania, Penn State Abington, Bucknell University and/or Lehigh University. In most cases, these gracious folks have shared their important works at multiple institutions. Thank you all for accepting my invitations over the years and for making university programming a centerpiece of my institutional service throughout my professional career. I believe that some of the most important work that I do as a scholar is to expose my students to extraordinary thinkers, activists, artists, poets, novelists, and scholars. My hope is that this collection shares these experiences with an even broader audience.

In Media Res actually began as a conference, a series of events, papers, performances, and lectures delivered at Bucknell University in the spring of 2009. Some of the most energetic students that I have ever engaged were undergraduates at Bucknell during the four years that I just so happened to be there. "In Media Res," the conference, realized those efforts to critically engage university programming through the collective agency of students thoroughly committed to social justice, both on campus and beyond. Mahdi Woodard, Nadia Sasso, Andrew Yaspan, and too many others to name here were instrumental in developing the intellectually engaged community that would ultimately organize the conference and make this volume possible. I have to also acknowledge my extraordinary colleagues at Bucknell—especially Shara McCallum, Linden Lewis, Nina Banks, Jim Lavine, Carmen Gillespie and the entire English Department. There are also many people who participated in the "In Media Res" conference or who have given their time and effort to accept an invitation from me and speak or perform on a campus at which I have worked over the years. Unfortunately we could not include all of their work; I wish we could have collected two volumes. Special thanks to Barry Long, April Silver, Gbenga Akinnagbe, Martha Diaz, and so many others whose work I genuinely admire.

This volume could also not have been completed without great support from my current colleagues at Lehigh University. Faculty in the Africana Studies Program, Bill Scott, Ted Morgan, Seth Moglen, Saladin Ambar, Vera Fennell, Bruce Whitehouse, Stephanie Powell Watts, Kashi Johnson, Berrisford Boothe, Kwame Essien, Darius Williams, Susan Kart, Imaani El-Burki, and Monica Miller have all worked diligently to help realize our programmatic vision. THANK YOU! I would also like to acknowledge and thank Donald Hall, the dean of our College of Arts and Sciences (CAS). Support from CAS enabled me to finish this project, and for that I am truly grateful.

I am also truly grateful for the time, patience, and editorial support from everyone at Bucknell University Press, especially Greg Clingham. Throughout this process, I often struggled to meet deadlines, keep in contact with all of the contributors, and generally execute the logistics of editing a volume. Bronwen Durocher was my editorial assistant for this project. Bronwen's work ethic, her attention to detail, and her outstanding organizational skills all helped to make this volume possible. Thank you so much for all of your emails, editorial suggestions, and logistical support.

Finally I want to thank my FAMILY—my children, Breanna and James, and my life partner, Belinda. Without your patience with me and your love for me, NONE of this would be possible. I LOVE YOU.

Introduction
Into the Midst of Things
James Braxton Peterson

Organizing programs for university communities continues to be one of the most challenging aspects of the academic profession. Many students feel as if the programming on college campuses has pronounced "in medias res" qualities. Backgrounds on the lives of invited speakers are some how left out of the biographies and other promotional materials made available for their visits. Related stories regarding these speakers' experiences and accomplishments are likewise absent from the materials promoting their campus appearances. Students, staff, and faculty understand these events as a challenge to their intellectual community. They collectively feel the imperative to question these and other campus narratives. They feel the critical need for a thoughtful, well-researched response. Students recognize contextual fragmentation in the world—and see the need to address moments of political disparity and informational flux. Generally speaking, they know that when narratives of history, culture, and/or religion represent only fractions of a whole, or fragments of a truth, that they have to pick up the conversation in the only place that they can—in the middle. Students do their homework and unlike a lecture series where the authority of the speakers dominates the discourse, the college and university programs upon which this project is based became one way for students to proactively engage in intellectual exchanges, the themes of which they could claim authorship. The rules of truncated speaker biographies and the acceptance of a moderated, superficial Q & A must be subject to sustained critique. Students and staff at all of the institutions at which I have had an opportunity to work organize forums designed to discuss the lectures delivered by campus speakers before and/or after their arrival. Students' efforts to engage served as a catalyst to a range of programs, symposia, speakers, and an "In Media Res" conference—programs designed to account for the middle-of-the-game nature of traditional university programming; the general feeling being that entering in the midst of things reduces the discourse to a litany of miscues and misunderstandings.

The Latin phrase, *in medias res* literally translates as "in the middle of things" or "into the middle of affairs." It is ironically considered a literary convention—ironic because the term stems from the oral tradition of performing epics such as the *Iliad* and the *Odyssey*. "The origin of the device lies in the traditional nature of early Greek literature: the audience was familiar with the stories and the singers could therefore start at whatever point they thought most effective."[1] The challenge for students on college campuses in the twenty-first century is that too often their limited familiarity with programmatic narratives precludes them from fully understanding the "in medias res" quality of too many college or university offerings. A narrative that begins *in medias res* requires the use of other literary (or verbal as it were) techniques to make the story whole. Some of these include flashbacks, flashing forward, analepsis, and other anachronistic strategies. Technically speaking, the aforementioned examples of invited lecturers/performers and the discourses that did or did not emerge (with respect to the narratives that might have better contextualized them) do not immediately qualify as examples of the literary technique known as in medias res. In order for them to be identified as such they would have had to have been intentionally and strategically executed. There would have been some flashbacks or other analeptic approaches that fleshed out the lives of these speakers and performers. Instead—and here's where the experiences and efforts referenced above match up well with the literary device—the university community enters these dialogues, ideologies, performances, and lectures at crucial moments in both the university's historical narrative as well as in the narratives of the lives of the lecturer/speaker/performer in question.

The images, speeches, conference papers, academic essays, and creative writing collected in this volume represent programs produced and organized on college campuses (throughout the state of Pennsylvania) in the active spirit of progressive student engagement. The content of this collection also represents the efforts of students who assumed the charge to make their educational experience more intellectually and politically satisfying. Some of this effort requires a direct embrace of those issues and areas of inquiry for which an "in medias res" start does not necessarily disadvantage students. In the many programs represented by papers, speeches, stories, poems and essays in this project, those issues and areas of inquiry center on campus diversity especially as campus/university diversity relates to race, identity, and popular culture at the national and global levels. Universities will continue to experience the growing pains that attend certain diversity directives—especially the recruitment and retention of women faculty and faculty of color and the important task of admitting (and retaining) students of color and students from different socioeconomic backgrounds. They must do so by providing a sense of community for students who may not feel comfortable in the middle of nowhere. These crucial and critically momentous times offer university communities an opportunity to dig deeper into the lives, life's work, and ideologies of those who would contribute to the public sphere and social climate of our intellectual communities. In fact, this challenge invites a deeper and more profound engagement within the university community. The decision to critically and intellectually engage the intersections of various social issues—especially those that focus on race, gender, and popular culture and to do so at the university—has been made.

This volume wrestles with the sense of popular culture captured in Stuart Hall's formative essay on black popular culture. According to Hall: "[t]he role of the 'popular' in popular culture is to fix the authenticity of popular forms, rooting them in the experiences of popular communities from which they draw their strength, allowing us to see them as expressive of a particular subordinate social life that resists being constantly made over as low and outside."[2] Not all of the iterations of "the popular" in this volume fit neatly into the category of the "subordinate social life"; in fact many of the examples/subjects analyzed by the scholars, artists, and intellectuals in this volume are constitutive components of popular cultural texts that seem to serve traditional hegemonic purposes; many of these texts: Jay-Z's "Empire State of Mind," *A Few Good Men*, or the truncated Rodney King video are features of commodified culture. Hall is again instructive here, arguing that "as popular culture has historically become the dominant form of global culture, so it is at the same time the scene, *par excellence*, of commodification, of the industries where culture enters directly into the circuits of a dominant technology—the circuits of power and capital."[3]

In *Understanding Popular Culture*, John Fiske argues that: "popular forces transform cultural commodity into cultural resource, pluralize the meanings and pleasures it offers, evade or resist its disciplinary efforts, fracture its homogeneity or coherence, raid or poach its terrain."[4] The popular forces on campuses (across universities) demanded programs and/or speakers who would directly confront efforts to sublimate the full story of diversity, the history of oppression, or the righteous indignation of progressives in this neoliberal moment. Those popular forces are at least in part represented in the selections collected in this volume. Together, these selections function as a small part of the cultural resources that students (especially, but not only) require to "transform cultural commodity into cultural resource," to salvage narratives from the confusion of the "in medias res" effects on university programming. In effect, the selections collected here offer "other traditions of representation" to the university community and the world beyond.[5] Popular culture, race, and identity serve as coordinates through which new traditions of representation have and can be realized. And it is the programs that deal directly with the popular, especially where it intersects with issues of race, racism, and identity, that speak most poignantly of and to new traditions of representation.

The planning committee for one such program, a symposium from which several of the academic essays in this volume derive, decided to play on the phrase *in medias res* in two ways—one visible and one not so visible. First, we dropped the *s* from the Latin, "medias" to arrive at its etymological derivative, "media"—this play is not so original—but serves the purpose of highlighting the symposium's central concern with the platforms upon/through which so much of these narratives (histories, cultures, and experiences) are generated and perhaps the ways in which they are decimated or become reductive. The second play hinges on the alternate pronunciations of the Latin term for things or affairs. Res can be pronounced with a long *e* sound closely approximating the long *a* in the term, Race. "In Media Race," if you will, then sharpened the focus on the conceptual cornerstones of that effort: race, identity, and popular culture. This deconstruction of classic literary devices was a consistent point of discussion, some confusion, and even contention throughout the symposium planning process. More than once, colleagues and friends assisted us in its clarification and figurative distinction from/between the Latin original and the nuanced sense with which we decided to project it. I suppose that it is difficult to *signify* in Latin.

The contributors to this project recognize that we all enter these discussions "in medias res." The selections collected here function as a map—they are a key to understanding a vast web featuring a complicated strata of media, misogyny, racism, and politics—much of which we tend to ignore in favor of a sound bite, angry emails, a quick comeback, a provocative tweet, or a trendy Facebook cause. In the signifying spirit of the "In Media Res" symposium, the volume opens with Imani Perry's brilliant reclamation and redefinition of the notion of "empire" in Jay-Z and Alicia Keys' super popular single. Professor Perry's address, edited and essentially reproduced in its speakerly form here, wrestles with contemporary racial inequality through the veneer of the alleged post-racial moment. For Perry, the challenges presented by racial inequality have become somewhat obscured in our national discourse, partially because of the hopeful promise of the inaugural black presidency and partially because we are still willfully reluctant to critically discuss race in the public sphere. Perry plays on Jay-Z's hit single, "Empire State of Mind" to point to the presence of Hip Hop culture in our debates about race, to tether contemporary concepts of supremacy and inequality to nineteenth-century notions of imperialism, and to capture the force of the wide range of empirical data to which she refers in order to make her most salient points. Professor Perry's keynote did exactly what opening keynote addresses are supposed to do: she set the table for all of the discussions that followed. This fact was summarily evidenced in the number of times that her remarks were referenced and/or alluded to throughout the remainder of the symposium panels and programs.

"An Empire State of Mind" is (also) the opening for the entire collection, as well as the lead off for the "Head Matter" section. In part I, contributors wrestle with race, identity, and Hip Hop culture through literary, cultural, and visual imagery. For Tanji Gilliam, this critical engagement takes shape through her revisiting, some twenty years later, of the full version of the infamous Rodney King videotape. Gilliam rereads the King tape through the lens of Hip Hop culture and nation and she situates her reading within the discourses of technological media advancements and the construction of an imagined national community. In "Head on Straight, Mask on Crooked," Nicholas James attempts to pull back the mask from the enigmatic rap persona known (somewhat) popularly as MF Doom. In the process of this unveiling, James considers how, through the artistry of MF Doom, the black cultural legacy of wearing the mask finds purchase in Hip Hop culture. In the final essay of the "Head Matter" section, Will Boone historicizes certain figures within rap music and Hip Hop culture and the impact of superhero conventions upon Hip Hop—combining two of the most pervasive and dominant forms of popular culture in modern history.

Part II, creatively titled "Visual Matter," collects those *In Media Res* selections that critically engage photography, film, television, videotape, and some of the most compelling identity-defining imagery in recent memory. Paul M. Farber's essay engages new media images of the March on Washington on the occasion of the fiftieth anniversary of the march. Through a range of images and "digital projects," Farber wrestles with the ways in which photography is a medium for "historical memory related to the March." Emily Churilla's essay, "How Deep? Skin Deep?" dissects an episode of *House* in order to peel off the scabs of inherent gender biases that persist and sometimes thrive in contemporary culture. Many of these biased themes and images are ostensibly designed to challenge and critique traditional conceptualizations of gender. Scott St. Pierre's

"Faggoty/White/Uniform" interprets a comment made by Jack Nicholson's Colonel Jessup from the military film, *A Few Good Men*. St. Pierre excavates the ways in which the film trucks in homophobia through the queering of certain characters. He reads *A Few Good Men* as one popular commentary on and reflection of the recently abolished policy known as "Don't Ask, Don't Tell."

In part III, "Global Flows," contributors look beyond our national borders in order to explore the intersections of race, subjugated identity, and globalized culture. Suheir Hammad is one of the most critically acclaimed poets of her time, but her words are as timeless as they are popularly pertinent. If only there were some way to share with readers the power and energetic cogency of her live performance. In her live performances she makes intimate connections with her entire audience—not one look, word, or expression is wasted. From the moment she took the stage, she checked her microphone in the poetic voice of the narrator from her now classic poem, "Mic Check."[6] Although it is not included here, the selections herein convey Hammad's poetic depth and the value of poetry in these critical discourses on racial identity from perspectives beyond our national borders. Belinda Monique Waller-Peterson's essay on the "Communal Womb" in *Sankofa* takes a closer, critical look at Haile Gerima's (understudied) documentation of slavery, loss, recovery, memory, and redemption. *Sankofa* is a cinematic narrative of institutional slavery and of enslaved people in historic and contemporary cultures. Waller-Peterson employs an original concept—the communal womb—in order to understand the ways that enslaved communities, especially women, responded to and transcended the physically and spiritually destructive nature of the peculiar institution. Delores B. Phillips' contribution to the "Global Flows" section is a critical postcolonial analysis of masculinity and globalized Hip Hop identity in Guatam Malkani's *Londonstani*. Adam Mansbach's "'A True and Faithful Account of Mr. Ota Benga the Pygmy,' written by M. Berman, Zookeeper" chronicles the racialized body on display in a zoo, a somewhat fictional narrative consistent with our own tendencies to view the black body as spectacle.

Part IV of this collection, "Culture of Personality," features essays that grapple with the public and artistic personas of some well-known artists across various media. Sean Springer's essay, "Richard Pryor's Pain," explores the stages of Pryor's career and the near impossibility of projecting the complexity of his racial and existential pain through mediated comedic performances. Here again we come to understand that entering "in the middle" and through the "media" in which we view and contextualize our experiences and responses, we can become lost—or reductive. Springer, much like Gilliam in her excavation of the full Rodney King video, explores the representations of Pryor in order to uncover something new—something more complicated than either medium in which these figures appear. Wilfredo Gomez's "You Are Now Tuned Into the . . . Greatest" closely reads lyrics of rapper, Jay-Z juxtaposed with close readings of two of his most watched appearances on popular television. Through critical readings of Jay-Z's appearances on *The Oprah Winfrey Show* and *Real Time with Bill Maher*, readers will gain a deeper understanding of what Gomez calls the spectacle of the cool—as it applies to Jay-Z's artistic persona. The final essay in this section, Carrie Walker's "Disassembling the 'Matrix of Domination,'" dwells on the intersections of musical genre and gender politics in the dynamic artistic production of Janelle Monae. According to Walker, Monae embodies post–Hip Hop aesthetics through an agential manipulation of her body and the metaphor of the cyborg. As the second bookend or final coda to this collection of essays, I include a keynote speech, "Dreams of the Drum," delivered by Michael Eric Dyson at the Black Arts Festival held at Bucknell University in April 2010. Dr. Dyson's rhetorical mastery is on full display here as he weaves narratives of popular culture, signifying, and African American cultural history.

Throughout this collection you might note that many of the selections reflect my own scholarly interest in Hip Hop culture—especially Hip Hop music. But this coincidence is much more a product of student demand for Hip Hop generational programming, the submissions received for the "In Media Res" symposium, and the contributors who decided to add their informative essays to this compelling volume. Hip Hop culture (comprised of four foundational elements: graffiti art/visual aesthetics, breaking/B-boying/kinesthetic, DJ-ing/aural/audio aesthetics, and MC-ing/Rapping or verbal aesthetics) produces an apropos fit for the central themes of *In Media Res*. Race, identity, and "the popular" are major social, creative, and political concerns for the artists and constituents of Hip Hop culture. The fact that Hip Hop is also a culture that shamelessly interpolates other cultural products and that it is as effective at diminishing and truncating the human experience as it is at uplifting and edifying our humanity is the illegible signature without which a volume of this nature simply could not exist.

One final contributor, John Jennings, does not author any of the essays, but instead contributes several stunning sketches that visually capture the themes of several of the selections collected in this volume. These visually intricate images, and the various explications of audiovisual imagery, help to make this collection as reflective of the multimedia inclinations of the university programs represented here (and of our world) as textually possible. The scholarly, visual, and artistic ruminations collected here signify what my efforts to produce quality university programming brought to light—the importance of understanding our responsibility when we enter in the middle of things and the intellectual work required to offset the contextual vertigo of the "in medias res" effect. This collection is a contribution to the eternally unreachable whole narrative in which race, gender, media, and popular culture at academic institutions (and beyond) functions. Many of the university programs featuring scholars, speakers, poets, and performers were specifically designed to enhance the university community's engagement with these issues as they are introduced to the community. The collection you find before you features critical essays, academic papers, speeches, and creative work that represents the intellectual and artistic spirit of nearly a decade of university programs across multiple institutions, even as it gestures toward the broader issues at stake in the most significant intersectional discourses taking place all around us in the twenty-first century.

NOTES

1. Irene J. F. de Jong, "In Media Res," in *Routledge Encyclopedia of Narrative Theory*, ed. David Herman, Manfred Ahn, and Marie-Laure Ryan (New York: Routledge, 2005), 242.
2. Stuart Hall, "What is this 'black' in black popular culture?" in *Stuart Hall: Critical Dialogues in Cultural Studies*, ed. David Morley and Kuan-Hsing Chen (New York: Routledge, 1996), 469.
3. Ibid.
4. John Fiske, *Understanding Popular Culture* (Boston: Unwin Hyman, 1989), 28.
5. Hall, *Stuart Hall: Critical Dialogues in Cultural Studies*, 469.
6. Suheir Hammad, "Mic Check," in *ZaatarDiva* (New York: Cypher Books, 2008).

I

HEAD MATTER: THE MIND AND THE MASK

Part I explores race, identity, and popular culture through a series of essays, all of which attempt to explore individual and collective mentalities in the contemporary moment. At issue here is the construction of identities—self-identity as well as national identity. For Imani Perry, "Head Matter," takes the shape of a social scientific critique of an "empire" state of mind. Perry reads Jay-Z's optimism regarding Hip Hop's capacity to improve race relations as a privileging of cultural affinities over and above the statistical data that belie the artistic brilliance of Jay-Z and the kind of cultural miscegenation that popular Hip Hop music continues to produce. In short, the fact that majority culture imbibes Hip Hop culture does not translate into actual changes in policy, politics, and racism itself, whether that racism is intentional or completely unintended. The consequences of sustained racial inequality are as real as anything that Hip Hop music claims to be. Tanji Gilliam's piece on the Hip Hop nation and the Rodney King video suggests that oftentimes what remain hidden in popular media contexts can be vital touchstones for the multi-vocalic potential for Hip Hop national voices. The King video, (as well as the trial and the ensuing riots), mark a watershed moment for the Hip Hop generations' struggles with the US criminal and civil justice systems. The voices of the women who witnessed the brutal beating of Rodney King at the hands of the Los Angeles Police Department were edited out of the widely circulated version of the video and these voices—which Gilliam reads as discourse representing a Hip Hop nation—point to a critical collective identity and the requirement that we remain vigilant for silenced voices from Hip Hop within popular culture. Nicholas James' paper on MF DOOM, examines the rapper's use of the mask as a tool to subvert popular culture and mainstream Hip Hop culture. MF DOOM's mask obscures his identity, confounds the players in the music industry business, and subverts the power structures of popular culture and conventional artistic identity construction. James also situates MF DOOM's signifying use of the mask within the African American literary and cultural discourses on the mask—including, concepts such as double-consciousness, wearing the mask, and signifying. Will Boone's essay on superhero aesthetics in Hip Hop pushes the "wearing of the mask" in black culture and in Hip Hop to its logical conclusions. For Boone, rappers appropriate the aesthetics of comic book superheroes and American mafia figures in order to construct their artistic identities. These constructions appeal to generations of Hip Hop listeners who—like the artisans of Hip Hop—find powerful aesthetic attributes that are in turn compelling ways to configure power and in many cases masculinity itself. Each of the selections in this section embraces Hip Hop culture as an important lens through which to view race and identity in American popular culture.

1

An Empire State of Mind

Imani Perry

As some of you may know I have spent a good deal of my life thinking, writing about, and listening to Hip Hop—the music that expresses the identities of post civil rights generation people; the music that provided the soundtracks to our coming of age. Hip Hop is a music that grew with us, with ebbs and flows of brilliance and pragmatism. More recently, my book on contemporary racial inequality, *More Beautiful and More Terrible*, was published.[1] I was therefore more than a little interested to hear what Jay-Z had to say about the impact of Hip Hop on racism. He is quoted as having said:

> [Hip-hop] has changed America immensely . . . Hip-hop has done more than any leader, politician, or anyone to improve race relations. Racism is taught in the home . . . and it's very hard to teach racism to a teenager who idolizes, say, Snoop Dogg. It's hard to say, "That guy is less than you." The kid is like, "I like that guy, he's cool. How is he less than me?" That's why this generation is the least racist generation ever. You see it all the time. Go to any club. People are intermingling, hanging out, enjoying the same music.[2]

Jay-Z is a remarkable MC, a figure of transcendence and possibility, but I believe he got this one wrong. True, Hip Hop does some interesting things in terms of racial perceptions and cultural interactions. It opens some doors—some good, some bad, but I have to disagree with the brilliant MC. Hip Hop does not destroy the empire state of mind that undergirds American ideas of race. And perhaps that is because it (the

11

racial empire state of mind) isn't just taught and learned at home; it is taught (and learned) everywhere. Now obviously I am not using the term Empire State in the way that Jay Z does, to refer to New York City, in his hit single (featuring Alicia Keys). I mean empire as connected to the nineteenth-century idea of imperialism, and defined by *The Dictionary of Human Geography* as "the creation and maintenance of an unequal economic, cultural and territorial relationship, usually between states and often in the form of an empire, based on domination and subordination."[3] Such a sense of empire framed the ideology of white supremacy that justified global economic development by relying on concepts of the inferiority of those whose labor, lives, and bodies were exploited.

We have had enormous gains in this society since the days in which philosophies of empire or manifest destiny framed the United States and other global powers. In those years we have seen the liberation of the colonized states across the world. And at home, the Civil Rights Movement not only insisted upon equality before the law of all American citizens, but it also prompted the expansion of the rights that all citizens would have in the eyes of the federal government. The Civil Rights Movement broadened the pool of people of color who would have the prospect to immigrate to the United States and to enter its universities and institutions of employment. But we have not yet arrived at the post-racial promise in which idol worship, of a self-proclaimed pimp or a preternatural president, can counteract a long history of thinking about race.

To start this: I am going to give you some information about race in America, and everything I am about to tell you is substantiated by empirical research—not anecdote, not individual experience—but research about what happens to large groups of people. Consider the major factors in a person's life. You are born into a body that has certain facts about it: color, shape, organs, senses. The fact of what your body is, and what it will become, has no meaning independent of the society into which you are born. It is inherently arbitrary. But of course, since you are born into a society, the fact of your body has almost immediate meaning applied to it. What is more arbitrary than the color of one's skin? And yet, not just between, but within racial groups, over the course of life, it is apparent that there is an economic value to having lighter skin. People with lighter skin are paid more for the same work with identical qualifications as those with darker skin.[4] There is also meaning applied to the circumstances of your birth and to whom you belong. If you are born to someone poor and brown or black, you are at a greater risk of being separated from the people you love at a very early age due to the operations of gray economies in poor communities of color; undocumented labor markets which demand labor but punish presence; and a dysfunctional social welfare system which applies child removal policies in discriminatory fashion.[5]

You grow and live in one, two, several, or many communities. All of this happens inside the arbitrary body you were born into which faces its own obstacles as you journey from birth to death. Your path through life is an interactive one, and the results of your life are shaped by a dynamic set of variables including choices made by you and the many people you encounter and those with whom you share life. If you begin this journey as a black or brown child in the United States, from the very beginning of your life you are less likely to receive decent medical care or to experience quality education with teachers who have high expectations of you, and you are less likely to live in a safe community.[6] You are more likely to be exposed to environmental hazards,[7] to live in poverty, and to experience food insecurity.[8] You may become ill. And in that illness you will find that doctors are less likely to order necessary tests, or to investigate your illness fully. Regardless of your class, if you are African American, they may assume you will be noncompliant with treatment.[9]

If you are on this journey as an Asian, Latino, or black person in the United States, once you enter the employment market you will likely earn less than white counterparts with the exact same credentials,[10] and you will be less likely to be identified for promotion regardless of your skill.[11] You may go to purchase a home. If you are black or brown it is not unlikely that you will experience discrimination on the basis of your voice or speech pattern by realtors.[12] Because of where your home is, who your parents are and their ability or inability to provide you with financial support, you will likely find it much more challenging to purchase a home as a person of color.[13] You will have a higher interest rate for your mortgage, and you will see less appreciation in the value of your home in the years following your purchase. You are significantly more likely, if you are black or brown, to be unemployed or to have lost your home in the 2007–2008 economic crisis and throughout this painfully slow "recovery."

Perhaps you do something illegal. The likelihood that your car will be stopped because you were speeding is much higher if you are black or Latino.[14] The likelihood that your car will be searched is much higher if you are black.[15] The likelihood that a prosecutor will decide to pursue the case is much higher if you are black.[16] The likelihood that you will be convicted of a crime is higher and your sentence will likely be longer.[17] And if you are dark skinned it is even longer than if you are light skinned, if your features are African it is likely to be longer than if your features are European.[18] If you are black, then a criminal offense is more likely to lead to the denial of your right to vote for the rest of your life.[19] If you use drugs,[20] get into an altercation, fail to attend to your child,[21] or play your music too loud,[22] the consequences are demonstrably greater if you are black or brown than if you are white. But maybe you aren't a person who ever gets into trouble. You simply go about your daily life in clean-cut fashion. You turn on the television and see that people like you are overrepresented as criminals, jokesters, and social deviants.[23] You buy a car, a house, or some other consumer good, and you are charged more because you are black.[24] If you work in the service economy you get tipped less than whites[25] and if you are seeking service, the quality of services delivered are poorer.[26] You may find that the hair you are born with, the name you were given at birth, your features, your accent, are all sources of discrimination that you experience at work and in daily life.[27]

Add the following factors to this well-researched data: the intergenerational transfer of wealth, the fewer economic resources present in African American and Latino communities, the lower rates of quality health care and education, poverty, immigration status, and you will see the presence of inequality exponentially grow. But even if we just limit ourselves to observing a contemporary active practice of racial inequality, one can easily recognize that daily life and life outcomes are shaped by race. The greater question is how and why? All of these things I have identified are the product of choices made by individuals in response to other individuals. Doctors choose which tests to order; juries choose who to convict; producers choose which news stories to run; studio executives choose which projects to green-light; teachers decide which kids enter into accelerated classrooms and which enter into special education; social workers choose who stays with their families and who doesn't; restaurant owners choose to exploit cheap labor, and hire undocumented people who cannot risk complaining when they are cheated and abused. Choices. Choices. Choices. Chances are the individuals making these decisions would not identify themselves as bigots even though we can see the racial preferences embedded in their choices. Many are likely to be people who identify themselves as victims of discrimination themselves. This narrative, and the data that I have cited are offered as evidence that there are cumulative patterns to be found in the choices that individuals make, patterns that are often not readily identifiable if one looks at the actions or beliefs of an individual but rather emerge when one looks at how many individuals choose to act in the same way.

Clearly we are not post-racial, not even close. Rather, the ideas of racial superiority and inferiority that existed at the origins of our nation state continue to infect our culture, to haunt it with harrowing impact. But there is some good news. The good news is we do not want to be racist. Nobody wants to be racist. We want to see our society as a place where everyone receives a fair shake. Why then do we have such a gulf between aspiration and the realization of a society in which race does not significantly impact one's life? Why does it persist? There are a number of reasons. When we describe what racism is, we use an old-fashioned definition. We seem to think that racism has two components: First: the belief that a person will necessarily be a particular way because he or she belongs to a specific group. This is deterministic racism. The second is: the conscious animus directed towards another person because of his or her race; this is intentional racism. But the fact is, one can act in a bigoted fashion without having deterministic ideas about race. Just because you believe a person can be an *exception* to what you consider the *norm* does not mean that one does not act in a discriminatory fashion. One can hold open the prospect of innocence despite a presumption of guilt associated with a color. With respect to intentional animus, growing research in social cognition shows that people hold much more bias than they self report or self perceive against members of racial minority groups—most dramatically against African Americans. In short, one does not have to embrace bigotry for it to shape how we think and act.

Racial bias is a cultural norm. And that cultural norm is compounded by historical ignorance. Historical ignorance serves stereotypes and bigoted attitudes. As James A. Baldwin said "I am what time, circumstance, history, have made of me, certainly."[28] When we fill in the blanks as to why things are the way they are when it comes to race, without that history we resort to the stereotypes that are so familiar. I'll give you an example to illustrate my point: Take two snapshots in your mind, one of the inner city, one of an affluent suburb. Take the example of the cities in which we live: Go to urban areas of concentrated poverty and contrast them to manicured suburbs. Take a moment and think about why they're so different. Why do these people live in such radically different circumstances? The popular explanation attributes the life in the suburbs to hard work, diligence in schools, a family culture that values saving, married adults sharing household responsibilities, and the life in the ghetto is explained by the absence of those things. But there's a history that offers a much more compelling explanation.

In the 1930s, and in response to the Great Depression, the Federal Housing Administration was created. This federal agency assessed risk, and gave guidelines for mortgage lending. It also facilitated the transformation of mortgage terms. Instead of 50 percent down to be paid off over five years, you began to see the 10 percent down, twenty-to-thirty year mortgages that we see now. Add to this the 1940s expansion in home building and the G.I. Bill. Owning a home became a goal that could be realized for a much broader sector of society. But African Americans were excluded. They were excluded because the FHA manuals dictating the terms for mortgage lending used explicitly bigoted criteria for assessing the value and risk of homes. Thus, homes in black communities were worth less and the process for securing mortgages for them was more difficult. To make matters worse, much of the American landscape was covered by racially restrictive covenants. These were private land agreements where residents of a particular area or neighborhood agreed not to sell their homes to people of color. Some cities were up to 85 percent covered by restrictive covenants. So on the one hand, homes in black communities were devalued, on the other, African Americans were denied access to homes in white communities through private contracts. These contracts were declared unenforceable by the Supreme Court in 1948, but they continued to be adhered to and entered into until 1968 with the passage of the Fair Housing Act. It fueled the practice of redlining: Redlining refers to the practice of banks marking, in a red line, areas where they would not grant mortgages or otherwise invest, and race was routinely used to guide the borders of that line. This practice was common until the 1990s, notwithstanding federal legislation against discrimination in housing. And it is an ongoing practice of discrimination in the real estate industry. Those mid-twentieth-century years had a devastating impact. To this day, the greatest asset Americans have is usually the home. It provides money for inheritance, to pay for college educations, security and stability. The exclusion from the home ownership aspect of the American Dream, led to substantial gaps in wealth that existed alongside gaps in salary.

Along with the FHA discrimination in the 1930s, there was discrimination in education. And by this I do not simply mean segregated schools, or inequitable expenditures per pupil. I mean that many states did not provide public high schools for African American teenagers to attend, and they could not attend the ones for white students. At the same time, across the United States, there was the dramatic expansion of public education for white teenagers—this was particularly dramatic for recent immigrants, many of whom had virtually no prospect for education in their countries of origin, but by virtue of becoming American, and being a white American, they could attain a high school diploma, and purchase a home. Access to public high school did not become universal for African Americans until after the *Brown v. Board of Education* decision.[29]

So there is a wealth and an opportunity gap, inherited from previous generations, that partially explains the difference between the suburb and the inner city. Additionally, over the course of the twentieth century, African Americans were shuttled from one social experiment to another—urban renewal and slum clearance, moved for highways and public works—and rarely re-accommodated. As a response to restrictive covenants and pervasive residential discrimination they witnessed the creation of high rise public housing projects—a social welfare program that did not create assets like that which was created for white Americans—and then ultimately, the high rise project was realized to be another example of debilitating urban policy. Many of these *projects* were and are being demolished, yet again without accommodating all those displaced. And then there was the de-industrialization of the cities, the loss of working class employment accessible to people in the cities. This history altogether explains why the cities are poor and disenfranchised while the suburbs are comfortable and peaceful. If you do not know this history; if you are white and American you might say: "my grandfather worked hard, and came to this country with nothing but made something of himself" and wonder why my grandfather didn't do the same. But in fact my grandfather, a college-educated World War II veteran, and my grandmother both worked hard and long, but the home in which they raised their children, paid their mortgage, and worked hard for—because of redlining and restrictive covenants and discrimination—is worth in the area of $20,000 while comparable homes in the suburbs are worth ten times that amount.

This is just the tip of a very large iceberg of how historic discrimination shapes current landscapes. As James Baldwin once wrote, "American history is longer, larger, more various, more beautiful, and more terrible than anything anyone has ever said about it."[30] This is just one abbreviated story, one that, I think, you should know about, but I really tell you about it to illustrate a point. Be careful about making assumptions based upon what you see instead of what you know. If we want to achieve the racial egalitarianism that we claim to value, members of this society must constantly self-interrogate. This is a tall order. We have so much anxiety about bigotry that we often seek to confirm that our bigotries are not really bigotries, but rather about the moral or social failings of those we are bigoted against. We seek to assuage our guilt when we have social advantages by pretending that those advantages don't exist. But that isn't fair.

An earlier Baldwin quote in its entirety is as follows: "I am what time, circumstance, history, have made of me, certainly, but I am also, much more than that. So are we all. We can be more, and better."[31] In order to challenge the ways that the old lens, that empire state of mind, frames how we see and treat people according to race, we must constantly focus on telling more accurate, more nuanced, more complete stories about the reality of race. People often discount thinking when it comes to race. Either they say let's not talk about it, or they say let's act instead of talking so much. But as Ida B. Wells once said, "The people must know before they can act."[32] I charge you with acquiring knowledge. It is perhaps the most important intervention into racial inequality. At each moment that you presume a deficiency, a behavioral failing, a explanation for distinctions that is based in merit or value or labor, call it into question, look deeper, self-police—ask yourself about how you value people differently according to how they are defined. Consider these words an invitation to move beyond empire to a democratic state of mind.

NOTES

1. Imani Perry, *More Beautiful and More Terrible: The Embrace and Transcendence of Racial Inequality in the United States* (New York: New York University Press, 2011).
2. Shaheem Reid, "Jay-Z: Hip-Hop Has Done More Than Any Politician To Improve Race Relations," *MTV News*, March 20, 2009, http://www.mtv.com/news/articles/1607418/jay-z-hip-hop-has-done-more-than-any-politician-improve-race-relations.jhtml (accessed April 15, 2014).
3. Derek Gregory and others, eds., *The Dictionary of Human Geography*, 5th ed. (Malden, MA: Wiley-Blackwell, 2009), 373.
4. Jennifer Hochschild, "When Do People Not Protest Unfairness? The Case of Skin Color Discrimination," *Social Research* 73, no. 3 (Summer 2006): 473–98, 736. See also Eric Uhlmann, et al., "Subgroup Prejudice Based on Skin Color Among Hispanics in the United States and Latin America," *Social Cognition* 20, no. 3 (2002): 198–226, for strong evidence of color preferences among Hispanics.
5. See Dorothy Roberts, *Shattered Bonds: The Color of Child Welfare* (New York: Basic Civitas Books, 2002).
6. See Julie Landsman, "Confronting the Racism of Low Expectations: Subtle or Blatant, Racist Attitudes Poison Life at School," *Educational Leadership* 62, no. 3 (November 2004): 28–32; Sherry Marx, *Revealing the Invisible: Confronting Passive Racism in Teacher Education* (New York: Routledge, 2006). Also for a thorough understanding of the impact of teacher expectations see Rhona S. Weinstein, *Reaching Higher: The Power of Expectations in Schooling* (Cambridge, MA: Harvard University Press, 2004).
7. Robert D. Bullard, et al. "Toxic Wastes and Race at Twenty: 1987–2007: Grassroots Struggle to Dismantle Environmental Racism in the United States," *A Report Prepared for the United Church of Christ Justice and Witness Ministries* (Cleveland, OH: United Church of Christ, 2007), 1–160. Available online at http://www.ucc.org/assets/pdfs/toxic20.pdf (accessed April 14, 2014).
8. "Food Insecurity and Race," Share Our Strength for Multicultural Foodservice & Hospitality Alliance (MFHA), Symposium, 2005.
9. Brian D. Smedley, Adrienne Y. Stith, and Alan R. Nelson, *Unequal Treatment: Confronting Racial and Ethnic Disparities in Health Care* (Washington, DC: National Academies Press, 2003).
10. See Valerie A. Rawlston and William E. Spriggs, "Pay Equity 2000: Are We There Yet?" Washington, DC: National Urban League Institute for Opportunity and Equality, SRR-02-2001, April 2001; and Barbara Kilbourne, Paula England, and Kurt Beron, "Effects of Individual, Occupational, and Industrial Characteristics on Earnings: Intersections of Race and Gender," *Social Forces* 72, no. 4 (June 1994): 1149–76. For an overview see: Deborah M. Figart, "Pay Equity and Race/Ethnicity: An Annotated Bibliography," Hyattsville, MD: National Committee on Pay Equity, October 2001.
11. David J. Maume, Jr., "Glass Ceilings and Glass Escalators: Occupational Segregation and Race and Sex Differences in Managerial Promotions," *Work and Occupations* 26, no. 4 (November 1999): 483–509.
12. See John M. Yinger, *Closed Doors, Opportunities Lost: The Continuing Costs of Housing Discrimination* (New York: Russell Sage, 1995); and Kedamai Fisseha

and Nicholas Yannuzzi, "Linguistic Profiling: Pilot Studies on Restaurants, Car Dealerships and Apartment Rentals," unpublished article, dated January 12, 2007.

13. See Ira Katznelson, *When Affirmative Action was White: An Untold History of Racial Inequality in Twentieth-Century America* (New York: W. W. Norton, 2005).

14. David Cole, "Policing Race and Class," in *No Equal Justice: Race and Class in the American Criminal Justice System* (New York: New Press, 2000), 16–62.

15. Ibid.

16. David Cole, "Judgment and Discrimination," in *No Equal Justice: Race and Class in the American Criminal Justice System* (New York: New Press, 2000), 101–31.

17. David Cole, "The Color of Punishment," in *No Equal Justice: Race and Class in the American Criminal Justice System* (New York: New Press, 2000), 132–57.

18. Irene V. Blair, Charles M. Judd, and Kristine M. Chapleau, "The Influence of Afrocentric Facial Features in Criminal Sentencing," *Psychological Science* 15, no. 10 (October 2004): 674–79; and Irene V. Blair, Charles M. Judd, and Jennifer L. Fallman, "Attitudes and Social Cognition: The Automaticity of Race and Afrocentric Facial Features in Social Judgments," *Journal of Personality and Social Psychology* 87, no. 6 (December 2004): 763–78.

19. Jeff Manza and Christopher Uggen, *Locked Out: Felon Disenfranchisement and American Democracy* (New York: Oxford University Press, 2006); and Jamie Fellner and Marc Mauer, *Losing the Vote: The Impact of Felony Disenfranchisement Laws in the United States* (Washington, DC: Human Rights Watch and The Sentencing Project, 1998).

20. Ryan S. King, *Disparity by Geography: The War on Drugs in America's Cities*, (Washington, DC: Sentencing Project, 2008), http://www.sentencingproject.org/doc/publications/dp_drugarrestreport.pdf (accessed April 15, 2014).

21. See Roberts, *Shattered Bond*.

22. Disparities in public nuisance laws.

23. See generally Herman Gray, *Watching Race: Television and the Struggle for "Blackness"* (Minneapolis: University of Minnesota Press, 1995).

24. See the quantitative analysis of marketplace discrimination in Ian Ayres, *Pervasive Prejudice?: Unconventional Evidence of Race and Gender Discrimination* (Chicago: University of Chicago Press, 2001).

25. Michael Lynn, et al., "Consumer Racial Discrimination in Tipping: A Replication and Extension," *Journal of Applied Social Psychology* 38, no. 4 (April 2008): 1045–60, this study found that both white and black patrons tip black servers less than white servers, though the difference was more substantial among white patrons. Also see Ian Ayres, et al., "To Insure Prejudice: Racial Disparities in Taxicab Tipping," Yale Law School, Public Law Working Paper 50; and Yale Law & Economics Research Paper 276, May 3, 2005, http://islandia.law.yale.edu/ayres/toinsureprejudice.pdf (accessed April 15,2014), showing African American cab drivers are tipped on average one-third less than white drivers. This disparity existed for both black and white patrons.

26. Anne-Marie G. Harris, "Shopping While Black: Applying 42 U.S.C. § 1981 to Cases of Consumer Racial Profiling," *Boston College Third World Law Journal* 23, no. 1 (Winter 2003): 1–56.

27. While language based discrimination is unconstitutional as it is highly correlated to national origin discrimination, employers can justify discriminatory

practices on the basis of language if the employees accent or language "materially interferes" with job performance. However, since the burden on proof lies on claimants, victims of discrimination based upon accent face an uphill battle in pursuing a remedy. Employers are, on the other hand, allowed to discriminate against employees for wearing hairstyles that are easiest to maintain for those with naturally coily or tightly curled hair like dreadlocks and afros because these styles are considered mutable characteristics. In Philip Moss and Chris Tilly's book *Stories Employers Tell: Race, Skill, and Hiring in America* (New York: Russell Sage Foundation, 2001), the author cites employers distaste for African American language and communication styles.

28. James A. Baldwin, *Notes of a Native Son* (Boston: Beacon Press, 1955, repr. 1984).

29. U.S. Supreme Court, *Brown v. Board of Education of Topeka*, Opinion, May 17, 1954; Records of the Supreme Court of the United States, Record Group 267 (Washington, DC: Archives, 1954).

30. James A. Baldwin, speech delivered October 16, 1963, as "The Negro Child—His Self-Image"; originally published in *The Saturday Review*, December 21, 1963; repr. *The Price of the Ticket, Collected Nonfiction 1948–1985* (New York: St. Martin's, 1985).

31. J. A. Baldwin, *Notes of a Native Son*.

32. Ida B. Wells, *Southern Horrors: Lynch Law in All Its Phases* (New York: New York Age Print, 1892).

2

✥

Consolidating a Hip Hop Nation

Revisiting the Videotaped Police Beating of Rodney King, Twenty Years Later

Tanji Gilliam

Although *Black Power* and land ownership have been central demands of Black Nationalist movements in the United States, the fight for electoral representation has been the most realized aim, even if only for fleeting periods. Ironically, like black capitalism and black hypersexuality today, Black Nationalism is/was hyper-represented in history. The ideologies of Hip Hop nationalism emerge out of the adaptation of Black Nationalism as an available politic in the black community, throughout the history of that community within the United States. "All adaptations are political interventions, telling us something about the cultures that produced them."[1] Hip Hop is a black art form. It takes its social, historical, aesthetic, and political cues principally from this particular ethnic community. It is also overwhelmingly concerned with carving out a representational space for a Hip Hop nation. Hip Hop is certainly American in that it borrows from (or adapts) other ethnicities, and includes a mixture of ethnic groups among its cultural participants, but its influences are predominately black, and as a result, it self-identifies as a black art form, first and foremost. Thus it inherits and advances the accomplishments that Black Nationalists have made in uniting a racial community. "Adaptations," such as the Hip Hop nation, and Hip Hop nationalist-themed music and videos, "reconstruct history . . . by using the past to comment on the present."[2] Hip Hop nationalism is rooted in a sharp critique of the American nation and the social inequality it was founded upon, as well as the reiteration of these critiques during various periods of Black Nationalist fervor: the late 1800s, the 1920s, the 1960s and early 1970s most certainly, and the late 1980s and early 1990s.[3]

Video media serve as an appropriate model for the development of a Hip Hop or neo-black nation. Video is an expansive medium that enjoins multiple related imaging styles, including home videos, video art, commercial television, webcasts, and digital film.[4] Therefore in form, video is multilingual and multicultural, collecting various attributes of media with a common technical origin and history. Also, video is broken down into a democratic organization of component parts, including sound, visuals, characters, text, etc. Each of these component parts are organized in order to best articulate a particular theme. This assembly might serve as a model for a more democratic organization of political expression in the Hip Hop nation. Black Nationalist representations have, in the past, been far less polyrhythmic (with respect to their voice and multi-vocalic potential). Upsetting this trend results in a more wholly representative voice, particularly across gender lines. This chapter will explore how an isolated moment in Hip Hop video history, the Rodney King tape, can help us understand how Hip Hop's ideas about nationalism are adapted and re-represented. "Adaptation studies necessarily trouble and open disciplinary boundaries."[5] Though it is more customary to consider adaptations as works of literature recreated on film, translating the Rodney King video, or adapting it for literature, suggests a more democratic representational voice.

Historically, video has not always been evaluated as having a multimedia (sound and video) aesthetic, but this only further demonstrates hope for Hip Hop's new nationalist agenda. Formally, the term "video" represented the visual portion of television broadcasts exclusively.[6] Video was clearly superior to its accompanying sound (after all this was how television surpassed radio media), yet it was still reduced to a simple part of one imaging style: the television broadcast. However, with the introduction of high art video, the prominence of the Internet, and the global distribution of consumer video equipment, the medium is broader now, more intricate and diverse. The same can be hoped for with Hip Hop nationalism.

In *Imagined Communities*, Benedict Anderson argues that: "nation-ness is the most universally legitimate value in the political life of our time."[7] He arrives at this conclusion, from the context of post–World War II revolutionary and geopolitical frameworks such as the People's Republic of China and the Socialist Republic of Vietnam. For black America, democracy is the most relevant value; but Black Nationalism is far too often the political context within which "democracy" is both critiqued and pursued.[8] For the Hip Hop nation, the roots and "deep attachments" of nationalist ideologies are as steeped in the "dilemmas of helplessness" as any other contemporary society.[9] They can be traced back further than Anderson's proposed eighteenth century origin, to sixteenth century "crossing[s] of discrete historical forces," namely European enslavers and enslaved Africans.[10] The Hip Hop nation is an imagined community, in the way that Anderson developed the notion. It is a collective of disparate peoples that defines boundaries and polices them defiantly both within and without. It is likewise fraternal, organized, at the very least, for the continuance of an artistic culture and the persistence of an artistic community.[11] The idea of an imagined community however doesn't neatly fit, conceptually, with the rhetoric of the Hip Hop nation. In the Hip Hop nation the emphasis is on reality and an "imagined community" in some ways contradicts the emphasis on "realness" espoused within the culture. In the sphere of Hip Hop nationalism, regions, cities, neighborhoods, and crews are real cultural groupings that are affirmed as such in lyrics and other linguistic devices, symbols and other visuals.

Video has become one of the primary modes of representation that supports the sense of real communities and the imagined nation embraced by constituents of Hip Hop culture. This represents a distinct shift from former artistic media. If we consider painting for instance, reality is theorized as all but natural.[12] When a subject is painted, it is considered an "ahistorical sense of human reality" at best, a consideration granted by a minority of cultural theorists who accept the role of the painter in representing the fluid reality of history. Duke Ellington has noted, "Sometimes I imagine I paint, with watercolors or oils, a crystal-clear lake in the sky reflecting the shadows of invisible trees upside down beneath sun-kissed, cotton-candy snow."[13] The imaginative possibilities presented by Ellington for painting, may very well compliment the burdened "realness" of black musical art forms, including Hip Hop, as well as his own genre of jazz music. In *Ways of Seeing* John Berger wrestles with this comparison as well. According to Berger, all images, even photographs, which are often incorrectly presumed to be "mechanical records," reflect an artist's "way of seeing," or her/his own adaptation of reality.[14] Furthermore, the painting's message is intentionally altered for the purposes of various audiences.[15] The audience's perception of the work, and art in general, changes the meaning of the painting for each individual spectator.[16] "The domain to which painting is said to belong is that of perception."[17] The painter's task is to perceive reality and copy it. Mistakenly, some believe that the videographer's task, especially within the realm of Hip Hop culture, is considered to be recording reality and replaying it, unaltered and with complete respect to history. This is especially ironic given that Hip Hop artists are constantly critiqued for promoting stereotypes. Black film in particular, Valerie Smith has noted, and here I would extend her argument to incorporate black video, is constantly striving towards the portrayal of "authentic black subjects."[18] So much so, that when Hip Hop artists are consciously portraying black historical stereotypes, they are chastised for "real" longings for hypersexuality, criminality, and other social ills.

This emphasis on reality is not simply a function of Hip Hop video representations. It is not solely a feature that results from the culture's insistence; it is a characterization of video in general. Hip Hop has gravitated to the medium in such a manner because of this presumption, and despite its contemporaneous emergence. There were of course other, nonvideographic artistic mediums adopted by Hip Hop, and they could have been the more dominant voices of the Hip Hop generations, much like we see in the cultures of jazz or classical music. However, Hip Hop has gravitated towards video, even in the absence of the microphone (via commercials, interviews, television programming, etc.) because of its illusionary realism. The quest for realism in video is but an extension of this sought-after criteria in film, as video media is, of course, a derivation of film in both aesthetic and technical terms. The most common aesthetic criterion in film is that it be realistic.[19] Even when films consciously present fantasy or illusion, the expectation of the audience is that there be "realism in the illusion."[20] Despite the fact that realism is shaped by filmmakers (and videographers), it can be the basis through which spectators determine whether a film is believable or unbelievable.[21] Cinema and video audiences accept "an increasingly cinematic or mediated reality."[22] For video, this quest for realism is so prevalent that mass audiences (and critics) presume reality in its very form.[23]

The tension between the real and the imaginary, for video and for Hip Hop culture, obstructs the application of Anderson's theory from being comfortably assigned to the Hip Hop nation. Even when theorists other than Anderson are not explicitly referring to nationalism as an imaginary concept, the terminology is being thoroughly policed. There has been resistance among theorists to comfortably accept the idea of "cultural nationalism." According to Aijaz Ahmad, theoretical debates as well as global historical accounts are rendered all the more opaque when the category of "nationalism" is yoked together with the category of "culture" to produce the composite category of "cultural nationalism." Unlike the political category of the state, the regulatory and coercive category of law, institutional mechanisms such as political parties or class organizations like trade unions, "culture" generally and the literary/aesthetic realm in particular, are situated at a great remove from the economy and therefore, among all the superstructures, culture is the most easily available for idealization and theoretical slippage.[24]

The fact is that culture is a nebulous designation, and Hip Hop culture is fluid. However, to write off cultural nationalism altogether would be premature and dismissive. Unlike other cultures, Hip Hop is most certainly not "removed" from the economy. One commanding mechanism that produces the culture is a billion-dollar recording industry that greatly impacts the advertising strategies of multiple industries, including beverages, fast food, automobiles, and other consumer product offerings. Furthermore, radio and television programming, because of companies such as Clear Channel and Viacom, have an extraordinary impact on our national economy. Hip Hop economies are not entirely independent of these global corporate forces and the artists and constituents of the culture need to make better sense of how to translate economic growth into political power. Declaring cultural-national independence that is democratic, and therefore accessible for all classes and genders of the black nation, is not often a priority for prominent artists or political leaders. Within the context of cultural/black nationalism, imagined communities, and popular culture, the role of video has become powerful and pervasive. Videotaped events, first on handheld video cameras and more often now on cameras in phones, can emerge in the public sphere and shape popular culture and its constitutive communities. And as I suggest below, in some cases, videotaped events contribute to the consolidation of imagined culturally nationalist communities.

II

The videotaped police beating of Rodney King, because of its repetitive broadcasts, emerged in popular culture as an early 1990s echo and confirmation of outcries for social justice from a tentatively formed Hip Hop nation. These outcries were made by an increasingly educated, maturing, and newly re-politicized Hip Hop generation and by witnesses to the event itself. Rodney King became a symbol for the black male angst and political sensibility of a post–Public Enemy, early Gangsta rap moment in Hip Hop culture.[25] Because the beating took place in Los Angeles, it represented yet another vehicle for the cross-national reverberation of political ideas that East Coast cultural-nationalist emcees such as Melle Mel and Afrika Bambaataa had previously established and that West Coast *gangstas*, including Ice Cube and Ice-T, expanded upon.

American news and other media outlets opted not to disseminate the Rodney King tape in its original form. The original George Holliday version, archived in the Library of Congress, is significantly different, particularly with respect to length and pacing, from the footage that was edited and manipulated for the purposes of news networks and other video dissemination. It was edited and slowed down to accommodate *one* enhanced representation of the police brutality.[26] In the process of being both edited and slowed down, the sound on the video was removed (because it would have otherwise been rendered inaudible). By altering the sound of the videotape, important voices and viewpoints were excised. The framing of the video became a redirected vision of a victimized Rodney King and a brutal set of LAPD victimizers. The blows were exaggerated in the process of slowing the feed and King's body appeared even more languid and traumatized. This version, though discordant from the original that George Holliday videotaped, was effective on national news outlets in conveying a representation of heightened controversy. Later, as archival footage in the Bitches With Problems "Wanted" video, in Spike Lee's *Malcolm X*, and through discussions on other black cultural video programming such as *The Arsenio Hall Show* this same edited, sloweddown version became a symbol of white racial hatred against black people and justified a profound mistrust of the criminal justice system on the part of black Americans. This vision of the video representation is a significant one, chiefly because it was largely accepted as the actual happenings of that evening. Additionally, it was considered by many to be a complete vision of the atrocities committed and so it was presumed that all the information needed to represent that event were contained in this edited video. However, there are additional characters in the original, Holliday included, and the edited video differs greatly from the original as a result of their absence (and silencing).

A segment of the dialogue from the anonymous witnesses surrounding Holliday's camcorder reads as follows:

FEMALE 1. It's about 20 some cops out there beating on him.

FEMALE 2. They beatin' him to death. Lord have mercy. Look at him kicking. That is sickening.
They kicked him. They beat him.

MALE 1. He must have been on drugs or something.

FEMALE 1. He sittin' there lying on the ground with handcuffs on him.

FEMALE 2. On his feet too.

MALE 1. I'm going to tell my uncle about this. He's the police chief. He can sue for that can't he?

FEMALE 2. It's fifty of them out there for one man. Sickening.

MALE 1. But I heard if you resist the police . . .

FEMALE 2. That is sick.

MALE 1. You seen his face?

FEMALE 2. They beat him all on his face. They wasn't supposed to hit him on his face. They kicked him. I was looking at it. He's bloody as a hog over there. I'm trying to figure out how many of them is it. It's enough cops over there to fight an army. They should have went over there to fight Hussein like that.

FEMALE 3. I was standing hear watching when he got out. He had his hands on the car. That was awful. We over here paying taxes. They wasn't supposed to kick him in the face. Call the ambulance to come and get him.[27]

This excerpt from the full transcription only captures four speakers and there are at least two others that are inaudible. Also, present at the scene, and audible on the tape are both Spanish and English speakers. A police helicopter shining its light from above presents the greatest amount of noise distortion. Police sirens and radios also contribute to background noise. The nine-minute videotape begins with the police beating Rodney King. Viewers might presume that there was dialogue before the camcorder started recording. The video also never shows the audience members, with the exception of a few passing motorists that gape when they enter the frame. There are many more speakers with varying levels of audibility on the video, including the assailants and King himself, which we are unable to hear. What three of the four transcribed speakers say is unequivocally incriminating of the LAPD officers. The female speakers have clearly identified King as a victim of police brutality. There is some hesitation on the part of the male speaker however. His initial reaction is to assume that King was high and therefore somewhat complicit in his own victimization.[28] The male speaker recognizes that King could sue the LAPD and offers to inform his uncle, who happens to be a police chief. His final comment, "but I heard if you resist the police . . . ," is unfortunately only half-audible, leaving room for viewers to assume that he was still willing to find fault in King's actions.[29] The lone male voice is critical of King and seemingly willing to side on the part of the police officers. Perhaps this male speaker identifies with King. I say this not necessarily because he sees himself as a victim, but because he has likely been trained to view himself, through the eyes of police, as a suspect. The assumption here is harsh but it suggests a possible interpretation. Black males, and here only the voice of this male speaker has guided me to conjecture as to what race he is, are trained more so than any other race and gender to prepare for police encounters. The hopeful subtext of this training is that the black male will be so preparedly deferent and polite to police authority that his innocence will prevail.[30] Because King's innocence was not at all apparent to the LAPD officers at the scene, it is possible that the black male speaker, more so than the female speakers in the video, was willing to present excuses for the police brutality.

In contrast, the audible, defiant, and boldly resistant speech of the black female witnesses transcribed from the Holliday video present a discourse that is reflective of the countercultural messages of West coast Hip Hop music at the time. They are more than willing to admonish the officers in the video. FEMALE 2 refers to the brutality as "sickening." Both FEMALE 1 and 2 give an estimate of the number of police who are present, first twenty and then fifty, by doing so, they paint a picture of a lynch mob beating a defenseless man. They invoke imagery of past and present victimization. Familiarity with past narratives of state-violence against black bodies, including slavery, lynching, and earlier cases of police brutality informed the consciences of these women. Yet, hog slayings are explicitly made analogous in their exchange. After pointing out that he is hogtied, his hands and feet both handcuffed (with a rope extending from either end) FEMALE 2 laments, "he's bloody as a hog over there." Furthermore the brutality is likened to the Gulf War and the police mob is likened to the American army. "It's enough cops over there to fight an army," says FEMALE 2, very cynically, "they should have went over there to fight [Saddam] Hussein like that."

The frank discourse of the female witnesses is uncompromising. If the audio feed of the video were testimony in the trials of the LAPD officers who were present it would be both compelling and incriminating. As hearsay or idle-talk from other people, the defense attorneys would most certainly want it suppressed. As witness testimony, the prosecutors could find no stronger arguments for the brutality recorded on the Holliday video. Three black women, unrelated to either the victim or the perpetrators, who happened to be at the scene giving real time accounts of what happened; their testimony.[31] They were silenced by the news media, by future filmmakers and videographers, and subsequently by the American public. On the contrary, the arresting officer, Melanie Singer, was considered the "only significant woman in the case."[32] She at first testifies for the prosecution in the State trial against the officers, and then for the defense in the federal trial.[33] In both cases she testifies that the accused used excessive force, however she also testifies that King failed to respond to her orders after getting out of the car. This runs contrary to what FEMALE 3 said she witnessed, from the time that King exited his vehicle, up through the moments leading up to the tape. According to her comments on the video, King placed his hands on the car when he initially exited his vehicle.

This potential inconsistency exposes the dividing lines between an emergent collective sense of the Hip Hop nation and a criminal justice system—with urban police departments as its line of first offense. In the late 1980s and early 1990s when N.W.A.'s "Fuck the Police" and Ice T's "Cop Killer" were legally banned and artists were subject to scrutiny from national and regional police agents, it was both radical and normal for artists and constituents of Hip Hop to critique police in the media. But ultimately, police perpetrators in the Rodney King incident were acquitted. The ironies of the Rodney King tape then are two-fold. Because audiences had seen a muted version of the Holliday tape, and therefore had witnessed the principal action, many people believed they had effectively witnessed all of what happened. It did not matter whether you believed that King was victimized or on drugs or black and male and therefore guilty. The tape was viewed by millions of Americans, and the

American public felt they had a right to soundtrack what they witnessed. Thus they voiced the edited video that had been unvoiced. The full transcript of the Holliday video generally serves to make the point that so many, especially those in the Hip Hop nation, already believe(d): that the LA police officers in the video are guilty of violating Rodney King's civil and human rights. After the video was played repeatedly across national media platforms; after the trial and the jury returned a verdict, and after the streets of Los Angeles were riotous, the one voice the American public had been waiting to hear, the one witness who was present and had not, as of yet been voiced, Rodney King himself, spoke: "Can't we all just get along?" he asked. His statement is deemed by some to be prophetic, a clarion call directed at America's history of racism and intolerance. But it also tacitly supports ideological opposition to the Los Angeles riots and other forms of Hip Hop generation radicalism. Rodney King's question became one of the most quotable questions in pop cultural history but the tone and tenor of it played as unsupported idealism, especially for those most likely to be subjected to police brutality. He transforms in this inarticulate instance from a nationally sympathetic figure into the butt of a popular running joke. His idealism is mocked; his victimization is not questioned but public compassion for him disperses. In the face of his beating, and in the wake of continued injustice for black folks in the criminal justice system, King's "Can't we all just get along?" was an instant comedic sound bite for popular culture. Herein lies the second irony: that while the black American public was looking for King to give them an articulate, nationalist critique of an unjust system of justice, he opted for a flat, conservative, humanist approach to the situation. The critique that the public desired was delivered at the scene of the crime by women who witnessed it and complained about their own incongruous relationship with the American government ("we over here paying taxes") and they unabashedly drew borders between them and majority culture. The American media, and by default the larger public, silenced these voices in exchange for King's commentary and then flippantly turned it into a joke to hide their shame at the humility in King's rhetorical question.

Poet and scholar, Elizabeth Alexander argues that the Rodney King tape is a "traumatic" instance in American popular culture.[34] She lists the King "instance" within a timeline of 1990s video moments which include Marion Barry's arrest for smoking crack cocaine, the Clarence Thomas hearings, Mike Tyson's rape trial, the shooting death of Latasha Harlins, and Magic Johnson's and Arthur Ashe's press conferences announcing their HIV and AIDS statuses.[35] Alexander carefully presents the King tape as a popular media context for "consolidating group affiliations" among black people, particularly ones drawn across national and gender lines.[36] The Hip Hop nation represents a series of group affiliations loosely organized through an imagined community in which experiences like the Rodney King beating, videotape, trial, and commentary serve to enhance opportunities for consolidation against a deeply problematic justice system. Each of the videos that Alexander points to feature "black bodies in pain for public consumption."[37] The King video is an archetype of this phenomenon. Furthermore, Alexander suggests that white men are the "primary stagers and consumers," yet she also acknowledges that: "black people have been looking, too."[38] For Alexander, the edited version of the Holliday original functions as a "counter-narrative" reflecting a white American desire to "erase [black] bodily language," and create a new version of the King beating for our "national memory."[39] She speaks specifically to the void created by the lack of "first-person" spectatorship in the edited video, and defines the witnesses of the televised version as a community of viewers who empathized with King's victimization.[40] Alexander's reading of white men as the primary stagers/consumers of the edited tape underscores the racial problematic of our justice system, but it also encroaches upon the agency of King, the multiple black spectators transcribed in this chapter, and the potential for the King videotaped event to serve as a consolidating force for nationalist/imagined sentiments amongst the constituents of Hip Hop culture. Her characterization of the primary consumers of the tape as white males also belies the fact that "when the video broadcast first on local and then on national news programs, viewers of all races joined in condemning the police."[41] Like others, including Linda Williams and Paul Gilroy, Alexander does not refer to the dialogue of the Holliday original, nor does she address the presence of the additional spectators.[42] This absence or double silencing validates the cynicism with which artists and constituents of Hip Hop culture view mainstream media institutions and the entire criminal justice system. The publicly hidden, multi-vocal, dialogic quality of the unedited Holliday tape functions as a transcript for silenced responses to police brutality by/from the Hip Hop nation.

NOTES

1. Laurence Raw, "Mapping Adaptation Studies," reviews of *The Literature-Film Reader: Issues of Adaptation*, by James M. Welsh and Peter Lev; and *Cambridge Companion to Literature on Screen*, edited by Deborah Cartmell and Imelda Whelehan, *Literature Film Quarterly* 36, no. 3 (2008): 234.
2. Ibid.
3. In reverse chronological order, during the late 1980s and 1990s cultural-nationalist rap groups were prominent. See Imani Perry, *Prophets of The Hood: Politics and Poetics in Hip-Hop* (London and Durham, NC: Duke University Press, 2004), 28. The 1960s and 1970s witnessed Black Nationalist figures and groups such as Malcolm X and the Nation of Islam. See Ilyasah Shabazz, with Kim McLarin, *Growing Up X: A Memoir by the Daughter of Malcolm X* (New York: One

World, 2002). Garvey and the Universal Negro Improvement Association shared a "mass-based nationalism and emphasis on race pride," in the 1920s. See Robin D. G. Kelley, *Race Rebels: Culture, Politics, and the Black Working Class* (New York: Free Press, 1994), 107. Finally, in the late nineteenth century the all-black Women's Association of Philadelphia, was one among many organizations that supported Frederick Douglass' black nationalist politics. Erica Armstrong Dunbar, *A Fragile Freedom: African American Women and Emancipation in the Antebellum City* (London and New Haven, CT: Yale University Press, 2008), 95.

4. David Joselit, "The Video Public Sphere," *Art Journal* 59, no. 2 (Summer 2002): 46–53. I support the connections of these media here because they are presently shot on video. It is also significant that Tommy L. Lott supported extending the category of cinema to incorporate television. At this point documentary and narrative videos/films are similarly produced for television networks, which was Lott's justification for widening the definition of film. Tommy L. Lott, "A No-Theory Theory of Black Cinema," in *Representing Blackness: Issues in Film and Video*, ed. Valerie Smith (New Brunswick, NJ: Rutgers University Press, 2003), 91. Video artist Bruce Nauman, uses the terminology "films" and "video tapes" to apply to the same work of his. Bruce Nauman, "Interview with Michele De Angelus" in *Art In Theory, 1900–2000: An Anthology of Changing Ideas*, ed. Charles Harrison and Paul Wood (Maiden: Blackwell Publishing, 1992), 910.

5. Timothy Corrigan, "Literature on Screen, A History: In The Gap," in *The Cambridge Companion to Literature on Screen*, edited by Deborah Cartmell and Imelda Whelehan (Cambridge: Cambridge University Press, 2007), 42.

6. Phillip Brian Harper, "Marlon Riggs: The Subjective Position of Documentary Video," *Art Journal* 54, no. 4 (Winter 1995): 69–72. The preoccupation with this video element is evident in the fascination with technical improvements such as color TV, high-definition video, Blu-ray, etc. Lawrence Alloway, "The Arts and the Mass Media," in *Art In Theory, 1900–2000: An Anthology of Changing Ideas*, 716. In Edward Said, "Opponents, Audiences, Constituencies, and Community," in *Art In Theory, 1900–2000: An Anthology of Changing Ideas*, 1058, he defines television as "visual media," alongside commercial film, as opposed to visual and oral media, or audiovisual media. Whereas Dick Hebdige addresses the separate but related apparatuses of independent film and video productions, he still refers to them both as "image strands," ignoring the component parts of their "voice-overs" and "found sound," altogether. Dick Hebdige, "Digging for Britain: An Excavation in Seven Parts," in *Black British Cultural Studies: A Reader*, ed. Houston A. Baker, Jr., Manthia Diawara, and Ruth H. Lindeborg (Chicago and London: University of Chicago Press, 1996), 141. Ultimately the slippage in terminology expressed within this note, and note 4, results from what Hayden White considers an inherent problem with "technical terminology." Hayden White, "Historical Text As Literary Artifact," in *The History and Narrative Reader*, ed. Geoffrey Roberts (New York and London: Routledge, 2001), 231. According to White, "technical languages are familiarizing only to those who have been indoctrinated in their uses and only of those sets of events which the practitioners of a discipline have agreed to describe in a uniform technology." In the case of video, too much of video scholarship borrows language from film scholarship and because video, as a technology and as an art, succeeded film chronologically, even video artists muddy the distinctions between these two related mediums.

7. Benedict Anderson, *Imagined Communities: Reflections on the Origin and Spread of Nationalism* (London and New York: Verso, 1983), 3.

8. This idea is supported by Harold Cruse when he notes that, "For American society, the most crucial requirement at this point is a complete democratization of the national cultural ethos." Harold Cruse, *The Crisis of the Negro Intellectual: A Historical Analysis of the Failure of Black Leadership* (New York: Quill, 1984), 457. In Joy James, "Radicalizing Feminism," in *The Black Feminist Reader*, ed. Joy James and T. Denean Sharpley-Whiting (Malden, MA: Blackwell, 2000), 251, James warns against "neoradicalism" where "corporate flinders finance 'radical' conferences and 'lecture movements' and democratic power diminishes." Though James is speaking to "radical feminism" in general within her article, I believe the same cautions should apply to the coupling of black nationalism and democratic ideals also. Elsewhere black Americans accept "God's plan for America's democratic mission in the world," which includes black "suffering, oppression, and inequality." Melissa Victoria Harris-Perry, *Barbershops, Bibles, and BET: Everyday Talk and Black Political Thought* (Oxford and Princeton, NJ: Princeton University Press, 2004), 207.

9. Anderson, *Imagined Communities*, 4–5.

10. Ibid., 4.

11. Ibid., 6.

12. Norman Bryson, "The Natural Attitude," in *Visual Culture: The Reader*, ed. Jessica Evans and Stuart Hall (London, New Delhi, and Thousand Oaks, CA: Sage Publications, 1999), 26.

13. Robert G. O'Meally, *The Jazz Cadence of American Culture* (New York: Columbia University Press, 1998), 178.

14. John Berger, *Ways of Seeing* (London: BBC, 1972), 10.

15. Ibid., 25.

16. Ibid., 31.

17. Bryson, "The Natural Attitude," 27.

18. Valerie Smith, "Introduction," in *Representing Blackness*, 1.

19. Elizabeth Cowie, "Fantasia," in *Visual Culture: The Reader*, 366. Andre Bazin, trans. Hugh Gray, "The Ontology of the Photographic Image," *Film Quarterly* 13, no. 4 (Summer 1960): 6.

20. Cowie, "Fantasia," 366.

21. Ibid.

22. J. P. Telotte, "Heinlein, Verhoeven, and the Problem of the Real *Starship Troopers*," in *The Literature/Film Reader: Issues of Adaptation*, ed. James M. Welsh and Peter Lev (Lanham, MD: Scarecrow Press, 2007), 196.

23. Cowie, "Fantasia," 366.

24. Aijaz Ahmad, *In Theory: Classes, Nations, Literatures* (London: Verso, 1993), 7–8.

25. The videotaped incident of Rodney King's police brutality (1991) falls chronologically in between the videos for Public Enemy's "Fight The Power" (1989) and "Tour of a Black Planet" (1991), the *Rockline* and *Nightline* broadcasts where Chuck D protested the fact that King Day was not yet a national holiday (1992), the sit-down conversation between rapper Ice Cube and activist/scholar Angela Davis (1992), and the Los Angeles riots documentary video directed by Matthew McDaniels, *Birth of A Nation*, 4x29x92 (1993) that featured archival footage of Ice-T and N.W.A. Furthermore, it is "soundtracked" temporally by

the Source Classics: "No One Can Do It Better" (1989), "Grip It! On That Other Level" (1989), "AmeriKKKa's Most Wanted" (1990), "Death Certificate" (1991), and "The Chronic" (1992).

26. The George Holliday tape, in its original form is held in the Library of Congress archives; see note 27. It is publicly accessible in this venue, though clearly the archive's public is limited principally to academic researchers. The Library of Congress does not allow the duplication of any of their videos. This may have contributed to the failure of future videographers/filmmakers to reproduce the Holliday original as opposed to the news media adaptation. Yet the soundtrack of the Holliday original is as compelling and igniting as the visuals in the adaptation and it is therefore unfortunate that this soundtrack is removed.

27. *George Holliday's video of the Rodney King beating.* Collection: Copyright Collection (© registration no. PA 518–451). Call number: VAB 4242. Library of Congress control number (LCCN): 91789926.

28. King was later found to be under the influence of alcohol and marijuana. Linda Williams, *Playing the Race Card: Melodramas in Black and White From Uncle Tom to O. J. Simpson* (Princeton, NJ: Princeton University Press, 2001), 253.

29. *George Holliday's video of the Rodney King beating.* Collection: Copyright Collection (© registration no. PA 518–451). Call number: VAB 4242. Library of Congress control number (LCCN): 91789926.

30. Many anecdotes about this kind of preparedness have been discussed publicly around tragic murders of innocent black men based on racial profiling—Trayvon Martin, Sean Bell, Oscar Grant, etc.

31. The audio from the tape is a type of "testimony" in the sense of the black church tradition. This further underscores the silencing of these black female voices, here and in the larger sphere of Hip Hop. Female two even calls out, "Lord have mercy," in the religious tradition of black "witnesses."

32. Williams, *Playing the Race Card*, 279.

33. Ibid., 276.

34. Elizabeth Alexander, "Can You Be BLACK and Look at This?: Reading the Rodney King Video(s)," in *Black Male: Representations of Masculinity in Contemporary American Art*, ed. Thelma Golden (New York: Whitney Museum of American Art, 1994), 92–93.

35. Among the instances E. Alexander, "Can You Be BLACK . . . ," lists, the Arthur Ashe announcement and the Harlins homicide are the only ones that *The Source: The Magazine of Hip-Hop, Culture, and Politics* did not report. Furthermore, she refers to each of these instances as "videotap[ed] site[s] on which national trauma . . . has been traumatized." This is despite the fact that the criminal trial of Mike Tyson was not videotaped, his homecoming celebrations were.

36. Ibid., 91.

37. Ibid., 92–93.

38. Ibid., 92–93.

39. Ibid., 94–95.

40. Ibid., 100.

41. Williams, *Playing the Race Card*, 253.

42. Paul Gilroy, *Against Race: Imagining Political Culture Beyond the Color Line* (Cambridge, MA: Harvard University Press, 2000), 263; and Williams, *Playing the Race Card*, 253.

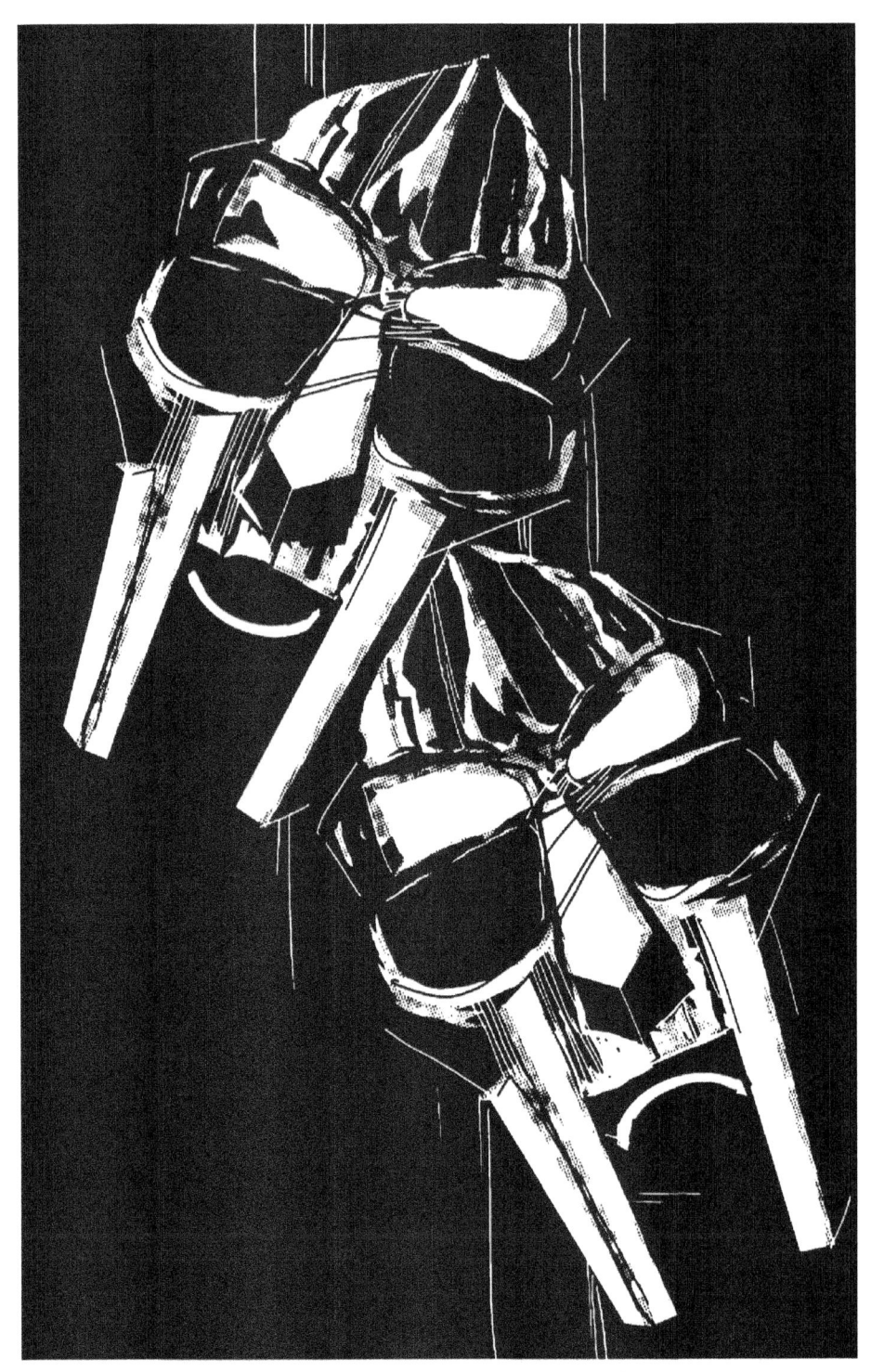

Figure 3.1. Born Like This Again
Computer Image, art by John Jennings

3

✥

Head on Straight, Mask on Crooked

MF DOOM and the Trope of the Mask

Nicholas James

In 2001, *Bl_ck B_st_rds,* an album recorded by the short-lived rap group KMD was remastered and rereleased under the independent label, Sub Verse Records. The album was predominantly ignored by the mainstream Hip Hop fan-base, as many independently released rap albums were at the turn of the century. Similar to many of its independent contemporaries, *Bl_ck B_st_rds* faded into obscurity without any significant attention given to it on the popular music scene. Seven years later, in October of 2008, when independent Hip Hop encountered new patrons in search of raw, authentic rap, aesthetically reminiscent of the Golden Age of Hip Hop, *Bl_ck B_st_rds* was rereleased again, this time under the label Metal Face Records.[1] Originally slated for release in 1994 by Elektra Records, the *Bl_ck B_st_rds* album cover depicts a cartoon drawing of a *Little Black Sambo* figure being hanged.[2] The cover art was deliberately contentious inviting critique and commentary on race and popular culture. The themes and the effect of this cover art were consistent with the ways that KMD constructed and projected their artistic identities. KMD's first and only commercial album, *Mr. Hood,* opines on social injustices, racial stereotypes, and various other cultural issues. But because this occurred at a time when the controversy over censorship and rap music was extraordinary, Elektra demanded that KMD front-man, Zev Love X, change the artwork of the album. Zev refused. *Bl_ck B_st_rds* was never commercially released to the mainstream. And eventually, Zev faded into obscurity.

In 1999, *Ego Trip's Book of Rap Lists* voted *Bl_ck B_st_rds*, with its "more pronounced musical and lyrical aggressiveness," as the most notable rap album never to be released.[3] Around the same time, Metal Face Records released *Operation: Doomsday* on a small budget with little to no promotion. The artist was a "newcomer" called MF DOOM. Ta-Nehisi Coates, an award winning writer and journalist, notes that MF DOOM "did literally what most rappers only do metaphorically: he wore a mask."[4] A decade later, at the time of the Metal Face Records' rerelease of *Bl_ck B_st_rds*, MF DOOM had established himself as one of the most well-known MCs in what aficionados refer to as the underground Hip Hop scene. Since *Operation: Doomsday*,[5] MF DOOM has produced a number of efforts, including the 2003 independent Hip Hop classic *Madvillainy*, a collaboration album with world-renowned producer Madlib (together, they are known as Madvillain); 2004's *MM . . FOOD*; a live album in 2005 called *Live from Planet X*; his most popular work, a collaborative piece with the oft-sought-after producer Danger Mouse, and in conjunction with [*adult swim*] of the Cartoon Network, called *The Mouse and the Mask*, also from 2005; and more recently, 2009's *Born Like This*.

By 2008, the audiences that were captivated by MF DOOM, a self-described super-villain, were also well aware that the man behind the mask was the former KMD front man, Zev Love X. For fans, critics, and scholars alike, this posed important questions regarding MF DOOM/ Zev Love X: given that his identity is no longer secret (if it ever was), what is the mask's significance now, and why continue to wear it? This chapter briefly explores critical connections between cultural theories and artistic identity construction in an effort to unveil the historical and figurative implications of the mask of MF DOOM, as well as its emergence as a trope in contemporary American media and popular/Hip Hop culture. The *Bl_ck B_st_rds* album cover, as its subsequent censoring indicates, and DOOM's mask-wearing signify the possibility that the haunting history of black artists in popular culture still draws breath in contemporary African American performance art, particularly here in underground Hip Hop.

The mask occupies contested space in the history of black/American theatre and literature; it becomes particularly complicated in Hip Hop culture and rap music. The mask has served many purposes—from its more subtle function in the Sugar Hill Gang/Cold Crush Brothers controversy over "Rapper's Delight" to its brilliant, social interpretation in the 1996 song "The Mask" by The Fugees. For rap artists such as Ghostface Killah and MF DOOM, the mask carries out a utilitarian purpose in that it literally obscures the faces of these artists, even as it simultaneously communicates symbolic and/or figurative meanings. The mask has had a consistent and complex capacity to figure and symbolize broader themes in the popular ethos of Hip Hop culture and in mainstream society. In his expressive memoir/treatise, *Covering: The Hidden Assault on our Civil Rights*, Kenji Yoshino discusses the unfortunate insistence on conformity in America and its harmful effects on the civil rights of American people—particularly those with acknowledged cultural differences based on race, ethnicity, gender, sexual orientation, and religion. Yoshino writes, "Everyone covers. To cover is to tone down a disfavored identity to fit into the mainstream."[6] Yoshino's argument is that covering, or assimilation to the "mainstream," is a standard American practice and regrettably a survival tool that must be altered in order to thwart the sociocultural modes that produce the need to conform. As a result, he proposes a paradigmatic shift in identity development/ construction, based on the preliminary authentication and preservation of one's self-identity. Owing to its conceptualization as a new methodology for civil rights, Yoshino's theory is suggestive for how the mask functions for constituents of Hip Hop culture, and how self-identity formation in Hip Hop compellingly compares to other canonized theories throughout history, particularly to those concerned with the conditions of black people in America. One such theory, worth briefly exploring is W. E. B. Du Bois' assessment of the "Negro" situation in America in his classic collection: *The Souls of Black Folk*.

Du Bois discusses the black, or "Negro" situation as it appears in the American South and paints a vivid picture of the "Negro's" social considerations throughout America. In "Of Our Spiritual Strivings," he introduces a theory of double-consciousness, a regularly cited definition of a condition internalized by black folk as they endeavor to make progress in a country where the "American Dream" does not apply to their kind. According to Du Bois: "[t]he Negro is sort of a seventh son, born with a veil, and gifted with second-sight in this American world,— a world which yields him no true self-consciousness, but only lets him see himself through the revelation of the other world,"[7] He goes on to suggest that it is "a peculiar sensation . . . measuring one's soul by the tape of a world that looks on in amused contempt and pity."[8] Note here that by "the revelation of the other world," Du Bois is referring to the panoramic view of society dictated by a mainstream culture of southern, and in many cases, northern whites, with whom black folk must conduct their everyday lives. He adds that "one ever feels his twoness,—an American, (and) a Negro."[9] The dilemma here is that the "American Negro" is self-conscious in ways that undermine her authentic sense of herself, according to mainstream American standards. In *Resistance, Parody, and Double-Consciousness in African American Theatre, 1895–1910,*

David Krasner adds that, "for Du Bois, double-consciousness is by and large, unhealthy."[10] Black people, according to Du Bois, will always carry the heavy burden of double-consciousness, a burden thrust upon them by the social protocol of the American mainstream. Du Bois also suggests that the "Negro's second-sight in this American world" is a gift, if it can be cultivated. This is a sensory approach to the African American experience in society. The "second-sight," or having a gift for intuition and/or clairvoyance in African American folklore, gives black folks advantages that the "other world" cannot comprehend. And the historical challenges to African American identity, community, and humanity itself continue to inform/shape socioeconomic conditions in the twenty-first century. One of the many challenges for black folk is how to deal with this burden of history.[11] Krasner argues that the aggravation of living a double-conscious life "culminates in a desire (as Du Bois writes) 'to make it possible for a man to be both a Negro and an American, without being cursed and spit upon by his fellows.'"[12]

Through his own critical engagement with Du Bois' theory of double-consciousness, Nathan Huggins argues that Du Bois' analysis "fails only to make explicit an important corollary: this "double-consciousness" opens to the Negro—through his own quest and passion—a unique insight into the vulnerable and unfulfilled soul of that other world; a possibility which, once grasped, liberates one forever from the snarls of that other world's measuring tape."[13] For Huggins, double-consciousness presents an opportunity for one to transcend the limitations of the other world, and become his own authentic self—this is especially significant for popular culture artists. For an artist like MF DOOM, this "unique insight" allows him to step outside of and away from the conventions of popular rap music. He can use his art, as performer and composer, to make a statement about the conditions of his craft and as a creative opportunity to both resist social norms and inform his audience.

Du Bois and Huggins suggest that an important relationship exists between self-consciousness, satire, and the American sociocultural world. And here Henry Louis Gates' notion of signifyin' is useful. Signifyin' "is the figurative difference between the literal and the metaphorical, between surface [or manifest] and latent [hidden or masked meaning] ... Signifyin(g) presupposes an 'encoded' intention to say one thing but mean quite another."[14] Gates explores and ultimately defines the outcomes of and subjective responses to double-consciousness. Paul Laurence Dunbar's classic poem, "We Wear the Mask" lyrically captures the encoded nature of the mask in the African American experiential tradition. "We wear the mask that grins and lies / It hides our cheeks and shades our eyes."[15] In an essay presenting the "dissident forms of black expression," Paul Gilroy views Dunbar's poem as an extraordinary moment for black aesthetic cultural history. According to Gilroy, Dunbar "comments acutely upon the institution of minstrelsy, while also managing to convey both the stresses and the opportunities that can arise from refining the ability to manipulate the expectations of whites who are misled by the consistency with which those whom they dominate (and on whom they depend) deploy the mask."[16] For Gilroy, the intense quality of agony and despair for black people in the theatre at the turn of the century, the pain to which Dunbar's "We Wear the Mask" alludes "is of special significance to contemporary black artists who operate within a more extensive cultural circuitry than the one Dunbar knew."[17] In other words, the range of social and artistic situations within which contemporary black artists might "wear the mask" has expanded; the "cultural circuitry" of the current moment presents a complex of subjective choices that artists must make in order to construct their identities and creative personas. In short, MF DOOM's mask-wearing is an important nuanced instance of artistic identity formation with deep connections to Du Boisian double-consciousness, Gates' notion of signifyin', the African American tradition of "wearing the mask," and the history of blackface minstrelsy.

The task of discerning the exact derivation of how blackface minstrelsy developed in the United States is mystifying. In terms of popular culture, the first blackface performance is usually traced back to the early theatre exhibitions of Shakespeare's *Othello*. In America though, minstrelsy arises from an artistic revolt against standard European musical forms (the customary classical and theological brands). In his ambitious study, *Black Like You*, John Strausbaugh suggests that minstrel performances constitute original forms of American music. He argues that southern "Negro" folk songs and new modes of instrumentation contributed to the blackface minstrelsy's origins as "blacks and whites admired and picked up each other's music and dances from the earliest colonial days." He proposes that, "the exchanges went both ways." However the racism that becomes indicative of the minstrel show converges with mainstream white America's detachment from or aversion to the possibility of "race-mixing," including integration and miscegenation, which Strausbaugh himself believed "would dilute the American stock."[18] The minstrel show is often viewed as the first authentic piece of American popular culture. Throughout the nineteenth and early twentieth centuries, minstrelsy was mainstream American popular culture and entertainment. Consisting mostly of white male performers dressed/masked in blackface, the minstrel show purposefully advanced degrading stereotypes that black folk, particularly black males, were lazy, shiftless, subservient, unintelligent, unintelligible, and exotic. During the post–Civil War years, the pleasurable presentation of authentic American music that catered to white audiences found amusement in representing racist assumptions, reflecting stereotypical behavior of black people. This theatrical misrepresentation of African American people, life, and culture was put on display as comic relief for white audiences, and constructed a framework for the roles of black performers that many believe still exists today. Within that framework, these misrepresentations continued in the emergence of American film, television, and now find purchase in the marketing of contemporary black popular culture (the Hip Hop generation).[19]

Over time, in an attempt to confound the mainstream conventions and prescribed positions, many black performers would mask themselves in blackface and create their own "minstrel shows." Krasner writes that "many black performers gained access to the theatre by imitating a misrepresentation of blackness constructed by whites . . . Black performers had to advertise themselves as "authentic" representatives, while simultaneously imitating counterfeit mannerisms and styles conjured up by whites."[20] Krasner defines this phenomenon as reinscription: "the manner in which black performers entered into blackface caricature and refashioned it,"[21] no doubt intending to find gainful employment, as well as a modicum of artistic and racial signifyin' through a craft in which they believed. Theoretically and practically, in the African and African American tradition, the mask has been in operation throughout much of history. Perhaps the most significant explication of the mask for the case of MF DOOM comes again from Henry Louis Gates, Jr., from a section titled "Black Structures of Feeling" in *Figures in Black*. In the context of his discussion of Esu Elegbara as both the trickster figure and the physical embodiment of signification, Gates employs the mask as a symbol of a complicated history. He writes, "it is the mask that attracts us to blackness . . . for therein is contained, as well as reflected, a coded, secret, hermetic world, a world discovered only by the initiate."[22]

In this context, MF DOOM's mask which, to borrow from Du Bois, yields him no true self-consciousness, or rather no true self-identity in this mercenary pop cultural, "other" world which still "looks on in amused contempt and pity," ultimately affords him the artistic underground identity he desires. In order to unravel the intricacies of MF DOOM's mask-wearing, one has to go beyond the broad-based, traditional approaches to black identity, and become an initiate as Gates proposes, delving into the abstract, the unconventional—precisely where MF DOOM thrives artistically. To be one of the few total initiates to the world of MF DOOM, one must have adept insight in various arenas, including comic books, science fiction, foreign and independent film, cartoons, current events, African American literature and its literary tradition, world history, etc. as well as the cultural history of Hip Hop. In the production of his own music, which indeed wears its own mask, MF DOOM writes and records songs, and creates whole compositions that totally disrupt the formulaic protocol for structuring popular mainstream singles and chart-topping albums in rap and popular music. Lines such as one where DOOM employs his mask in an effort to conceal his "raw flesh" provide rich opportunities for analysis. Exploring and analyzing the connection between this line from the song "Beef Rapp" and Yoshino's sense of covering and conformity suggest important insights into DOOM's artistic persona. DOOM's "raw flesh" lyric intimates that he does not have a face at all; that is, he has no skin beneath the mask. In the world of popular culture inhabited by MF DOOM, convention eradicates the skin/face off of the individual. Conformity dominates identity construction and in this context, one's ugliness can be countered by verbal or lyrical beauty and the absence of an individual face can be countered by wearing the mask. Still, DOOM's actual wearing of a mask suggests that he in some ways, artistically delves into an abstract arena where the artist literally becomes the mask.

MF DOOM, (né Daniel Dumile) was born in London, England and raised in Long Island, New York. In 1989 he was a featured guest on a song by then-popular rap duo 3rd Bass called "The Gas Face." "The Gas Face" poked fun at corruption, exploitation, and a host of other maladies present in popular culture and in the rap music industry. Everyone, from Adolf Hitler to MC Hammer, is targeted. KMD would drop its first album, *Mr. Hood*, in 1991. Zev Love X was the clear front person of the group. His own abstract consciousness was appealing, but not enough for KMD to be more than a blip on the radar screen of the pop music industry. The next two years would see the death of his brother, and KMD partner, Subroc, who was killed in a car accident. All of this preceded and eventually led up to Elektra Records' censoring of KMD's project, *Bl_ck B_stards*, due to its cover art. The cover art for *Bl_ck B_st_rds* puts into bold relief its lifeless, soulless, Sambo subject, noosed and suspended, presumably for an audience to view in awe, amazement, fear, or indifference. The animated image of the Sambo is typically associated with aloofness and carelessness—the blasé black male figure subject to violence for comedic effect, often portrayed in minstrel shows and early Hollywood films, when roles for African American actors were scarce. For KMD, the Sambo figure in the cover art represents the rapper, the "black bastard," in contemporary popular culture, who has to concede his own integrity and authenticity, or as

Kenji Yoshino suggests, to "cover" in order to attain acceptance by/ in the mainstream. For KMD, rap music is becoming, as Spike Lee's brilliant 2000 film *Bamboozled* might conclude, "The New Millennium Minstrel Show." The *Bl_ck B_stards* album cover functions as a critical symbol for Hip Hop at the close of its Golden Age (circa 1993). It metaphorically suggests what rapper/MC Nas would expound upon more than a decade later: that Hip Hop is dead.[23] More accurately stated, popular Hip Hop music no longer represents the underserved, culturally authentic populace from which the culture emerged. It implies that through a rapper's tacit agreement to "coon" (and cover) for mainstream acceptance he rids himself of his own authenticity. The ultimate outcome for these artists is a symbolic lynching, after having given mainstream popular culture just enough rope for the hanging, in exchange for apparent capital gains. One of the ironies here is that KMD's label, Elektra Records, forced the group to "cover" by changing the image of the album under threat of eventually shelving it. For Zev Love X though, the stalling of the album, and as a result, KMD's career, appeared to be a more honorable (if figurative) death.

After the *Bl_ck B_stards* saga, and the death of his brother/partner-in-rhyme, Subroc, Daniel Dumile decided that in order to resurrect his rap career, and possess control of his artistic identity, he would wear a mask. In a 2009 interview in *The New Yorker* called "The Mask of DOOM," MF DOOM explains that the mask "came out of necessity ... a visual always brings a first impression. But if there's going to be a first impression, I might as well use it to control the story. So why not do something like throw a mask on?"[24] In choosing the mask and the name MF DOOM, Dumile assumed the characterization and disposition of the super-villain, similar to the legendary Marvel Comics' character he resembles. MF DOOM, like Marvel's Dr. Doom, seeks to exact revenge on those responsible for the demise of his life in a figurative signifyin' sense. Viktor Vaughn, phonetically equivalent to Dr. Doom's alias (Victor Von), functions as one of MF DOOM's many alter egos. With superior intellect, keen foresight, and brute force, he seeks to outwit everyone and conquer everything in his path. Dr. Doom was also an inventor, and one of his most notable inventions was a machine intended to liberate his mother's soul from eternal damnation. During the energizing process, the machine exploded, leaving Dr. Doom's face scarred, forcing him to wear a mask. This mask contributes to his criminal-mythical existence, and allows him to design duplicates of himself called "Doombots."[25] MF DOOM, as rapper/super-villain, wreaks similar (if figurative) havoc across the domain of underground Hip Hop culture. And MF DOOM's mask-wearing allows him to introduce the possibility that Dumile himself has "Doombots" who sometimes stand in for him and perform his shows as MF DOOM.

The first couplet of "The Mask," from MF DOOM's most popular work, a collaborative effort with the esoteric producer Danger Mouse called "The Mouse and the Mask," and also the inspiration for and title of this paper, claims that his head is "on straight." But his mask is "crooked." This line definitively names the trope of the mask and intimates its functionality as a signifying practice. As I suggested earlier, Gates informs us that signifyin(g) implies "an 'encoded' intention to say one thing but mean quite another," and in effect, layer multiple meanings upon language in social-cultural contexts within which this layering serves the interests of the subject. MF DOOM's lyrics about his own mask articulate a commonly referenced problem with artists collecting compensation from promoters after performances. Dumile's head is on straight in this instance, meaning that he is focused on being compensated for his work, a focus that takes on broader cultural significance in the context of the historical exploitation and commodification of black art. The mask is always "on crooked" in the sense that it is not supposed to be neatly aligned with the identity of its wearer. In this verse, DOOM's crooked mask obscures the promoter's capacity to respect the lengths that DOOM is prepared to go to in order to collect what is owed to him for his artistic performance. The model of mental acuity, that is, straightness, and the mask of obscurity, that is, crookedness, works to configure the significance of wearing the mask as a subversive strategy in black popular culture, especially in the Hip Hop music industry.[26]

In 2008, there was some controversy around the absent-presence of MF DOOM, at live performances. In strikingly similar fashion to Doctor Doom's "Doombots," some believe that MF DOOM sent "DOOMposters" on stage, in mask, to perform entire sets at concerts. For MF DOOM, this is a requisite signifying practice, a natural extension of the mask-wearing that has become a staple of his artistic identity. However, in a web blog titled "An Open Letter to MF DOOM,"[27] Kno of the independent rap group CunninLynguists condemns MF DOOM for pulling these "DOOMposter" stunts, infuriating talent buyers, promoters, and venue operators, whom most independent rap artists actually depend on to earn a living. Kno is, of course, criticizing DOOM for affecting his ability to work in the underground/independent Hip Hop music scene. Kno writes "people don't buy much music anymore. Touring is what allows artists . . . to meet our fans, fuel our art and put money into our projects and pockets."[28] He goes on to argue that the potential to arrange and reserve performance opportunities is becoming scant, at best, and that MF DOOM's "act" is only hurting the reputation of the independent rap artist. Kno makes a convincing argument, one that makes sense given DOOM's "head on straight/mask on crooked" lyrics. But those same lyrics suggest that there is a pivotal method to MF DOOM's madness. Coates writes, "If Dumile had his way, he would take it further. He jokes that he'd like to dart backstage after a performance, take off the mask, and then wade into the crowd—beer in hand—and applaud his own work." To which, MF DOOM remarks "I'm the writer, I'm the director."[29] The exhibition of the "DOOMposters" demonstrates more critical significance than simply duping the audience or impeding the progress of other independent rappers. In effect, DOOM's mask-wearing trickery allows him to perform in multiple venues simultaneously; it subtly critiques his own audience for their inability to discern his artistic voice; and it further enhances the signifyin' mystique of wearing the mask in the first place.

The artistry of MF DOOM connects to a profound history of subversion in black literature, performance, and culture. In critical ways, MF DOOM represents these rich traditions in Hip Hop culture. The historical and theoretical thread throughout black popular culture produces fascinating links for the signifying legacy that MF DOOM inherits. The presence of MF DOOM's mask-wearing tactics in the contexts of race, identity, and popular culture allow for important connections between black art history and the construction of identity for the Hip Hop generation. Hip Hop culture, much like other black arts movements, is a traditional extension of previous black artistic and cultural discourses. In the same ways in which jazz, the blues, and soul musical forms are linked to several categorical elements crucial to cultural movements (the Harlem Renaissance, Civil Rights, and Black Power movements for example), Hip Hop music is an important component of the Hip Hop generation's expressive resistance to hegemony. This contemporary hegemony for Bakari Kitwana takes shape as: "high rates of suicide and imprisonment, police brutality, the generation gap, the war of the sexes, blacks selling black hatred, among others."[30] At its best, Hip Hop music provides a platform for voices that speak to contemporary black crises. Part of what separates MF DOOM from other Hip Hop artists, who embrace themes of resistance, is the unique parallel his character shares with the origins of black popular culture. Performers during the minstrel era, the dawn of American popular culture, reinscribed standard notions and stereotypes of black culture, and in so doing, provided for themselves and developed signifying practices within their craft. MF DOOM does the same through his subversive, super-villainous mask—obscuring and altering the image of the rapper, and reconstructing it in order to challenge identity conventions in popular Hip Hop music. In an interview with *Village Voice*, Dumile once said, "The oppressors usually look at the people they're oppressing as the villains. But the oppressed are the heroes to the people . . . I'll be the villain. I'll be the hero to the hip-hop world."[31] This is the persona under review—an artist in tune with his critical role, in control of his own boundless creative universe, and fully aware of his own practical joke on society.

NOTES

1. The Golden Age of Hip Hop typically refers to a time in history, roughly 1986–1994, where rap music first experienced and sustained mainstream success, yet remained culturally authentic.

2. *Little Black Sambo* is a controversial children's story written in 1899 by Helen Bannerman. Viewed as a stereotypical depiction of black children, the story has been criticized and demonized throughout its history.

3. Sacha Jenkins, et al., *Ego Trip's Book of Rap Lists* (New York: St. Martin's Press, 1999), 156.

4. Ta-Nehisi Coates, "The Mask of DOOM: A Nonconformist Rapper's Second Act," *New Yorker*, September 21, 2009, 52.

5. MF DOOM, *Operation: Doomsday*, April 20, 1999, Fondle 'Em Records, Sub Verse Music (compact disc). Ironically (or not), was also rereleased in October of 2008, again by Metal Face Records.

6. Kenji Yoshino, *Covering: The Hidden Assault on Our Civil Rights* (New York: Random House, 2006), ix.

7. W. E. B. Du Bois, *The Souls of Black Folk*, in *Three Negro Classics*, introduction by John Hope Franklin (New York: Avon Books, 1965), 214–15.

8. Ibid., 215.

9. Ibid.

10. David Krasner, *Resistance, Parody, and Double-Consciousness in African American Theatre, 1895–1910* (New York: St. Martin's Press, 1997), 52.

11. Du Bois, *Souls of Black Folk* (1965), 3. Throughout the history of African descendants in America, different designations and identifiers have been given and created to represent and characterize black people. Each title carries distinction and holds different, multilayered cultural representations, from "negro" to the "n-word."

12. W. E. B. Du Bois, quoted in Krasner, *Resistance*, 8–9.

13. Nathan Huggins, *Harlem Renaissance* (New York: Oxford University Press, 1971), 245.

14. Henry Louis Gates, Jr., *The Signifying Monkey: A Theory of African-American Literary Criticism* (New York: Oxford University Press, 1988), 82.

15. Paul Laurence Dunbar, "We Wear the Mask," in *Lyrics of Lowly Life* (New York: Dodd Mead, 1896), 167.

16. Paul Gilroy, "'To Be Real': The Dissident Forms of Black Expressive Culture," in *Let's Get It On: The Politics of Black Performance*, ed. Catherine Ugwu (Seattle, WA: Bay Press, 1995), 16.

17. Ibid., 17.

18. John Strausbaugh, *Black Like You: Blackface, Whiteface, Insult & Imitation in American Popular Culture* (New York: Jeremy P. Tarcher/Penguin, 2006; repr. 2007), 70, 71, and 64.

19. Submitted by Bakari Kitwana, the "Hip Hop Generation," comprises young black people born between 1965 and 1984. He posits that this generation succeeds the civil rights generation, yet faces different social challenges such as "disproportionate incarceration and unemployment rates." (*The Hip Hop Generation: Young Blacks and the Crisis in African-American Culture* [New York: Basic Civitas, 2002]).

20. Krasner, *Resistance*, 25.

21. Ibid.

22. Henry Louis Gates, Jr., *Figures in Black: Words, Signs, and the "Racial" Self* (New York: Oxford University Press, 1987), 167.

23. Nas, *Hip Hop is Dead*, Def Jam, December 19, 2006 (compact disc).

24. Coates' interview, "The Mask of DOOM," 53.

25. Viktor Vaughn, "Doctor Doom (Victor Von Doom)," *Marvel Universe*, http://marvel.com/universe/Doctor_Doom_Victor_von_Doom) (accessed February 19, 2010).

26. This is reminiscent of *The Autobiography of an Ex-Colored Man*. Originally written anonymously, this narrative sketches a character attempting to discover an identity, while simultaneously accounting for the Negro race in America, and navigating existent white stereotypes and conventions, circa 1912. These contrasting perspectives of identity come to life through the narrator's realization of the limitations and possibilities of "blackness" in America. James Weldon Johnson writes: "I know I am playing with fire, and I feel the thrill which accompanies that most fascinating pastime; and, back of it all, I think I find a sort of savage and diabolical desire to gather up all the little tragedies of my life, and turn them into a practical joke on society," (Weldon, *The Autobiography of an Ex-Colored Man*. In *Three Negro Classics*, introduction by John Hope Franklin [New York: Avon Books, 1965], 393). This passage becomes a vehicle of signification, generating an impulse to "gather up all the little tragedies" of MF DOOM's life, and negotiate the impetus and potential for his own "practical joke on society." My suggestion here is that the "Ex-Colored Man," in anonymity, represented no black man and every black man. Through wearing the mask, any black person can dare to identify with, and interpret herself or himself as the archetypal trickster figure in African American culture. MF DOOM fits into this "trickster figure" role effortlessly. His mask can operate however he wishes, and with whatever pretense, but what's under the mask (and at times, detached from the mask) is always intact.

27. Kno, "An Open Letter to MF DOOM," *QN5* (blog), posted August 13, 2008, http://www.qn5.com/blog/entry/an-open-letter-to-mf-doom/ (accessed November 9, 2009).

28. Ibid., n.p.

29. Coates' interview, "The Mask of DOOM," 54.
30. Bakari, *Hip Hop Generation*, xi.
31. Ben Westoff, "Private Enemy: Two New York Rappers Dreamed of Stardom. MF Doom Got It. MF Grimm Didn't," *Villagevoice.com*, October 31, 2006, http://www.villagevoice.com/2006-10-31/music/private-enemy (accessed April 13, 2014).

Figure 4.1. Super G
Computer Image, art by John Jennings

4

✢

Superhero Aesthetics in Hip Hop Culture
Will Boone

Comic books and superheroes have been cited as early influences on hip hop aesthetics.[1] This chapter explores the interface between superhero aesthetics, artistic identity construction and Hip Hop culture. The influence of comic book superheroes is reflected in all of the elements of Hip Hop culture including: graffiti, breaking/B-boying, MC-ing, and DJ-ing. Superheroes have played a central role in American youth and popular culture since the 1930s and 1940s, a period widely regarded as the Golden Age of comic books.[2] In *Comic Book Culture: An Illustrated History*, Ron Goulart defines the Golden Age of comic books as "running from the late 1930s, marked by the advent of Superman and his earliest imitators, through the deluge of costumed crime fighters and into the late 1940s, by which time the majority of superhumans had just faded away."[3] One question that emerges from the juxtaposition of superheroes and certain personas in rap music and Hip Hop culture is: what are the significant implications with respect to identity for Hip Hop culture's appropriation of superheroes?

Early Hip Hop pioneers such as DJ Kool Herc, Grandmaster Flash, Kool Keith, and The Fantastic Romantic 5 are all examples of the influence of superhero and comic book culture on Hip Hop culture.[4] The emergent and then fleeting popularity of DeAndre Way (aka Soulja Boy) and the success of his viral hit "Crank That" underscores the ongoing centrality of superhero aesthetics in Hip Hop.[5] Hip Hop artists' appropriation of superhero aesthetics, as with previous African American

49

music forms, is about deconstructing identity, as well as questioning and revising "accepted notions of reality."[6] This appropriation is not a wholesale transliteration of superhero iconography and aesthetics. Instead, Hip Hop artists excerpt attributes and monikers of superheroes and certain comic book narratives for their own artistic personas. My focus here is on the sampling of comic book superhero aesthetics within Hip Hop culture.[7] My goal is to unravel some of the underlying sociocultural tensions and assumptions about superhero narratives as they relate to race, class, and Hip Hop culture in order to better understand the *hidden transcripts* within Hip Hop texts. I am concerned with three fundamental questions: (1) What does the embrace and sampling of certain superheroes reveal about the development of Hip Hop aesthetics? That is, what are some of the motivations—at least from a racial and/or subjective identity perspective—behind Hip Hop's embrace of superhero aesthetics?; (2) How is superhero mythology utilized and refashioned within Hip Hop culture?; and (3) What are the ways in which Hip Hop artists have reappropriated superhero iconography (that is, themes, motifs, etc.)? At issue here are the ways that Hip Hop artists project superhero iconography, aesthetics, and conventions through dress, attitude, lyrical content, and other forms of reappropriation. At least since 1987, Hip Hop aesthetics have vacillated between the poles of superhero and super-villain character traits. MCs, DJs, B-boys, and graffiti artists sample superhero iconography and conventions in various ways (for example, masking, signifying, dual-identity aesthetics, lyrical sampling, etc.), consistent with the wide range of cultural and identity-oriented practices across the African American experience.

African American heroes, icons, tropes, and archetypes serve as important links to the roles that African American culture played in the development of Hip Hop. In *Black Culture and Black Consciousness: Afro-American Folk Thought from Slavery to Freedom*, Lawrence W. Levine views folk heroes and lore as functional modes of expression for African Americans.[8] He argues that the meaning behind the selection of African American heroes is always in flux. Similarly, the iconography of identity in Hip Hop is constantly shifting, reflecting (and responding to) social-cultural attitudes and sensibilities of the constituents of Hip Hop culture. Hip Hop culture's affinity for superheroes is partially linked to its African American heritage. Hip Hop art is often times some form of bricolage[9]; it samples from all available texts.[10] Along with African American pop cultural icons in sports and entertainment, comic book superheroes and super-villains are Hip Hop artists' preferred iconographic selections. Hip Hop's embrace of specific superheroes reflects the influence and importance of folk heroes in American and African American culture. Moreover, Hip Hop culture's remix of superhero aesthetics and its reliance upon superhero identity tend to perpetuate hypermasculinty and/or reinforce established patriarchal norms (for example, black male privilege, domestic violence, the objectification of women, etc.).

African American icons and archetypes such as Muhammad Ali, Richard Pryor, and/or the badman trope itself provide the sociocultural and subjective contexts for certain aesthetic choices within Hip Hop culture. American pop culture icons, including comic book superheroes of European descent, also inform and shape rappers' aesthetic choices. Until the 1990s, there were a limited number of African American superheroes. The vast majority of superheroes were white and male.[11] On one level, the sampling of superhero conventions in Hip Hop is a reclamation and celebration of the black superhero. But superhero allusions in Hip Hop music also serve to signify on and critique the dearth of African American superheroes in popular culture. This critique should not reduce Hip Hop culture's appropriation of popular superheroes to political criticism or some form of cultural coping mechanism. Robin D. Kelley, *Yo' Mama's DisFunktional*, argues that "hip hop must be understood as a sonic force more than anything else."[12] In other words, the appropriation of superhero conventions in Hip Hop culture can be as much about aesthetics and the production of art as it can be about sociopolitical critique.

Hip Hop activates superhero aesthetics through style, hyperbole, the superhero mission to save their community, and/or Hip Hop itself, the utilization of the badman/badwoman trope and the dual-identity (or codename), and superior—that is, superheroic lyrical ability. Although Hip Hop's embrace of comic book superheroes reflects trends in American popular culture in general, the ways in which Hip Hop aesthetics employ superhero narratives is unique. Traditional superheroes are not radical revolutionaries seeking to overthrow the government.[13] For many MCs, undermining the status quo is an expressed intention or goal of their music. In popular Hip Hop music, the use of the superhero is more about deconstructing American meta-narratives as opposed to reifying Western ideals via traditional superheroes. Superhero conventions and Hip Hop culture are two of the most pervasive and dominant forms of twentieth century, American popular culture. Juxtaposing superhero aesthetics and Hip Hop provides historical context for a particular worldview—mapping the intersection of certain key figures and tropes within Hip Hop music and the ways that they interface with the constructs of race, gender, and popular culture.

The popular and pervasive nature of superhero iconography coupled with African American folkloric traditions within a post-industrial, racially stratified society sets the stage for Hip Hop's aesthetic appropriation of superhero mythology and iconography. In *Superhero: the Secret Origin of a Genre*, Peter Coogan argues that there are three primary conventions or definitional characteristics of the superhero: mission, power, and identity.[14] Comic book superhero references are present in every element of Hip Hop culture including graffiti and DJ-ing. The B-boy and B-girl, by definition, possess superhuman abilities. Whether the B-boy is a dancer, MC, DJ, scholar, or graffiti artist, the expectation is that the individual be highly skilled.[15] The emphasis here is on lyrical allusions and the trajectory of certain rap personas within Hip Hop culture. Hip Hop culture builds upon previous formulations of American masculinity portrayed in superhero narratives.[16] Comic book conventions closely parallel conceptualizations of African American masculinity, including some well-circulated African American stereotypes.[17] In *Heroes and Villains*, Mike Alsford situates heroes and villains within a larger sociopolitical framework. He posits that heroes and villains are "iconic receptacles" that represent cultural values.[18] Hip Hop's reappropriation of certain heroic narratives reflects certain ideas and formulations about identity within the culture. In "Sacred-Secular Icons," Gregor Goethals discusses heroes as models within contemporary society.[19] However, the majority of superheroes that are sampled within Hip Hop are not African American. On the surface, it appears that Hip Hop's appropriation of superheroes of European descent is an attempt to disrupt, revise, and transcend traditional racial constructs.[20] Although Hip Hop's sampling of superhero identity can be viewed as social resistance and/or political critique, it is equally productive to view superhero aesthetics in Hip Hop as "stylistic and aesthetic convention."[21] Within a Hip Hop cultural context, adornment and brand affiliation can inscribe "superpowers of attitude and protection."[22]

In order to consider the trajectories of superhero iconography within Hip Hop aesthetics, I divide the eras of superhero influence in Hip Hop culture into five periods. Each period is marked by specific icons and figures of the timeframe in question. Period 1 (1973–1979) spans from Kool Herc to Grandmaster Flash. Period 2 (1980–1989) is marked by artists such as Kool Keith, Clark Kent, Luke Skywalker, and N.W.A. Period 3 (1991–1999) includes Redman, Wu-Tang Clan, Big Pun, Jeru the Damaja, MF DOOM, Foxy Brown, C-Murder, Capone-N-Noreaga, Mos Def, Jay-Z, and Ghostface Killah (aka Tony Starks/Iron Man). David Banner (akin to Bruce Banner/Hulk), Rick Ross, 50 Cent, Rah Digga, Jean Grae (as in the X-Men's Jean Gray), and Soulja Boy represent period 4 (2000–2007).[23] Period 3 represents an apogee of Hip Hop lyrical output. It elucidates the most salient remixes of superhero iconography since Hip Hop's emergence. Conversely and throughout these same time periods, Hip Hop narratives began to sample Mafioso-style aesthetics. These periods are not mutually exclusive nor do they represent rigidly divided categories. The purpose of this taxonomy is to elucidate the consistent influence that superhero iconography has had on artistic identity construction in Hip Hop culture, over time. As Hip Hop narratives shifted toward tragic realism and late-capitalist urban naturalism during the late 1980s and early 1990s, there was a decrease in the influence of superhero iconography within Hip Hop aesthetics, which was only to reemerge in the new millennium. From the late 1980s to the present, Hip Hop iconography and aesthetics have generated imagery of the superhero and the super-gangster. Collectively, superheroes, super-villains and super-gangsters are enmeshed within Hip Hop aesthetics and represent a range of artistic subject positions in Hip Hop culture.

Periods 2 and 3 coincide with the proliferation of gangsta motifs and allusions.[24] Luke Skywalker and DJ Clark Kent emerged alongside N.W.A., Schoolly D, and Scarface. By period 3, gangsta aesthetics and iconography, particularly "mafia-style" iconography, were firmly enmeshed within Hip Hop culture.[25] Whereas artists such as Redman, Big Pun, Wu-tang Clan, and MF DOOM drew heavily from superhero aesthetics, other artists and labels such as Naughty by Nature, Death Row Records, Bad Boy Records, The Notorious B.I.G., and Smif-N-Wessun embraced a deliberately gangsta iconography during the early to mid-1990s. Periods 2 and 3 coincide with what some Hip Hop scholars have labeled as the "Golden Era" of Hip Hop music.[26] Notably, these periods are skewed along gender lines. Until 2000, women MCs such as Foxy Brown, Lauryn Hill, Queen Latifah, Lil' Kim, and Rah Digga borrowed more heavily from the fashion world, the blues, and/or Black Nationalist iconography than they did from superhero aesthetics. Superpowers, more specifically the embodiment of physical might and strength, are an important feature of superhero conventions in Hip Hop culture. In regard to gender dynamics in Hip Hop culture, superpowers are significant because male MCs' use of superpowers—on one level—is an attempt to revise and reclaim discursive patriarchal power in a racialized, capitalist society. The minimal use of superhero conventions by women MCs, then, can be linked to the male-centric milieu of Hip Hop culture, as superhero aesthetics closely parallel traditional gender dynamics in society. Critical gender discourses (as well as feminist critiques of Hip Hop's patriarchy) more often occur between women who happen to be spoken word, Neo-soul, and R&B artists and their male counterparts in Hip Hop. This is due, at least partially, to the dearth of women in mainstream Hip Hop music. Women in Hip Hop negotiate the tension between limited artistic power and the pervasive use of superhero conventions in the music and culture.[27] Because superhero conventions rely so heavily on (super) power, African American women MCs such as Lauryn Hill, for example, focus more on losing and reclaiming power in a racist, patriarchal society rather than overpowering or controlling their physical environment.[28] Other women MCs, (for example, Nikki Minaj, Iggy Azalea, and Kreayshawn) reengage the hypermasculine gaze within Hip Hop culture and reinterpret sexual agency with varying degrees of critical productivity. In *The Hip Hop Wars,* Tricia Rose explains it this way: "many young women parrot the sexist ideas that are so widely circulated in hip hop; it's key to belonging."[29]

In terms of women MCs, superheroine aesthetics have provided a discursive space to reconcile inter-gender tensions in Hip Hop culture. Jean Grae's remix of a superhero persona iterates the subtle nuances of Hip Hop culture's embrace of superhero *and* super-villain aesthetics. Grae's rap persona is a reappropriation of Marvel Comics' superheroine Jean Grey/Marvel Girl. Jean Grey was a member of the original X-Men and was married to the team's original leader, Cyclops/Scott Summers. Jean Grey's marriage to Cyclops should not be understated. Superheroine aesthetics and narratives in Hip Hop culture (and in comics) tend to be less narcissistic and more communal, placing value on interpersonal relations, focusing more on love (and love loss), and generally tend to be more empathetic in tone.[30] On *Evil Jeanius,* an underground release by Grae that serves as a companion album to the officially released *Jeanius,* she underscores the complexities and nuances of super-villain and superheroine/superhero aesthetics in Hip Hop culture. On *Jeanius',* "Don't Rush Me," Grae struggles with the reality that her superheroine alter ego is forced to conceal her identity.[31] In these lyrics she plays on the wearing of the mask donned by superheroes and the wearing of an emotional mask more akin to Paul L. Dunbar's classic poem: "We Wear the Mask." (The nuances of which are more thoroughly explored in Nick James' chapter in this volume—"Head on Straight, Mask on Crooked"). Note here also that the Jean Grey of X-Men fame does not wear a mask. Grae's pairing of *Jeanius* and *Evil Jeanius* models the character arc of the X-Men's Jean Grey. Through a series of narratives and fantastic circumstances, Jean Grey eventually becomes host to the Phoenix force—"a sentient cosmic entity of limitless power."[32] The Phoenix force eventually overpowers her mind and she becomes the ultimate super-villain—Dark Phoenix. Jean Grae, the Hip Hop artist, plays on this cosmic-comic duality throughout her recorded work. She combines these ongoing allusions with one of the most well-known superheroines using allusions to the badwoman trope and African American iconography, and simultaneously aligning her narrative with traditional Hip Hop aesthetics.[33] Grae's alter ego possesses telekinetic superpowers—claiming that she can "bend spoons" by looking at them. She also reflects certain badman/badwoman themes as well, with references to drinking from a flask and referring to herself as "the bad ma'am."[34] The Jean Grae/Jean Grey example is significant for superheroine aesthetics in Hip Hop culture because she models a popular accessible allusion to a superhero that reflects her creative moniker and certain aspects of her artistic persona. The Jean Grae/Jean Grey example also offers lyrical proof that some women MCs appear to be concerned (like their male counterparts) in the heroic mission to save their community and all of Hip Hop culture, and they are more open to revealing emotions such as pain, grief, and love loss.[35]

In *The Tanning of America: How Hip Hop Created a Culture That Wrote the Rules of the New Economy*, Steve Stoute argues that by the 1980s rappers replaced sports heroes as the preferred icons for working-class, inner-city youth.[36] For Stoute, Hip Hop culture generated and shaped an economy that remains deeply influenced by the aesthetic choices of the culture's most popular and successful artists. In this context, creative decisions to embrace superhero iconography have become a part of the formula for popular success in the Hip Hop music industry—including music, fashion, artists' merchandise, touring, and a bevy of consumer products and promotional campaigns. According to Stoute, Hip Hop culture "began to fulfill the same functions that religious institutions have served throughout history."[37] While equating religious institutions with Hip Hop culture may be an overly simplistic assertion, the abiding impressions of superhero iconography on the artistry of Hip Hop music is undeniably present and characteristically reflective of certain elements of traditional religious institutions. Newark, New Jersey MC, Redman, utilizes multiple identities and superhero conventions in his narratives.[38] Redman borrows heavily from superhero aesthetics and conventions (particularly dual identity and superpowers), but it is his canny use of African American folkloric signifiers that activate superhero conventions within his lyrical body of work.[39] In an interview he explains the significance of superhero-influenced identities in Hip Hop. When asked what advice he would give to aspiring emcees, he advises them to return to superheroic identity constructions:

> But the first couple of mother f***ers that retract and start becoming superheroes again, and what I mean by superheroes is what I mean by names you can remember for the longest like Salt N Pepa, Big Daddy Kane, Biz Markie, Rakim, LL Cool J . . . The legends. See those are superhero names. Even when it came to the next generation up, like then when it came to '92 and '94 it was like with Wu-Tang, Redman, Busta Rhymes, Keith Murray. Those are big—those are superhero names . . . Like Redman. Those are big superhero names right now.[40]

Here Redman reiterates the importance of superhero iconography within Hip Hop culture. He also explicitly acknowledges the influence of superhero aesthetics on his own artistic persona. Consider "A Day of Sooperman Lover," where Redman signifies on the concept of smoking to suggest that he figuratively murders the competition.[41] Redman's use of an African American, folkloric signifier, in this case the badman trope, accentuates certain superhero aesthetics in his narratives. When Redman suggests that he is more powerful than "King-Kong" for example, he is tapping into the badman trope, boasting of superheroic physical strength and incorporating the African American tradition of signifying and toasting into his narrative.[42] Redman deploys superhero imagery and dual-identity techniques, but he also consistently returns to themes of realism as a way to reflect the socioeconomic conditions of the environments in Newark, New Jersey.[43] Redman also reminds the listener that he is involved in theatrical performance and hyperbole, in order to establish a superhero identity within a Hip Hop context. In effect, Redman links superhero mythos to certain socioeconomic realities.[44] Redman the "hip hop superhero"—despite superhuman abilities—also makes lyrical allusions to labor and a working-class struggle.[45] Within a Hip Hop worldview, particularly with respect to identity construction, the negotiation of work and "play" is an important aspect of reconciling the dual-identity conventions of superheroes.[46] Robin Kelley argues that several factors, including unemployment and the decline of youth programs have "altered the terrain of play and creative expression for black youth."[47] In Hip Hop lyrics, rapping superheroes do not necessarily have the same privileges or access to resources as their mainstream counterparts. Hip Hop superheroes like Redman's "Sooperman Lover" are unable to transcend the economic struggles of their community, despite their superpowers.[48] In the story worlds of DC Comics, Clark Kent, and Bruce Wayne, for example, are either gainfully employed and/or enjoy high-class status in society. Many of Hip Hop's reappropriated superhero characters generally have mundane jobs and are working class.

Aside from the dual-identity and the codename, the conventional superhero mission is one of the most appealing characteristics of superhero aesthetics in the construction of artistic personas in Hip Hop. The superhero's mission is central to the superhero's identity. Whenever the emphasis is on protecting the community, the mission narrative is closely aligned to Black Nationalist/Black Power politics.[49] It is within these "hidden transcripts" featuring Black Nationalist/Black Power rhetoric, in the post-industrial, post–civil rights environment, that superhero aesthetics take shape in Hip Hop culture.[50] A "hip hop superhero," then, can be viewed as a synthesis of comic superhero mythology, African American popular culture iconography, American popular culture sensibilities, and the African American folk tradition, all filtered through Hip Hop aesthetics.

The lyrics of Brooklyn-based MC Jeru the Damaja highlight the internal fissure within Hip Hop during the mid-1990s between gangster and "conscious" iconography and imagery. He also directly engages superhero iconography through the construction of his alter ego, the Black Prophet, and his mission to "save" Hip Hop from the limited themes of gangsterism and consumerism. Jeru's use of the Black Prophet alter ego links his narrative to superhero aesthetics not only through his reappropriation of the original "Prophet's" identity as an alter ego, but also through his focus on the mission to "save" Hip Hop culture from itself—particularly its newfound formulaic popularity driven by gangster and consumer themes. Jeru's Black Prophet assumes the mission of saving Hip Hop from ignorance and self-destruction.[51] Jeru's lyrics intermingle superhero aesthetics and conventions with inner-city imagery and Kung Fu cinema references. In the DJ Premier–produced classic "Come Clean," Jeru puts forth a scathing critique of the rise of "gangsta" imagery in Hip Hop culture, highlighting the aesthetic tension in Hip Hop between "fake gangsta MC's" and more progressive MCs. Throughout the song he remixes Kung Fu cinema iconography within a Hip Hop conceptual framework that fully employs superhero convention in the lyrical narrative.[52] Another song, Jeru's "Ain't The Devil Happy" aptly illustrates the interface between superhero aesthetics and Hip Hop aesthetics, critiquing both American capitalism and the Superman figure.[53] Jeru's allusion to "Men of Steel" serves as a site to critique (and revise) the superhero trope in Hip Hop and, more specifically, the Superman superhero figure. His appropriation of superhero imagery operates as a critique and revision of Superman's invincibility, as well as a critique of hyper-consumption and materialism. If "Men of Steel" weather and rust, then the identity construction of superheroic capabilities in Hip Hop culture is likewise vulnerable. For Jeru, this critique of superhero conventions within Hip Hop music is also a critique of the ways in which hypermasculinity overdetermines identity construction amongst the artists and constituents of Hip Hop culture.

Jay-Z (another Brooklyn-born Hip Hop artist) illustrates the material value of superhuman abilities/superpowers within Hip Hop culture on *The Blueprint 2: The Gift and the Curse*. On "Hovi Baby" (2002), he establishes the narrative within the context of the invincibility of his former label, Roc-A-Fella Records. On the chorus, Jay-Z introduces the listener to his alter ego, J. Hova. J-Hova is indestructible, "unbreakable."[54] Jay-Z's claim to invincibility reflects more of what Imani Perry (chapter 1) refers to as his "Empire State of Mind." That is, superhuman ability for Jay-Z almost always translates or is translatable into his own capital accumulation and material wealth. Boasting about superhuman abilities is one of the central themes of Hip Hop narratives. Superman, the ultimate American superhero, serves as a common trope in many of these narratives.[55] In this example, developmental parallels between Jay-Z and the Superman character are worth noting, as Superman has changed over time, but like Jay-Z "he will not retire."[56] Jay-Z announced his retirement from making studio albums in 2003, only to come out of retirement three years later with the release of *Kingdom Come*.[57]

On "Kingdom Come," the title track of the album, Jay-Z relates his mission to save Hip Hop; his usual boasts of entrepreneurial success; and 1980s drug tales via the Superman persona.[58] Jay-Z appropriates the Superman/Clark Kent persona as a metaphor for his superhuman lyrical ability that underwrites his exceptional material success in the Hip Hop music business. For Jay-Z, the recording booth is symbolic of the economically transformative power of Hip Hop music. Whereas a telephone booth—a representation of the intrinsic link between technology and superpowers in Superman narratives—served as the conduit for Clark Kent's transformation into Superman, Jay-Z replaces the telephone booth with the recording booth as a transformative pathway to superhero emceeing ability, and—in turn, the material success that accompanies that ability.

Jay-Z pushes the Superman analogy and the superheroic mission narrative further in "Kingdom Come" by proclaiming that he is "Not only N.Y.C.'s [he is] Hip Hop's savior."[59] On "Kingdom Come," Jay-Z also makes an allusion to Clark Kent, Superman's alter ego, in order to complete the superhero analogy and highlight his prowess as a lyricist and businessman. Jay-Z's varied accomplishments underscore the multiple layers of meaning in his activation of a superhero mythos.[60] The use of a codename or dual-identity is a foundational component of most superhero conventions within Hip Hop culture. Though the codename "clearly marks the superhero as different from his predecessors, the heroic identities of these characters do not firmly externalize either their alter ego's character or biography."[61] From Jean Grae to Jay-Z, codenames and monikers are integral elements of the construction of the rapper/MCs artistic persona.[62] Hip Hop artists' use of dual identity seeks to create "new narrative[s] of mythic identity" through renaming (that is, alter ego construction) and through the reappropriation of superhero iconography.[63] I have attempted to offer a few examples of how superhero aesthetics, in this case the appropriation of superhero identity, operate within a Hip Hop context, but throughout the periodic developments of superhero aesthetics within Hip Hop culture, some of these same artists as well as many others, incorporated certain American gangster themes into their processes of identity construction as well.

N.W.A is often credited with the paradigmatic shift in Hip Hop musical content toward so-called "gangsta rap."[64] The release of N.W.A's *N.W.A and the Posse* in 1987 marked a shift away from comic book superhero aesthetics in Hip Hop culture, as gangsta iconography was not so subtlety incorporated into Hip Hop's aesthetic worldview. By 1991, Hip Hop artists began to more directly associate themselves with antiheroes and super-villains. At issue here are not only the aesthetic implications of Hip Hop's embrace of the super-villain, but also the philosophical implications for artistic identity construction as well as Hip Hop's rejection—at least partially—of the superhero metaphor. On the surface, Hip Hop's embrace of the super-villain can be misinterpreted as lawless amorality or nihilism without proper socioeconomic context. Upon closer examination, though, it can be argued that villains, especially within the context of underground economies that are the cultural context of so much Hip Hop content, have "more well-defined values than heroes."[65] Moreover, Hip Hop's aesthetic and thematic embrace of the super-villain also coincides with the embrace of the Mafioso-styled villain in mainstream popular culture. The popularity of gangster narratives such as *The Godfather* rests on Mario Puzo and Francis Ford Coppola's treatment of Don Corleone.[66] From this perspective, the villain can be viewed as: (1) proactive; (2) a paternalistic protector; and (3) a dedicated and devoted agent of change, committed to a no-holds-barred approach to the "common good."[67] Jeffrey Ogbar posits that between 1992 and 1995, rappers "helped romanticize the organized crime 'mafia style.'"[68] The gangster archetype—though present before the late 1980s within African American culture—was refashioned and reinterpreted within Hip Hop culture. Crack cocaine, the growth of the prison industrial complex, and the proliferation and promotion of violent imagery in popular culture all aided in the prominence of the gangster archetype in Hip Hop.[69] By 1997, gangster iconography was firmly enmeshed in Hip Hop culture. Groups like CNN (Capone-N-Noreaga), Tupac's Outlawz (featuring Kadafi, Fatal Hussien, and Mussolini), Scarface, Irv Gotti, et al., represented a full embrace of gangster aesthetics within the culture. In *Performing Identity/Performing Culture*, Greg Dimitriadis discusses the importance of the gangster archetype in American culture:

> The violent outlaw, living his life outside of the dominant cultural constraints, solving his problems through power and domination, is a character-type with roots deep in American popular lore. Indeed, the gangster holds a very special place in the American popular imagination. He embodies such capitalist values as rugged individualism, rampant materialism, [and] strength through physical force.[70]

The outlaw and badman are prominent archetypes within American and African American culture. The transference of these two archetypes into Hip Hop aesthetics subtly reinscribes the appeal of superhero iconography signified through the lyrics and words of Hip Hop culture. By 2000, artists such as Mack 10, Daz Dillinger, and C-Murder signaled an entrenchment of gangsta iconography in popular Hip Hop music. And just over a decade earlier, the murder of Kelvin "50 Cent" Martin on

October 24, 1987 foreshadowed the birth of a new Hip Hop icon: Curtis "50 Cent" Jackson. Kelvin "50 Cent" Martin was prominently featured on the back cover of Eric B. and Rakim's classic album, *Paid in Full*, and through his role as a leader in the underground economy of inner-city New York he had become a local folk hero prior to his murder. The emergence of Curtis "50 Cent" Jackson marks a major shift in superhero *and* gangster iconography and iconology within Hip Hop. 50 Cent's reappropriation of the notorious 1980s criminal, Kelvin "50 Cent" Martin, reified in his mixtape sensation, "How to Rob," exemplifies a new iteration of superhero aesthetics in Hip Hop culture. 50 Cent the rapper referenced real life, criminal narratives, and identities that signaled a new iconography; one that relied less on superhero aesthetics and more on gangsta motifs. The fact that Curtis Jackson was shot nine times and survived an attempted murder led to the public acceptance of his authentic superhuman narrative; a narrative that 50 Cent had no problem promoting in conjunction with his first major label release in 2003.

The release of 50 Cent's debut album *Get Rich or Die Tryin*[71] represented the mainstreaming of gangster motifs on the one hand and a new reading of superhero aesthetics in Hip Hop on the other. 50 Cent fully embraced gangsta culture, and reinscribed a tried and true Hip Hop archetype.[72] He also identifies with the heroic and hyper-gangster figure within Hip Hop culture. In 50 Cent's story world, the superhero does not "save the day."[73] The fact that 50 Cent survives nine gunshot wounds and his superhero physique are also important factors in his emergence as a global superstar. The first song on *Get Rich or Die Tryin*, "What Up Gangster?" was 50 Cent's "introduction" to the commercial audience, debuting at number one on the Billboard 200 chart. The song is an ode to gangster culture, with references to both the Bloods and the Crips in the chorus.[74] The opening line of the song serves as an important rhetorical and cultural marker for 50 Cent's narrative. He appropriates and then summarily rejects the Superman iconography in the first lines,[75] supplanting it with gangsta references to guns and bulletproof vests. He clearly targets a hardcore, gangsta demographic, yet his articulation of gangsta sensibilities is also anchored in superhero sensibilities.

50 Cent's "In Da Club" music video, directed by Phillip Atwell, borrows from *The Six Million Dollar Man* television show. The video, set in the Shady/Aftermath Artist Development Center, played on the television series' central concept of rebuilding a man by giving him superhuman, in this case bionic, capabilities. After being critically wounded and figuratively left for dead by many in the music industry, the "In Da Club" music video suggests that by signing to Shady/Aftermath Records and utilizing Dr. Dre's musical production skills and Eminem's social cache as a popular mainstream MC, 50 Cent's music career (and physical body) could be

"rebuilt" and made better.[76] Nonetheless, it is 50 Cent's lyrical reconfiguration of superhero–super-villain aesthetics and conventions within the process of constructing his artistic identity that marks a moment wherein Hip Hop culture rereads its embrace of superhero mythology.[77] Though the super-villain stands in opposition to the superhero, within Hip Hop aesthetics, the strict binary between bad and good dissolve, especially when filtered through African American folk cultural traditions—namely the blues and the badman trope. In practice, Hip Hop does not adopt superhero narratives uncritically and it is not unique in this regard as comics, film, and popular music also critique and revise hero-villain narratives in their reappropriation of superhero aesthetics.

In Hip Hop culture, the badman/badwoman serves as a "reconstituted trickster."[78] In *To the Break of Dawn: A Freestyle on the Hip Hop Aesthetic*, William Jelani Cobb declares that the trickster in Hip Hop is secondary to the Thug Iconography regularly associated with artists such as Tupac, 50 Cent, and others.

> The trickster is secondary in hip hop; in this arena the boulevard 'hood— at least since the inception of Topic's ghetto ontology "thug life"—has reigned supreme. And the lauded Thug Icon is nothing if not the remix version of the blues' Bad Nigger archetype. Whereas the bad nigger and the trickster exist as parallel types in the blues, the thug alone has become the patron deity of hip hop.[79]

Cobb's emphasis on the Thug Icon may obscure trends in American popular culture and media in general that have impacted shifts in Hip Hop iconography. One clarifying insight here is that the super-villain can be viewed as an extension of the badman trope especially as it is reinterpreted through Hip Hop culture.[80] The residue of the badman figure is present in Hip Hop through hypermasculine posturing and the ritualization of naming.[81] In Hip Hop, the badman and super-villain are often conflated. Nonetheless, the super-villain—as with the superhero—is a reflection of the society from which he emerges: "[The super-villain] represents an inversion of [societal] values. But more than that a super-villain has the ability to enact that inversion, to bring the normal activities of a society to a halt and force a hero to arise to defend those virtues." [82] The super-villain exists alongside blaxploitation imagery, Black Nationalist representations of African American men in the twentieth century, and the gansta rap figures of the 1990s and beyond.

Gangsta iconography has been present in Hip Hop culture since its inception.[83] N.W.A. elevated West Coast realism to the forefront of Hip Hop narratives. They tapped into the badman trope as they popularized the use of gangsta aesthetics in Hip Hop culture.[84] Since Hip Hop initially emerges as counter culture, the super-villain as social agent or critic is important to its aesthetic formations. In many ways, the super-villain—with his desire to usurp the status quo and break society's laws—is *more* in line with Hip Hop's sociopolitical mores than the superhero. Artists such as Big Pun (Punisher), MF DOOM, and Ghostface (aka Iron Man/Tony Starks) borrow heavily from super-villain narratives.[85] For these artists, super-villains often have superiority complexes that originate from childhood trauma. Such childhood experiences leave the super-villain emotionally scarred:

> [The supervillain] creates a superiority complex that most often emerges as a defense mechanism to make up for feelings of inferiority and inadequacy that arose from maltreatment received when he was younger, often in childhood, that made him feel inferior—they are defective physically or socially (or both) and are only superior mentally. They are, as therapists say, in love with the story of their wound, unable to get past whatever happened in their past and turn their energies toward healing or redemptive therapy.[86]

For poor, urban youth, societal and familial factors such as poverty, socioeconomic discrimination, the long, sordid history of racial discrimination, and/or permanent scars from traumatic violence in inner-city America create an imagined community within Hip Hop culture and the narratives of badmen and super-villains. In this sense, the badman trope informs Hip Hop's embrace of the super-villain. Much of the super-villain's appeal in Hip Hop is linked to the super-villain's critical criminal mind. Criminal behavior is another characteristic of the super-villain/badman that has been creatively embedded in Hip Hop aesthetic discourse. Ogbar argues that "the prison industrial complex, with its wide-reaching power, has become an indelible part of black and Latino youth consciousness as they forge creative outlets in hip hop."[87] The super-villain approaches crime artistically, linking the super-villain—in an aesthetic sense—to the gangsta ethos in Hip Hop culture. For the super-villain, "crime is a theatrical art, with actors, audience, and performance and it can be appreciated aesthetically. The criminal, the super-villain is the impresario who puts on a show for the world that is far superior to the pecuniary plunderings of ordinary bad guys."[88] The super-villain trope elevates the criminality of badman archetypes in Hip Hop culture to the status of high art.

In comic books and in Hip Hop culture there are only slight ideological and psychological distinctions between the hero and the villain.[89] On his debut album *Capital Punishment* (1998), Big Punisher (Big Pun) boldly frames his artistic persona within the conceptual framework of the super-villain.[90] On the album's title track "Capital Punishment," Big Pun unabashedly embraces criminality.[91] In his music he celebrates crime and appears to derive pleasure from performing criminal acts.[92] Big Pun draws from superhero identity conventions, but he also taps into African

American folklore. Pun's use of the African American badman trope, satire, and superhero aesthetics mark his artistic contributions to Hip Hop culture.[93] On "Capital Punishment," he evokes the devil and conjures surreal imagery in his embrace of criminality.[94] Big Pun's remix of the antihero highlights the importance of African American cultural forms and super-villain aesthetics in Hip Hop culture. For Pun and other MCs listed here the embrace of the super-villain in Hip Hop is an extension of the badman trope. Because Hip Hop is rooted in African American culture practices such as toasting, signifying, and the dozens, the super-villain was easily accessible and recognizable for Hip Hop artisans. The rise of the super-villain, then, represents a revision of the superhero as opposed to a rebuke of it; it also marks a shift toward more realistic representations of superheroes in general. Ultimately the super-villain's appeal lies partially in his principled commitment to changing his society. Whereas superheroes maintain the status quo, super-villains often represent the radical aspects of the comic book story world.

Although not as prominent a feature of the music as it was in the 1990s, Hip Hop culture continues to borrow from superhero mythology, aesthetics, and iconography. Hip Hop artists' posturing and style, along with certain artists' repositioning of superhero motifs and conventions within the context of artistic identity construction, offer a rereading of superhero narratives and an interpretive restructuring of American popular culture texts. The influence of superhero aesthetics has ebbed and flowed in response to and in communication with coinciding developments in the socioeconomic landscape, popular culture, and comic book (and) superhero cultures. That said, through television, movies, and/or comic books Hip Hop Culture has borrowed heavily from superhero aesthetics. Because Hip Hop is grounded in African American culture, the icons and archetypes that it has absorbed represent the radical, socioeconomically appropriate, and aesthetically pleasing aspects of superhero identities and conventions for the Hip Hop community. Archetypes and icons that have emerged within Hip Hop represent an extension of previous African American and American archetypes, heroes, heroines, and icons. Part of the attraction of superhero conventions for Hip Hop artists (and fans) is connected to the fact that many of these conventions parallel traditional representations of American masculinity. The simultaneous use of African American cultural practices such as the badman trope inform superhero conventions within a Hip Hop artistic framework. The power of Hip Hop culture lies in its ability to meld disparate—and sometimes competing—worldviews, theories, etc. simultaneously, while developing a new sociocultural context with layers of meaning for the construction of identity. Hip Hop's remix of superhero conventions has led to a distinct type of superhero within Hip Hop culture. The Hip Hop superhero is part trickster, part hustler, part businessperson, and part visionary. But, more importantly, the Hip Hop superhero, as well as the super-villain, is either the product of or in some ways committed to cultural and socioeconomic change. This can take shape as policing or changing the trajectory of Hip Hop aesthetics, reclaiming or saving his or her community, or changing the political status quo. Superhero (and super-villain) aesthetics have been remixed by Hip Hop culture through dual-identity, hyperbole, brand affiliation, lyrical allusion, the mission narratives, boasts about superior artistic skills, and the use of the badman trope. The Hip Hop superhero—or at the very least the presence of superhero conventions in Hip Hop—will continue to influence the aesthetic trajectory of artistic identity formation in the culture.

NOTES

1. In *Black Noise: Rap Music and Black Culture in Contemporary America*, Tricia Rose explains Hip Hop texts often "appropriate and sometimes critique verbal and visual elements . . . from popular commercial culture especially television, comic books, and karate movies" ([Middletown, CT: Wesleyan University Press, 1994], 40). Rose argues that the concepts of "flow, layering, and rupture as demonstrated on the body and hip hop's lyrical, musical, and visual works" surface on the stylistic and aesthetic level (39).

2. According to Thomas Heyd, "aesthetics is concerned with the qualitative dimension of perception and the incorporation of perceivable properties in systems of value and meaning that integrate them with cultural processes" (*Aesthetics and Rock Art*, ed. Thomas Heyd and John Clegg [Farnham: Ashgate 2005], 54).

3. Ron Goulart, *Comic Book Culture: An Illustrated History* (Portland, OR: Collectors Press, 2000), 43.

4. These MCs borrow identity and nominative traits from superhero characters, including: Hercules, Flash Gordon, Kool Keith (who also utilized the alter persona Dr. Doom and Dr. Octagon), and The Fantastic Four.

5. In February 2006, a fifteen-year-old boy—DeAndre Way—posted "Crank That (Soulja Boy)" on his MySpace page. The song "Crank That (Soulja Boy)" is rife with sexist innuendo and spawned a dance craze among youth. Nonetheless, the success of "Crank That (Soulja Boy)" highlights a shift in Hip Hop production, distribution, and marketing (Soulja Boy, *Soulja Boy Tell 'Em*, October 2, 2007, Collipark Music [compact disc]).

6. In *Blutopia: Visions of the Future and Revisions of the Past in the Work of SUN RA, Duke Ellington, and Anthony Braxton*, Graham Lock argues that Sun Ra "was more interested in questioning concepts of reality (and proposing an alternative) than in questioning accepted notions of sanity, ([Durham, NC: Duke University Press, 1999], 59).

7. I utilize the term *sampling* to connote the reappropriation of texts, dress, images, iconography, technology, et al. within Hip Hop. In Hip Hop America,

Nelson George expands on this definition of "sampling," connoting an embrace of "new sounds, bending found technology to a creator's will in search of new forms of rhythm to inspire and please listeners" (*Hip Hop America* [New York: Penguin, 1998], 96).

8. Lawrence W. Levine, *Black Culture and Black Consciousness: Afro-American Folk Thought from Slavery to Freedom* (Oxford and New York: Oxford University Press, 1997), 370. "The enduring plight of black Americans produced a continuing need for a folklore which would permit them to express their hostilities and aspirations and for folk heroes whose exploits would allow them to transcend their situation. Thus it might be argued that all Afro-American folk heroes sprang from the same causes and reflected identical needs . . . Nevertheless, the specific ways in which hostilities are expressed and transcendence symbolized are revealing . . . The appearance of new heroes, the alteration of old ones, and the blending of the new and the old that went on continually have a great deal to say about the changes in black situation and consciousness that [are] occurring . . . Neither the heroes nor the consciousness that mold[s] them remain[s] static."

Although African American iconography has always been fluid and flexible, whether these icons are religious or secular in origin, they all "sprang from the same causes and reflected identical needs." The African American folkloric tradition relies upon folk heroes that provide ready-discursive and aesthetic space for Hip Hop culture to engage, edify, and revise icons and archetypes to suit its needs.

9. Zittoun discusses contemporary manifestations of bricolage, linking its use, at least from a historical perspective, to religiosity. Zittoun repositions bricolage within a contemporary context, detaching it from Levi-Strauss' heavy-handed, esoteric analysis of bricolage, while viewing bricolage as a "symbolic resource." She explains, "as the *bricoleur*, or handyman, the user has to destroy existing meanings and construct new ones with bits of cultural elements." *Transitions: Development Through Symbolic Resources*, edited by Tania Zittoun, [Charlotte, NC: Information Age Publishing, 2006], 128.

10. When discussing Malcolm McLaren, Jeff Chang states Hip Hop is "pastiche, bricolage" (*Can't Stop Won't Stop: A History of the Hip Hop Generation* [New York: St Martin's Press, 2005], 162).

11. All-Negro Comics, Inc., a publisher formed in 1947, which featured Ace Harlem and Lion Man. Lobo, widely considered the first African American superhero, emerged in 1965.

12. Robin D. G. Kelley, *Yo' Mama's DisFunktional: Fighting the Culture Wars in Urban America* (Boston and New York: Beacon Press, 1997), 38.

13. In *Superman on the Couch: What Superheroes Really Tell Us about Ourselves and Our Society*, Danny Fingeroth purports "superheroes generally agree that the laws of the land need to be upheld. They believe that democracy is the best form of government democracy" ([New York: Continuum International Publishing, 2007], 160).

14. According to Peter Coogan, "superpowers are one of the most identifiable elements of the superhero genre" (*Superhero: The Secret Origin of a Genre* [Austin, TX; Monkey Brains Books, 2006), 31].

15. Morgan declares "creativity in hip hop is a celebration and recognition of well-developed skills that are relentlessly and incessantly practiced and evaluated" (ibid., 82).

16. Comic book superheroes, in the tradition of American heroic mythology and the folklore that precedes them, serve as receptacles for and embodiments of American masculinity. Jeffrey A. Brown adds an additional layer of meaning to the reading of comic book superhero mythology. He asserts that black masculinity parallels comic book conventions of masculinity, ("Comic Book Masculinity and the New Black Superhero," *African American Review* 33, no. 1 [Spring 1999]: 26).

17. In "Black Skins' and White Masks: Comic Books and the Secret of Race," Marc Singer explains "Comics still perpetuate stereotypes, either through token characters who exist purely to signify racial clichés or through a far more subtle system of absence and erasure that serves to obscure minority groups . . . However, superhero comics also possess a highly adaptable set of conventions . . . " (*African American Review* 36, no. 1 [Spring, 2002]: 118).

18. In *Heroes and Villains*, Mike Alsford situates heroes and villains within a larger sociopolitical framework ([Waco, TX: Baylor University Press, 2006], 2).

19. "The notion that someone is able to cope or deal with life in an extraordinary and exemplary way provides comfort and inspiration to a boring and disillusioned existence . . . Saints and heroes took on a special power as representative figures that offer, at the least, a vicarious experience for less privileged human kind." (Gregor Goethals, "Sacred-Secular Icons," in *Icons of America*, ed. Ray B. Browne and Marshall Fishwick [Bowling Green, OH: Popular Press, 1978], 2).

20. Fingeroth implores that "each generation will redefine the superhero according to its needs" (*Superman on the Couch*, 172). It is fair to reason that the Hip Hop generation would redefine superhero to suit the demands of the post-industrial, post–civil rights environment.

21. Robin Kelley, *Race Rebels: Culture, Politics, and the Black Working Class* (New York: Free Press, 1994), 37.

22. In *The Tanning of America: How Hip Hop Created a Culture That Rewrote the Rules of the New Economy*, Steve Stoute proffers that Los Angeles youth attained a degree of "superpowers" when they adorned Los Angeles Raiders gear *because* it was worn by hardcore, gangster pioneers N.W.A. More specifically, he posits that young peoples' affinity for Raiders gear was due to the "brash mind-set of the Raiders" coupled with the "outlaw mentality" of N.W.A. ([New York: Gotham Books, 2011], 46).

23. The release of Soulja's Boy's "Crank That" in 2007 marks the end of period 4. By 2008, with the release of Rick Ross's *Trilla* and the release of Lil Wayne's *Tha Carter III*—the contours and currents of superhero aesthetics—though still present in Hip Hop culture—once again, began to recede. (Soulja Boy, *Soulja Boy Tell 'Em*, October 2, 2007, Collipark Music [compact disc]).

24. Bikari Kitwana points out in *The Hip Hop Generation: Young Blacks and the Crisis in African American Culture*, that "Black gangster films," for example, also shaped the Hip Hop "generation's consciousness" ([New York: Basic Civitas, 2002], 139).

25. Jeffrey O. G. Ogbar, *Hip-Hop Revolution: The Culture and Politics of Rap* (Lawrence: University Press of Kansas, 2007), 112.

26. Many Hip Hop scholars have put forth postulations of the "Golden Era" of Hip Hop. I argue that these analyses are too broad chronologically and thematically. For example, William Jelani Cobb identifies the Golden Age as 1984–1992

(*To the Break of Dawn: A Freestyle on the Hip Hop Aesthetic* [New York: New York University Press, 2007], 41).

27. On "Everything is Everything," superhuman ability, the badman/badwoman trope, and Kemetic iconography foreground superhero aesthetics (*The Miseducation of Lauryn Hill*, August 25, 1998, Sony Records [compact disc]).

28. On "When It Hurts So Bad," for example, Lauryn Hill taps into blues modalities. In this ode to lost love, she sings that she has essentially given up her power as a woman to sustain a relationship with her lover.

29. Tricia Rose, *The Hip Hop Wars: What We Talk About When We Talk About Hip Hop—and Why It Matters* (New York: Basic Civitas Books, 2008), 174.

30. On "Take It Back" *Evil Jeanius*, Jean Grae spits, that she is "restless" and her heart is filled with sadness. (*The Evil Jeanius*, September 30, 2008, Babygrande Records [compact disc]).

31. On "Don't Rush Me," Grae makes an allusion to masking her true feelings and emotion. (Jean Grae, "Don't Rush Me," *Jeanius*, July 8, 2008, Blacksmith Records [compact disc]).

32. *The Marvel Comics Encyclopedia: The Complete Guide to the Characters of the Marvel Universe*, ed. Alastair Dougall, et al. (New York and London: DK Publishing, 2008), 136.

33. On "Lights Out," *Evil Jeanius*, Grae illustrates the importance placed upon intermingling African American iconography and superhero aesthetics. The lyrics reference Blaxploitation film era icon *The Mack*. It is also worth noting that Jean Grae is clearly alluding to a figurative assault and not a literal one; directed at adversaries, detractors, and haters ("talk smack").

34. Ibid.

35. "Still A Love Song," *Evil Jeanius*, is an allusion to Grae's love for Hip Hop. In this case, Hip Hop culture is personified as a male, love interest.

36. Stoute, *Tanning of America*, 32.

37. Stoute argues it was Hip Hop culture's "impoverished-yet-unapologetic mind-set" that became the hip hop religion's unifying concept" (ibid., 32).

38. In 1966, Noburu Tsuburaya created Ultraman, a space-policeman. It premiered on Japanese television on April 9, 1967. August Ragone describes Redman as "an incorporeal intergalactic refugee . . . meld[ed] with Officer Sakomizu of the SIA, and together they protect mankind as Redman." Ragone points out that Redman is "where the concept of the henshin hero (transforming hero) first took shape—two beings inhabiting one body, the human living day-to-day, the superhuman being called forth in times of extreme danger" (*Eiji Tsuburaya: Master of Monsters: Defending the Earth with Ultraman, Godzilla, and Friends in the Golden Age of Japanese Science Fiction Film* [San Francisco: Chronicle Books, 2011], 114).

39. Lock discusses Sun Ra's use of "Black Atlantic mythologies." Lock describes Ra as a "self made myth" shaped by a kind of symbiotic dialogue, an intertextual relationship, with the main narrative threads of African American history" (*Blutopia*, 74). I distinguish, here, between Lock's "Black Atlantic" from Gilroy's—though both useful, as both concepts are still widely debated.

40. Brolin Winning interview, "Redman: Still Smokin," March 14, 2007. http://www.tv.com/news/redman-still-smokin-9042/.

41. Redman, "A Day of Sooperman Lover," *Whut? Thee Album*, September 22, 1992, Def Jam (compact disc).
42. Kelley explains, rap music's gritty realism, storytelling, and straight-up signifyin(g) is not always clear to listeners, nor is it supposed to be" (*Race Rebels*, 38).
43. Newark was representative of many post-industrial urban centers during the mid-1990s. Mark Anthony Neal asserts, Hip Hop represents "a concerted effort by young urban blacks to use mass-culture to facilitate communal discourse across a fractured and dislocated national community" (*What the Music Said: Black Popular Music and Black Public Culture* [London: Routledge, 1999], 136).
44. Redman highlights his need to negotiate labor, work, and play.
45. Redman interjects a dialogue around returning back to lunch break at his job late and the threat of having to file for unemployment as a result.
46. Here I juxtapose play and crime fighting.
47. Kelley, *Race Rebels*, 46.
48. The "Sooperman Lover" series features songs across several of Redman's albums. Although I do not go in depth in my analysis here, the songs tend to feature a homophobic reveal of a transgendered love interest. Superhero conventions' service to traditional modes of masculinity included both homophobia and misogyny.
49. Peter Coogan, "The Definition of the Superhero," in *Super/Heroes: From Hercules to Superman*, ed. Wendy Haslem, et al. (Washington, DC: New Academia, 2007), 25.
50. Richard Iton implores a "nuanced and precise" analysis of resistance to uncover meaning in "specifically hidden transcripts" (*In Search of the Black Fantastic: Politics and Popular Culture in the Post–Civil Rights Era* [Oxford: Oxford University Press, 2008], 102).
51. Prophet, the comic book character, was created by white writer Stephen Platt and debuted on October 1, 1993.
52. Jeru the Damaja references Kung Fu iconography as a way of informing his brand of superhero aesthetics. He cites Sam Sneed of the *Drunken Master* Kung Fu film and Kung Fu movie mogul Run Run Shaw in "Come Clean" (*The Sun Rises in the East*, May 24, 1994, Fontana Island [compact disc]).
53. Lyrics from Jeru, "Ain't The Devil Happy," *The Sun Rises in the East*.
54. Jay-Z, "Hovi Baby," *The Blueprint 2: The Gift & the Curse*, November 12, 2002 Roc-A-Fella/Island Def Jam (compact disc).
55. Ibid.
56. Fingeroth, *Superman on the Couch*, 34.
57. Josh Tyrangiel briefly discusses Jay-Z's maturation and coming out of retirement ("The Un-Retirement of Jay-Z," *Time*, November 24, 2006, http://www.time.com/time/arts/article/0,8599,1562881,00.html [accessed April 13, 2014]).
58. Jay-Z, "Kingdom Come," *Kingdom Come*, Roc-A-Fella Records, 2003.
59. By declaring that he's "hip hop's Savior," Jay-Z (or J-Hova) employs hyperbole through the use of double entendre and also taps into the superhero mission: saving (New York) Hip Hop.
60. Julius Bailey suggests "the range of [Jay-Z's]accomplishments" elucidates the "varied contexts in which he can be studied," (*Jay-Z: Essays on Hip Hop's Philosopher King* [Jefferson, NC: McFarland, 2011], 4).

61. Coogan, *Superhero*, 32.
62. Fingeroth explains dual identity within a contemporary, technocratic society. He cites criminals, "graffiti artists," and political terrorists like the KKK as persons that would want to conceal their identity (*Superman on the Couch*, 48).
63. Eithne Quinn explains, "artists reoriented and extended the mythic tales of thes past, keeping hold of the bold surrealism, while incorporating a documentary style" (*Nuthin' But a "G" Thang: The Culture and Commerce of Gangsta Rap* [New York: Columbia University Press, 2005], 97).
64. Ogbar, *Hip-Hop Revolution*, 44.
65. Fingeroth explains that we view Don Corleone and the gangsters in *The Godfather* series as heroes because Puzo and Coppola's scripts "bring us inside their minds, making us realize that perhaps we, in similar situations, might behave in the same way" (*Superman on the Couch*, 165).
66. Fingeroth explains that we view Don Corleone and the gangsters in The Godfather series as heroes because Puzo and Coppola's scripts "bring us inside their minds, making us realize that perhaps we, in similar situations, might behave in the same way" (ibid.).
67. Ibid.
68. Ogbar further nuances the gangsta aesthetic, marking an embrace of "Mafioso-styled" imagery and iconography in Hip Hop. He cites groups such as Don Corleone rap group, Nas' alter ego Nas "Escobar," and Snoop Doggy Dogg's 1996 sophomore LP—*The Doggfather*—as examples (*Hip-Hop Revolution*, 112).
69. Ogbar argues that even though African Americans lag behind whites in many categories, we must hold artists accountable by looking at "artists' agency" (*Hip-Hop Revolution*, 174).
70. Dimitriadis, *Performing Identity/Performing Culture: Hip Hop as Text, Pedagogy, and Lived Practice* (New York: Peter Lang, 2001), 188.
71. 50 Cent, "What Up Gangsta," *Get Rich or Die Tryin*, Interscope Records, 2003.
72. In a May 25, 2003 *Los Angeles Times* article, Baz Dreisinger pontificates on the hypothetical creation of "a superhero named 50 Cent." He suggests that the superhero 50 Cent's "costume would not be a cape but a blue bulletproof vest."
73. Fingeroth observes that the role of the "secret identity has become less significant" due to "the greater insistence on certain types of realism in superhero fiction" (*Superman on the Couch*, 59).
74. Lyrics from 50 Cent, "What Up Gangsta," *Get Rich or Die Tryin*, February 6, 2003, Interscope Records (compact disc), in which he makes veiled references to the Los Angeles–based Bloods and Crips street gangs.
75. Ibid.
76. 50 Cent's *Get Rich or Die Tryin* was certified six times platinum by the Recording Industry Association of America (ibid.).
77. Redman references Spider-Man and Batman and supplants these figures in an urban environment. Redman's farcical tale also includes numerous references to illicit drug use and drug dealing (ibid.)
78. Cobb, *Break of Dawn*, 30.
79. Ibid.
80. Quinn, *Nuthin' But a "G" Thang*, puts forth a folkloristic view, describing "gangsta's badman incarnations" as "productive reworkings of Stagolee lore"

(23). He explains "rather than narrating badman exploits, gangsta rappers actually assumed his role" (25).

81. Quinn argues that badman lore is "felt . . . in [rap music through] verbal sparring, macho posturing, and a heightened insistence on self (and group) naming and reputation. Gangsta [rap] is distinguished by its more explicit, full-blown adoption of these themes," (ibid., 97).

82. Coogan, *Superhero*, 61.

83. In the groundbreaking film *Wild Style* (1983), the rap duo Double Trouble can be seen brandishing fake firearms in the finale scene. Legendary Brooklyn stick-up kid Kelvin "50 Cent" Martin was prominently featured on the back of Eric B. and Rakim's seminal *Paid in Full* (1987).

84. On "Respiration," Black Star simultaneously engaged and rejected the superhero iconography, while highlighting the post-industrial and the post-modern landscape as a backdrop for a reconceptualization of superhero aesthetics in their narrative. The line "No Batman and Robin" is an example of how superheroes and superpowers are not enough to transcend the realities of a post-industrial, post–civil rights landscape, in this case, police corruption (*Mos Def & Talib Kweli are Black Star*, August 18, 1998, Rawkus/UMDG [compact disc]).

85. Coogan has identified five types of supervillain: the mad scientist (the lab), the criminal mastermind, and the inverted-superhero are most common in Hip Hop narratives (*Superhero*, 84).

86. Coogan, *Superhero*, 84.

87. Ogbar, *Hip-Hop Revolution*, 173.

88. Coogan, *Superhero*, 80.

89. Fingeroth explains that the super-villain is more committed to change than the hero. He reports "With the notable exception of the proactive Batman and Punisher, most heroes are reactive . . . What makes Batman a hero is the relative restraint he shows compared to the Punisher," (*Superman on the Couch*, 166).

90. Big Pun, on "Twinz" (Deep Cover '98)." Big Punisher rhymes in ways that place him squarely along the trajectory of the supervillain trope (*Capital Punishment*, August 24, 1999, Relativity [compact disc]).

91. Big Pun on "Capital Punishment" puts forth a hyperbolic narrative of criminal behavior, superhuman strength, and torture (ibid.).

92. Big Pun declares himself an "abomination." He builds heavily upon the badman tropes, as well as makes homoerotic, masochistic threats to his opponents and enemies (ibid.).

93. On "Super Lyrical," Pun raps about battling Jesus (or hay-soos) and makes numerous, metaphoric threats to his opponents via his lethal lyrical skills (*Capital Punishment*, August 24, 1999, Relativity [compact disc]).

94. Big Pun, "Capital Punishment."

II

VISUAL MATTER

Part II explores race, identity, and popular culture from a series of essays that wrestle with Internet images/imagery, a television program, and a film. Each selection interrogates some form of visual media in order to examine the ways that "Visual Matter" informs popular discourses on racial, gendered, and sexual identities. Paul M. Farber's "I Have a Meme" explores the digital visual culture that emerged in order to commemorate the fiftieth anniversary of the March on Washington. For Farber, "emergent photographic technologies" are transformative but also tend to reinscribe traditional practices of photography. This duality does not prevent a grassroots interaction with new media interpretations of the 1963 March on Washington. Emily Churilla's essay on the "Skin Deep" episode of the television show, *House*, turns again toward national public culture and popular discourses on gender/gendered identity. Churilla argues that publics form around television programs and the discourses that revolve around the story worlds' audiovisual pop cultural texts. The "Skin Deep" episode of *House* presents an intriguing opportunity to discern the ways in which popular culture facilitates the shaming of certain "deviant" gender identities. Scott St. Pierre's "Faggoty/White/Uniform" revisits the immensely popular film, *A Few Good Men*. While St. Pierre concedes that the very existence of the film develops out of the context of shifting popular ideas regarding the "Don't Ask, Don't Tell" policy, he also argues that the film reinscribes certain conceptualizations of gay identity and the limited ways that popular culture informs our understanding of Lesbian, Gay, Bisexual, Transgendered, and Queer (LGBTQ) identities. Each essay in this section implicitly understands the powerfully influential capacity of visual media to determine identity politics in popular culture and in public discourses.

Figure 5.1. I Have a Meme
Computer Image, art by John Jennings

5

✢

I Have a Meme

Photography, Interactive Memory, and Digital Commemorations of the March on Washington

Paul M. Farber

In August 2013, on the occasion of the fiftieth anniversary of the March on Washington for Jobs and Freedom, the United States Postal Service (USPS) announced they would produce a stamp honoring the legacy of the great 1963 gathering on behalf of racial democracy on the National Mall. The stamp would be composed as a virtual mosaic of uploaded personal digital images. Several weeks before the actual anniversary on August 28, the USPS requested that public online audiences—including friends of their Facebook page—upload images of themselves in order to populate the pixels of this stamp. Days before the actual March anniversary, they held an event to officially launch the stamp, with the mantra that, "Equality has a stamp of its own today."[1] On the day of its public unveiling, actress Gabrielle Union, in person at the ceremony hosted by the Newseum in Washington, DC, offered her own image as the final piece to complete this composite. The finished result appears as an impressionistic painterly view of imagined Marchers, but with historically accurate protest placards and a Washington Monument towering over the scene. Conjuring a nonspecific, generic, yet highly recognizable image resembling a documentary photograph of the March, the Postal Service presents us with an artifact not of the original March but one for the commemoration fifty years later.[2]

For producers of such a public history, the broader commemorative strategies for the fiftieth anniversary of the March included a revisiting of its historic photography and the promise of participation through digital pathways. The commemorative stamp acts as a compelling site of memory, aspiring to capture the March's shared and enduring national significance. However, the collective "selfie" imprint of the stamp is instructive as well, as its designers attempted to honor, if not build upon, the collective aims of the 1963 original gathering. The event in 1963 marked a profound achievement in grassroots organizing. The March's architects brought together a wide ideological spectrum and geographically scattered set of civil rights organizations, politicians, trade unions, religious communities, and educational groups despite rifts and internecine squabbles in order to organize a collective contestation of the repressive racialized status quo. Despite all of these historical underpinnings, this commemorative stamp features a public gathered yet split by the cellular distinction of their individual images. Each participant shared their own image, subsumed into the appropriately honorific act of constructing a March-related stamp, but without clear distinction on the interrelated legacy of the achievements and unresolved longings of the original Marchers themselves. The creators of this image approach commemoration through imagined collectivity while obscuring the actual likenesses of both the original marchers and the digital participants.[3]

As a project of crowdsourcing, the producers of this artifact frame interactivity through personal or branded registers. Its designers allude to historical linkages, drawing our attention to the 1963 Marchers by way of a contemporary digital crowd, but without the primary aim or effect of forging new collectives of social action. That may be beyond the scope of such an interactive postal project; however, like the official fiftieth anniversary commemoration on the National Mall—which was broken into two separate large-scale public gatherings on August 25 and 28, respectively, and partitioned into credential-only areas of VIP accessibility—both the stamp and commemorative events serve as a prompt for assessing the state of any social collectivity that claims the original March as its touchstone. Digital interactivity and commemorative action, as such, remain exercises in consumer choice that do not necessarily entail critical reproduction or furthering of the causes of racial and economic justice. The result is an image that draws on the photographic history of the March without a singular visual referent or a trajectory beyond its own consumption. Such an artifact prompts the following questions: What are the goals of any commemoration of the March on Washington that incorporates historic photography? Who (or what) are the current owners, guarantors, or constituents if shared within our digital culture? And what are the multiple pathways to approach a nuanced, evolving crowdsourced history of the March?

By examining the role of photography as a central component of an enhanced history of the March in the weeks that led up to and followed its fiftieth commemoration, in this essay I consider a variety of digital projects that interpret the March's collective legacy through the pursuit of digital interactivity. Beyond the commemorative March postal stamp, I trace the sourcing of and traffic in historic photographs to investigate the forces that shape and control photographic innovation, accessibility, and critical action—through iconic March images, major media commemorative platforms, and grassroots usages of March photographs for digital activism. I argue such attempts foster interaction under the interests of both an augmented public history of the March and present-day needs of their sponsors. Further, I contend that while emergent photographic technologies may be thought of as transforming the nature of photographs and images for events deemed historical, such new productions do not replace but rather recode older practices and mythologies of the medium—they function unevenly in regard to bringing forward the Marchers' original aims of racial justice and democracy. Ultimately, the digital layers of March memory continue to invite corporate sponsorship—as well as novel forms of collective ownership of the grassroots histories and unforeseen legacies of the March on Washington.

Photographs from the March on Washington have gained status in American culture as iconic images. Robert Hariman and John Luis Lucaites define iconic political photographs as those that "work in several registers of ritual and response . . . They are reproduced widely and placed prominently in both public and private settings, and they are used to orient the individual with a context of collective identity, obligation, and power."[4] Hariman and Lucaites write of the production, circulation, and afterlife of photographs (including images from the Depression, VJ Day, Vietnam War, Challenger Explosion, and Tiananmen Square), which become visual shorthand for the historical record and evolving discourses around public history.

Photographs and images of the 1963 March now routinely appear in historical and arts museums, documentary programs, historical studies, and television advertisements; abstracted images based on photographic documentation, like the USPS stamp, include designs on civic memorials, souvenirs, and vernacular tourist photography on the National Mall. Included among the range of iconic images of the March are those captured by Associated Press (AP) and other newswire photographers. Others are powerful and deliberate images from the bodies of work of noted photo documentarians such as Bob Adelman, Bruce Davidson, Leonard Freed, and Danny Lyon, including shots of Dr. Martin Luther King, Jr. and members of the organizing groups, including the Student Nonviolent Coordinating Committee (SNCC). In some instances, displays of iconic imagery from the March are derived from stills or short loops of televisual news footage.

One primary subject of iconic images from the March includes Dr. King, one of the day's keynote speakers, in a variety of poses, often with his hand outstretched, set against the sweeping crowd of over 200,000 assembled on the Mall. Such images are now commonplace in visual representations of US history. They have gained iconic stature—a profound shift given the March's questionable, if not maligned, status in the weeks leading up to the event by a host of politicians, journalists, and critics of civil rights reforms. Additional challenging aspects to such an elevated position include the political maneuvering at the height of the turbulent summer and fall of racial violence of 1963, the unresolved nature of many of the Marchers' demands in the ensuing years following the March, the decades-long debates surrounding the nationalized memorialization of Dr. King, and the precarious state of the larger movement's accomplishments in voting rights through the present day. And yet, the iconography of the March photographs featuring Dr. King and others, largely of the crowd, summons both honorific recall and, increasingly, possibilities for reinterpretation. Whether we are reading the massive display of handheld signs in the crowd, the text or transcripts from the day's keynote speeches, or the captioned photographs that rendered such scenes in hometown and national newspapers in the days after, the iconicity begins to emerge from the sum of media forms related to the event. To be truly iconic, according to Hariman and Lucaites, the centrality of a given image must also "acquire their own histories of appropriation and commentary . . . they have more than documentary value, for they bear witness to something that exceeds words."[5] The relationship between text and image is crucial to an understanding of the day's historical evocations, but also the way photographic images have significantly shaped public history of the March in a variety of shifting contexts, namely the historical period in which they are invoked.

As iconic images circulate and are remixed in digital realms, as is commonplace in the memes of contemporary culture, their public function or historical relevance evolve. The meme, popularized as a loose collection of online expressions circulated in image or video (often with text overlaid) on a given topic or theme, is analogous to the iconic in that it confers validity through collective iteration and variation. The use of a meme to explain the mutability and transferability of culture precedes the Internet.[6] Limor Schifman notes, "Internet memes can be treated as (post)modern folklore, in which shared norms and values are constructed through cultural artifacts such as Photoshopped images or urban legends." Shifman argues, "we live in an era driven by a *hypermemetic logic*, in which almost every major public event sprouts a stream of memes." She adds, in a "so-called participatory culture," that the difference between older forms of memetic culture and those that are shared digitally is the role of the producer—"the performative self"—who consumes, then produces fodder ripe for memetic sharing. Her examples draw on a number of contemporary popular memes, some of which borrow from iconic or historical content, often either in the public domain or easily sourced through a simple Google Image search. We could qualify the arguments made about iconic or memetic images to accommodate for historical events that precede the digital era, which are brought forward by new users. We may also be cautious concerning which archives are ripe for memetic circulation, whether due to copyright, accessibility, or legitimacy.[7]

The interplay between forms of mediation, as well as sponsors or underwriters of "participatory culture," is crucial to our understanding of the resilience of March images now situated as landmarks in national memory. Despite the myriad long-term usage and elevation of March photographs, those previously looking for useable and transferrable media may have previously favored other modes of representation. Writing about photography's uses in 1963, Maurice Berger suggests, "While still pictures were an undeniably powerful medium for documenting important events, they could do little to communicate the words, cadences or inferences of a speech. In that area, television excelled." He notes the ways televisual pictures and satellite technology made the March an early national live televisual news event. Further, the release of audio proceedings from the days' speeches and performances—by Folkways and Motown Records—circulated sound footage of the day into public consciousness decades earlier. But Berger adds, "where television sometimes fails . . . the photograph excels. It demands our sustained attention, teasing out the complexities, the incongruities . . . and the ironies of ostensibly straightforward circumstances."[8] In other words, photography demands interpretation in a way that TV or audio coverage does not. Berger reminds us to heed the evocative power of photography, and to view its conveyances as participating in the creation of icons more complex than the photographs themselves. As such, the iconic images that emerge from the March are constituted through concrete representations of the day; but they are also functioning as access points to the day's deeper contexts of strife and contestations of racial rule, especially relevant for reconsideration in what scholar Salamishah Tillet deems the "post–civil rights imagination."[9] Even as the March emerges and stands as a national story of cohesion, photographs may also lead us to the depictions of such strain or the connections to our present day civil rights struggles. Online portals including layering techniques for digitized images from the March also invite critical scrutiny and possibility through promised participation.

The summer preceding the fiftieth anniversary marked a return to viewing the photography of the day—not merely as filler or background for other cultural productions, but as a reconsideration of the evocative power of the medium. A number of prominent national venues, including the Smithsonian and Library of Congress hosted photographic exhibitions of both well-known and vernacular March visuals. Multiple national media outlets, including the *New York Times*, offered exclusive online slideshows or ready-made memes drawing on the March's photographic traces, especially to highlight the identities and stories of former Marchers. The National Park Service teamed with digital firm Organic for the website We Are Still Marching.[10] What marked many of these attempts was not just a return to seeing the March but a promise of its recoding: the goal of enhanced digital photographic viewing and the March's evolving status as an iconic moment in American history inspired a number of attempts to recall the March digitally, to render the legacy of analog photographs and archives as interactive terrains. If we follow Berger's line of thinking in one sense, the enhancement of photography under the service of other visual media could address some of those shortcomings of photos as historical data, especially gaps or silences evident in reports of the day (such as the lack of women speakers on the day's main program or threats of vigilante violence aimed at Marchers); however, his important formulation that viewers of photographs may "tease out the complexities and incongruities" remains an unresolved function of the enterprise of new photographic online multimedia. Expanding on the March's story of unprecedented collective grassroots empowerment is one such arena that could be explored through expansions into digital layering and social media, but not its inevitable outcome.

The rapid shifts in the developing field of photography over the last decade, especially its social and historical uses, build on previous era's innovations of accelerated photographic capture, dissemination, and framing. Elsewhere, I have previously argued to consider the endurance of photographic prints in new media through Jay David Bolter and Richard Grusin's notion of "remediation," in which new media producers "attempt to engage, transcend, or erase their antecedents."[11] The March on Washington commemorations were fueled by hopeful yet ambivalent expanded uses of photography, and not always unproductively. The multiple digital projects commemorated the event but regularly overlooked grassroots historical linkages, while attempting to update a given photograph's use value through devised scenarios of crowd participation. Several prominent digital offerings centered on King's dream as imagined in August 1963 and how it has evolved through the present day. However many of these digital offerings are produced without the possibilities for interaction, or attention to the estrangement or discontinuity that could be specifically addressed through new media techniques.

Photography continues to be used to render the March's emergent themes, in particular to cast the dream in pictorial terms. For commemorative projects functioning under the promise of interactivity, the political implications of the photographs are tracked into particular meanings when used by multinational news corporations in this new digital landscape. In the weeks leading up to the March's fiftieth anniversary, a number of prominent national news outlets presented programming that bridged traditional forums of broadcast and print with digital offerings. ABC News, for example, layered a memorable photograph of Dr. King originally taken by AP photographer Timothy Clary for their "interactive" website. Circular buttons beckon invitations to augment this image with pop out elements of the March's history. ABC draws on their own rich news archive to include video footage of newscasts from the day of the March and other information, included in caption-sized tidbits. Visitors can learn trivia about the March within a space of a small caption window. Such a visual framing from this particular image relies on the framing of the event through the pairing of Dr. King and a mass collective of gathered marchers, but views the latter as a crowd beyond individual or nuanced distinction. Furthermore, the credit line also fails to mention the photographer's name or source, and instead solely credits the digital production artists. Their digital labor is certainly worth acknowledgment, but also raises the question: Who created *this* image? Authorship is not granted for the original photographer, nor anyone who publically interfaces with this work. Interactivity is ultimately emphasized for the digital producers/architects of this piece, whose impressive and dynamic augmentation also produces a static layer for consumption. Viewers are opened up to but tracked toward particular glimpses within this selected photograph. The emphasis of this project ultimately animates the archive of ABC News, with open access for customers of their coverage and modes of sought-after click-through for its advertisers.

In another major network's augmentation project, NBC's #DreamDay series, the network created content for both its televisual and online audiences. This was promoted by the parent brand, NBC, and its subsidiary MSNBC. #DreamDay functions around recognizable March images, including ready-made memetic images, with a quote from Dr. King, a view of the crowd again from a distance, and a yellow border that conjures the wax pencil used on old negative contact sheets by photographers of the analog era to signal an important shot. NBC quotes Dr. King on this ready-made viral image: "We cannot walk alone. And as we walk, we must make the pledge that we shall always march ahead. We cannot turn back." The quotation, however is not credited to Dr. King, but rather assumed. Together, this puts forth collectivity in content and the framing as a gesture, aspiring toward viral dissemination—and yet the photograph also conveys a massive yet blurry crowd. On the website for the broader initiative, a virtual exhibition space stages simultaneously older historic photographs, mostly of Dr. King, and user-generated digital media content, many from NBC personalities, celebrities, and others uploaded and branded with the #DreamDay hashtag. The dream becomes a collective prompt, without a sense of specificity or continuity beyond the anniversary. Important to note, the sponsorship line, on the top right hand below the task bar, is understated, presented by name but without a logo: "Bank of America is proud to honor Dr. King's legacy." Bank of America is the financial outfit that has settled multiple cases for improper racially motivated lending and hiring practices.[12] This is not the first civil rights project to have a bank fund its operations, and perhaps such a partner in the marketplace may ensure greater power or reach to convey this history. But this also suggests a cost of doing business with civil rights legacy projects, in which photography serves as a form of currency in the exchange. NBC's *#DreamDay* draws on photography's "evidential force," as Roland Barthes suggests of the medium. In place of an accounting for the grassroots political legacies of the actual March, feasibility and profit bear out as a top priority alongside digital commemoration.

Beyond television networks, *Time Magazine* produced the documentary and website, "One Man. One March. One Speech. One Dream." The title is somewhat misleading, as the content focus is less channeled through exceptional individualism than a broad, impressive display of photographic forums and constituents. There are extensive narrative sections connected by a range of historical slideshows that give a sense of a larger arc of the movement beyond that day, and critically approach the way photographs furnish our memory of the day, and the later trajectories and gaps in memory. They draw on a vast archive of *Time*, *Life*, and other licensed content, including never-before-published works, and painful images, of Birmingham's 16th Street Baptist Church bombing a month later, along with urgent essays by Maya Angelou, Michele Norris, and others.[13]

To be certain, the Time documentary offering does engage a view of the March from the ground up. As a handful of amateur photographers were on the scene, Time collected their photographs to tell stories of the crowd. The design and accompanying slideshow conjures the layout of the Instagram app, and reminds us of one of the major changes from 1963 to now: being a photographer is a flexible identity. We readily approach photography as alternating subjects, shooters, and readers. In a parallel move, the developers of Instagram posted a special March on Washington page on their blog for the commemorative date, with the heading, "Marking 50 Years Since MLK's March on Washington,"[14] which gathered uploaded content with their suggested hashtag #MOW50. What legacy will these new images have, beyond the commemorative appeal or the satisfying of "FOMO," the "Fear of Missing Out," for digital users that share but gather collectively in different terms? What will they furnish or inspire?

Despite the sprawling sense of archival representation and historical knowledge on *Time*'s site, again a question of sponsorship, of who powers the venture, is important to consider. The sponsor field is empty months after the launch of the site, like a vacant storefront, but during the lead-up to the March anniversary the chief sponsor was high-end watch company Rolex. We are reminded here that the iconic nature of March images may be serviced in selling products and leveraged here for luxury.

Major media projects—like those of ABC, NBC, and *Time*—function as a look back on the history of the day without a broadening of the context available to historical memory far beyond their brands. The goal of dynamic commemorative interactivity is undermined and at times trivialized by corporate consumer exchange. From corporate sponsorships to grassroots deployments, photography of the March has continued to play a role in our still emergent conception of democracy through the long progression of the Civil Rights Movement. Drawing on its iconic status and serving differing needs determined by the market, March photographic images continue to evolve in our national imagination. Enhancement through digital techniques may also work to expand our notion of historical reflection, and reinterpretation, in the service of greater public access and goals of a corporate parent company. Or, others may employ historic photographs in the service of leveraging their enduring authority toward what Tillet refers to as "critical patriotism," an aesthetic approach that "neither encourages idolatry to the nation's past nor blind loyalty to the state," but through "dissidence and dissent . . . re-engages the metadiscourse of American democracy."[15] Tillet reminds us to consider repurposed historical tropes and material toward present-day engagements with civic participation and estrangement.

The fiftieth anniversary of the March not only included moments to celebrate the serious contributions of the Marchers and the larger Civil Rights Movement, but also to critically engage contemporary power structures. For example, a significant ambivalence marks the uses of March-related imagery with respect to the nation's first black President Barack Obama. Upon his election in 2008, many online memes conjured the March, placing Dr. King and President Obama in shared contexts, with images from the 1963 gathering offering a historical anchor. Such visuals widely circulated online, and also were printed on a wide body of souvenir t-shirts and hats as well. In one example from a large number of improvised images, an unknown digital artist offers Obama's election as a realization of King's dream, enacted in one series through a juxtaposition that serves to choreograph a karmic high five between the two leaders replacing the directed reach of King's arm from the March crowd to the President. Others reaffirm such visions, and include text declaring Obama the realization and embodiment of King's dream. Graphic remixes such as this function well within memetic cultures in that that they both reiterate visual knowledge as well as seek to revise historical understandings. While many of these improvised artifacts still exist and could be seen on the National Mall during the commemoration festivities, alternately, through the same convention of photographic overlay and viral sharing, we see a critical juxtaposition in the later years of his presidency—the emergence of the meme featuring similar images, albeit with President Obama pointing a finger, and with the text underneath: *I have a dream* and *I have a drone*. In this context, whether this image is viewed online as a meme or printed out for improvised protest signage, the March holds a complicated place in our national memory as well as our racial discourse. The archive of the March's memory is still compelling, still effective, and still being leveraged by a number of parties claiming ownership, or at least access to the legacy of the March, its debts and the dreams, by routing through its historic photographs.[16]

If artists and activists together can collaborate through Tillet's notion of critical patriotism, we can also consider new uses of photography toward honoring the contributions of the Marchers and carrying on the mantle of their work through its fiftieth anniversary. We may consider, then, the March in terms of significant and unlikely endurance in the national registers of history. We may also reflect upon the 1963 Marchers and leaders occupying the national capital through protest that represented critical coalition building and offered unique opportunities for embodiment and presence in the face of precarity, violence, and indifference. This essay demonstrates a sampling of the sorts of visual transmissions of March images for public history at the fiftieth anniversary, whether utilized for corporate dissemination or toward the evolution of the March toward racial, economic, gender, and sexual forms of social justice.

A case in relief: During the summer of 2013, youth activists known as the Dream Defenders gained national attention when galvanizing youth in Florida to action in response to the slaying of Trayvon Martin and the acquittal of his killer George Zimmerman. The Dream Defenders sought immediately to occupy the state capital and open public discussion of "Stand Your Ground" laws, but also conjured the dream in order to identify and train new leadership toward a reinvigorated Civil Rights Movement. They regularly used social media forums and tools of digital overlay to appropriate the rhetoric, strategies, and imagery of earlier civil rights protests and social action. Their rise to prominence likely resulted in their director, Phillip Agnew, being offered a speaking position at the commemorative fiftieth anniversary March on the National Mall in August 2013. When Agnew was unexplainably bumped from the program, along with another youth leader Sophia Campos of

United We Dream, due to timing issues, the group did not waver in their attempt to be heard and seen. The following day, bridging the site specificity of the Mall, the historic value of the photograph, and the possibilities of virally inclined media, they appropriated the legacy of the original March and a photographic image taken in 1963, as part of their own website's subpage, Our March.[17]

Sampling the image of young Austin Clinton Brown, then nine years old, of Gainesville, Georgia originally taken by an uncredited AP photographer, is repurposed for "#OurMarch," a digital campaign that included footage from Agnew and an invitation to an online "march" and exchange of ideas through social media. The content of this image, though subsumed without caption or credit to an original photographer, is leveraged toward the goal of social action. Though they fail to explicitly cite the original photographic constituents (photographer and subject), Dream Defenders achieved a regular feat for a new generation of *memers*, activists who streamline site-specific and online forms of social action, and are enabled when interpreting and reusing materials of cultural or historical import. In this case, they refocused the iconic photographic memory of the March, not to account retroactively but with contemporary participatory activism in mind. They did so to create a virtual and political space to connect, to organize, to innovate, and to continue marching. The photographic archive of the March, in this instance, belongs to those who bring forward its historical holdings, and reinterpret the contexts of the struggle and social transformation.

NOTES

I am grateful to the friends and scholars who gave me feedback on various drafts of this essay. In particular, I am grateful to James Braxton Peterson, Salamishah Tillet, William Hodgson, James Huckenpahler, and Amanda Robiolio for their insights. I also thank the participants of the American Studies Association roundtable, *A Debt and a Dream: The Afterlives of the March on Washington* (Michael Eric Dyson, Joshua Guild, Danielle McGuire, Salamishah Tillet, and Toussaint Losier), all of whom shared generative dialogue about the March's legacies following the fiftieth anniversary commemoration.

1. USPS, News Release, "Postal Service Issues March on Washington Stamp," August 23, 2013, no. 13-067, http://about.usps.com/news/national-releases/2013/pr13_067.htm (accessed October 1, 2013).

2. In addition, the notion of the stamp as keepsake is furthered by the consumer options for purchase, including on press sheets, t-shirts, and in a "Civil Rights Bundle" grouped with stamps marking the Emancipation Proclamation and honoring Rosa Parks.

3. For more on the grassroots history of the March on Washington, see Patrik Henry Bass, *Like a Mighty Stream: The March on Washington, August 28, 1963* (Philadelphia: Running Press, 2002); Charles C. Euchner, *Nobody Turn Me Around: A People's History of the 1963 March on Washington* (Boston: Beacon Press, 2010); Leonard Freed, Julian Bond, Michael Eric Dyson, and Paul M. Farber, *This is The Day: The March on Washington* (Los Angeles: J. Paul Getty Museum, 2013); and William Powell Jones, *The March on Washington: Jobs, Freedom, and the Forgotten History of Civil Rights* (New York: W. W. Norton, 2013).

4. Robert Hariman and John Luis Lucaites, *No Caption Needed: Iconic Photographs, Public Culture, and Liberal Democracy* (Chicago: University of Chicago Press, 2007), 1.

5. Ibid.

6. For more on the predigital memetic qualities of Dr. Martin Luther King, Jr.'s "I Have A Dream" speech, see NPR, "Dr. Martin Luther King Jr. and the Public Imagination," January 18, 2013, http://www.onthemedia.org/story/263577-dr-martin-luther-king-jr-and-public-imagination/ (accessed October 1, 2013).

7. Limor Shifman, *Memes in Digital Culture* (Cambridge, MA: MIT Press, 2014), 4, 15.

8. Maurice Berger, "A Momentous Day Driven by Ordinary People," (blog) *New York Times* LENS, http://lens.blogs.nytimes.com/2013/08/22/a-momentous-day-driven-by-ordinary-people/?_php=true&_type=blogs&_r=0 (accessed October 1, 2013).

9. Salamishah Tillet, *Sites of Slavery: Citizenship and Racial Democracy in the Post–Civil Rights Imagination* (Durham, NC: Duke University Press, 2012).

10. See Smithsonian National Museum of American History, "Changing America: The Emancipation Proclamation, 1863 and the March on Washington, 1963," http://americanhistory.si.edu/exhibitions/changing-america (accessed October 1, 2013; Library of Congress, "A Day Like No Other: Commemorating the 50th Anniversary of the March on Washington," http://www.loc.gov/exhibits/march-on-washington/ (accessed October 1, 2013); "Witnesses to History, 50 Years Later," *New York Times*, http://www.nytimes.com/interactive/2013/08/23/us/march-on-washington-anniversary-memories.html?_r=0 (accessed October 1, 2013); National Park Service, "We Are Still Marching," http://www.wearestillmarching.com (accessed October 1, 2013.) Full disclosure: I was a contributor of annotations for the National Park Service project.

11. Paul M. Farber, "The Last Rites of D'Angelo Barksdale: The Life and Afterlife of Photography in The Wire," *Criticism* 52, nos. 3–4 (2010): 413–39; Jay David Bolter and Richard Grusin, *Remediation: Understanding New Media* (London and Cambridge, MA: MIT Press, 2001).

12. See US Department of Labor, "Judge orders Bank of America to Pay Almost $2.2 Million for Racial Discrimination against More than 1,100 African-American Job Seekers," News Release, no. 13-1967-NAT, http://www.dol.gov/opa/media/press/ofccp/OFCCP20131967.htm (accessed October 1, 2013); or Natalie Sherman, "Group Alleges Racial Disparities in Bank of America Practices at Foreclosed Baltimore Homes," *Baltimore Sun*, October 1, 2013, http://articles.baltimoresun.com/2013-11-15/business/bs-bz-boa-suit-20131115_1_nfha-minority-areas-complaint (accessed October 1, 2013).

13. "One Man. One March. One Speech. One Dream," *Time Magazine*, #ONE-DREAM website, http://content.time.com/time/onedream/ (accessed October 1, 2013).

14. "Marking 50 Years Since MLK's March on Washington," Instagram (blog), http://blog.instagram.com/post/59618165996/mow50, (accessed October 1, 2013).

15. Tillet, *Sites of Slavery*, 11.

16. As noted, co-production is a key feature of memetic culture. However, recognized authorship remains elusive in regard to specific meme images. Meme authors regularly draw on copyrighted material, and thus claims of ownership or originality often are not framed as facets of meme creation. To trace the development of a given meme, readers may consult Meme online aggregators such as BuzzFeed, Reddit, or Know Your Meme.

17. Dream Defenders, "Our March," http://dreamdefenders.org/ourmarch/ (accessed October 1, 2013).

6

✤

How Deep? Skin Deep?

A Case Study on Shameful National Orientations

Emily Churilla

Shame has a long history of critical engagement in literary theory and the social sciences. As a subject of inquiry, shame has reemerged in recent years though its popularity has remained, for the most part, relegated to the realm of psychoanalysis and, more recently queer studies. While increasing attention is being placed on what—and how—bodies feel, it is essential that we also examine how a national public is constructed of feeling bodies that must necessarily and individually orient themselves toward objects they feel *about* in multiple and often conflicting ways. In the following pages I will explore some of the ways that individual affect and feeling form communities via media interaction thereby writing them as public sentiments. Focusing on what I am calling a *case study*, an interaction with popular media that highlights how orientation and inclusion operates through phenomenological reorientation of shame by the public, I will explain how one becomes integrated into a public in the act of turning away or toward. Rather than considering this public-building as an act that centers on defining and reinforcing borders, considering collective orientation instead, offers new possibilities in how sentiment circulates and coalesces from and into dominant discourse and facilitates affective subjugation of those deemed other in some way. Furthermore, tracing orientation allows us new means of action in light of such subjugation; rhetoric that focuses on inclusion/exclusion always necessarily falls back onto that of becoming permeable or expanding borders, processes that still perpetuate a deviant. Take, for example, the ever-expanding series of letters added to LGBT to LGBTIQQA for intersex, queer, questioning, and asexual, or the ongoing battle for gay marriage which, sadly, will still leave many individuals in nonnormative relationships of all sorts outside legal safety nets. It is the nature of publics, as I will explore below, to be a borderless collaboration through participation which gives the illusion of bordered belonging or not belonging; additionally I will argue that affective national belonging can operate much the same way. Focusing on an episode of the television show *House M.D.* titled "Skin Deep,"[1] I will highlight the malleability and pervasiveness of using shame as it pertains to gender and gender deviancy specifically and how normativity's effective shaming of that other allows a return to its haven of pride and security. Additionally, I am interested in the way even the act of viewing the episode in question creates an interactive, observantly regulatory, normative public-building process.

SHAME AND THE TURN TO NORMALCY

In our contemporary United States, national public-formations often fall back on the rhetoric of *national pride* or *national shame*, though these categories are not mutually exclusive nor does pride or shame rule out or surpass other affects such as fear, love, hatred, or disgust. There are practical reasons for my concentration on shame in this paper such as the unwieldiness of examining the depth and the enormous range of emotions we experience in any sort of a collective, but also because a shame/pride dichotomy is prevalent in so many of the stories and events that shape our social imaginary and this prevalence warrants a closer look. By examining the affective turns of this dichotomy within a national public we might better understand how the nation as a public operates beyond its laws and institutions and is enacted by the community that these laws and institutions imagines. Our emotions form as great a part of our world as our tangible items and identity markers as they help dictate what it is we form curiosities about, care for, and assume authority or knowledge over. These emotions, in turn, shape and are shaped by the national public.

Silvan S. Tomkins, in "Shame-Humiliation and Contempt-Disgust," writes that shame is a response individuals experience in the gaze of another—an *Other* body—in an act that causes the one who feels shame to turn inward by such actions as dropping the eyes, reducing facial communication, and hanging the head.[2] These are actions that Tomkins believes make shame an "affect linked with love and identification," so that "shame can only be created where there is a hierarchical relation between the shamed person and an object of love."[3] Here, the individual who feels shame does not live up to the real or imagined standards of the love object resulting in a failure to "cope successfully" with a challenge.[4] To further explicate this, in *The Cultural Politics of Emotion*, Sara Ahmed writes:

> The idealization of another is presumed if the other's look matters to me. At the same time, it is "an ideal" that binds me to another who might be assumed to be "with me" as well as "like me" (sharing my ideals) . . . [such an ideal] defined as an ego ideal, as "the self" that a self would like to be. Hence the conflict of shame has been characterized as a conflict between the ego and the ego ideal, in contrast to guilt, where the conflict is between the super ego and the ego.[5]

Without a desire to identify with another, without a love or desire to be accepted by that other, an individual cannot feel shame: we cannot be shamed by an individual we feel contempt, hate, or disgust for, as the desire to identify with that individual is not there.

On a collective level, this rule of shaming applies just as it does to the individual body. Following Hegel's *Lectures on the Philosophy of World History*, the state becomes a principle instrument in developing history and historiography. The state not only provides for the discourse of history but also helps to produce it. Through the development of history, the state produces a historical discourse, but through the discourse of shame, that national history is produced—as individuals are excluded from history because of the use of shame in the creation of a national identity. We cannot be shamed by people or nations that we feel politically, morally, and/ or economically superior to; we can only be shamed by our allies and equals. This collective shame can be thought of as something that binds a nation together through the notion of national shame—a shame that we all feel and can experience together just as we experience national pride or a national identity.

In *Publics and Counterpublics* Michael Warner writes: "publics are essentially intertextual, frameworks for understanding texts. . . all interwoven not just by citational references but by the incorporation of a reflexive circulatory field in the mode of address and consumption."[6] Considering the nation as a type of public, a framework for understanding other texts beyond the text that the nation is in and of itself, may help to focus our perspective—or our *orientation*. And though Warner makes the distinction between a national collective and a public, I do think it important to consider the nation (as it is articulated by the collusion of same-directed sentiment) as a type of public that is self-produced—which is possible if we accept that the nation is a text.[7] For when we turn away from our strange sons and daughters or our neighbors who do not have skin color or hair texture like ours we do not simply turn toward, or into, ourselves as we fortify our fences, upgrade our door locks, or rewrite our wills. Rather, we turn towards *something* (or some*one*), in fact—oftentimes something that has also turned away from the same people or objects that we have.[8] But our participation in this collective does not end here. To orient (or to *turn*) ourselves toward this something, thus aligning ourselves with it and others who make the same turn, means that we may now use this collective of things as a lens to read and interpret other texts that we encounter.

To further explicate this, I return to Sara Ahmed who, in *Queer Phenomenology: Orientations, Objects, Others*, demonstrates how bodies can come to be temporally and spatially shaped and framed through the repetition of social norms. In this work Ahmed writes that:

> The field of positive action, of what this or that body does do, also defines a field of inaction, of actions that are possible but that are not taken up, or even actions that are not possible because of what has been taken up. Such histories of action of "take up" shape the bodily horizon of bodies ... So, for instance, if the action of writing is associated with the masculine body, then it is this body that tends to inhabit the space for writing. The space for writing—say, the study—then tends to extend such bodies and may even take their shape. Gender becomes naturalized as a property of bodies, objects, and spaces partly through the "loop" of this repetition, which leads bodies in some directions more than others as if that direction came from within the body and explains which way it turns.[9]

We might push this further: as normative gender takes up the ideological space of the nation (and we are all familiar with the notion of the normative family as the microcosm of the nation) the nation is written as such— as if it is naturally, intrinsically, and normatively constructed. What becomes evident here is how national discourse writes through this process of the individual turning away from something—diverting one's eyes away from queer bodies in public, for example—and why this belongs within its own network of understanding.[10] Our viewing of gender and race, as either normal or not normal, and safe or not safe, is mediated by the alliances we make with the nation or the publics concerned with such distinctions as we turn away from or too the *something*. Here the masculine body inhabits the space for writing just as a normative-gendered body inhabits the space of the nation. The inhabitation process comes not from the body but from the repetition of directionality, an orienting loop that only gives the illusion of inclusion/exclusion or inside/outside. The normative national subject then is no longer formed through a confrontation with its deviant other but through a confrontation with the mythical ideal that has been predefined through association.

With this in mind I suggest we view national inhabitation not as an issue of inside and outside but as one that operates as a field of vision. The field of vision dictates what is seen and unseen; knowing what to look for or turn toward and knowing when to look or turn away—thereby demonstrating one's ability to be able to determine what the mythical ideal is. This becomes crucial in maintaining one's path of normative national subjectivity. By considering orientation in this way we may more accurately contend with the circulation and the displacement of shame. Here I am strangely reminded of Ophelia's words after Hamlet rejects her. Ophelia's exclamations at once reflect her disgrace and recognize something queer in Hamlet:

> And I, of ladies most deject and wretched,
> That suck'd the honey of his music vows,
> Now see that noble and most sovereign reason,
> Like sweet bells jangles, out of tune and harsh;
> That unmatch'd form and feature of blown youth
> Blasted with ecstasy: O, woe is me.
> To have seen what I have seen, see what I see![11]

Ophelia notes that what Hamlet once was he is no longer and this has precipitated a turn from her. But it is also significant that in the image she had seen in the past, likened to the sound of sweet bells jangling, there was something crucial that remained unseen by her (the bells were out of tune and harsh). Because she was not able to see his discordance she has been shamed and thrown off path. The King, however, picks up this unseen affect in the next few lines as he speaks, "What he spake . . . was not like madness / There's something in his soul."[12] That something is monstrous and threatening to the state—and though Hamlet turns away from Denmark, it is also he who is turned away from. For both Ophelia and the King, vigilance and the ability to read and identify Hamlet's unseen "something" is vital for both them; it is this same ability to read and identify that facilitates Ahmed's "'loop' . . . that leads as if the direction came from within" or Warner's "circulatory . . . modes of address and consumption."

The use and meaning of the term monstrous here is derived from Judith Halberstam's work in *Skin Shows: Gothic Horror and the Technology of Monsters*. In this text, Halberstam argues that "postmodern horror lies just beneath the surface, it lurks in dark alleys, it hides behind a rational science, it buries itself in respectable bodies . . . horror resides at the level of the skin itself."[13] The monstrous is produced by its embodiment of the respectable body and the fear it creates thereby proffers the notion that monsters look, really, just like you and me. And though we tend to think of the skin as a boundary that controls what comes in or out, here it acts less as a border and more as a textual realm, constructed by notions of normalcy rather than already existing as an agent of filtration against the deviant.[14] If horror exists "at the level of the skin itself" it is not because the skin itself holds markers of the horrific (it is not green or blue or black, nor is covered in boils, nor rotting away like the skin of zombies and other monstrous creatures in popular cinema) but rather because of the skin's powers to confuse, disorient, and refract. The true horror is the potential misidentification of the deviant and, therefore, the pseudoscientific processes of identification of gender deviancy's minor markers become all the more important to those who are only able to define themselves via the strict definition of male and female. The horror and shame that normativity feels when unable to diagnose deviancy at the surface level of the skin is demonstrated to us through *House*'s unfolding plot.

THE ULTIMATE WOMAN

In the Season Two episode of *House M.D.* entitled "Skin Deep," Dr. House begins treatment for heroin addiction on a fifteen year old supermodel, Alex. On the surface (or skin deep), Alex is beautiful as defined by Western norms, having long blond hair, high cheekbones, and a tall and thin physique; automatically the viewer understands that the episode will ask him or her to look beneath the surface, beyond any skin-deep perceptions. The plot begins to unfold when, during hospitalized treatment for her addiction, Alex suffers an unidentified heart complication and emerges from it displaying symptoms of anterograde amnesia, a problem that inhibits her from storing new information in her long-term memory. Believing she is suffering from Post-Traumatic Stress Disorder (PTSD) as a result of sexual abuse, House confronts Alex's father who admits he had sex with her "one time." However, when she exhibits symptoms that exclude, or contraindicate, the diagnosis of PTSD, House soon becomes convinced she has cancer and sets out to discover its location. When House, along with his assistant Cameron, discover the cancer that is causing her problems, the final twist is revealed and House explains to his patient and her father:

> *He* has cancer, on his left testicle . . . *you've* got male pseudohermaphroditism. See, we all start out as girls and then we're differentiated based on our genes. The ovaries develop into testes and drop. But in about 1 in 150,000 pregnancies a fetus with an XY chromosome, a boy, develops into something else. Like *you*. Your testes never descended because you're immune to testosterone. You're pure estrogen, which is why you get heightened female characteristics; clear skin, great breasts. The ultimate woman is a man.[15]

House's diagnosis is that Alex has androgen insensitivity syndrome, or AIS, an X-chromosomal linked condition that results in the "abnormal" masculinization of external genitalia of genetically male individuals. Individuals with complete androgen insensitivity syndrome (CAIS) develop female external genitalia—including clitoris and labia—and often people with AIS do not find out about their condition until a gynecological exam reveals it when they do not menstruate around the time of puberty.

In disbelief and as a way to reject this revelation Alex gets up from her hospital bed and strips off her gown, exposing to House (and several onlookers outside the hospital room) her "ultimate woman[ly]" body. The viewer, of course, only sees a perfectly sculpted back torso and top of the buttocks. Were we left with this image we might be asked to question gender (as the back shot certainly *looks* feminine) but instead we are refocused by the camera's angle onto Alex's shame. Alex's father turns away from her to look contemplatively out the window while Alex slowly covers her body and looks over her shoulder and back to her father. I am not as interested in the way that the notion of gender was linked to biological sex in this episode, or even the way that a scriptive or discursive process was implemented in order to recuperate traditional gender values. Both of these are important topics of discussion, but what is also interesting here is how the episode must work to orient *House*'s viewers toward normative conceptualizations of gender and away from its deviant, Alex. One endpoint for this discussion is to determine how these normalizing discursive practices are used to resituate *House*'s viewers as a homogenous viewing public that can come together and *agree* on something. Alex's gender deviancy becomes a shameful marker that works to turn the viewer (and her father) away from her and toward a normative collective; even Alex's father's act of looking out the window focuses him towards the normative collective. Normativity, remember, is unseen. Whiteness, heternormativity—these are invisible whereas deviancy is always the spectacle. Shame is relevant here because Alex, while positioned as shameful to the episode's viewers, does not recognize her own shame, at least not until the end; this facilitates the need for others to make the turn from her shame. In addition, this disrecognition of personal shame posits her as both monstrous and deviant.

Because the plot in part revolves around Cameron reporting Alex's father for molestation a social worker arrives at the hospital to speak with both patient and father. Both father and daughter deny the abuse ever took place and without evidence the social worker abandons the case. Cameron enters Alex's room only moments after the social worker leaves and it is here where the viewer begins the turning away from Alex (as the victim) and toward her father and the nation. We might even imagine Alex's father to be representative of the nation: for not only is he a white male father, but he is the one that is effectively damaged by the disguised intervention of the perverse body. Viewers will conclude that Alex is guilty of seducing her father since they are informed that he did not willingly participate in the sex act. Alex reveals that she "had to get him drunk," thereby suggesting a language of coercion that interestingly incorporates aspects of both the femme fatale and the college co-ed date rapist.[16] And to heighten the distancing or turning that the viewer begins to experience in this moment, Alex also appears much stronger or healthier in this scene than she has in previous ones. Her twitching has stopped and the makeup that darkens her eyes and yellows her skin is lessened here; her hair is less matted, she is not panting or struggling to speak. She appears resolute, confident, and perhaps even defiant, as she holds her head high, speaks directly, and makes eye contact with Cameron. She does not appear shameful and she does not demonstrate the physical markers of being shamed. And because of these intensifications, both physical and of her will, the show's viewing public begins to feel less sympathetic toward Alex. Instead, the public views *her* as perverse and not the father who slept with his fifteen-year-old daughter. Additionally, in this scene we discover that Alex not only seduced her father but has been sexually aggressive prior to this encounter—at age fifteen she has "taken" multiple partners to advance her career. Alex explains: "by sleeping with him now he lets me do whatever I want . . . I also slept with my photographer, my financial manager, and my tutor. If I hadn't I'd still be getting Cs posing for newspaper ads back in Detroit."[17] Demonstrating that not only can this perfect woman not be a product of nature, this scene also posits that Alex's overt sexuality is, when off the catwalk and beyond the male gaze, perversely oriented.

The distinction is thus: hypersexuality in the female body is acceptable when it is the product of the penetrating male gaze. Dr. House's blunt and vocal observations of her body and attractiveness are acceptable means of sexualizing the female body because his comments are informed by the gaze that defines Alex's body as sexual. Alex's sexuality becomes perversely oriented in the way she queers House's gaze, refracting (not mirroring) it back to him. She feeds on his gaze for her own benefit. This feeding is a queering of the power dynamic; one that allows her to take some of the power that is being exerted on her for her own uses. Again the end of the episode has Alex stripping off her hospital gown to House and several onlookers. Viewers might question if this isn't a futile act to reclaim some of the power that was taken from her by the violent gendering she just received.

If the ultimate woman is a man, albeit one that is lacking (testosterone), then she must parasitically feed on whole or real men to gain access to power, fame, and good grades. But even if this parasitical feeding may only threaten *House*'s male viewer, Alex's admission of being pretty and not smart also works to situate her as unnatural to its female viewers.

Natural female beauty is often espoused as real femininity; femininity, however, is never considered as natural as masculinity often because of the many props that women must use in order to perform femininity: makeup and hair products, restrictive clothing, high heels, breast implants, etc. And while I'm certain that many women, for one reason or another, might feel sympathetic to Alex's feelings here, the fact that her statement is a veiled lament only heightens the idea that beauty is lesser somehow than being smart (which is perceived as natural). This is one instance of many where viewers are asked to see Alex as not simply a *physically* sick individual. Time and again throughout the episode Alex is presented as the perfect woman. Alex's physical features, described as a "heart-shaped ass" and breasts that are "love apples handcrafted by God" are tellingly described as more erotic than natural—hearts and the sinful forbidden fruit. House and his male assistants place a bet on whether or not her breasts are, in fact, real.[18] The point, of course, is that in the end we are supposed to be left with the same question.

Also, throughout the episode the audience is asked to play the familiar game of "is this really a man or a woman?" Her gender ambiguous name, Alex (though we might imagine it being short for Alexandra or the like), coupled with other subtle cues, become signposts along the way. After the grand revelation that Alex is (chromosomally) a man (boy) the audience is tempted to return to these red flags, certain that there was some sort of uncanny *a priori* awareness or clue to her deviancy. This deviancy is one that viewers *should* have seen all along, even if it is something that is a legitimate medical condition, and in this way the episode acts eerily as a training program to help its viewers appropriately identify otherness.

Alex becomes a monster to the viewing public and her monstrousness ultimately boils down to fear or doubt in the ability to determine if she is *in fact* a man.[19] Alex has infiltrated everyday life, hidden in a skin that is too perfect, too beautiful, to actually be a woman. The perfect woman is not a man, as House claims, but rather a monster—and all the more monstrous and shameful for making us feel such horror. Furthermore, the game viewers participate in when we piece together these signposts becomes a distracting mechanism to keep us focused on just how we might tell the difference between Alex and a *real* woman while diminishing any concerns we might have regarding her victim status. This has the effect of positioning Alex not simply as spectacle, but specimen—that is, a specimen of scientific study where we are the scientist-judges. We might also argue that Alex further exemplifies a Halberstamian monster when we consider the emphasis on science from the quote that began this section. But the monstrous, for Halberstam, is also produced by its embodiment of the respectable body and the fear it creates thereby stems the notion that monsters look, really, just like you and me. Alex's monstrousness, then, boils down to our own fear of our inability to tell if she is a woman or a man. She has infiltrated our everyday life, hidden in a skin that is too perfect, too beautiful, to actually be a woman. In either case, however, Alex is decidedly not normative and therefore is a threat to the public and/or national order with respect to gender.

Note well that Alex is in a clinical setting, having a battery of tests run on her—and she is quite literally under the microscope. Through the machinery of the set and the setting, "Skin Deep" instructs us to judge the specimen with testicles and breasts, prompting viewers to look for the markers of deviancy, disclose that they/we might know someone who has pseudohermaphroditism, or just tell a good story of "someone who knows some guy who dresses like a girl." However, this is not simply about the firsthand experiences of the victims themselves but the experience everyone (supposedly) shares as citizens of the United States and how that experience marks membership in this citizenry. American social imaginary resides in the mythology of gender normativity; articulating relationships to the nation via experience with it allows a public articulation of judgment over those who do not fit within normative gender roles. Situating Alex as deviant and less than human (by becoming a monstrous specimen) is necessary to set up what is at stake in the moment of turning away. Again, Alex's father turns away not in shame but from his perceptions of and reaction to the horror of her body, reinscribing his own normalcy. His shame and perverseness in sleeping with his daughter is overcome by the moment of revelation in the narration that she's a he—and the moment of revelation is only such a moment because of how horrific a revelation it actually is. As House explains at the end, at least there's no worry about a repeat offence of molestation from the father: "Now it's gross!" The unfolding narratives of the episode go to great lengths to position Alex as having something wrong with her that exceeds her health issues while subtly demonstrating her father's remorse for his actions.

This dynamic of remorse and trauma is evident when Cameron presses her on her interaction with her father, reasoning that her deviant behavior is the result of prior harm: "After your father slept with you, you were traumatized." Alex responds, "my dad was last. You've never taken a run at your boss, or professor, or somebody else you needed?" She positions herself as having agency in her sexual experiences, effectively negating possible accusations of rape at least as it is defined by consent, if not by age. On the other hand, House presses Alex's father into admitting the sex act ostensibly out of love when he asks: "Do you love her enough to admit that you slept with her? Psychological conditions can manifest themselves in physical problems. Sometimes these can be extreme enough to kill. There are treatments, but only if there's a diagnosis. Are you going to admit that you slept with your daughter or are you just gonna let her die?"

and her father replies, simply, "One time."[20] The grossness, or monstrousness, of Alex's body absolves her father from his actions; the possibility of his shame in having sex with his daughter is foreclosed by his own disgust and horror in her body. His shame, then, derives from not being able to see her markers of deviancy.

Outside *House*, notions of monstrosity and shame play out much the same way. Hate crimes enacted on transgendered individuals are often justified through the language of panic, fear, shame, and horror when their cases make their way into the public. For example, consider the case of Scott Amedure's 1995 murder by Jonathan Schmitz after Amedure announced he had a secret crush on Schmitz on the *Jenny Jones Show*. Asserting a defense based on Edward J. Kempf's definition of homosexual panic in his 1920 book *Psychopathology*, Schmitz admitted to feeling "humiliated" and "embarrassed" by Amedure's confession and asked the jury to identify with his position in the narrative. Since the jury found Schmitz guilty of second-degree murder instead of the prosecution's first-degree murder charge, we can conclude that many of the jurors identified with Schmitz. The "Skin Deep" *House M.D.* episode, airing in 2006, was three years before the first ever US conviction of a hate crime against a nonnormative gendered individual. In this case, Allen Andrade was convicted of beating Angie Zapata to death with a fire extinguisher on July 17, 2008 after learning that she was transgender; he attempted to claim he was in a state of violent temporary insanity stemming from panic upon learning of her gendered state.[21]

A more recent and related nonfiction incident seemed to be uncannily anticipated by *House*'s writers. Appearing at number ninety-eight in *FHM*s "100 Sexiest Women in the World 2011" was nineteen-year-old Andrej Pejić. And initially accompanying Pejić's photograph was the caption, worth quoting at length:

> Did you spot it? The missing "s" in "he"? Or perhaps the Adam's apple was a giveaway?
> Don't worry if you weren't quick enough at playing detective, you are not alone. Andrej has been confusing the male gender since he was 14 . . . Although his sexual identity is ambiguous, designers are hailing him as the next big thing. We think 'thing' is quite accurate . . . Having managed to get away with [his looks] in campaigns for Marc Jacobs and Jean Paul Gaultier, the blonde gender-bender has jumped the gun again in hoping he might one day be signed as a Victoria's Secret Model. (Pass the sick bucket).[22]

Of course, almost a month after the list was published, critical attention from *The Guardian* and *Huffington Post* among others invoked a formal statement from *FHM*; the editors of the magazine ultimately retracted the original post. My focus here is on the language of the caption and the manner in which it closely follows *House*'s detective play (opening with the question of observance, "Did you spot it?") and unfolding into the dehumanizing of Pejić into thing. Furthermore, the statement "pass the sick bucket" mirrors House's reaction and points to his desire to resituate the shame of deviancy on Alex. Just as Alex's father must turn himself away from her monstrousness, so must the writer of Pejić's caption symbolically vomit in response to the deviant fluidity and difference in someone's gender.

The alignment between Schmitz and his jury, and the conventional gender norms to which Alex's father responds are necessary in maintaining a strongly oriented and ordered gendered schema from which the nation can operate. This may be in part explained by theorizations of self-formation through confrontation of otherness—that the self is not possible without the other—and therefore dichotomies of gender normalcy and deviancy arise. But something must account for the hate and disgust that is evident in these encounters or the depiction of them. Neither Schmitz, *FHM*'s readers, nor Alex's father could see that there was something wrong with their object of lust and they became disoriented in relation to their mythical ideal. Their acts of violence (murder, turning away, and vomiting) are frantic attempts to realign with the normative. Gender normative orientation is socially conscripted. It is passed down from one generation to the next and most are socialized to think about gender norms at early ages. Moreover, shame, the failure of the self to live up to the self's ideal (whether this is a failure to see or of one's desires that rest in seeing), is disorienting. Shame in this way is a recognition that one is off the path of the ideal self and offtrack in relation to the nation's ideal.

Similar to Schmitz's jury or *FHM*'s reader, *House*'s viewer is positioned to see Alex as the psychologically sick perpetrator, an aggressive hypersexual object for a gender normative gaze. Alex is a perverse specimen. She is both ashamed and a shameful figure in the "Skin Deep" episode. Her incompleteness (she lacks both womanness and manness) is exposed. Her illness and the revelation of her deviant body become causal factors in the reorientation of her father and the viewing public. Alex's shame and deviancy rearticulates a heteronormative orientation. Perhaps her cancer can be justified as a lesson from God, much like AIDS was said to be for gays and drug addicts in the 1980s or Hurricane Katrina was said to be for the poorest folks of New Orleans. Ultimately Alex's body is portrayed as disruptive, disorienting, and shameful, and her punishment for this is the redirection of shame back onto her so that her father and the viewing public can maintain certain heteronormative conventions.

The "Skin Deep" episode works to position Alex as a deviant specimen, and as an unnatural other. Both the physical turning away from her body within the episode *and* the turning away from her deviant body by viewers require the episode's normative narrative trajectory and well-plotted reveal. This kind of shame compels reaction, even if only internal or mental, and the reactions must necessarily go beyond misguided and unproductive pronoun debates and games of pin-the-gender-on-the-deviant. The contemplation of societal gender norms is a more challenging activity than simply turning away from a shameful body or turning off the television. If as a society we are to grapple with the gendered other in some serious way, then the mechanics of the "Skin Deep" episode will reveal for us the entrenched nature of conventional gender norms. Within the episode these norms trump incest, rape, and the very visual presentation of Alex's body. In the end Alex recognizes her shame by covering her body, retreating into herself, and looking back longingly at those who have turned away from her (in) shame. All the while, the public, safe in its conventions of straightness and heteronormative orientations, can simply click the off television or change the channel.

NOTES

1. "Skin Deep," *House M.D.*, directed by James Hayman (Los Angeles: NBC Universal Television, 2006).
2. Silvan S. Tomkins, "Shame-Humiliation and Contempt-Disgust," *Shame and Its Sisters: A Silvan Tomkins Reader*, ed. Eve Kosofsky Sedgwick, et al. (Durham, NC: Duke University Press, 1995), 137.
3. Ibid., 137.
4. Sara Ahmed, *The Cultural Politics of Emotion*, (New York: Routledge, 2004), 133.
5. Ibid., 106.
6. Michael Warner, *Publics and Counterpublics* (New York: Zone Books, 2005), 16.
7. M. Warner writes that "Publics differ from nations, races, professions, and any other group that, though not requiring co-presence, saturate identity. Belonging to a public seems to require at least minimal participation, even if it is patient or notional, rather than a permanent state of being" (ibid., 71) and continues later that while "a nation, for example, includes its members all the time, no matter what . . . whether or not they are awake or asleep, sober or drunk, sane or deranged, alert or comatose" a public "exists only by virtue of address, it must predicate some degree of attention, however nominal, from its members" (ibid., 87). I disagree with this last statement, at least in a particular context. A nation forms through repetition of a particular type of proper citizenry that exceeds a legal definition: a "real" citizen is that person who not only holds the documents but is one who is folded into the national body through his or her strict adherence to and reinforcement of normality.
8. M. Warner warns us, however, that this *something* is not necessarily an object (or an object *of*) as he critiques historical and literary modes of analysis: "Analysis can never simply begin with the text as its object . . . Publics are among the conditions of textuality, specifying that certain stretches of language are understood to be 'texts' with certain properties" (ibid., 16).

9. Sara Ahmed, *Queer Phenomenology: Orientations, Objects, Others*. (Durham, NC: Duke University Press, 2006), 58.

10. As Lauren Berlant in *The Female Complaint: The Unfinished Business of Sentimentality in American Culture* writes, "What makes a public sphere intimate is an expectation that the consumers of its particular stuff *already* share a worldview and emotional knowledge that they have derived from a broadly common historical experience. A certain circularity structures an intimate public, therefore: its consumer participants are perceived to be marked by a commonly lived history; its narratives and things are deemed expressive of that history while also shaping its conventions of belonging . . . it flourishes as a porous, affective scene of identification among strangers that promises a certain experience of belonging and provides a complex of consolation, confirmation, discipline and discussion about how to live as an *x*" ([Durham, NC: Duke University Press, 2008], vii).

11. William Shakespeare, *Hamlet*, in *The Norton Shakespeare*, ed. Stephen Greenblatt, et al. (New York: W. W. Norton, 1997), 1707, lines 154–60.

12. Ibid., 1707, lines 162–63.

13. Judith Halberstam, *Skin Shows: Gothic Horror and the Technology of Monsters* (Durham, NC: Duke University Press, 1995).

14. See Judith Butler, *Bodies That Matter: On the Discursive Limits of "Sex"* (New York: Routledge, 1993). I am also reminded of Sara Ahmed's observation that the "skin connects as well as contains" through touch and sensation (*Queer Phenomenology*, 54).

15. "Skin Deep," *House M.D.*, directed by James Hayman (Los Angeles: NBC Universal Television, 2006).

16. Ibid.

17. Ibid.

18. Ibid.

19. I place this in italics to highlight the impossibility of a factual sex.

20. "Skin Deep," *House M.D.*, directed by James Hayman (Los Angeles: NBC Universal Television, 2006).

21. For further reading, see Michigan Court of Appeals, *People v. Schmitz*, 586 NW2d 766, 678 (1998). Also, for an extended review of the Homosexual Panic Defense (HPD), please see Kara S. Suffredini, "Pride and Prejudice: The Homosexual Panic Defense," *Boston College Third World Law Journal* 21, no. 2 (May 2001): 279–314.

22. FHM, "100 Sexiest Women in the World 2011," *FHM: Good News for Men*, May 5, 2011.

7

✢

Faggoty/White/Uniform

Gays in the Military and
A Few Good Men

Scott St. Pierre

This essay argues that it is not an historical coincidence that Rob Reiner's film version of Aaron Sorkin's successful Broadway play, *A Few Good Men*, premiered late in 1992, shortly after the presidential election of Bill Clinton. Clinton's campaign had promised substantial reform of the US military's controversial practice of excluding soldiers from service based on sexual orientation.[1] However, as we know today, Clinton's reform efforts famously fizzled (after a very public confrontation with Congress) into the politically problematic and intellectually dishonest "Don't Ask, Don't Tell," an invasive policy that banned open "homosexuals" outright and that mandated "separa[tion] from the armed forces" for any service member who discloses or is discovered to "demonstrate a propensity or intent to engage in homosexual acts."[2] "Don't Ask, Don't Tell" operated voraciously unabated until fairly recently—late September of 2011 to be precise—in stark contrast to what seemed to be the campaign promises of Barack Obama, another popular, supposedly reform-minded Democratic president. Some estimates have put the total number of soldiers discharged under the policy at over 13,000. Yet its continued implementation under the first years of the Obama administration perhaps should not be surprising given a political environment that continues to cast doubt on the motives of progressive reformers whose own squishy rhetoric of sexual inclusion is routinely interpreted as evidence of their unwillingness or inability to "keep us safe."[3] I contend that this problematic trend—of many American left politicians' persistent reluctance to seem weak by, paradoxically, "fiercely advocating" on behalf of lesbians and gays—undergirds Reiner's film adaptation and continues to inform American left politics today (despite, I would argue, the eventual repeal of "Don't Ask, Don't Tell").[4]

Such contorted political logic, I argue, is central not only to Obama's current administration (on a range of issues), but is also integral to the politics and structural logic of *A Few Good Men*. For though Reiner's film is ostensibly about the ethics and legality of military hazing and military self-policing, the film's own conflicted sympathy for lesbian and gay soldiers provides an instructive example for ongoing debates in the public arena about abandoning "Don't Ask, Don't Tell."[5] Instead of genuinely focusing on the rights of gays and lesbians in the military, this film narrows its focus. Instead, homosexuality in the military is the battleground over which two heteronormative men vie for the right to define "strength" and "national security." In other words, *A Few Good Men* is a remarkably relevant text to be reviewed today. This iteration of the debate, then, recapitulates a familiar left approach to gays in the military that at once seems eager to advocate on behalf of homosexual service members, but at the same time finds itself terrified to seem weak by doing just that. Such discourse remains beholden to the "strong" patriarchal, misogynistic, and homophobic authority of its would-be villains. The film, then, despite the defeat of its antagonists in the short term (including a memorable turn by Jack Nicholson, who tells us with conviction and seems poised for victory before his downfall that "You want me on that wall; You need me on that wall!"), reinscribes the petrifying/petrified logic of many American politicians. That is because it allows the charming, reassuring voice of conservatism, despite some setbacks, to advocate convincingly for the continued exclusion of homosexuals in what amounts to a reactionary apologia for the calcified fear of military "integration." The film clearly encourages its audience to root for some minorities, including women, racial minorities, and the uneducated, rural poor. Nonetheless it cannot or will not, in a move that anticipates Clinton's capitulation and perhaps Obama's early hesitation, hold the line for gay and lesbian service members for fear it may mark the film's liberal sympathies as irredeemably "soft" on defense.[6]

In spite of the procedural nature of the classic courtroom drama, the film's plot is fairly straightforward. Three navy lawyers, Tom Cruise's Lieutenant Kaffee, Demi Moore's Lieutenant Commander Galloway, and Kevin Pollak's Lieutenant Weinberg, successfully defend two junior enlisted marines after they accidentally kill a fellow soldier in a hazing incident gone wrong. The hazing, or "Code Red," is meticulously covered up by their senior officers, including Nicholson's smugly grinning, cigar chomping Colonel Jessup. And the crime is laid at the feet of the two marines who they claim killed in order to cover up evidence of another, earlier crime. Yet the film is also curiously saturated with sexual preoccupations that divide the protagonists and the antagonists along the lines not only of practical, plot-driven motivations, but also of sexual ideologies. Jessup and his men chuckle darkly, for instance, after the colonel informs Kaffee that procuring oral sex from Galloway will solve all of his problems. The navy lawyers respond only with pained, speechless disgust. Jessup explains: "There is nothing on this earth sexier, believe me gentlemen, than a woman you have to salute in the morning. Promote 'em all, I say, 'cause this is true: if you haven't gotten a blowjob from a superior officer, well, you're just letting the best in life pass you by." Jessup's astonishingly coarse remark is a key moment in the film. Firstly, in this moment Jessup signals his antagonism. He shifts from the warm, friendly, and helpful company man into the film's pompous villain. Yet the sexual manner in which Jessup activates that shift is especially noteworthy, giving film viewers pause to wonder why sexual politics should rear up so insistently.[7] For one thing, Jessup underscores division within the military itself, a division that pits the powerfully conservative forces of the colonel and his men on one side and a group of relatively weak liberal reformers on the other. That group is represented here as a stereotypically fractious coalition nearly brought down by its own bickering. The defense includes a Harvard-educated son of a prominent civil rights attorney, Cruise's Kaffee, an assertive woman in uniform, Moore's Galloway, and a cautious, wonky Jew, Pollack's Weinberg.

The comment, though, also emphasizes Jessup's—and by extension the conservative faction he represents—aggressive misogyny and homophobia. It is actually an extremely rich way of boasting of his own authority, while simultaneously denigrating Galloway's talents (and implicitly those of the entire US Navy) as limited to the oral variety. The marine men are the ones who act. In the navy, however, they just use their mouths.[8] He is also tacitly suggesting (and of course makes explicit in his later comment on Kaffee's attire) that he thinks the navy man is at best half a man and at worst half a fag. Of course many soldiers do get blowjobs from one another—and those men who do it with men are liable to discharge—but Jessup's implication is that Kaffee just plain isn't man enough to be in the military. "You know," he says, "it just hit me—she *outranks* you, Danny." Kaffe is thus emasculated in the marines' eyes by his own subordinate position to a woman. And by the logic of these marines, such feminized men also, associated as they are with the mouth, are just all talk.[9]

From the rhetorical perspective of the filmmakers, this exchange is obviously meant to play up Jessup's villainy in the eyes of its soft-lefty audience. Jessup is a "bad" guy because he disrespects women and is mean to Tom Cruise. Yet Jessup continues to press the matter of sexuality in a curiously insistent way that suggests something else is going on here other than a meanness divorced of any contextual signification. Jessup ends this early confrontation by menacingly repeating his otherwise irrelevant charge: "I can deal with the bullets, and the bombs, and the blood. I don't want money, and I don't want medals. What I do want is for you to stand there in that faggoty white uniform and with your Harvard mouth extend me some fucking courtesy." The audience is actually already aware that Kaffee hates the uniform, but the point is clear. The entrenched conservative element of the military is suspicious of faggots and those liberals who would dare to challenge its hegemony are themselves weak, effete, too concerned with trivial things and pleadings for "special rights" to be able to handle what Jessup can: bullets, bombs, and blood.

If, however, the film takes a skeptical stand on the homophobia of a certain kind of military man, it also presents a surprisingly rosy vision of race. One of the key friendships in the film, after all, is between the two men on trial—Dawson, an African American "recruiting poster marine," and Downey, his uneducated, Caucasian naïf buddy. And Santiago, the marine the two men accidentally kill, is murdered not out of any apparent racial or ethnic animus, but for other reasons concerning sexuality that I will come to in a moment. This is a film that seems to think race matters very little any more; it is a subject over which no one spends even a moment's pause. The implication, I think, is that the forced military integration of the mid-twentieth century actually worked, that it led to a racially egalitarian military. This fact, of course, is also embodied by the figure of the African American judge who presides over Dawson and Downey's trial. The audience might wonder, then, if the film is suggesting by extension that a related, top-down (from the civilian commanders rather than rank and file officers) integration of the military—this time one involving gays and lesbians—might meet with the same fortuitous results.

This oversimplified analogy between the circumstances of African American and gay/lesbian soldiers has been critiqued in theoretically supple ways by a number of critics for creating a false dichotomy that would suggest that the categories of African American and homosexual are mutually exclusive. In other words, such thinking falsely assumes that all African Americans are heterosexual and that all homosexuals are white.[10] Alycee J. Lane, for example, criticizes the advocates and the opponents of lifting the military anti-gay ban for often engaging in this problematically simplistic conflation and decontextualization.[11] According to Lane, as a result of such decontextualization,

> How race continues to be central to the operations and organizational structure of the military; how it is implicated in gay and lesbian politics; and how the opposition, in its offensive against gay rights advocates, relied on what

has been the conservative and far right's use of race over the past thirty years to dismantle civil rights as a whole, were rendered unspeakable.[12]

In other words, for proponents of lifting the ban, the strategy of arguing for an analogy between the situation of racial segregation in the military and the military's anti-gay policy uses African Americans as a means to an end without really demonstrating much interest in the politics of race and its intersections with gender and sexuality.[13] So while such claims do make a good faith effort to advance gay and lesbian civil rights, those who make them "might have believed that decontextualization helped them to establish the basis for claiming equivalent victimization, [yet] it actually demonstrated the extent to which white (male) privilege structured that position. In other words, the attempts to erase race only made more poignant the fact that some people had the privilege to do so."[14]

Advocates of lifting the ban, of course, were and are not the only ones who have often relied upon this faulty thinking to make their case. Opponents of gays and lesbians in the military have also invoked the desegregation/sexual orientation comparison for even more troubling purposes. As Lane rightly points out about the debates of the early 1990s, "those who opposed lifting the military's ban on gays and lesbians relied on being able to fuse race to the gay/military issue, and they ensured this through their decontextualization of black bodies, exemplified by *their* references to the 'end' of racism."[15] This is an important observation, and one whose logic we find recapitulated in *A Few Good Men*. For Jessup partakes of exactly this line of argumentation when he finds out who Kaffee is: the son of a successful civil rights attorney and a former attorney general. Jessup practically glows in recounting one of the elder Kaffee's victories: "Jefferson versus Madison County School District. They didn't want a little black girl to go to an all white school. Lionel Kaffee said, 'We'll just see about that.'" Jessup's approving remarks point to an "end of racism" worldview, one in which there is not much left to be done on the subject of race. The end of racism position strengthens Jessup's hand, as Lane suggests, by allowing him to conceive of himself as a benevolent and "right thinking" man, but one who is then doubly justified in his suspicion of other "special interest" groups like homosexual soldiers who would supposedly endanger his unit's safety.[16] In other words, by presenting himself as an ardent supporter of racial equality, Jessup preemptively armors himself against charges of bigotry. Yet what Lane's work helps to illuminate in the film is how each possible position on the issue of gays and lesbians in the military, whether for or against, is nonetheless characterized by a problematic indifference to the very real concerns of how race continues to operate both within the military and within American cultural life.

It may not seem as though the film is thinking about these kinds of cultural debates at all, but I would suggest that the film actually repeatedly signals a deep, but conflicted imbrication in such discourse. After all, the underlying crime that sets the film in motion is precipitated by a young, fey marine named Santiago, who can't for the life of him meet the physical, social, or ethical standards expected of marines. What little we discover about Santiago—a crucially dense, purposefully opaque site of meaning for the film's politics ("From now on Willy is Private Santiago," Kaffee at one point counsels his clients, "You start calling him Willy and all of a sudden he's a person who's got a mother who's gonna miss him.")—is that he is a weakling. He is an outsider who sits alone at meals because his peers ostracize him. And ultimately he is a traitor who, when he cannot succeed in the military, breaks the all important "code" of the men ("unit, corps, God, country") by ratting on a squad-mate to the outside civilian authorities about an illegal shot across enemy lines. As one reviewer of the stage version put it, Santiago is "a complainer whose lack of esprit threatens his unit's image."[17] He is, in short, a caricature of reactionary fears about gay soldiers. He is (all at once) not up to the job, disruptive of unit morale and camaraderie, and finally a turncoat who betrays the corps as his last option. And as Janet E. Halley points out in her exhaustive account of the gays in the military debate, this caricature actually deflects any legitimate discussions about social justice by depicting the gay soldier as not up to the job, as essentially a threat to our national security.[18] And this idea is part of a history that, as Jabir K. Puar points out, draws on

> The historical convergences between queers and terror: homosexuals have been seen as traitors to the nation, figures of espionage and double agents, associated with communists during the McCarthy era, and, as with suicide bombers, have brought on and desired death through the AIDS pandemic (both suicide bomber and gay man always figure as already dying, a decaying or corroding masculinity).[19]

Santiago follows this pattern exactly, from the corrosion of traditional masculinity down to his own violent sexualized death.

Though we feel sorry for Santiago, and sorry also for his grieving parents, we can't help but think yes, of course this person does not belong in the marines. He is "substandard" as Jessup later terms him. Santiago's death is later explained away as the result of a mysterious "condition" that causes his death when the accused soldiers "accidentally ... stuff a rag down his throat." But the "accidental" nature of his death ameliorates the guilt of the marines on trial and makes our acceptance of this death much more palatable. Still, the fact that his death is revealed to be an accident does not totally soothe the discomfort of watching a hazing incident that is all too reminiscent of a sexualized hate crime. Santiago is woken in the night, bound, and gagged before being orally penetrated by his attackers, a fully "appropriate" and homophobic punishment given the logic of the film's representation of him and his crimes. Of course, I do not wish to simply assert that Santiago is gay. In its representation of him in these specific terms, the film creates him as a dense nucleus of anxiety about gay identity, a homosexuality that he may not embody at the level of story but that he nonetheless signifies in the film's anxious political economy.

Even in death Santiago continues to function not as a real human being with a mother (Kaffee's formulation), but as a problem for the military, as a distraction, according to Jessup's logic, to the real work of defending the nation. The dramatic tension of the film lies not in the question of whether Santiago's death will be avenged or not; we never meet his grieving mother even though we do meet Dawson's parents and even Downey's Aunt Ginny. Instead the drama of the film is embodied in the question of whether Jessup is right in his claims about defending a nation. Is it necessary to sacrifice or "separate" Santiago (and the homosexual soldiers he represents) in order to keep America "safe?"[20] Halley astutely argues that deploying this question of safety allows people like Jessup to make the case that his approach to running the military "can hardly express any animus toward any real social group, [because he] can claim that [his] project is nonnormative or even anormative, conjoined with the related claim that the military itself (like an insurance scheme) is a special-purpose social aggregation immune from most constraints applicable to other civic actors."[21] In other words, as we see in Jessup and Kaffee's final, famous showdown on the witness stand, Jessup is able to stake the convincing claim that the military's role as a special-purpose institution, one devoted to defending the nation, protects/insulates it *a priori* from accusations of discrimination, discrimination against homosexuals or anything else, for that matter. Jessup neatly exempts himself from the debate: "Have you ever served time in an infantry unit, son? Ever served in a forward area? Ever put your life in another man's hands, ask him to put his life in yours? We follow orders, son. We follow orders or people die. It's that simple." The ground Jessup stakes out is one that cannot be bothered by the supposedly petty claims of progressive social agendas, because it operates on a single, simple and practically indisputable principle. (Never mind that Dawson and Downey *did* follow Jessup's orders and that's what killed Santiago).

This is where the film finds itself sadly conflicted. And this is what Jessup means when he bellows the film's most famous, much parodied line: "You can't handle the truth!" The truth, he rightly says, is that though the film seems to have a soft spot for gay and lesbian service members, that sensitivity comes face to face with the hard reality of its dedication to a nationalistic program that is, as Puar argues, itself inherently heterosexist. The truth is that despite liberal fantasies, Jessup's personal contempt for "faggots" is not the real obstacle to integration for gay and lesbian men and women. The problem is not just to change the minds of a few resistant old-timers. Rather, as Puar says, "for contemporary forms of U.S. nationalism and patriotism, the production of gay and queer bodies is crucial to the deployment of nationalism, insofar as these perverse bodies reiterate heterosexuality as the norm."[22] In other words, though I would wager the filmmakers themselves meant for this project to be sympathetic to gays and lesbians, their incessant "incitement to discourse" about homosexuality, to borrow Foucault's famous phrase, is in cahoots with the fundamentally heteronormative project of US nationalism. This liberal agenda unintentionally, then, becomes another instance of fuel for the fire of rampant neoliberal nationalism, a project that at this historical moment sees homosexual bodies only and always opportunistically.[23] The film is, like many American politicians on the left, that heteronormative, nationalistic project's consort.[24]

The dominance of the nationalistic project in this film (with its fetishization of safety and strength) over the representation of homosexuality and the military can hardly be overstated. The showdown between Kaffee and Jessup is a microcosm of the play of power that circuits through the loaded oppositions of strength/weakness and safety/danger that shape the gays in the military debate. Opponents of lifting the military ban on homosexual soldiers most frequently emphasized the claim that a change to the law would weaken the military and put Americans in danger. This is essentially the position Kaffee finds himself in at the conclusion of his first meeting with Jessup: standing weak and insecure in his "faggoty white uniform." Jessup, in contrast, projects strength and safety precisely because he subscribes to conservative doctrines. As he explains, "I run my unit how I run my unit. You want to investigate me, roll the dice and take your chances. I eat breakfast three hundred yards away from four thousand Cubans who are trained to kill me, so don't think for one second that you can come down here, flash a badge, and make me nervous." His macho disgust for this liberal trio's reformist agenda is paired with the colonel's reassuring confidence, the sense that though this guy may be a jerk, he has the courage and the competence to keep Americans safe. And Jessup himself explicitly ties that project to his own conservative policies. The practice of Code Red—"enlisted men disciplining their own"—that sparked the whole case, for example, has been banned by Jessup's superiors because of its barbarism. However, Jessup says that "On the record I tell you that I discourage the practice in accordance with the commander's directive. Off the record I tell you that it is an invaluable part of close infantry training, and if it happens to go on without my knowledge, so be it." For Jessup, the old way, the way of tradition, is not just tacitly accepted but, as viewers will find out, is actively endorsed. From his perspective, outsiders who attempt to impose a new way on his old guard do nothing but undermine those "invaluable" traditions that are essential to a strong military and a safe nation.

In its early acts, the film seems set to tackle this structural conflict on a large scale, to indict a systematic resistance to change. The showdown between Kaffee and Jessup is primed to be an effective intervention into the system by the filmmakers. However, I would suggest that by its end, this critique collapses under the weight of its own unacknowledged affinity for the structural conservatism Jessup represents. The central dilemma of the film's final act is played out in the famous set-piece battle of Kaffee's cross-examination of the colonel back on the witness stand in Washington, DC. In the scenes before this clash of the box office titans, Kaffee is all but ready to concede the trial, as a key witness who would have testified that Jessup ordered the Code Red has just killed himself. Kaffee, recognizing that he has no evidence to disprove Jessup's testimony, is resolutely opposed to challenging his word on the stand, arguing that "after falsely accusing a highly decorated marine officer of conspiracy and perjury, Lieutenant Kaffee will have a long and prosperous career teaching typewriter maintenance at the Rocco Columbo School for Women." He fears that he will be relegated to yet another feminized position as just a teacher. His character's ethical dilemma is whether he has the personal courage to go up against the colonel for what he believes is right even if it means ruining his own career. Kaffee of course finds his courage and does indeed get Jessup to admit his culpability in the charged courtroom scene. But this final, personal struggle is the film's political Achilles heel. It marks the transition from what could have been, should have been, the film's broader, genuinely liberal call for reform into just one man's struggle with his conscience. And in doing so, the film collapses what could have been a meaningful political critique into Kaffee's neoliberal crisis of doing what's right versus keeping a great job. The political therefore becomes merely the personal, that is, merely the self-interested.[25]

This shift from authentic political critique to what I have characterized as a clichéd interest in whether or not the protagonist will "do the right thing" has important implications for what the film has to say about the military's anti-gay policy. Kaffee's transformation from his earlier position of weakness in his first meeting with Jessup is accompanied by a significant costume change: he has traded in the faggoty white uniform for his sober and confident dress blues. He has, in essence, finally assumed his "proper" gender role by distancing himself from the comparatively "immature" attitude and attire he sported earlier in the film. And that transformation, that abandonment, signals the film's ultimate capitulation to Jessup's position in its own neoliberal incarnation. For example, on his defeat, Jessup erupts, shouting, "You fuckin' people. You have no idea how to defend a nation. All you did was weaken a country today Kaffee. That's all you did. You put people's lives in danger. Sweet dreams, son." And if Nicholson's performance here is itself a bit campy, I would argue that the film does not discount Jessup nor his words. Indeed, it operates instead by exchanging Kaffee for Jessup, by having Kaffee assume Jessup's own rhetorical invocation of strength and safety in his response: "Don't call me son. I'm a lawyer and an officer in the United States Navy. And you're under arrest, you son of a bitch." In this overdetermined antipathy to the oedipal situation, Kaffee does not dispute the colonel's premise, that institutional reform of the military will put people's lives in danger.[26] Instead he co-opts Jessup's strength, and that strength comes at the price of jettisoning his association with gays and lesbians. Kaffee rises as the strong man, but in so doing he reveals the American left's own dangerous infatuation with that strength, its willingness to sell out on reform. Such a move exists in order to secure for itself the aura of strength of which it had previously been so critical.

It is crucial to recognize that the real-life debate about homosexual soldiers during the early months of the Clinton administration shared many similarities with the scenario presented in *A Few Good Men*. I do not wish to draw too close an analogy, for of course the two situations are not the same, but it is worth considering how and why they have certain affinities. One obvious correspondence is that the battle between Clinton and a contentious Congress that eventually resulted in "Don't Ask, Don't Tell" pitted a young upstart, Clinton, against the entrenched opinions of opponents to reform led by conservative Democratic senator Sam Nunn of Georgia. And as Halley points out, the "victory" Clinton achieved with "Don't Ask, Don't Tell" is on the order of the one achieved by Kaffee, that is, a hollow one that refuses to admit its own ultimate complicity with the conservative forces it pretends to oppose. As Halley explains,

> "Don't ask" was the issue on which Clinton staked most, fought longest, had his single identifiable victory, and engaged in his most delusional refusals to acknowledge how meager his victory was and how massive were the accompanying losses. He achieved "don't ask" at the expense of "don't tell," and thus agreed to a pervasive and intimate system of status-based regulation.[27]

In other words, like Kaffee, Clinton's own conflict over strength and security resulted not in the dramatic reform he seems to have initially favored, but rather with a reification of the troubling reactionary agenda he had once wanted to topple. Thus Clinton's personal strength is won at the expense of progressive reform and his commitment to "keeping us safe" is guaranteed with a policy that doubles down on status-based discrimination against lesbians and gays within the military.

Based on this pattern, it was alarming to see Obama approach the same issue mostly in his second term of office with these familiar, problematic and failed terms. In the early years of his presidency, Obama repeatedly declared "Don't Ask, Don't Tell" a misguided policy but has used the same reading of security and strength as the basis for making that call. That is, he has often argued that discharging lesbian and gay soldiers makes the US military less strong and that continuing to do so makes Americans less safe. Unsurprisingly, this claim is most often embodied in the guise of the now familiar "Arabic linguist" discharged for his homosexual status.[28] That Obama continues to engage in the debate in the same old terms of strength/safety signals an inability for politicians like him, as was the case in *A Few Good Men*, to let go of a fetishization of power, in effect an inability to really think differently. Because Obama repeated the claim that discharging homosexual soldiers was bad policy because it made the military less strong, he merely inverted Jessup's logic. Obama, like Kaffee and Clinton, has not yet shown that he wants to be a fierce advocate who can make the case for civic transformation without relying on a heterocentric notion of strength. He does not want to wear the faggoty white uniform. Instead, like his forbearers, he seems only to want to topple the colonel so that he can assume his heterocentric position of power. Until our leaders can begin to articulate antihomophobic political goals in a different way, the debate over gays and lesbians in the military will sadly only continue to serve the same heterosexist and nationalistic projects as it has done for years. And despite an "ally" in the White House, we will have moved only incrementally closer to rethinking the relationship between homosexuality, civil rights, and the military in any terms other than what makes "us" more or less "safe."

POSTSCRIPT

Since my initial presentation of the work in progress that was to become this essay, some things have changed while other important things have not. Most obviously, Barack Obama did indeed sign a congressional bill to repeal "Don't Ask, Don't Tell" in December of 2010. The policy officially ended on September 20, 2011.

The almost two full years of the Obama presidency in which the policy remained in effect were tumultuous ones for pro-repeal activists. In fact the period was marked by several high-profile protests and arrests. And while many of those same activists celebrated the official repeal of the policy, I want to in conclusion offer a word of caution. For as I've said, some important things *have not* changed. Notice in particular these remarks from US vice president Joe Biden on the occasion of the repeal bill signing in 2010:

> This fulfills an important campaign promise the President and I made, and many have on this stage made, and many of you have fought for, for a long time, in repealing a policy that actually weakens our national security, diminished our ability to have military readiness, and violates the fundamental American principle of fairness and equality.[29]

Biden's remarks continue to traffic in the same problematic language I have been describing. Though he later goes on to highlight the contribution to social justice he believes the bill will bring, Biden leads with and builds his case for the bill precisely through the same old appeal to national security and the maintenance of a strong defense. Obama himself does the same: "The law I'm about to sign will strengthen our national security and uphold the ideals that our fighting men and women risk their lives to defend."[30] Is it not the case that even in the wake of repeal, these remarks continue to represent a dangerous infatuation with military strength from the political left? That is, though our laws may have changed, how far afield have we come really from the fetishization of strength and safety that are so problematic to conceiving a truly egalitarian state?

NOTES

Many thanks to John Fisher, my co-panelist Atiya Stokes-Brown, and the audience of the "In Media Res" symposium at Bucknell University. Questions and comments on my initial presentation of this work were extremely valuable to my thinking about the issues contained here.

1. Aaron Sorkin, *A Few Good Men*, DVD, directed by Rob Reiner (Culver City, CA: Sony Pictures, 1992; 2001). All subsequent references in the text are to the same.

2. U.S. House, *National Defense Authorization Act For Fiscal Year 1994*, U.S. Code 10 (1994), § 654.

3. According to a report by the Congressional Research Service, "Prior to the 1993 compromise, the number of individuals discharged for homosexuality was generally declining. Since that time, the number of discharges for same-sex conduct has generally increased until recently. However, analysis of these data shows no statistically significant difference in discharge rates for these two periods." David F. Burrelli, *"Don't Ask, Don't Tell:" The Law and Military Policy on Same-Sex Behavior*, CRS Report R40782 (Washington, DC: Congressional Research Service, 2010).

4. Many news outlets have continued to emphasize that "Mr. Obama campaigned as a 'fierce advocate' of equal rights for gays" but that "the President's re-

lationship with the gay community has been a conflicted one." Sheryl Gay Stolberg, "Obama Pledges Again to End 'Don't Ask, Don't Tell,'" *New York Times*, October 10, 2009, A24, http://www.nytimes.com/2009/10/11/us/politics/11speech.html (accessed December 20, 2009). Others, principally on the right, have characterized Obama's "conflicted" relationship as the tell-tale mark of presidential weakness. Pat Buchanan, for example, though hardly a voice of moderation has argued that Obama has largely "capitulated" to "the gay rights and the more militant gay rights community" and that as a result "we have a very weak president . . . the man is not a strong leader." (Pat Buchanan, quoted by Mamta Trivedi, *Hardball with Chris Matthews*, MSNBC, first broadcast February 23, 2011).

5. Though the policy has been repealed, that has not stopped several presidential contenders from vowing to reverse the repeal under a new administration. U.S. House, *Don't Ask, Don't Tell Repeal Act of 2010*, Public Law 111–321, 111th Cong. (December 22, 2010), repeal *U.S. Code* 10 (1994), § 654.

6. At the time I presented an earlier version of this paper at Bucknell University in November 2009, the Obama administration had made no indication that it imminently planned action on the subject of "Don't Ask, Don't Tell."

7. One explanation is that, as Judith Butler argues, "it is not merely the quiet and furtive repression of lesbians and gays that is required for the military citizen to emerge" since "by forcing homosexuals into publicity, the military inadvertently intensifies and proliferates the discourse on homosexuality." ("Status, Conduct, Word, and Deed: A Response to Janet Halley," *GLQ* 3, nos. 2–3 [1996]: 258).

8. Kieffer Sutherland's marine character levies a similar charge: "No, I like all you Navy boys. Every time we've gotta go someplace and fight, you fellas always give us a ride."

9. We already know that Kaffee has been characterized as a fast-talking hack of a lawyer. Even Galloway reprimands him during the team's visit to Cuba for his dedication to talk and lack of action: "Are you going to do any actual investigating," she asks, "or are you just going to take the guided tour?" Kaffee is thus associated, in all quarters, with the mouth or *talk* over and above masculine *action*.

10. Roderick A. Ferguson in his critique of homonormativity and race goes further to argue that "gay rights, inasmuch as it pushes for military inclusion, is only about encouraging" what he characterizes as "the brutal disciplinary measures of the U.S. government" abroad and "the fascist and panoptic techniques of discipline against Arab and Muslim immigrants as well as against Arab Americans" domestically. While I agree with this statement as a reading of comments made by Andrew Sullivan that Ferguson discusses, I would question his assertion that the push for military inclusion is "*only* about" encouraging these projects, a reading that is reductive about the lived experience of many, for example, who may see the military as the only practical way out of otherwise terrorizing lives devoid of other opportunities for escape ("Race-ing Homonormativity: Citizenship, Sociology, and Gay Identity," in *Black Queer Studies: A Critical Anthology*, ed. E. Patrick Johnson and Mae G. Henderson [Durham, NC: Duke University Press, 2005], 64). For a discussion of how demobilization of large numbers of US soldiers following World War II led many lesbians and gay men to resettle their lives in more opportune locales, and to build more productive, more politically empowered, and more personally rewarding lives, see John D'Emilio, *Sexual Politics, Sexual*

Communities: The Making of a Homosexual Minority in the United States, 1940–1970 (Chicago: University of Chicago Press, 1983), 23–39.

11. Alycee J. Lane, "Black Bodies/Gay Bodies: The Politics of Race in the Gay/Military Battle," *Callaloo* 17, no. 4 (Fall 1994): 1074–88.

12. Ibid., 1075.

13. I attribute this political stance to the filmmakers (and especially the screenwriter Aaron Sorkin) on the basis of my understanding of the film's rhetorical position on the issue of gays in the military. Sorkin seems to reiterate this position in a 2000 episode of his popular television program *The West Wing* entitled "Take Out the Trash Day." In the episode, the apparently conservative Midwestern father of a murdered gay man modeled after Matthew Shepherd stuns the series regulars with a damning critique of their own self-perceived progressivism as nothing more than garden variety neoliberal cowardice. Asked by the Press Secretary C. J. Cregg about his position on a proposed hates crimes bill, the father explodes:

> The hate crimes bill is fine. Who gives a damn? It's fine. I don't care. If you ask me, we shouldn't be making laws against what's in a person's head but who gives a damn? I don't understand how this President, who I voted for, I don't understand how he can take such a completely weak-ass position on gay rights . . . Gays in the military, same-sex marriage, gay adoption, boards of education—where the hell is he? I want to know what qualities necessary to being a parent this President feels my son lacked? I want to know from this President, who has served not one day in uniform—I had two tours in Vietnam. I want to know what qualities necessary to being a soldier this President feels my son lacked? Lady, I'm not embarrassed my son was gay. My government is.

This extraordinarily sympathetic character's moving plea serves to reiterate Sorkin's apparent commitment to repealing the anti-gay ban, but it also serves as a sort of reflection on or self-critique of his earlier work. For while I have criticized *A Few Good Men*'s take on the issue as overly beholden to the "strong" conservative values of its antagonists, this later work likewise seems to be a similar critique of the complacency of self-congratulatory liberals like those who populate *The West Wing* (and possibly even of the younger Sorkin himself), who find themselves with a constituency, one made up not just of gay soldiers, that is still waiting eagerly for its fierce advocate. We must note, however, that even this critique is still preoccupied with seeing the debate in terms of strength, as the President is described as "weak-ass" in contrast to the father's own muscular pro-gay rights agenda. (Aaron Sorkin, "Take Out the Trash Day," *The West Wing: The Complete First Season*, DVD, directed by Thomas Schlamme et al. [January 26, 2000; Burbank, CA: Warner Home Video, 2003].)

14. Lane, "Black Bodies/Gay Bodies," 1077.

15. Ibid., 1080.

16. Ibid.

17. "Of Men and Angels," *Commonweal*, March 9, 1990, 150.

18. Janet E. Halley, *Don't: A Reader's Guide to the Military's Anti-Gay Policy* (Durham, NC: Duke University Press, 1999).

19. Jasbir K. Puar, *Terrorist Assemblages: Homonationalism in Queer Times* (Durham, NC: Duke University Press, 2007), xxiii.

20. It is important to note that Jessup never specifies from what he is keeping us safe. Presumably it is those Cubans who guard the other side of the fence he is charged with protecting. But Jessup is also guarding another fence, a fence that continues to keep people of some sexual identities inside and others outside.

21. Halley, *Don't*, 48.

22. Puar, *Terrorist Assemblages*, 39.

23. My understanding of our current neoliberal moment's deep entanglement with heteronormative and indeed homonormative agendas is derived from Lisa Duggan, *The Twilight of Equality? Neoliberalism, Cultural Politics, and the Attack on Democracy* (Boston: Beacon Press, 2003).

24. For a description of the politics of homonormativity and nationalism, what Puar terms "homonationalism," see Puar, *Terrorist Assemblages*, 2, 38–39.

25. I of course do not mean here to denigrate the important decades-old feminist claim that "the personal is the political." My use of the phrase here is meant to contrast productively that authentically progressive idea with what we might identify as Kaffee's own economic self-interest, a self-interest that is held up in a fraudulent way by the film as some sort of heroic act.

26. Much of Kaffee's anxiety is attributed at various points in the film to his relationship with his father and his own inability to satisfy his father's desires. That Jessup calls Kaffee "son" and that Kaffee resists that label so strongly suggests that the film thinks that Kaffee has finally achieved a position of "mature" sexuality. He rejects the infantile position Jessup places him in and finally "grows" out of the kind of "immature" sexuality—grandiose, narcissistic, uninterested in women—that our culture traditionally associates with homosexuality.

27. Halley, *Don't*, 48.

28. Though I haven't the space to do it here, there is much more to be said about the implicit association between homosexuality, terrorism, and "the orient" that is contained in that bizarre and terrifying rhetorical creature.

29. U.S. Department of the Interior, Remarks by the President and Vice President at Signing of the *Don't Ask, Don't Tell Repeal Act of 2010*, December 22, 2010. http://www.whitehouse.gov/the-press-office/2010/12/22/remarks-president-and-vice-president-signing-dont-ask-dont-tell-repeal-a (accessed April 22, 2014).

30. Ibid.

III

GLOBAL FLOWS

Part III is distinct from others in this volume as it includes two academic essays as well as two creative selections as bookends to the section: the first, several poems from poet, Suheir Hammad and the last, a short story from Adam Mansbach. The purpose of the writing collected in this section is to explore critical and creative ideas about identity and popular culture beyond the boundaries of the United States. Hammad's selections reflect her complex identity as a Jordanian born, Palestinian American woman, whose parents were Palestinian refugees that migrated to Brooklyn, New York. Hammad came of age during the emergence of the Hip Hop generation and the era of the War on Terror—spurred by events that took place in New York City on September 11, 2001. Her poetry represents her identity and reflects all of the aforementioned complexities. Belinda Monique Waller-Peterson's essay on the "communal womb" and Haile Gerima's *Sankofa* returns to the film in order to critically excavate the signal role of ancestral mediation in remembering, reclaiming, and returning to sites of history and in particular here, the role of Africans in organized resistance to the transatlantic slave trade. For Waller-Peterson, the communal womb is a site at the site of reclamation (or in this case "the return") where the community refigures conceptualizations of and constructions of women's bodies—particularly here in the context of the brutalization and commodification of women's bodies in the transatlantic slave trade. Delores B. Phillips' essay on "South East Asian Hip Hop Wannabes" shifts the sites to London, England and triangulates the identities of *Londonstani's* main characters with notions of hypermasculinity in Hip Hop culture, and their own London-based Southeast Asian heritage. Phillips deftly explores the cross-sections of postcolonial studies and popular culture as she rethinks the ways in which American popular culture—in this case, Hip Hop—transforms and is transformed as it circulates through postcolonial youthful cultures around the globe. The protagonists of the novel "navigate varying degrees of alienation and affiliation between their parents' cultures of origin and England, [turning] to an outside cultural assemblage: African American Hip Hop and its obsessive interest in hypermasculinity, with its sexual prowess, physical toughness, and conspicuous consumption." The final selection here is a previously published short story penned by Adam Mansbach. In the story, Mansbach meditates on the repressive Western tradition of putting black bodies on display for public and popular consumption. In this case, readers experience this phenomenon through the eyes of a zookeeper who is responsible for Mr. Ota Benga—a pygmy who is captured, caged, and put on display like any other animal in the zoo. These selections work together in their dedication to critically and creatively exploring how bodies of color are contained, displayed, and interpreted in popular culture and the global public sphere.

8

✛

Selected Poems

Suheir Hammad

A Prayer Band

every thing

you ever paid for
you ever worked on
you ever received

every thing

you ever gave away
you ever held on to
you ever forgot about

every single thing is one
of every single thing and all
things are gone

every thing i can think to do
to say i feel
is buoyant

every thing is below water
every thing is eroding
every thing is hungry

there is no thing to eat
there is water every where
and there is no thing clean to drink

the children aren't talking

the nurses have stopped believing
anyone is coming for us

the parish fire chief will never again tell anyone that
help is coming

now is the time of rags
now is the indigo of loss
now is the need for cavalry[1]

new orleans

i fell in love with your fine ass poor boys sweating frying catfish
blackened life thick women glossy seasoning bourbon indians
beads grit history of races and losers who still won

new orleans
i dreamt of living lush within your shuttered eyes
a closet of yellow dresses a breeze on my neck
writing poems for do right men and a daughter of refugees

i have known of displacement
and the tides pulling every thing
that could not be carried within
and some of that too

a jamaican man sings
those who can afford to run will run
what about those who can't
they will have to stay

end of the month tropical depression turned storm

someone whose beloved has drowned
knows what water can do
what water will do to once animated things

a new orleans man pleads
we have to steal from each other to eat
another gun in hand says we will protect what we have
what belongs to us

i have known of fleeing desperate
with children on hips in arms on backs
of house keys strung on necks
of water weighed shoes disintegrated official papers
leases certificates births deaths taxes

i have known of high ways which lead nowhere
of aches in teeth in heads in hands tied

i have known of women raped by strangers by neighbors
of a hunger in human

i have known of promises to return
to where you come from
but first any bus going any where

tonight the tigris and the mississippi moan
for each other as sisters
full of unnatural things
flooded with predators and prayers

all language bankrupt

how long before hope begins to eat itself
how many flags must be waved
when does a man let go of his wife's hand in order to hold his child

who says this is not the america they know

what america do they know

were the poor people so poor they could not be seen

were the black people so many they could not be counted

this is not a charge
this is a conviction

if death levels us all
then life plays favorites

and life it seems is constructed
of budgets contracts deployments of wards
and automobiles of superstition and tourism
and gasoline but mostly insurance

and insurance it seems is only bought
and only with what cannot be carried within
and some of that too

a city of slave bricked streets
a city of chapel rooms
a city of haints

a crescent city

where will the jazz funeral be held

when will the children talk

tonight it is the dead
and dying who are left
and those who would rather not
promise themselves they will return

they will be there
after everything is gone
and when the saints come
marching like spring
to save us all[2]

mahmoud darwish

an earth in our throats a song a scale higher than walls
our broken land we call home in song a poem
in my hands an empty basket a bottle

august this month of faeries casting men molding earth
how to raise a man drowned how to answer death with birth

a poem
in my hands flowers a joint
my country in my throat

i am one of seven brides
married to sea foam smoking praying bodies married to the last
sky to poetry before she was language after he entered me

he has gone somewhere else the space between
our footsteps the farthest mosque to the country between us
the country in our throats he's gone through the alchemist's diary
over the map of love he went to the ones we have been
waiting for hands washing water to the one drop to parting seas to rivers

to lavender fields where the horses are not left alone
to where the butterfly rests her burden

in my throat a song that is his country
in my hands a poem that is earth

the poet carried his nation and nothing
but paper to write never sent letters
the poet carried his country in his throat
wine cigarettes women drowning song

the people carried the poet through years
through tears through passports through airports
the people carried the poet over seas
under tongues turned foreign language

in an african mediterranean sea deeper still there is our face
peace unto the blessed mirror of the page
peace unto the holy echo of the memorized
peace unto to all of palestine peace perfect peace

he has gone to the country of my dreams to the earth in the attic a time
between ashes and rose home to the men in the sun the temperature of

this water the salt of this sea find him in your father's knees distance
between sisters his mother's bread scent of his beloved's hair
there is the poet there in the words under the words under the fig tree

there are the thousand and one nights and the thirteenth bullet
there is the desire if only the sea could sleep
there is the dar which is home
there is the wish which is wish
there is the map which is body
there is the land which carried me

in my hands an oud a book
in my throat a people his song[3]

Jabaliya

    a woman wears a bell carries a light calls searches
    through madness of deir yessin calls for rafah for bread
    orange peel under nails blue glass under feet gathers
    children in zeitoun sitting with dead mothers she unearths
    tunnels and buries sun onto trauma a score and a day rings
    a bell she is dizzy more than yesterday less than
    tomorrow a zig zag back dawaiyma back humming suba

    back shatilla back ramleh back jenin back il khalil back il quds
    all of it all underground in ancestral chests she rings
    a bell promising something she can't see faith is that
    faith is this all over the land under the belly
    of wind she perfumed the love of a burning sea

    concentrating refugee camp
    crescent targeted red

    a girl's charred cold face dog eaten body
    angels rounded into lock down shelled injured shock

    weapons for advancing armies clearing forests sprayed onto a city
    o sage tree human skin contact explosion these are our children

    she chimes through nablus back yaffa backs shot under
    spotlight phosphorous murdered libeled public relations

    public

    relation

    a bell fired in jericho rings through blasted windows a woman
    carries bones in bags under eyes disbelieving becoming
    numb dumbed by numbers front and back gaza onto gaza
    for gaza am sorry gaza am sorry she sings for the whole
    powerless world her notes pitch perfect the bell a death toll.[4]

rafah

there is a music to this all
the din has an order of orders
a human touch behind all arms
all of it manufactured stars above all

something melting a dove molting mourning through dusk

one child after another gathered if possible
washed where possible wrapped there is always cloth
all the while prayed on then pried from the women
always the women in the hot houses of a winter's war
the cameras leave with the men and the bodies always
the women somehow somehow putting tea on fire
gathering the living children if possible
washing them when possible praying on them
through their hair into their palms onto dear life

something fusing into dawn feathers shed eyes

people in a high valence state
that's when breathing feeds burns
that's where settlers take high ground
that's how villages bulldozed betwixt
holidays before your eyes
high violence holy children lamb
an experience no longer inherited
actual
earth in scorched concrete
heart in smoking beat.[5]

NOTES

All poems by Suheir Hammad.

1. "A Prayer Band," 2010.
2. "new orleans," 2010.
3. "mahmoud darwish," 2010.
4. "Jabaliya" reprinted with permission from *Born Palestinian Born Black and The Gaza Suite*, New York: UpSet Press, 2010.
5. "rafah" reprinted with permission from *Born Palestinian Born Black and The Gaza Suite*, New York: UpSet Press, 2010.

9

✢

The Communal Womb in Haile Gerima's *Sankofa*
Belinda Monique Waller-Peterson

Sankofa is an Akan word that means "to return to fetch something that has been forgotten."[1] In general it is represented by the sankofa bird that dips her beak into her tail as a reflection of this definition. In his 1993 film, *Sankofa*, Ethiopian filmmaker, Haile Gerima, sought to reveal what he believes is one of the deliberately hidden truths of slavery: that enslaved blacks were active participants in securing their freedom through subversive and violent acts of rebellion. In his 1994 interview with Pamela Woolford, Gerima states, "I brought out the individual identities and motives of the characters, transforming the 'happy slaves' into an African race opposed to this whole idea, by making the history of slavery full of resistance, full of rebellion."[2] Gerima reports that he met resistance from Hollywood when he sought financing for *Sankofa* because his depiction of slave unrest and slave-generated rebellion is a counter-narrative to its predecessors, including *Roots*, which, according to Gerima, depicts a traditionally nonthreatening picture of slavery. Subsequently, *Sankofa* did not receive enough funding to be screened at large cinemas and its success was dependent on small film houses and communities that raised enough money to screen it locally. Gerima was able to finance the production of a limited number of copies of *Sankofa* but a fire in the warehouse where the film was stored destroyed approximately 10,000 copies, an emotional setback for Gerima as well as the actors and production crew.[3]

Gerima's resistance narrative regarding the production and distribution of *Sankofa* underscores his belief that uncovering Africa and African history is essential to the overall healing of society and transformation of the world.[4] Gerima seems to suggest that history and collective memory serve to spiritually and culturally transform African people through a connection to a past rich in tradition and ancestry. This belief informs his urgency about the need for films like *Sankofa*. The depiction of African and African American history and collective memory at the heart of *Sankofa* presents a unique opportunity to explore a concept that I call the communal womb, as well as wom(b)anism, and Karla F. C. Holloway's notion of ancestral mediation in *Moorings and Metaphors*. In this essay I utilize the term wom(b)anism to read, excavate, and critically engage the presence of what I refer to as the communal womb in *Sankofa*.[5] Thus wom(b)anism is an interpretive tool and critical approach that I employ in order to excavate the communal womb motifs and narratives. The term wom(b)anism evolves from Alice Walker's womanist definition and branches out to interrogate specific references to and manifestations of the womb in novels and films.[6] Wom(b)anism is the term that I have created to describe the interpretive framework through which readers can identify iterations of the communal womb. Wom(b)anism combines aspects of the black womanist ethos with an expressed interest in seeking out literary depictions of or references to the womb in black women's writing and in other media that wrestle with representations of black womanhood. The communal womb then is a particularly significant result of wom(b)anist readings. The communal womb emerges from wom(b)anist readings and consists of the following three elements: (1) textual moments in black literature that involve an ancestral mediator—a figure defined by Holloway; (2) a character who is faced with a crisis that involves her womb; and (3) the nature and consequences of the character's relationship to her community. The ancestral mediator is at the center of the dynamism and agency of the communal womb and as such this figure is worth discussing in detail. Gerima's focus on marginalized women exemplifies my study of wom(b)anism and foregrounds the necessity to fully conceptualize the significance of black women's roles in history and literature.

Sankofa offers an understanding and openness to one's history that unveils the crucial role that women and the womb play in the construction and deconstruction of their communities. Within *Sankofa*, the communal womb and ancestral mediation provide a crucial linking of black women and their threatened wombs to the communities that are separated from and pitted against them. The communal womb also exposes an intricate relationship of women to one another, a relationship fostered on shared experiences exclusive to women. Wom(b)anism necessarily continues the holistic inclusion of marginalized women and their threatened wombs so that their narratives can be explored and contextualized within history and literature.

Part of the project of *Sankofa* is to recover the obscured and marginalized narratives of black women in slavery. *Sankofa* chronicles the narrative of Mona who is possessed by Shola, after she enters the slave castle during her photo shoot. Mona's cultural disconnection from Africa prompts her to be possessed by the spirit, Shola, who takes her back to slavery where she lives as Shola. Ultimately, Mona connects to and acknowledges her history through her experiences as Shola and returns to her present moment reborn with a more nuanced understanding of the brutal reality of American slavery. NuNu is central to Mona/Shola's spiritual reclamation and acts as her ancestral mediator. NuNu also mediates on behalf of another slave woman Kuta, who is beaten to death by an overseer while she is far along in her pregnancy. *Sankofa* informs my study of the communal womb as it suggests that life-threatening violence perpetrated against black women and their wombs is connected to the spiritual health and survival of black communities and the recovery of African and African American history. This essay provides a brief summary of *Sankofa*, engages the critical conversation about the film, and explicates specific communal womb scenes and the implications of reading a film such as *Sankofa* with a theory that privileges the woman and her womb. This essay also argues for the recovery of the central role that women played in the resistance to the institution of slavery, a theme that has thus far been obscured by critical discourse surrounding the film. Foregrounding Shola, NuNu, and Kuta's narratives in relation to the communal womb and African Asante history honors the spirit of *Sankofa* and, more importantly, the legacy of female leaders and warriors who established African clans and led their people in resistance to oppressive institutions.

Criticism about Gerima's film tends to focus on African tradition, symbolism, and *Sankofa*'s historical accuracy. Collectively, scholars that write about *Sankofa* attempt to tease out African metaphors, symbols, traditions, and cultures that Gerima utilizes to confront what he describes as the presentation of dehumanized black people who are incapable of advocating on their own behalf.[7] But, with the exception of Sandra M. Grayson's "Spirits of Asona Ancestors Come: Reading Asante Signs in Haile Gerima's *Sankofa*," there is scarce discussion about the role of women or the womb in *Sankofa*. The silence around the women in *Sankofa* necessitates further exploration of how women, specifically NuNu, provide a crucial link to African history. The reluctance of these scholars to identify the nuanced relationship that develops between Mona/Shola and NuNu inhibits a more complex reading and understanding of NuNu's mediating role in Mona/Shola's life. This critical oversight reinforces a reading of *Sankofa* in which Shola's love interest, Shango, is the sole catalyst for Shola's unrest and rebellion and NuNu is simply a mother figure on the plantation. However, NuNu's character and her impact on the community are imperative to *Sankofa's* historical recovery of African culture and tradition. A wom(b)anist reading of *Sankofa* foregrounds and contextualizes NuNu's significance as an ancestral mediator, her vital role as a resistance leader within her community, and her place in a broader historical narrative that includes the African Asante clan.[8]

Sankofa creates a space for women as leaders of rebellions, active bearers and disseminators of history, and meditative presences that transcend time and place. Throughout *Sankofa*, Gerima destabilizes visual text and language including metaphors and symbols significant to the cultural, spiritual, and physical recovery of black women. Gerima empowers the sankofa bird and NuNu's invocation of Asona ancestors to historically inform Mona/Shola of her ancestral roots.[9] NuNu's use of African language reinforces her historical connection to African cultures and traditions and denounces American religious and social practices. NuNu uses this language at the secret Maroon meeting to address the Asona ancestors. Through NuNu's invocation and mediation, cultural memory and place of origin moor black women to a rich tapestry of diasporic ancestral women. According to Holloway's discussion of the ancestral mediator, the fractured biographies and histories of black women contribute to the construction of time as a flexible, fluid concept. Time is neither fixed nor static. The collapse of time makes plausible the unconstrained intervention of the ancestral mediator on the behalf of fragmented black women throughout the New World, the African diaspora, and Africa. NuNu's interventions and mediations are not bound to time constraints and she demonstrates this with her knowledge of events in the past and in the future. She operates inside and outside of time and place. Holloway also argues "the idea of ancestry revises the histories that it reenacts through its intimate mediation of history and memory."[10] Thus the women who are marginalized by the written record of history are empowered and central in texts such as *Sankofa* that privilege the recovery of women's narratives. These are all significant components of Holloway's construction of the ancestral mediator and my definition of the communal womb.

I

The centralization of women within the narratives of *Sankofa* can be evidenced by the various scenes that grapple with the womb, maternal loss, and the role of the ancestral mediator in reconciling the affected woman with her community. *Sankofa's* communal womb–imagery begins when Mona enters the dungeon of the Elmina Castle at the insistence of Sankofa who demands that she return to the past. The dungeon represents the womb as a tomb. The Portuguese built Elmina Castle, which is located in Ghana, in 1482 and it is the first fort built on the West African coast.[11]

Elmina's association as the final destination for African slaves prior to their embarkation to the New World situates Mona's possession by the spirit Shola within a historical narrative of suffering and loss of identity attached to the castle; the castle becomes a signifier of slavery and the Middle Passage. The dungeon of the castle acts as a metaphorical womb that conceives a hybrid form of slavery in which slaves are not solely property, according to the pre–New World definition of slavery, but chattel that functions in the same way as livestock.[12]

Mona's entrance into this historically dead womb, which is brought to life by Sankofa's incantations and drumming, signals her acknowledgement of her psychological and emotional disconnection from her African roots and the complicated history of her African foremothers. This disconnection allows her to pose in front of and around Elmina Castle in a photo shoot without considering the grotesque legacy of sexual exploitation of black women that was produced within the castle. Mona's disconnection also impedes her from understanding the ways in which her "modeling" for the white man who insists she become even more sexually provocative desecrates the sacred castle grounds. However, once Mona descends into the dungeon and the womb comes alive around her, she faces African men, women, and children, huddled together in chains. The dungeon acts as both womb and tomb that erases the identities of the Africans that are in it; families are separated, languages intermingled, traditions disregarded, and bodies are dehumanized. These images are so disturbing to Mona that she runs through the dungeon screaming, searching for a way out. Though initially she willingly returns to the dead womb of her African mothers, she is unprepared for the uncensored reality that materializes around her.

What Mona experiences in the dungeon is the possession of her body by the spirit of Shola. The conflation of the African ritual of possession and the narrative reconstructing slavery in the castle force Mona to confront slavery through the eyes of an ancestor who has already experienced it. Peter I. Ukpokodu asserts in "African Heritage from the Lenses of African American Theatre and Film" that Sankofa's refrains of "sankofa," and "spirits of the dead rise and possess the living," invoke the presence of the spirit of Shola.[13] Shola's possession of Mona's body occurs after Mona denies her African heritage and she desecrates the Elmina Castle; when Mona attempts to leave the castle and opens the dungeon doors, the black and white slave traders drag her back and she yells that she's an American. Mona's refusal to identify herself in relation to her African ancestors parallels Shola's refusal to identify herself in relation to the field slaves and rebel slaves (later in the film). Mona and Shola share a disconnection from their foremothers, which prevents them from protecting themselves from emotional and sexual exploitation. They have no knowledge of the history of resistance that is woven through the narratives of their ancestral mothers. Mona and Shola psychologically separate themselves from black women that resist categorical definition by dominant social and religious structures.

Shola's possession of Mona's body provides the opportunity for both women to reconcile themselves to their African history with the intervention of their ancestral mediator NuNu. Mona's possession is complete once the slave traders rip her shirt off and brand her back. Mona's scarred flesh becomes a symbol of her previously denied sexual commoditization. This moment mirrors the communal womb scene that occurs later in the film between NuNu and Kuta in which NuNu harkens to the other slaves to form a protective circle around her so that she can deliver Kuta's baby. The absence of an ancestral mediator at the moment of Mona's transfiguration requires the communal participation of the slaves who are present in the dungeon with her; they form a protective circle around her as she falls to the floor after the branding and the community embraces her as one of their own.

Shola reemerges from the womb of the dungeon on the Lafayette Plantation as a house slave who loves a rebellious field slave named Shango and struggles with the sexual abuse she endures at the hands of her owner. Shola identifies NuNu as one of the people who can guide her towards self-discovery, a connection with her community, and the purpose of resistance against the slave institution. Shola's love interest, Shango, also teaches her cultural rituals and traditions, and encourages her to rebel against their slave owners and rebuke their traditions and values. Shola identifies Shango as one of the two people who initiates her spirit of rebellion stating that after Shango puts the sankofa bird necklace around her neck, she knows that she will be a rebel. While Shango contributes to Shola's awakening, his presence in Shola's life does not function in the same way as NuNu's. NuNu embraces Shola in the same manner that she embraces the slave children. NuNu provides Shola with tales that encourage her belief in African culture and reinforce Shola's connection to Africa. NuNu shares her childhood experiences in Africa with the children and the slave community as a way of maintaining an image of their collective metaphorical home.

NuNu's maternal embrace of Kuta's son mirrors her embrace of Shola at another crucial moment in the text when she mediates at the site of Shola's battered womb. NuNu tearfully tells Shola that Afriye was raped on the slave ship and bore a hateful child; it is then that Shola realizes that NuNu is Afriye the Porcupine. NuNu's narrative acts as the catalyst for Shola's unrest and self-recognition and provides an important connection between Shola and NuNu at the site of their traumatized wombs. Contrary to scholar Sylvie Kandé's argument in "Look Homeward, Angel: Maroons and Mulattos in Haile Gerima's *Sankofa*," that Shango alone "convinces scrupulous Shola of the necessity of violent action (she kills a planter in the cane field)," I submit that the shared experience of sexual exploitation between Shola and NuNu as well as Shola's ability to identify NuNu's true name and history forces Shola to reject her own identity as a victim.[14] Shola understands NuNu's sadness and torment because Shola's owner repeatedly rapes her. It is through this shared experience of sexual exploitation that Shola recognizes the meaning of resistance. She subsequently idolizes NuNu as an example of strength, knowledge, and determination. Certainly Shola and NuNu's sexually abusive narratives are not exclusive to them alone, for as Hortense J. Spillers asserts in "Mama's Baby, Papa's Maybe: An American Grammar Book," "the captive body becomes the source of an irresistible, destructive sensuality."[15] Similarly, bell hooks states in *Ain't I a Woman*, that "rape was a common method of torture slavers used to subdue recalcitrant black women."[16] Shola's rejection of victimhood enables her to claim ownership of her womb; she murders her owner the next time he attempts to rape her. Shola's assertion of agency and self-recognition culminates in her physical death and the subsequent rebirth of Mona with a newly formed historical consciousness.

Note well here the importance of Shola's assertion of agency over her rapist in relation to NuNu's intervention unveiling a connection between Shola's act of agency over her womb and NuNu's interventional assistance in the posthumous act of agency regarding Kuta's (communal) womb. NuNu enables Shola to identify her place in a larger narrative of African women rebels and leaders whose bodies have been sexually abused. Once Shola attains this information, she can no longer be placated with Father Raphael's insistence that prayer and faith will make her life better. In fact, the harder she prays the more sexually abusive her owner becomes. NuNu's intervention binds Shola to a larger narrative of sexual exploitation that predates both women; one whose "political aim ... was to obtain absolute allegiance and obedience to the white imperialistic order."[17] The awareness of these narratives causes Shola to flee the plantation. Here the similarities between Shola and Kuta begin to emerge. Both women flee the plantation for the sake of their wombs: Shola's sexually battered womb, and Kuta's pregnant womb.

Once they are captured, both women are hung by their hands and beaten in a manner of retribution that is consistent with their reasons for running. Kuta's nine-month pregnant body is stretched out, arms overhead, and beaten.[18] The overseer makes no considerations for her pregnancy and forces her to assume the same position as the other slaves.[19] The deliberate omission of this consideration with respect to Kuta's condition is a direct response to her attempt to deliver her son as a free black; an act so heinous from the perspective of the institution of slavery that she must be beaten to death. Likewise, Shola's naked body is stretched out, arms overhead, in front of her owner, Father Raphael, and Joe. Because Shola's running away is associated with her rejection of her sexual abuse and religious indoctrination, her owner displays her nakedness to sexually humiliate her and Father Raphael simultaneously presses a large cross into her chest and demands her renewed commitment to Catholicism. The black female slave was subject to the unrestricted sexual desires of white men within the institution of slavery and any effort she made to resist sexual relations was met with violence and public humiliation.[20] Shola's owner cuts out some of the plaits that NuNu put in her hair, condemns her for congregating with the other black slaves, and attempts to reclaim her body by beating her. Joe's presence in this scene attempts to reinforce the dominant power structure; he is NuNu's antithesis and the product of the sexual and religious colonization of the black female slave via the rape of NuNu/Afriye. Joe's presence attempts to reinforce the inevitable sexual violation of black women and it suggests that the new, mixed race African American is complicit in the destruction of rebellious and resistant African spirits. He is present at Kuta's murder and Shola's beating. Joe also murders his mother NuNu.

Finally, Shola's murder of her rapist completes her spiritual journey; she severs the sexually abusive narrative with her machete before it is implied that she is killed and her soul travels back to Africa to join Mona in the dungeon of Elmina Castle. NuNu's intervention on behalf of Shola allows Shola to come to terms with her own sexual abuse and the constant destruction of her womb at the hands of her owner and results in a more resolute, self-aware Shola who returns and becomes Mona (again). The conflation of the two women (Mona/Shola) emerges from the womb of the dungeon as a newborn baby through the birth canal with the learned experiences of an adult. Though she is disoriented, Mona/Shola recognizes the elder woman—who covers her with a quilt—as "mama," further acknowledging her historical understanding of her place in African culture as well as the role of her foremothers and ancestral mediators. The woman covers Mona's nakedness, offering her the dignity and respect that was not afforded to her by the photographer or to Shola by her owner—particularly in the scene where she is stripped, proselytized, and beaten. Mona's cultural awakening is complete and Shola's spiritual journey is complete; both women have achieved a wholeness that respectively allows each to proceed with her life and allow her soul to rest in peace.

II

Gerima portrays NuNu as the embodiment of resistance through her actions in the text as well as her ability to defy the conventions of science.

This creates a space for a radical and incredibly wom(b)anist presentation of the black woman's role in slavery (as opposed to the passive victim of sexual abuse who allows the men to fight the battles). Gerima counters the argument that he deliberately challenged gender roles on his characters and says "in Jamaica, in Surinam, men and women took different positions at different places to lead a rebellion. And I guess I didn't get caught up with this whole politically required gender theme, maybe I was freer to make that happen."[21] However, it appears that it is precisely his knowledge of the co-gendered leadership within slave rebellions that allows him to foreground NuNu's narrative and let her character drive the story. For example, NuNu invokes the Asona ancestors to watch over the slaves and connects their rebellious actions to those of the Asante clan, led by Queen Mother Yaa Asantewa. Grayson makes important connections between the two women and recalls that historically Queen Mother Yaa Asantewa initiated what is now known as the Yaa Asantewa War against the British when they sought to gain control over the Golden Stool.[22]

NuNu is one of the central figures at Lafayette Plantation, the other is Shola, and two tales persist about her; she killed her former slave owner by staring at him, and after her death, a buzzard flew her body back to Africa. In both narratives, NuNu possesses supernatural characteristics that allow her to manipulate and defy the constraints of the human body. NuNu's story is one of the first stories told when Mona arrives in the past as Shola, and one of the last stories told before Mona returns to Africa. Several scenes in *Sankofa*, detailed throughout the chapter, assert that Gerima creates a woman-centered text positioning NuNu as a central figure, or Queen Mother, who leads the other slaves on the plantation in spiritual and physical rebellion against the religious and plantation practices that attempt to oppress the slaves, destroy the communal womb, and debilitate the community.

NuNu intervenes, physically and spiritually, at critical junctures in the text when violence against black bodies is imminent. NuNu and Jumma, another slave woman, stand at the edge of the sugar cane field where they witness Kuta (who is visibly pregnant) and the other runaway slaves' punishment for attempting to escape. NuNu's presence is obligatory because her healing abilities are required in the aftermath of such brutally violent occasions. She is knowledgeable about herbs and communicates with and invokes the presence of African gods/goddesses in order to fulfill her role as the healer within a community that constantly experiences violence and physical degradation. NuNu's presence also invokes an ancestral authority and informs her community about how they should interpret and react to the capture and punishment of Kuta and the others. NuNu understands that Kuta's beating is an affront to the entire slave community, a direct and deliberate assault on its womb, and its space of creativity, reproduction, and sustenance. NuNu's knowledge of the complexity of Kuta's actions, and the hypersensitivity of the community preceding the beatings, underscores the necessity for NuNu's relatively close proximity to Kuta as well as her imposing presence in the scene itself. From the moment the head slaves hoist Kuta's arms over her head, NuNu's stance is defensive and protective; she stands ready with her herbs, waiting to physically reclaim Kuta's battered body.

The involvement of two black head slaves in Kuta's beating complicates NuNu's mediation; Noble Ali whips Kuta while NuNu's son, Joe, counts. Like NuNu, they are aware of the impact that their actions have on the community; they understand that Kuta's pregnant body symbolizes the condition of black motherhood in slavery and the physical aggression that they unleash on her is a direct attack on the black slave community. Joe's history of denouncing his mother for the religious teachings and practices of the Catholic Church and Noble Ali's childhood separation from his mother as a result of her sale positions each man in a contentious relationship with black motherhood. Joe and Ali's complicated histories warrant their emotional distance, however, neither man is able to reconcile himself to the destruction of black female flesh or the black maternal body as evidenced by their attempts to relinquish their tasks and the trepidation with which they carry them out. Noble Ali hesitantly beats Kuta and stops at one point to look to NuNu. Joe hesitantly and wincingly counts, avoiding eye contact with anyone, especially NuNu. Ultimately, it is only through the overseer's threat of physical abuse and death that each man is able to carry out his task.

Noble Ali and Joe's deference to NuNu highlights the impact she has on all members of the slave community, regardless of their individual commitment and loyalty. While Joe avoids looking in NuNu's direction, Noble Ali tempers his actions in accordance to NuNu's authority and looks to her for understanding and guidance in the midst of beating Kuta. After thirty-nine lashes, Ali seems to realize that they have committed an unforgiveable transgression against Kuta's maternal body and the community. NuNu's physical stance and attitude become weighed down with the enormity of the egregious actions of Noble Ali and Joe. It is here that NuNu's intervention begins and she utilizes her deadly gaze to strike Ali to the ground after the forty-fourth lashing. NuNu attempts to mediate on behalf of Kuta's unprotected womb as she recognizes that Kuta's life is in mortal danger. Ukpokodu notes that Noble Ali's forced beating of Kuta, and his demoralization at the hands of the overseer constitute the most "humiliating aspects" of this scene, however, I disagree and assert that this de-centering of Kuta's own mental and physical suffering is precisely what *Sankofa* is trying to expose.[23] While Noble Ali is certainly humiliated and demoralized, Kuta's humiliation, demoralization, and physical annihilation must be considered as central and key to this scene. NuNu acknowledges the compromising and conflicting position that Ali's job as head slave places him in; like the other slaves, he must navigate the power structure of the plantation. However, as a head slave Ali must enforce the rules and distribute punishments according to the owner's specifications. At this point in the text, neither Noble Ali nor Joe have control over what they are expected to do by the owner and overseers, thus their actions are in constant opposition to the health and continuity of their slave community.

NuNu physically cries out for Kuta's womb as the centralizing, unifying thread of the slave community. Kuta's murder is the physical manifestation of a secreted component of American history—the annihilation of black female flesh and utter disregard for the black maternal body. Spillers' assessment of the condition of black female flesh and bodies in slavery conceptually engages the significance of Kuta's death and NuNu's subsequent intervention. Spillers builds an argument that the black captive body—the slave body, becomes the site of "cultural and political maneuver[s], not at all gender-related, gender-specific," which manifests as the "actual mutilation, dismemberment, and exile" of black bodies and the "seared, divided, ripped-apartness," of black flesh.[24] Spillers draws a clear distinction between the bodies that were stolen by Europeans from Western Africa with the help of African slave traders and the flesh that was physically tortured and destroyed saying "this body whose flesh carries the female and the male to the frontiers of survival bears in person the marks of a cultural text whose inside has been turned outside."[25] Kuta's physical condition as an expectant slave mother lays bare her vulnerability as a woman in bondage and her classification as something other than human and female. The deconstruction and removal of the female identity for black slaves propels them into a condition in which they are without gender. This condition subjects them to the same physical brutalization that the black male slave body endures and destabilizes the concepts of maternity and motherhood. In the absence of these categories within the slave institution, women such as NuNu are central figures who are present to intervene on behalf of the black female body and black female flesh; gender-related and gender-specific.

NuNu cries out in anger and frustration for the black flesh that generates acts of violence and sexuality from power structures and individuals acting on behalf of those structures. In another instance of linking African history with slaves that are severed from it, NuNu harkens to the Africans who walked on water and flew away back to Africa in the face of the perils and oppression of slavery and plantation life. She yells, "You know this is the only chain they have on us. You know because of this flesh, this meat. We would fly in the air. We would swim in the river, walk under the sea and soon we will be home. We will be home." In the moment preceding her physical intervention at Kuta's womb, NuNu prayerfully advocates for all of the slaves who must continue to endure the atrocities and abuses committed against their flesh. She serves as a source of reassurance to her community at a moment when the overseer literally beats the spiritual integrity away from its flesh and body. NuNu pounds on her chest in defiance and declares that they (religious and slave institutions) can never destroy her soul. NuNu acknowledges that the temporary condition of the black body in slavery engenders violence against the flesh and death without dignity. Yet she advocates for and reinforces resistance narratives as a means of transcending slavery.

In a measured act of resistance and assertion of black maternity and motherhood, NuNu cuts Kuta's dead body down from the wooden joists where it hangs. She calls out to the African god Akyemfo to assist her as she intervenes on behalf of the dead mother who is about to take her unborn child, and she calls out to the slave community to physically gather around her. The enslaved Africans, comprised of men and women, form a circle of protection around NuNu and Kuta, machetes in hand, facing the overseers and black head slaves who have their guns drawn. The enslaved Africans place their bodies in physical peril for the sake of the baby inside of Kuta and NuNu performs a crude cesarean section to deliver the baby alive. NuNu's invocation of Akyemfo, for spiritual counsel, and Nana Akonadi, the good mother, are consistent with her defiant act of saving the life of the baby that was destined to die according to the overseer. Her actions momentarily invert the power structure of the plantation. Though the outcome of NuNu's intercession is not the restoration of Kuta's life, NuNu's mediation at Kuta's womb reconciles members of the community to one another; they stand united around NuNu during her mediation/intervention, and Kuta's baby becomes a symbol of resistance and communal unity for all of the enslaved Africans, including Noble Ali who laments his actions and later joins the Maroons. It is important to clarify that Ali joins the Maroons later in the text as a result of the attempted sale of NuNu, not as a result of his beating of Kuta. His reconciliation with the enslaved community occurs when he acknowledges his role in Kuta's death to NuNu and allows her to swaddle the baby to his back to signal his renewed loyalty to the other slaves. Following Kuta's death, NuNu claims the baby boy as her own and names him Kwame, which means "the witness." Spillers also engages the conditions that necessitate this restructuring of slavery stating that the erasure of identity from the black body becomes a necessary component of slavery that enables slave traders and slave owners to commit and justify acts of brutality.[26] The physical destruction of Kuta's womb is a signifier for the entitlement that slave owners' felt in regards to their slaves as property. Kuta's death constitutes a financial loss for her owner but does not register as a moral dilemma or as a contradiction to religious teachings. The removal of identifying markers such as gender allows for Kuta's physical and maternal obliteration.

Critical emphasis on masculine resistance in *Sankofa* is rampant. For example, Kandé emphasizes the male leadership of the Maroon societies and situates the narrative within this historical context. However, I agree with Grayson and argue that NuNu's authoritative position in *Sankofa* reflects aspects of the historic African Asante clan, which had female rulers who led their people into war and refused to succumb to British colonization.[27] Grayson infers that NuNu is a descendant of the Asante clan from her incantation that speaks to the Asona ancestors. I would like to advance Grayson's assessment by claiming that a wom(b)anist interpretation of NuNu's placement within the Asante clan suggests that she functions to galvanize and lead the community. Her historical presence solidifies the role of the ancestral mediator within a lineage of ancestral figures who fought to maintain their communities. The importance of reading texts through a wom(b)anist lens is underscored in *Sankofa* as Gerima attempts to reveal and portray one of the truths about the history of slavery and the function of slaves in their own emancipation and the role women have in these rebellions. *Sankofa* relies heavily on the idea of resistance and confrontation as tools utilized by the enslaved in order to liberate themselves from an oppressive religious indoctrination and institutional slavery. Enslaved Africans organized revolts between the sixteenth and nineteenth centuries throughout the African diaspora; they refused to passively yield to oppressive religious and slave institutions.[28] In *Sankofa*, these institutions threaten Mona/Shola's existence and require the intervention of NuNu, who must also embody the spirit of resistance and defiance in order to withstand the patriarchal systems she encounters. I agree with Grayson that NuNu mirrors the historical Queen Mother (female ruler) Yaa Asantewa, and subsequently in the film she leads the other slaves in a rebellion against the plantation. NuNu also refutes the authority of the Catholic Church and the plantation by practicing African religious traditions and actively participating as a leader of the rebel slave group, the Maroons.

The women in *Sankofa* are the resistance leaders and their actions and interventions drive the plot of the film. This is not to say that men do not also offer leadership and resistance in the film as well. The distinction that I draw is based on my primary example, NuNu. This distinction is crucial because, in general, critical conversation about *Sankofa* relegates the women in the film to the roles of victims. This severe limitation prohibits women from claiming agency over their bodies, and their powerful roles in enslaved communities. This is not, however, to suggest that historically slave women had legal rights over their bodies. The structure of the slave institution removed human and legal rights by classifying slaves (including slave women) as chattel and property.[29] For instance, a 1798 Maryland legislative enactment states: "In case the personal property of a ward shall consist of specific articles, such as slaves, working beasts, animals of any kind, stock, furniture, plates, books, and so forth, the Court if it shall deem it advantageous to the ward, may at any time, pass an order of sale thereof."[30] Slaves are listed among animals and household items, completely removed from any semblance of humanity or personhood. By establishing NuNu as an ancestral mediator, a wom(b)anist reading of *Sankofa* reveals a more accurate depiction of slave rebellion, which was not limited by gender hierarchies.[31] Her actions create a counter-narrative to the institutional oppression of religion and plantation life that attempt to dominate and colonize the slaves. NuNu provides the slave community with more than a call to action; she teaches, heals, fights, and steals slaves away from the plantation to live with the Maroons. NuNu's actions require a reading of her character as a primary resistance leader. In addition, it is her physical presence in the lives of women whose wombs are being threatened that signals a particular act of resistance against oppressive institutional structures.

III

In addition to reclaiming the past and "making the history of slavery full of resistance, full of rebellion," Gerima centralizes women within this rehistoricized narrative and allows the ancestral mediator to intervene on behalf of the women, their threatened wombs, and the communities that are affected by the gendered violence of institutional slavery. The limited criticism of the film opens the space for dialogue about the communal womb and ancestral mediation alongside issues of religion, sexuality, social hierarchies, and African culture. While scholar Samuel Ayedime Kafewo states that in the end Mona "runs to hide behind the old man [Sankofa], backing away from the photographer," and "shields herself behind the old man on her way to take her pride of place among the African heroes and heroines," this assertion negates Shola's act of agency as well as her resistance to a dominant narrative created by her rapist in which she was the victim.[32] As a result of Shola's actions, Mona does not have to hide behind Sankofa; she has her own strength. Mona is also not the victim of "Gerima's camera-phallus" as Kandé suggests because Mona, through her connection with Shola and NuNu, is able to transcend the dominant sexual gaze of a white male society that is represented by the photographer's camera and the slave owner.[33] As a result of NuNu's mediation at the site of Shola's womb, Mona and Shola emerge from the womb of the castle with the potential for wholeness. They acknowledge NuNu as they sit down with the other men and women of the diaspora at the water's edge to pay homage to their African ancestors and she acknowledges *them*.

Sankofa's depiction of the communal womb manifests through the collective memory of a mythological Africa. NuNu initiates this memory with her stories of Afriye the porcupine and her invocation of Asona ancestors. NuNu's intervention foregrounds the marginalized narratives of the women in *Sankofa*, which center on their battered wombs. NuNu's intervening presence at Shola and Kuta's wombs provides a direct historical connection to African culture and results in the possibility of wholeness for Shola/Mona. Thus *Sankofa* unveils the crucial role of women within their slave communities. That crucial role is centered on complex and nuanced manifestations of the communal womb because the womb, woman, and community are all under direct attack. For NuNu, the communal womb consists of her violent rape during middle passage (a womb of sorts for the entire institution of slavery), the ways in which the product of that rape, Joe, becomes a walking signifier of the tensions between the black wom(b)an and the institution of slavery, and finally, the narratives that NuNu employs to communicate transcendence to the children of the community in the face of the brutal reality of slavery. For Kuta, the communal womb consists of her desire to confront the institution of slavery directly by escaping. Her escape is a double confrontation with the institution because her womb has a specific commodity value within the institution. Her communal womb narrative then culminates in the posthumous reclamation of the child. Lastly, Mona/Shola's communal womb consists of her transportation through time and place via the womb/tomb of Elmina Castle in Ghana and the subsequent brutal rape that she endures. NuNu's intervention into Shola's recovery of self and Kuta's beating/murder ultimately set the stage for Mona/Shola's rebirth through the womb/tomb as a woman with a more informed understanding of her history and the lives of her enslaved ancestors. Utilizing wom(b)anism as an interpretive tool and critical approach to excavate communal womb motifs and narratives allows scholars and readers to engage literary depictions of and/or references to the womb in black women's writing that wrestle with representations of black womanhood and the womb, rewrite gendered/racialized stereotypes, and attempt to reconcile women with their communities.

NOTES

1. Sandra M. Grayson, "'Spirits of Asona Ancestors Come': Reading Asante Signs in Haile Gerima's *Sankofa*," *CLA Journal* 42, no. 2 (1998): 212–27.

2. Pamela Woolford, "Filming Slavery: A Conversation with Haile Gerima," *Transition* 64 (1994): 92.

3. Lyle Muhammad, "SANKOFA FIRE! Arson fire destroys over 10,000 copies of landmark film," November 5, 2009, http://afgen.com/sankofa.html.

4. Woolford, "Filming Slavery," 94.

5. Wom(b)anism is a womb-centered reading and interpretation of texts that feature the womb. Salamishah Tillet mentions the latter in *Sites of Slavery: Citizenship and Racial Democracy in the Post–Civil Right Imagination* (Durham: Duke University Press, 2012), 122.

6. Alice Walker coined and defined the term womanist in her landmark collection of essays, *In Search of Our Mother's Gardens: Womanist Prose* (San Diego: Harcourt, Inc., 1983), xi.

7. Ibid., 92, 93.

8. The Asante connection is originally noted in Grayson's "Spirits of Asona Ancestors Come," 212–27.

9. Grayson notes that "Asona is the name for one of the Asante clans, called the 'fox' clan," (ibid., 220).

10. Karla F. C. Holloway, *Moorings & Metaphors: Figures of Culture and Gender in Black Women's Literature* (New Brunswick, NJ: Rutgers University Press, 1992), 122.

11. Sylvie Kandé, "Look Homeward, Angel: Maroons and Mulattos in Haile Gerima's *Sankofa*," *Research in African Literatures* 29, no. 2 (Summer 1998): 134.

12. Hortense J. Spillers, "Mama's Baby, Papa's Maybe: An American Grammar Book," *Diacritics: A Review of Contemporary Criticism* 17, no. 2 (Summer 1987): 79.

13. Peter I. Ukpokodu states that possession occurs in response to incantation and drumming and calls forth a "higher force" to "occupy the body" of a living person. The occupied body has the characteristics of the god, ancestor or spirit that inhabits it, in Mona's case she becomes Shola, a house slave on the Lafayette Plantation who is repeatedly raped by her owner. ("African Heritage from the Lenses of African-American Theatre and Film," *Journal of Dramatic Theory and Criticism* 16, no. 2 [Spring 2002]: 71).

14. Kandé, "Look Homeward, Angel," 134.

15. Spillers, "Mama's Baby, Papa's Maybe," 67.

16. bell hooks, *Ain't I a Woman?: Black Women and Feminism* (Boston and Cambridge, MA: South End Press, 1981), 18.

17. Ibid., 27.

18. In the opening chapter of Fred Douglass' narrative, he recounts his childhood experience of witnessing the brutal beating of his Aunt Hester. He refers to this scene as the "blood-stained gate of slavery." As a seven-year-old child Douglass was mortified by the brutality of the beating itself. The master tied her arms up to a joist, similar to Kuta and Shola. She was stripped, and Douglass understood the awful sexual implications of the beating. (Frederick Douglass, *Narrative of the Life of Frederick Douglass, An American Slave* (1845) (New York, NY: Penguin Classics, 1982), 51–52.

19. This practice for beating pregnant slaves is noted by a former slave in bell hooks' *Ain't I a Woman?*

20. Ibid., 27.

21. Woolford, "Filming Slavery," 96.
22. Grayson states that the word stool is used to designate the position of the king or chief. Asante stool history chronicles the matrilineage of the Asante clans. Grayson includes documentation from the British Governor which reinforces the significance of The Golden Stool stating: "the Stool . . . contained the soul . . . of the Ashanti." ("Spirits of Asona Ancestors Come," 222.)
23. Ukpokodu, "African Heritage from the Lenses of African-American Theatre and Film," 71.
24. Spillers, "Mama's Baby, Papa's Maybe," 67.
25. Ibid.
26. Ibid., 79.
27. Grayson, "Spirits of Asona Ancestors Come," 220.
28. Kandé, 131.
29. Spillers, "Mama's Baby, Papa's Maybe," 75.
30. Quoted in ibid., 79.
31. Woolford, "Filming Slavery," 64.
32. Samuel Ayedime Kafewo, "Exploring Narratives of the Trans-Atlantic Slave Trade in *Amistad* and *Sankofa*," *Africa and Trans-Atlantic Memories: Literary and Aesthetic Manifestations of Diaspora and History*, eds. Naana Opoku-Agyemang, Paul E. Lovejoy, and David V. Trotman (Trenton, NJ: 2008), 147–159.
33. Kandé, "Look Homeward, Angel," 140.

10

✛

South Asian Hip Hop Wannabes and the Chavs Who Love Them

The Blackening of British Culture in Gautam Malkani's Londonstani

Delores B. Phillips

Gautam Malkani's tragicomic novel *Londonstani* features characters that conform to a particular identity template; one that is wrought with an abiding anxiety that ultimately reflects aspects of Paul Gilroy's conceptualization of postcolonial melancholia. Jas, the novel's protagonist, only awkwardly fits into the cool clique of three young South Asian men, Hardjit, Ravi, and Amit, who attend his school and represent the power and élan that Jas lacks. They embody the performativity of Hip Hop culture, consuming its cultural production and then faithfully reinscribing it, using their bodies as its codex. Meanwhile, Jas reenacts both their South Asian cultural mannerisms as well as those of the Hip Hop culture that his peers emulate, thereby representing a secondary layer of removal from a range of authenticities and postures of belonging. Both Jas and his crew adopt Hip Hop culture tactically, deploying their sense of the culture as potent signifiers of masculinity that in turn represent a strategy for assuming cultural power in the novel. *Londonstani* foregrounds Hip Hop culture's investment in hypermasculinity as a means of negotiating the cultural contours of postmodern, multicultural Britain. Jas, the novel's protagonist, is a white male seeking identification with a group of South Asian men who themselves seek identification with African American masculine identity within Hip Hop culture.[1] To navigate varying degrees of alienation and affiliation between their parents' cultures of origin and England, Jas' crew turns to an outside cultural assemblage: African American Hip Hop and its obsessive interest in hypermasculinity, with its sexual prowess, physical toughness, and conspicuous consumption. Meanwhile, Jas attempts to distance himself from his own impotent British whiteness as he too negotiates the cultural shifts of an increasingly multiethnic England. In an effort to shore up his own masculinity, he embarks upon a quixotic quest for brownness, turning to both South Asian as well as Hip Hop masculinity in a move that exposes him as enacting, not cultural assimilation, but cultural displacement. Regrettably, he finds that the space of British brownness is a space that has no room for him, as his own attempt to inhabit a culturally chameleonic space creates a fiction of which Jas refuses to be disabused. His desire is to be a brown boy, but his white skin cheats him of this wish, no matter how brown he wants his life to be. In this way, Hip Hop masculinity offers only an ambivalent means of sublimating the frictions felt by both white and brown men in multicultural England.

This essay examines how the characters in *Londonstani* adopt and adapt to the features of the hypermasculine Hip Hop formations to which they pay homage, interrogating how and why they diligently follow the Hip Hop script. This essay is therefore situated at the crossroads of racial identity, cultural affiliation, and media and pop culture. The novel's depictions of hypermasculinity stand at the intersection that brings together the chav, the rudeboy, the desi, and the gangsta. Neither Hip Hop, nor chav, nor rudeboy, nor desi culture is monolithic. Gautam Malkani's actual struggle within his own group as to naming themselves when he was an adolescent exemplifies the difficult negotiation between multiple sites of identification and belonging that make labeling hybridized youth subcultures so problematic. It is for this reason that the cultural categories that define masculine postures in this essay ultimately break down—and not because they are poorly performed. Additionally, the adoption and shedding of these postures is tactical, as characters tactically deploy them as a means of maximizing masculine power.

I adopt the broad definitions of these stereotypes for the purposes of this essay. The gangsta is the immediately recognizable, African American Hip Hop badman. The rudeboy is another badman imported from the Caribbean (and later appropriated by the skinhead movement in many of its panracial forms) and comparable to the African American gangsta because of his associations with underprivileged, discontented youth culture. The gangsta and the rudeboy share close associations with musical forms—the gangsta with Hip Hop and the rudeboy with ska, rocksteady, and dancehall. The desi stands apposite of these two figures: the archetype of South Asian masculine competence, his stylishness is a marker of his success in the same way that the gangsta's affluence indicates his ability to transcend his impoverished origins. While the term often can apply to both genders, the desi in *Londonstani* embodies a perfectly executed, muscular masculinity (described in fuller detail below). The chav, however, is an inversion of these paradigms. Similar to the American whigger: poor, uneducated, and archetypally white, the chav body is a noisome reenactment of the gangsta, lifted wholesale from his contexts in the United States and deposited in the British estates. Chav characters in film and television usually feature white actors playing white characters emulating black Americans—and behaving with a measure of cultural ineptitude coupled with social incompetence, as chavs are depicted as shiftless, jobless, indolent, and self-indulgent. According to Imogen Tyler in "Chav Mum, Chav Scum," the chav stereotype that arises repeatedly in British humor serves a social purpose that deploys revulsion and mockery as a means of clearly demarcating the boundaries between classes in Britain. About this Tyler writes, "Laughing at chavs is a way of naming, managing and authorizing class disgust, contempt, and anxiety."[2] In texts featuring this character type, Hip Hop's inherent cool becomes the subject of an import/export renegotiation of difference by deconstructing race and regrafting it onto class. While the chav's physical trappings and language may constitute a new form of blackface for some critics, the laugh-factor perhaps more accurately lies in a degree of class snobbery that scapegoats the chav body as it blunders through its clumsy cross-cultural interactions. Moreover, it potentially reveals a discomfort with a lack of cultural authenticity, tenuous connection with areas of cultural expertise, and the ham-fisted deployment of cultural stereotypes.

The version of the desi is one that I take from the pages of the novel. His is the competent masculinity of the South Asian immigrant best exemplified on Bollywood posters and in the magazines that Hardjit reads. Sanjay, the boys' criminal mentor who connects their traffic in jailbroken cell phones to a much larger framework of organized crime, embodies perfect desiness: he lives in a lavish apartment, owns luxury cars, and trains Jas in the nuances of masculine poise and interactions with the opposite sex. The rudeboy is a trickier assemblage as he has a history embedded in the Jamaican diaspora, skinhead subculture, and the fraught racial politics of 1970s and 1980s England. For the purposes of this essay he is the man who emerges from the list of Rudeboy Rules that Jas offers the reader and alludes to the panethnic participants in urban youth culture, with features of the highly charged racial and cultural politics that mark his movements from Jamaica to the United Kingdom throughout the second half of the twentieth century. The novel reveals these distinctions as artificial, exposing the slippages between them and making it impossible to map them with absolute surety.

Londonstani is narrated from the first-person perspective, following Jas' plight as an adolescent Londoner of ambivalent cultural and racial identity. Throughout the novel, Jas' cultural persona is an assemblage of rap ethos, South Asian linguistic and cultural mannerisms, and, later, the more general, global trappings of wealth and privilege. While the other members of his crew combine these cultural inflections into effortless, well-articulated, semi-coherent wholes (which I will problematize in detail below), Jas stumbles and bumbles through the text, awkwardly reenacting a range of postures in ways that underscore his anxieties about his own risk of exposure—anxieties that are justified via the novel's conclusion. Jas loses everything: friends, girlfriends, access to easy money and the privilege that accompanies it. The text foregrounds what an inattentive reader assumes to be his brownness—Malkani drops hints, but does not expose Jas' putative whiteness until the novel's final pages. The long, shameful name that he will not pronounce early in the text is not a lengthy South Asian name, but is instead a very British one: Jason Bartholomew-Cliveden.[3] The revelation that Jas is white challenges the reader to rethink her cultural expectations and to evaluate her stance on the state of race in multicultural Britain.[4]

Somewhere between the gangsta, the rudeboy, the chav, and the desi, *Londonstani*'s men take shape with the "Rudeboy Rules" that they use to define themselves and shape their behavior so that it conforms with the Hip Hop stereotypes that they attempt to reproduce. Of particular importance here is the manner in which race is displaced in *Londonstani*, not in favor of class, but in favor of ethnicity. The politics of difference tap the rhetoric of African American disenfranchisement and its complex reclamation of cultural power, and for the same end. In a London blemished by Enoch Powell's 1968 "Rivers of Blood" speech, submerged in the social contexts of the rise of the National Front in the 1970s and early 1980s, and more recently in the conflagration of violence in the 2001 Oldham race riots, the adoption of Hip Hop culture and rap machismo by South Asian men in London at the turn of the twenty-first century represents a violent affront to white exclusionism and English cultural protectionism. Additionally, the adoption of African American Hip Hop mannerisms adds yet another volatile element to the increasingly complex cultural fabric of a multicultural Britain. As these young men find themselves as second-generation citizens of the South Asian diaspora, they seek belonging, not in an increasingly imaginary East, but in a transnational, transatlantic cultural space. In these contexts, race, nation, and ethnicity constitute the variables that redistribute power differences that in turn structure the performances of masculinity.

STRIKING THE POSE:
LONDONSTANI AND HIP HOP GESTURES

The clever manipulation of American pop and Hip Hop references in the novel is a playful redeployment of the music, working both metaphorically and literally as cultural referents. For example, DJ turntables metaphorize the scratching of a sari rubbing against itself as Hardjit's mother serves the boys pakoras.[5] The technological modernity and cross-cultural traffic signified by the DJ turntable contrasts sharply against the culturally atavistic referents of the sari, a traditional Indian garment worn by women, and the pakora, an everyday Indian snack. In this way, the novel draws into close proximity the clashing cultural values that drive its core conflicts. Musical allusions proliferate in the text and serve as cultural signposts signifying the boys' acumen in repurposing the nuances of the music for maximum affect. In other words, rap and pop songs become a secondary language that the boys use to translate their thoughts and desires to a listening audience, a layer of performance that signifies the range of the cultural scripts that they follow. For example, in addition to the DMX that blares from Ravi's (mother's) BMW, "I'll be Missing You" by Puff Daddy and Faith Evans—a eulogy written for Biggie Smalls—is played at Arun's funeral. Mixed musical genres also mark out culturally hybrid spaces in clubs. The musical shift between Arabic beats and LL Cool J's "Doin' It" combine cultural idioms and act as a foil for characters who attempt to pass fluidly between them—and often fail.[6] The text even uses Hip Hop clues to drop hints that Jas is white long before his whiteness is revealed: for example, Samira compares Jas' dancing to Justin Timberlake.[7] Similar to Eminem, Justin Timberlake represents an infusion of whiteness into Hip Hop, and is one of the clues leading to the ultimate revelation that, in spite of his pretense toward brownness, Jas is betrayed by his white skin and its associations with a mode of Britishness that he consistently attempts to resist. Hip Hop references also work discursively. Later in the novel, a discussion about westernization takes place over a basketball game between Jas and Arun.[8] While it certainly alludes to the centrality of basketball within Hip Hop culture, it may also refract the importance of Rucker Park to Hip Hop history, as well as its placement at the center of a class-based culture war in the New York projects. At Rucker Park, Hip Hop and rap artists gather annually in an event that is equal parts sporting match, concert, and cultural celebration—and this cornerstone of African American culture has come under assault in recent years as Harlem undergoes gentrification.[9] Serving as a microcosm for the protagonist's arc in the novel, cultural negotiation takes place on the court as Jas attempts to liberate Arun from the strictures of his upbringing and his mother's expectations. Whereas contested ground in Harlem constitutes a macrocosmic negotiation of race, class, and history, the basketball game in London is a negotiation of race, class, gender, and diaspora on a much smaller scale.

The most readily observable display of the group's absorption of a Hip Hop cultural affect is in their use of language. The novel's glossary decodes the various lexicons in which the boys speak, breaking this chapter into two parts. Terms such as "da," "dat," "dem," "dey," "dis," "wat," "wid," and "yo" appear in a separate section. Instead of sharing space in the general glossary (which is entitled "Glossary") these terms appear in a section labeled "Grammar." The text segregates imported inflections into distinct cultural spaces with South Asian and British colloquialisms overlaying a grammatical structure shaped by African American Vernacular English.[10] South Asian words drape themselves across African American syntax. Ravi's grammar is stamped indelibly by the culture he consumes.[11] For example, while complaining about the interruption of his efforts to "chirps" [sic] a girl he desires to bed, Ravi says, "Why da fuck he do dat for? Why da fuck he make us leave dem ladies behind, bhanchod?"[12] Hardjit replies, "Dey was too old 4 yo ass anyway."[13] "Why ... he do dat," "Why ... he make us," and "Dey was" become the grammatical scaffolding upon which the boys hang text message acronyms and Hindi swear words.

While not indexed in the glossary, other African American linguistic mannerisms characterize the dialogue in the novel. When teasing Hardjit about possibly mixing his Playboys in among the stack of Bollywood magazines beside the laundry hamper, Ravi suggests that "Maybe it'd even help yo mum n dad, you know, get jiggy wid it,"[14] indirectly referencing the 1997 hit single by Will Smith. This alignment with American cultures takes place in the company of other miscegenated cultural moments. The group of boys speak English marked by African American vernacular idioms, even as they salivate over images of South Asian film stars—Ravi almost literally, as he mimes licking Hardjit's poster of Kareena Kapoor. The narrative voice in the novel is also marked by a broader range of African American speech mannerisms, as Jas says that "Hardjit would've smacked them for dissin him, dissin his house, dissin his mum's magazines an dissin bitches in general. Truth is, we weren't actually dissin nothin."[15] Cultures of desire collide these sociolinguistic moments: material, ethnic, racial, national. All are negotiated here by the logic of the "dis" and how it outlines the boundaries of respectability.

In addition to Hip Hop Nation Language the novel's dialogue also includes text message acronyms. In the same scene in his bedroom, Hardjit threatens Ravi in an explosive mixture of inflections: "Fuckin get yo mouth off ma door, u perve, or I'ma glue yo tongue 2 da inside a da door frame n slam dis muthafucka shut. I mean it, Ravi, u best jus ease up on dissin ma shit today b4 I smack u again."[16] The inclusion of acronyms performs the doubled service of phonetically outlining the transgressive linguistic space of dialects marked out by class and race, as well as working as a dialect that does not appear in spoken English but instead arises out of the need for efficient exchanges between mobile devices. In addition to deconstructing oral linguistic forms, the acronyms deconstruct written language. The phonetic and grammatical subversions in the dialogue in the novel also deconstruct class privilege: the boys adopt the posture and the language of an oppressed minority underclass, tapping into a rich, potent language to give voice to their own strandedness both within and between cultures in Britain; but the CDs they purchase that teach them these postures and the phones that they use to communicate in these acronyms—and to learn their grammar—are themselves markers of middle-class consumer culture that they can easily afford, with or without their engagement with the illicit trade in unblocked mobile phones. Ravi's mother Kavita owns the lilac BMW that Ravi touts as his own. The money the crew makes is discretionary income that they spend on music, magazines, clubbing, and clothes. However, beyond the leisure time that they spend in ways that ape the plight of the unemployed both in England and abroad, there exist structural differences in privilege and power that represent a disconnect between the rap and Hip Hop culture with which they identify and the lives that they lead. For example, as Jas works diligently to assume the mantle of the disenfranchised, his father can successfully fight with the examining board to arrange Jas' retakes of his A-level examinations when he fails them.[17] Jad's father works diligently on his son's behalf to ensure that arson does not blemish his record with an arrest after Jas torches his father's warehouse in an effort to make good on his promise to deliver a shipment of mobile phones.[18]

These disconnections offer fertile ground for new linguistic affiliations, signifying a complex (and in some ways superficial) knowledge of Hip Hop culture as well as a profound ignorance of its roots. As they speak in its tongues, the boys disconnect cultural grammar from gangland origins. When bragging of past (possibly illusory) sexual conquests, Ravi crows in approval of Amit's boasts of penis size and promiscuity, "Wikid man, you b da dog."[19] Hardjit challenges Amit's claims of sexual dominance by saying, "Nah, blud, I sayin I *know* u makin dis shit up." While ostensibly a text message acronym and a use of the invariant *be* for habitual aspect,[20] the use of "b" as a verb and the appellation "blud" also offer a refraction of gang affiliations, decontextualized. Where such language—particularly the term "blud"—once constituted passwords that would ensure safe passage through strictly demarcated terrain in 1980s' South Central Los Angeles, they appear here stripped of their past exigence. Furthermore, detached from its opposite, "cuz," "blud" now stands apposite "bredren," the Caribbean linguistic mannerism that functions in the text as its close compatriot: the yardie and the gangsta close ranks in the text.[21]

The group's linguistic mastery also creates complete scripts that the boys can readily quote but, again, take utterly out of context. Confronted by Mr. Ashwood for attempting to steal his mobile phone, Ravi stands up in the face of authority, adopting a "gangsta-rap pose[]" and saying, "Yeh, man, nobody mess wid us, we bad muthafuckas. Da gangsta, da killa, n da dope dealer," giving a "lick-o-shot flick with his right hand" (a move largely abandoned in the United States by the early 1990s, but still alive and well in representations of chav culture at the time of this writing).[22] To keep the Hip Hop pose from resulting in an actual arrest, Jas must act as an interpreter. In the first of many such scenes, the Hip Hop pose in *Londonstani* is here revealed for what it is: a posture, an articulation of mannerisms that can be packaged via CD and music video and is subject to movement across global cultural flows. The Hip Hop Nation Language that the boys speak and the allusions that they invoke distort the street consciousness that gave rise to the language they speak and the music they reference for two reasons. The first is that their allusions are detached from Hip Hop's originary contexts in the urban United States. The boys therefore seek to inhabit Hip Hop character types. The second (closely related to the first) is that Ravi, Hardjit, Jas, and Amit do not participate in the evolution or extension of the Hip Hop Nation's national boundaries. Instead, they participate in endless forms of mimicry. According to H. Samy Alim, the street is "the site, soul, sound, and center of the Hip Hop Culture-World."[23] *Londonstani*'s men do not participate in the cultural connectivity that energizes the linguistic idiom that they so diligently imitate.

The young men's gender norms embrace those of the rappers whom they idolize, entering into the fraught terrain of the exploitation and objectification of women. The boys' bluster includes boasts of penis size, virility, and sexual prowess. The banter of the young men in *Londonstani* includes fending off accusations of impotence and laying claim to feminine flesh, using the demeaning appellations of "bitches n hos" to label women.[24] This exchange participates in the ritualized objectification of women that is a stereotypical component of Hip Hop culture, even as Hardjit claims to have higher standards than his friends. However, Hardjit's manner with women he does not know gives the lie to this statement, as he participates in the pageantry of the Hip Hop courtship ritual. Rather than seductive, the crew's interactions with the opposite sex in these moments are demonstrative and confrontational—indeed, almost combative. Audio drive-bys constitute a principal tactic. For example, as the crew rides in Ravi's (mother's) BMW, they pass a provocatively dressed young woman walking down a London street and, with their flashy car, fancy clothes, Hip Hop style, good looks, and loud music, stage a visual and audio assault. Her dress constitutes the coded catalyst that initiates the engagement: a short skirt and high boots. In response, Ravi slows the car and Hardjit cranks up DMX's "Ruff Ryders' Anthem" as he displays his own toned biceps, framed by a garishly painted luxury car.[25] As the young men drive past women, they use rap music and conspicuous consumption to make a vibrant display of their virility, a performance that they stage repeatedly in the novel.

The Hip Hop cultures in the text follow the regimented masculinities that include the preening of the body and constant, conscientious attendance to its postures. Hardjit is the text's most devoted acolyte. Jas admires his "designer desiness, with his perfectly groomed garms that made it look like he went shopping with P Diddy."[26] This meticulous attention to self is its own discipline constituted of scripted rituals. Chapter 6 opens with Hardjit peering into a mirror, obeying "one a his urges to go shape his facial hair in the big magnifying mirror above the sink," hunting for the inevitable stray hairs that trespass across the sharp lines of his goatee and the Adidas stripes razored into his eyebrows.[27] With microscopic attentiveness to detail (obsessively shaping his beard in a bathroom repurposed for that specific task), Hardjit deploys an artfully formed and performed masculinity that the novel tropes as crossing gender binaries. For example, Hardjit arrives fashionably late to a fight with a rival after carefully selecting clothes to maximize the effect of his entrance.[28] At the gym with his crew, also Hardjit instructs Jas in how to shape his body, providing detailed advice to enable Jas, not to get stronger, but to get bigger, to shape his body for the gaze of others.[29] While this certainly aligns with a more general theorizing of the role of exercise culture, metrosexuality, and masculinity in the United States, in these moments the sculpting of the body is also in keeping with the "cool pose" required of Hip Hop masculinity. Also defined as "restrained masculinity," the cool pose is described by Richard Majors and Janet Mancini Billson as "emotionless, stoic, and unflinching," a tactical diffidence designed to "offset an externally imposed 'zero' image."[30] Included in the cool pose are requirements of style that resist the scripts of impoverishment that oppress black masculine bodies in the United States. A complement to the verbal styling that includes playing the dozens, battlin, and flow is the nonverbal dimension of styling that includes control of facial expressions, wearing the latest, most expressive hair styles, sporting his own walk and dance, and driving the right car and wearing the right clothes.[31] The self-styling required of the cool pose requires a high degree of rigor and control. The scripting of masculinity in *Londonstani* obeys the structure of this rigorous disciplining of the self. The boys wear name brands that the text meticulously details, and Hardjit's excessive preening and neurotic attention to detail are in line with the impression management required by Hip Hop masculinity in the United States. If the black man "paint[s] a self-portrait in colorful, vivid strokes that makes [him] 'somebody,'"[32] then Hardjit appropriates and magnifies this aspect of black masculinity, and for much the same purpose. He wishes to transform his body into an expression of cultural power as a way of resisting dominant social idioms. However, *Londonstani* renders this posture ironic: young men of means adopt the postures of the dispossessed, and with an obsessive interest in even the smallest details such as a hair out of place or the motion of an arm. The microscopic attentiveness to even the most minute aspects of self-stylization refracts and exaggerates the presentation of self that is a component of the cool pose. However, these young men are not subject to the material disenfranchisement that shapes the lives of the African American counterparts they imitate. Instead, their social difficulties arise from spaces of cultural hybridity and not from economic oppression. In fact, the yard in front of Hardjit's five-bedroom house has a double driveway, and its proximity to the airport requires the installation of surround-sound speakers—an expensive remedy for the problem of noise. Rather than the class-based lack of power that characterizes the plight of black men in the United States, Hardjit must instead contend with his own odd positioning in Britain, where his cultural identifications are troubled by desis who act like goras, gora Jas who acts like desis who act black, and parents who adhere to cultural norms that his peer group finds increasingly alien.[33] Hardjit's unsettling encounter with the desi at the stoplight (examined in detail below) reveals his own troubled relationship with South Asian culture in London. His obsessive control over his own image therefore combats the sense of alienation that this encounter reveals by simplifying the terms of engagement.

If Hardjit disciplines his body, then Jas must discipline his gaze. As attentive as Jas is to the posing of Hardjit's musculature and the fashioning of Hardjit's body, Jas must be equally attentive to watching who watches him watching. He must protect his gaze so that he can protect his heterosexuality and, by extension, his masculinity as it is interpreted along the poles of a false sexual binary. As Ravi races recklessly down the street, Hardjit grips the door frame so that his bulging biceps—and his black D&G vest—are displayed to the view of onlookers they pass. Jas admires the intricate, microscopic adjustments that Hardjit makes to his appearance as he flexes his muscles ever so slightly in ways that appear to be an effortless display of masculine power. Jas must also guard his admiration, closeting it by looking surreptitiously. "Luckily, Hardjit din't notice me watchin him feel his biceps. Otherwise he'd have rinsed me for being gay or a gora lover, or both. I'd caught him enough times feelin his arms an just generally checkin himself out in mirrors an tinted car windows an somehow he always made me feel like I was the batty boy" (19). As Hardjit is hyperaware of the positioning of his body, Jas is hyperaware of the eyes of others meeting his own. In this moment, the homosexual is rendered as the equivalent of the cultural outsider; to be interpreted as gay maroons Jas in his unwanted whiteness. When looking at Hardjit's pants to see whether he has concealed a bar from his weight set to use as a weapon, Hardjit spots Jas looking at his crotch and calls him a batty boy.[34] Accusations of homosexuality constitute a potent weapon in the text, and Jas must carefully navigate the sexual terrain before him, in keeping with Hip Hop culture's sexual norms.[35] As a body inhabiting the cultural border, Jas' hyperawareness of the homosexual threat guards against classifications that are paradoxically requisite to the categories of masculinity he wishes to inhabit. Matthew Oware writes, "Although homophobic references are employed to demean and belittle male rivals and gays and lesbians, gay and lesbian sexual identities are indispensible to promoting a heteronormative masculinity."[36] In an interview with Jeff Chang, Tim'm provides the explanation that underwrites Oware's understanding of Hip Hop hetero brotherhood, stating, "Hip-hop heteros rely heavily on the inappropriate faggot in order to even exist. In a really twisted sort of way, they rely on the verbal bashing of fags in order to substantiate their manhood ... It's really funny, actually. Sadly, hard edge and masculinity almost always means you hate fags."[37] Because the Hip Hop hetero is also in the company of the Bollywood hero (Rudeboy Rule #7)[38] homophobic machismos compound, with the locus of abjection centering on the poncey gay gora or the coconut who imitates him. As he is already white and is straining against that whiteness (even participating in the beating of the white boy in the opening pages of the novel) he must also resist the emasculating effect of being labeled as gay, which means that he must carefully manage the contours of his desire—and participate in the bashing of fags.

Furthermore, as the encounter with Mr. Ashwood underscores and as their alignment with Sanjay illustrates, the boys have an interest in perpetuating the Hip Hop archetype of the badman: the pimp, the killer, the hustler, the dealer. Oware describes his function as a Hip Hop archetype:

[T]he badman is feared by whites and middleclass black society for his nonconformity, eschewing established rules, norms, or laws of society. Rather, he moves to his own tune and "is an outlaw, challenging a societal order antithetical to the expression of African American humanity. He is a rebel to society, living on the margins of a black community that at once regards him as a hero and a threat." Drug dealers, hustlers, pimps, and players adhere and abide by badman behavior. All emphasize their sexual and physical prowess, fully embracing misogyny and homophobia as part of their character. Under the guise of "strong black men" or "real men," gangsta rap artists uphold and perpetuate this aspect of masculinity.[39]

However, rather than trade in flesh, weapons, or drugs, the boys trade in cell phones. Still their small-time criminal activities constitute a rebellion against the class and privilege of their parents. More critically, they rebel against the cultural confines of the proper desi. They do not wish to be like the goras or the "poncey, gora-loving coconut" whose cultural allegiance with the white, middle-class, British mainstream suffers the additional layer of castigation by being characterized as a fawning, obsequious homosexual.[40] However, as Amit's brother Arun's suicide dramatizes, the group—including Jas—does not wish to be confined within their parent's cultural profile, as cultural hybridity makes untenable pure categories of difference. The badman therefore allows the crew to inhabit the margins and to conform to the Bollywood heroism that is also a necessary component of their cultural identification. The crew's version of the badman is so convincing that even the black kids at school fear their violence.[41]

Although it can offer nothing but confusion between genders, the Hip Hop creed's homosocial structures offer a ready template for understanding the dismay that Jas' friends feel by his multiple levels of betrayal. His crimes are many: his meddling in Amit's "complicated family shit" kills Amit's brother Arun; caught with Samira, Jas' transgression might be a violation of communal allegiances or, more likely, he has crossed lines of both community and race. He has violated the pact between men, and his crew's rejection works within the Hip Hop cultural code that has shaped their behavior throughout the text. This is in keeping with Hip Hop culture's depictions of the homosocial bonds that ensure the survival of African American men in the hazardous terrain of thug life. A consistent theme in rap is the need to rally to the defense of one's friends, acknowledgment of debts of gratitude for mutual protection and support, and the mourning of their loss.[42] It is perhaps for this reason why Jas' betrayal is so shocking to the group. Cultural transgressions are codified along multiple axes of belonging and exclusion.

THE UTILITY OF LEGITIMIZATION AND THE EXPOSURE OF THE HIP HOP POSE

Outlining the disconnection between South Asian identity and Hip Hop culture and white Britishness assumes that cultural values are absolute, and that the terms of engagement with cultural norms and mannerisms always remain the same as they travel across borders. They are not, and they do not. Jas and his friends pursue the Rudeboy Rules and the Hip Hop creed for a reason far beyond a mere desire for cool. Hip Hop and rap grant them access to specific forms of empowerment in ways that expose the raw wounds of diasporic longing, and not for the old ways of a mother country to which they can never return (although the avid consumption of Bollywood magazines inclines toward this longing). Instead, because the boys must negotiate a fractured landscape of cultural influences, Hip Hop represents a global voice that speaks to them in a language they understand. Ravi, Har(d)jit[43] and Amit find themselves in a fluid, hybrid space in London. Arun, Amit's brother, is involved in the archetypal "family-related shit" representative of what happens to the children of immigrants: his parents wish to conduct the arrangement of his marriage in accordance with Hindu customs as Arun balks. Neither belonging to the England of the goras they beat up nor to the culture of their parents, the boys graft onto their own understanding of South Asian culture (informed by Bollywood magazines and bhangra beats) African American cultural norms that speak to their sense of disenfranchisement.

The crew's gravitation toward African American culture represents a broader trend that makes ambiguous the cultural definitions of black Britishness. In the 1980s, the category stretched to include, not just African and Afro-Caribbean people in Britain, but also South Asians. As both African and South Asian British cultural production exposed the desire for cultural anchors to help artists make sense of difference, "British Asians seemed to find resources of hope from across the Atlantic as much as people who could directly trace their history to the slave plantations of the Caribbean."[44] Other authors who write in multiethnic Britain also reached across the sea to tap into the power of African American culture and its offerings of solidarity:

> [Author] Hanif Kureishi, who has a Pakistani father and white English mother, writes of his teenage years covering his suburban London bedroom in Black Panther imagery and finding in African American writing both "good, just anger" and a "political commitment to a different kind of whole society." Even given the very different composition of black British communities, the valence of African American culture offered a route into the thorny business of consolidating minority identity.[45]

However, the solidarity that unites African American cultural models with a uniform body of black Britons that include all nonwhite bodies from the post-imperial periphery had to yield to the multiple modes of difference within the category. In the late 1980s and early 1990s, sociologist Tariq Modood mounted a critique of the inclusion of British Asians in an African American–inflected black Britishness, arguing that this category offers little specific political utility or opportunities for cultural pride to Asian Britons.[46] Modood challenges the blackness of Asian bodies in Britain as a political category that collapses difference, but the men in *Londonstani* deconstruct the distinctions between black Britishnesses and reinforce a nonhegemonic, variegated blackness that is marked by a proliferation of self-conscious cultural mannerisms.

Jas and his crew clearly associate themselves with an authentic identity, even though it shuttles between cultural poles. When challenging a desi in the car next to them, Hardjit yells: "Fuckin batty boy, u sound like a poncey gora. Wat's wrong wid'chyu, sala kutta? U 2 embarrass'd to b a desi? Embarrass'd a your own culture, huh?"[47] Ironically, the challenge to authentic cultural belonging originates from a site of cultural hybridity. Furthermore, it is leveled along the vector of language—a hybrid formation reflecting Hardjit's amalgamation of cultural influences. However, this is a consequence of the manner in which the adoption of Hip Hop and rap mannerisms and, by extension, African American culture, also results in an adoption of claims to authenticity. Authenticity itself becomes the coveted object of desire. Additionally, the rhetoric of abuse identifies the desi as a poncey gora, the gay white body shunned by Hardjit's crew. However, this ironic relationship with the "coconut" body of the poncey gora desi reveals the dysfunction that disorders Hardjit's assemblage of cultural identifiers. This dysfunction is literalized by the spaces within which he assembles them: his house contains a nonfunctional bathroom dedicated only to grooming facial hair.[48] Similarly to Ravi's car, this room complicates the notions of privilege: the extra room and the leisurely pursuit of self-grooming mark out this privilege, but this bathroom does not work as well as the other two in the home. It is therefore repurposed to allude to the privilege that it initially signifies.

The crew's alignment with Hip Hop allows rap's cultural valences of authenticity to reverberate with South Asian cultural practices. The boys are indeed surrounded by the hybrid musical forms of bhangra, Arabic beats, and jungle. Nebulous forms of authenticity ripple outward, not only toward South Asian, but across the Atlantic:

> America is believed to be at the cutting edge of generic innovation in hip-hop. The combination of being the cradle of the music and the progenitor of its subsequent developments lent a sense of American hip-hop as the authentic article. Even though a precise definition of "authenticity" was not forthcoming, this potent mix of "origin" and "diversity" seemed to act, on first impressions, as a talisman of authenticity and credibility.[49]

As Hip Hop is charged with authenticity, the manner in which the boys graft its masculinity onto their own in an effort to interpret their place in multicultural London attempts to leverage its credibility but in ways that disarrange, indeed derange its content. However, the wholesale adoption of rap and Hip Hop culture points toward a measure of cultural ineptitude. Even with the models of Arabic and bhangra beats, the boys cannot adapt the forms of masculinity they consume into something new, reenacting an anxiety that pervades the import of Hip Hop culture in Britain. Tony Mitchell connects this to British consumption and market pressures that affected the distribution of homegrown Hip Hop artists; *Londonstani* exemplifies the same disconnection between Hip Hop and listener that concerns some of the critics of the form. Mitchell writes, "While many rappers could not help but begin by imitating the styles and accents of their US heroes, there were many who realized that to merely transpose US forms would rob U.K. hip hop of the ability to speak for a disenfranchised British constituency in the way that US hip hop so successfully spoke to, and for, its audience."[50] While the characters in *Londonstani* actually stop making music as DJ-ing becomes so common that they can no longer earn as much money as they would make selling unblocked cell phones, they still exhibit the adoption of a "slurred hybrid" that "locate[s] rap somewhere in the middle of the Atlantic Ocean."[51] Set decades after the first wave of rappers in the United Kingdom, *Londonstani* still exhibits an ambivalent relationship with mixed cultural expression—an ambivalence underscored by the prominence of British Hip Hop crews such as London Posse, II Tone Committee, and Hijack, all of whom participate in a vibrant homegrown Hip Hop scene with a lengthy pedigree.

Meanwhile, Jas, suffering an identity crisis of more metaphysical proportions, does not wish to belong to a privileged gora England—even though he is a privileged gora. He drifts toward an immigrant Britain, a more color-neutral space, a cultural fabric comprised of cultural contributions from South Asia, the Caribbean, African America, and the British lower classes. Jas hopes that, by hanging with the right crowds, speaking across their dialects, mastering their cultural idioms and reproducing them in their plural simultaneity, he can earn his belonging. But, as hints scattered throughout the text suggest, he cannot. The Britishness invoked by his white skin is something that no amount of buying power can completely cover; therefore, his claims to belonging will always be subject to contestation. The urban youth interviewed by Briggs and Cobley clearly distinguish how worn identity differs between identities that are lived somatically, and it is something that whites do now know how to do, as buying power stands in for the ineffable aspects of cultural identification. "It is recognized that white youth appropriate 'black' styles and that this is based most frequently on commodity consumption alone. Yet such appropriations based on the purchase of goods do not guarantee subcultural equivalence. One of the study's interviewees says: 'You can't go out and buy yourself £50 trainers and get a black image. It's a walk, a talk.'"[52] Even if Jas can walk the walk, he cannot talk the talk.

Part of his problem is articulated in how inarticulate he really is. Throughout the text, he exhibits an ambivalent relationship with language. Even Rudeboy Rule #4 cannot help him: "According to Hardjit, it don't matter if the proper word for something sounds fuckin ridiculous. If it's the proper word then it's the proper word."[53] In attempting to parse Hip Hop grammar, Jas cannot accommodate the arbitrariness of African American linguistic idiom, and he points out how words such as "yard," "crib," and "The Shit" never match their objects.[54] Here, Jas outlines the uncomfortable fit of the language he must speak in order to belong. His ambivalence with language is far-reaching, however. Throughout the text, Jas stumbles over his tongue, and cannot even bear to reveal his own name.[55] In this way, Jas is constantly in anticipatory hush mode.[56] Always at the butt end of every joke, Jas lacks the verbal inventiveness that Alim identifies as Hip Hop language's primary strengths.[57] In fact, he resists Hip Hop language's dexterity as it confounds his understanding, because its relationship with White British Mainstream English[58] lacks a logic that he can readily apprehend.

As long as Jas listens to the music, apes the mannerisms, obeys the dress code, and follows the rules then his involvement in spheres of difference are not threatening. He can keep quiet most of the time, absorbing and behaving, avoiding the betrayal of his treacherous tongue. His engagement with South Asian and Hip Hop cultures obeys the same laws of cultural appeasement as the adoption of Hip Hop cultural mannerisms of his South Asian counterparts. Ravi's mother allows her son to drive her BMW so that he does not bring home a BMW of his own: a black, Muslim, or white girl.[59] Wearing Hip Hop culture and adopting South Asian cultural norms are the equivalent of driving the BMW; dating Samira and meddling in Arun's affairs are the equivalent of Jas bringing one home.

At the end of the novel, Jas, whose whiteness is concealed throughout the novel, is finally unveiled as a chav. His cultural capital exhausts itself in a mockery of cool and cultural incompetence. It is revealed that his diligent efforts throughout the novel are to darken his whiteness: invisible to the reader, he is the "hypervisible 'filthy white[]'" standing at a borderline of cultural exchange:

> This borderline whiteness is evidenced through claims that chavs appropriate black American popular culture through their clothing, music, and forms of speech, and have geographical, familial and sexual intimacy with working-class blacks and Asians and immigrant populations.[60]

Once the novel reveals his whiteness, Jas' brownness shifts registers. He is no longer brown because he is actually black British—in any of its forms. His body is instead made brown (upon terracing the text) by its intimacy with cultures of brownness, its proximity to other brown bodies, and his desire for them. The principal difference is that meddling with real organized crime has, for a short time, exposed Jas as a black British man who is not really black. His "poncey gora-ness" is not a denomination that he must evade; it is instead a state that he cannot shed. Rather than a fragile cultural state of which he can be divested with a verbal assault, brown ethnicity is a category into which he struggles to belong—a struggle he loses.

But the failure of negotiation does not belong solely to Jas. As he is the point of focalization of the entire narrative, the reader is completely within his frames of reference. However, the deployment of Hip Hop points toward a broader problem of cultural appeasement. Hip Hop culture is defanged here, made lightweight and almost jocular, as it is exposed through the difficulty of cultural negotiation and the complexities of masculinity. Meanwhile, concessions and negotiations keep difference in manageable dimensions. Ravi's purple BMW is part of an elaborate pretense, and is ultimately revealed as such. Paraded with some pomp early in the novel, the lilac panty excuse for the color of the car is a sham that the K4VITA license plate reveals: his claim that he picks up girls whose purple underwear matches the color is an alibi for the effeminate paint job on the car which actually belongs to his mother.[61] Similarly, the fight between Hardjit and Tariq is principally a performance for the benefit of an audience of his peers, with Hardjit even helping Tariq up off of the ground after knocking him flat.[62] As the "feds" come to bust up the fight, Davinder's crew merrily jump about, singing "Dat's Da Sound A Da Police" by KRS-One and dancing around.[63] As a set of easily replicable cultural mannerisms, Hip Hop becomes farce.

The farcical nature of their engagement with hip hop is revealed in their encounters with Sanjay, who is the real deal. When the crew first sees Sanjay's flat, its opulence stuns them almost into speechlessness.[64] Recommended to him by their teacher, Mr. Ashwood, who ironically hopes that Sanjay's example can reform the boys, Sanjay assesses their real criminality as the pretense that it is—and even identifies them as wannabes like most kids.[65] Even though Rudeboy Rule #2 stipulates that "[h]avin the blingest mobile fone in the house is a rudeboy's birthright. Not just for style, but also cos fones were invented for rudeboys,"[66] Jas eventually distinguishes the group from the hardcore rap lifestyle that blasts forth from the radio in the car. He says that they "in't wannabe badass gangstas or someshit . . . We just provided a service."[67] Even though unblocking mobile phones is illegal, Jas knows that their activity constitutes not even a blip on the radar of the police.

The crew's Hip Hop indoctrination fails them as they involve themselves in real organized crime. The shift is signified in two ways in the text, both of which involve mass media images. The first involves the rap imagery that the boys consume. For example, when the boys first visit his home, Sanjay changes the television channel "from MTV to MTV Base, which meant goodbye 50 Cent an hello Snoop Dogg."[68] In this moment, Sanjay marks a return to the old school—a mature, established rap style that signifies the boys' transition into organized crime and Sanjay's placement as their mentor. The second involves images of the mafia, the template that shapes rap culture's depictions of organized criminality. After Arun's funeral, having failed to deliver the promised cell phones, Jas visits Sanjay's house. As he enters, he finds Sanjay watching *The*

Sopranos on DVD. Displaying Photoshopped images of Jas having sex with Samira, Sanjay coerces Jas' participation in the arson of his father's warehouse and the stock of phones that it contains. The DVD plays in the background as he reveals how the boys are part of a larger criminal scheme that exploits their labor.[69]

Sanjay is able to coerce the crew's labor because he knows what the boys only suspect: their Hip Hop sham is but a ripple in a larger wave of cultural momentum. Instructing them in Bling Bling Economics, Sanjay reveals the context that the boys miss, and attempts to indoctrinate them into the axes of power that can make them wealthy men.[70] Cultural values that exist ostensibly on the periphery are actually moving toward the center as youth subculture becomes mainstream, and its key contribution to the mainstream is material comfort. This is its lasting stamp upon mainstream culture, which will not retreat from standards of material comfort even as people evolve past its idiosyncratic features.[71] Furthermore, the embeddedness of this material standard extends beyond the confines of Hip Hop culture and has to do with the larger framework of popular culture, consumption, and desire—and the ubiquity of urban music and MTV. He reveals what Briggs and Cobley's study of Hip Hop culture in London exposes: Sanjay makes the connection between production and consumption as they inflect youth culture in London. In their ethnographic study of urban youth culture, Briggs and Cobley's subjects stated that identity cannot simply be bought and worn—that there is something much more essential to cultural identity. They observe that, for urban youth, "Consumption . . . is repeatedly seen as an *artifice* in contrast to the perceived *authenticity* of much American rap and hip-hop."[72] Lacking a stake in the politics of authenticity that mobilizes its consumption, Sanjay lays bare the mechanics of its cultural flows and exposes how the crew can use them to turn a hefty profit. Its worship of affluence actually places the crew's Hip Hop cultural expression at odds with the very culture that purports to offer them a clear sense of belonging. Sanjay offers them a realignment, detaching cultural signifiers such as cars and clothes from Hip Hop and reattaching them to the cultures of wealth that Hip Hop culture covets.

The young men in *Londonstani* represent a cultural mélange of which Hip Hop culture is only a part.[73] As gender cannot occur in a vacuum and is a contingent cultural value based on specific performances of difference, masculinity does not simply collapse into a single, unvariegated performance of machismo. Instead, multiple machismos contest with and complement one another. Masculinities proliferate, and it is this volatility that complicates Jas' attempts to fit in as revealed by his furtive sexual liaisons with Samira and his own poor performances of the African American rapper, the suave ladies' man, and the South Asian *badmash*.[74] It is also this volatility that eventually results in Jas' ultimate exile by the novel's conclusion, as he betrays the group both by dating Samira and by giving Amit's brother Arun the advice that results in Arun's self-poisoning by the ingestion of an entire bottle of aspirin.[75] Crossing boundaries yields isolation for Jas and culture shock for a reader who does not know that she must resist reading along the novel's grain.

Alas, Jas is just a chav: the British analogue to the laughable white poser who looks foolish as he tries to talk, walk, and dance black in the United States.[76] The figure of the chav is a staple in British humor. Sacha Baron Cohen's Ali G uses the chav's putative anti-intellectuality to critique radical political stances in the United States and in Britain. Meanwhile, Hip Hop's hyperemphasized gender roles cut to the quick both ways in *The Catherine Tate Show*, a British sketch comedy in which the titular comedienne depicts a range of cultural stereotypes—including the chav. High school–aged Lauren courts her chav beau Ryan, by whom she is alternately adored and spurned and who razors slashes into his eyebrows. Badly executing their interpretations of a variety of Hip Hop performers and making critical mistakes about American idioms, her crew's adoption of Hip Hop postures make a flamboyant farce of their wedding in the series' final episode. Lauren and her best friend Liese ape a viral wedding video by dancing down the aisle to Missy Elliott's "Pass That Dutch" as Ryan wears gold fronts at the altar and sports a white suit and diffident masculinity inspired by P Diddy. In another sketch comedy show titled *Little Britain*, chav mum Vicky Pollard refracts Posh Spice and the archetypal fly girl with her metallic athletic suits, knee pads, and roller skates, viciously satirizing the British version of the welfare queen: she is lazy, slovenly, inarticulate, interested principally in her appearance and interpersonal drama with the other girls of her school, shoplifts, lives on the dole, and tries to abandon her unwanted baby. By themselves, these examples represent ill-ease with urban youth culture and its easy cross-cultural traffic. The commodification of the chav body represents, to some degree, the commodification of Hip Hop culture and its trappings into a packageable assemblage readily subject to exportation. Once situated within a new cultural space, Hip Hop referents take on renewed cultural vigor. Taken in tandem with David Cameron's announcement at the February 2011 Munich Security Conference, however, the lampooning of chav body represents a more disturbing castigation of a failed policy of state multiculturalism.[77]

A middle-class pretender to brownness, Jas imbeds himself in a lexicon of chav bodies that sublimate British anxieties about multiculturalism, class, and race. Similar to the chav body, his multiple failures in the text represent a retreat toward cultural orthodoxies that reorder the cultural derangements that proliferate at the beginning of the novel. His chav body constitutes the catalyst that deconstructs the multicultural British citizen—and the failed political commitment that regulates his attitudes. By the novel's conclusion, Jas is restored to Britishness and his crew has retreated into the communal fold as their brownness requires them to close ranks against him. Gautam Malkani describes his book as "the story of a bunch of 19-year-old middle-class mummy's boys trying to be men— which they do by asserting their cut-and-paste ethnic identities; by blending their machismo with consumerism; [and] by trying to talk and act as if their affluent corner of a London suburb is some kind of gritty ghetto[.]" However, more than a consideration of "how ethnicity is used to bolster machismo," I would suggest that the novel proffers an inversion of this relationship: the wholesale importation of key features of American Hip Hop machismo offers a means by which these "mummy's boys" can attempt to navigate the difficult terrain of male adolescence in general, but more critically it offers tools to navigate the difficult terrain of male adolescence imbricated in the ever-emergent complexities of multiethnic Britain. Additionally, the boys grate against more than simply the infantalization of their mothers. They also grate against the larger, much more discomfiting framework of cultural expectations and social structures of which ethnicity, race, and gender are but relatively small loci of alienation and estrangement.

But these masculine postures—South Asian Hip Hop wannabes and the chavs who love them—are ultimately revealed as farce, something for which the ethnographic study that was the novel's previous incarnation perhaps lacked room. The dissertation that was to be the initial articulation of Malkani's observations about urban youth culture among adolescent South Asian men might have been unable to accommodate the nuanced commentary that the novel makes about the poser, the faker who slips into their midst and whose presence troubles empowerment and authority even as it faithfully reproduces the same scripts that South Asian men use to make intelligible their own ethnic presence in England. This means that the power of Hip Hop culture's contribution to the boys' effort entails great risk and ultimately cannot deliver. Note that this is an effort in which Malkani putatively participates as he includes himself in the "us" of the Londonstani, those who want to "reassimilate with mainstream society, but on [their] own terms and from a position of greater self-esteem—and how that bodes well for society"; the novel's principal contribution to an understanding of these relations is perhaps revelatory only of cultures of failure.[78] There is little increase in self-esteem. Jas' friends close ranks against him, galvanized by the cultural bonds with which they have such an ambivalent relationship: it is at Arun's funeral— a communal cultural gathering—that the reader learns of Jas' exile. Although its musical choices are marked by the features of the pop and Hip

Hop cultures they consume, the united front that Amit, Ravi, and Hardjit present at the funeral signifies a cultural retreat for the South Asian men in the novel as they define themselves principally as *desi*, ejecting the contamination of difference and aligning themselves along the vector of religion and ethnicity, and not that of the international masculinity to which Jas attempted to subscribe. The loss of self-esteem is particularly humbling for Jas who ends the novel alone in a hospital bed, having lost both friends and girlfriend. Yet he spurns his family's attempt to embrace him. His shameful name is one that he sees but still will not claim: it leaps off of the clipboard on which the hospital has written it and sticks, unwanted, to his appallingly white skin. In the end, far from redemptive or salutary, the flirtation with imported, fetishized cultures of difference leave the young men of Londonstani betrayed: Jas by the very diffidence that he admires in Samira; the crew by Jas' sneaking and meddling; Jas by the crew's violent expulsion of his (tenuous) presence; and all of them by the Hip Hop pose's hollow promise and the false pact they forge with it, along that creaking bridge across oceans that sways precariously under the heavy burdens they ask it to bear.

NOTES

1. Gautam Malkani's essay, *Londonstani*, interests itself in African American Hip Hop because it is these artists upon which the novel draws to establish its Hip Hop credentials. This analysis does not disavow the rich musical tradition of British Hip Hop, ably charted in Andy Wood's article "'Original London Style': London Posse and the Birth of British Hip Hop," *Atlantic Studies* 6, no. 2 (August 2009): 175–90. Wood maps the origins of a uniquely British form that draws upon British musical influences rather than mimicking US or Caribbean musical forms. In this way, British Hip Hop offers young black Londoners a cultural voice of their own—and its origin in the 1980s means that this is not a brand new development.

Meanwhile, Hip Hop's global spread offers a voice to many groups, many of which tap its political power as a potent articulation of counterhegemonic resistance. Kim Adam's case study examines its spread in the urban subcultures of Puerto Rico, Chile, and Japan, noting how local populations across the globe inflect music that expresses inner-city black experiences to speak to urban experiences around the world. A potent example of this is the Hungarian animated film *Nyócker!* (dubbed as *The District!*), a film in which adolescent members of the Romani, Hungarian, Chinese, and Arab communities square off against each other lyrically and finally engage in a cooperative relationship only when their community is threatened by George W. Bush. Elsewhere, G-Town, a Hip Hop crew from Shu'afat Refugee Camp in Jerusalem, model themselves after Tupac as their music gives voice to the plight of disenfranchised young Palestinian men. Hip Hop has also politicized the voices of Afro-Brazilians (Bernd Reiter and Gladys Mitchell, "Embracing Hip Hop as Their Own: Hip Hop and Black Racial Identity in Brazil," *Studies in Latin American Popular Culture* 27 [2008]: 151–165). In the US, Hip Hop provides South Asian Americans with tools to address their own "differential disempowerment" (Jeff Chang, "Race, Class, Conflict and Empowerment: On Ice Cube's 'Black Korea,'" *Amerasia Journal* 2 [1993]: 87. Cited in Ajay Nair and Murali Balaji, *Desi Rap : Hip-hop and South Asian America*, [Lanham, MD: Lexington Books, 2008], viii) a motive shared by the South Asian men in Gautam Malkani's *Londonstani* (New York: Penguin Press, 2006).

2. Imogen Tyler, "'Chav Mum, Chav Scum,'" *Feminist Media Studies* 8, no.1 (2008): 23.

3. A number of studies suggest that Britishness and whiteness are synonymous cultural values and that multicultural Britain has done little to disturb the connection between them—a connection that, I would add, becomes even more fixed the closer to Englishness the body drifts. See Alexandra Campbell's study, "Without 'You' I'm Nothing: Making White Britishness Online" for an updated interrogation of the manner in which whiteness and Britishness are codified as one and the same in everyday discourse (*Social Semiotics* 18, no. 4 [2008]: 409–24). See also the infamous Tram Rant: for over two minutes, a white British woman spews a lengthy, hate-filled diatribe that declares that none of the black and brown people on the tram are British and that they sully the cultural fabric of a pure England. A noteworthy feature of her rant—which quickly went viral—is that she interchangeably uses "English" and "British" as coterminous values signifying whiteness and cultural authenticity.

4. Paul Gilroy's *Postcolonial Melancholia* articulates the post-racial fantasy that potentially hinders meaningful advances in intercultural relations in Britain (New York: Columbia University Press, 2005).

5. Malkani, *Londonstani*, 67.

6. Ibid., 219.

7. Ibid., 220.

8. Ibid., 230.

9. For Neal Shoemaker, homegrown Harlem historian and proprietor of Harlem Heritage Tours, Rucker Park is an example of the tension between revisionist treatments of the past and gentrification in the present. The annual games at Rucker Park are a celebrated event in Hip Hop history, but currently are a source of neighborhood friction as the surrounding public housing buildings are sold to private developers and converted into expensive condominiums. According to Shoemaker, the culture war is fought on the battleground of noise ordinances and event permits (personal interview, 18 April 2009).

For a comprehensive history of Rucker Park, see Vincent M. Mallozzi, *Asphalt Gods: An Oral History of the Rucker Tournament* (New York: Doubleday, 2003).

10. A full linguistic analysis of *Londonstani* is beyond the scope of this essay. However, the novel's use of Hip Hop Nation Language and its normalization of the grammar and lexicon of African American linguistic forms point toward the same subversive linguistic politics that are at play in the United States. H. Samy Alim's work in *Roc the Mic Right: The Language of Hip Hop Culture* (New York: Routledge, 2006) provides a basis for interrogating the shape of Hip Hop linguistics in this text.

11. It is important to note that Malkani uses a range of lexicons to mark how hardcore the characters are. Ravi speaks in one, Hardjit in another, Jas in yet

another, and so on. On his website, Gautam Malkani provides a style guide, "Londonstani Style Guide," http://www.gautammalkani.com/style_guide.pdf (accessed April 22, 2014).
12. Bhanchod (also spelled bhenchod) means "sister-fucker" in Hindi.
13. Malkani, *Londonstani*, 207.
14. Ibid., 52.
15. Ibid., 55.
16. Ibid.
17. Ibid., 330.
18. Ibid., 329–31.
19. Ibid., 20.
20. Ibid., 55.
21. The yardie is a figuration of Caribbean masculine toughness, distinct from the Hip Hop gangsta by its affiliation with Jamaican cultural mannerisms.
22. Malkani, *Londonstani*, 118.
23. Alim, *Roc the Mic Right*, 113.
24. Malkani, *Londonstani*, 20.
25. Ibid., 19.
26. Ibid., 4.
27. Ibid., 58.
28. Ibid., 83.
29. Ibid., 182–87.
30. Richard Majors and Janet Mancini Billson, *Cool Pose: The Dilemmas of Black Manhood in America* (New York: Touchstone Books, 1992), 4–5.
31. Ibid., 69–85.
32. Ibid., 84.
33. Ibid., gora is a pejorative term for a white person.
34. "Batty boy" is a pejorative Jamaican patois term for homosexual men.
35. Among others. South Asian masculinity has its own fraught relationship with the homosexual body, as homosexual acts between consenting adults was finally decriminalized only in 2009 with the overturn of a statute in section 377 of the Indian Penal code. ("Gay sex decriminalised in India," *BBC News*, July 2, 2009, http://news.bbc.co.uk/2/hi/8129836.stm [accessed April 22, 2014]). Homophobic heterosexual machismo therefore has at least two cultural vectors in *Londonstani*; Hip Hop culture is but one.
36. Matthew Oware, "Brotherly Love: Homosociality and Black Masculinity in Gangsta Rap Music," *Journal of African American Studies* 15, no.1 (2011): 25.
37. Tim'm West, interview by Jeff Chang, *Total Chaos: The Art and Aesthetics of Hip Hop* (New York: Basic Civitas Books, 2006) 203.
38. Malkani, *Londonstani*, 60.
39. Oware, "Brotherly Love," 25–26.
40. In "Notes on a Native Son," Eldridge Cleaver will vilify James Baldwin along a similar vector of homophobic blackness, challenging Baldwin's claim to an authentic blackness by demonizing him as a homosexual who offers himself bodily to the appetites of white men (in *Soul on Ice* [New York: McGraw-Hill, 1999], 122–37).
41. Malkani, *Londonstani*, 5.
42. Oware, "Brotherly Love," 30.

43. While this essay conforms to the novel's spelling of Hardjit's name with a d, both Mr. Ashwood and Jas' father reveal that the d is an inclusion chosen by Harjit, who toughens his name by literally hardening it.
44. Dave Gunning and Abigail Ward, "Tracing Black America in Black British Culture." *Atlantic Studies* 6, no. 2 (August 2009): 152.
45. Ibid.
46. See Tariq Modood, "Political Blackness and British Asians," *Sociology* 28, no. 4 (1994): 859–876.
47. Malkani, *Londonstani*, 22. A "ponce" is a pejorative term for the snobby poser who apes the privilege and culture of the upper classes. However, it also carries with it nuances of the castigation of the homosexual male body, similarly to "faggot."
48. Ibid., 58.
49. Adam Briggs and Paul Cobley, "'I Like My Shit Sagged': Fashion, 'Black Musics' and Subcultures," *Journal of Youth Studies* 2, no. 3 (October 1999), 341.
50. Tony Mitchell, *Global Noise: Rap and Hip Hop Outside the USA* (Middletown, Conn: Wesleyan University Press, 2001) 92.
51. Ibid., 94.
52. Briggs and Cobley, "I Like My Shit Sagged," 344.
53. Malkani, *Londonstani*, 44.
54. Ibid.
55. Ibid., 24.
56. Hush mode: "when you get clowned and not have remark or comeback for that person. To be dumbfounded. Usually used when instigating or talking about a fight or argument" (Alim, *Roc the Mic Right*, 63).
57. Ibid., 65.
58. Here and elsewhere in this essay, I must stress that I qualify Ramy's acronym WME (white mainstream English) by adding that his study confines itself to US expressions of blackness. With Hip Hop's global reach, Ramy's rubric still applies, but juxtaposes itself against a range of linguistic modes: white mainstream British English, South Asian British English, as well as the other subcultural lexicons that proliferate in multicultural Britain.
59. Malkani, *Londonstani*, 326.
60. Tyler, "Chav Mum, Chav Scum," 25–26.
61. Malkani, *Londonstani*, 14–15, 24.
62. Ibid., 105.
63. Ibid., 107.
64. Ibid., 148.
65. Ibid., 158–160.
66. Ibid., 40.
67. Ibid., 61.
68. Ibid., 159.
69. Ibid., 286–307.
70. Ibid., 162.
71. Ibid., 163–64.
72. Briggs and Cobley, "I Like My Shit Sagged," 347.

73. And which is subject to commodification, reification, and endless, parodic repetition, as gleeful fans of this novel, *The Catherine Tate Show*, Ali G, and *Little Britain* will eagerly attest.
74. Where the gangsta is the Hip Hop badman, the badmash is the South Asian version.
75. Malkani, *Londonstani*, 273.
76. Majors and Billson, *Cool Pose*, 72.
77. At this meeting, British Prime Minister David Cameron announced the failure of the decades-old policy of state-sanctioned multicultural tolerance, citing terrorist attacks within Britain by British citizens as proof of that failure. In response, Cameron suggests that Britain "[make] sure that immigrants speak the language of their new home and ensur[e] that people are educated in the elements of a common culture and curriculum." He adds:

> Back home, we're introducing National Citizen Service: a two-month programme for sixteen-year-olds from different backgrounds to live and work together. I also believe we should encourage meaningful and active participation in society, by shifting the balance of power away from the state and towards the people. That way, common purpose can be formed as people come together and work together in their neighbourhoods. It will also help build stronger pride in local identity, so people feel free to say, "Yes, I am a Muslim, I am a Hindu, I am Christian, but I am also a Londoner or a Berliner too." It's that identity, that feeling of belonging in our countries, that I believe is the key to achieving true cohesion.

(David Cameron, "PM's Speech at Munich Security Conference," Number 10, 5 February 2011, https://www.gov.uk/government/speeches/pms-speech-at-munich-security-conference, [accessed 5 June 2014].)

78. Gautam Malkani, "About Londonstani," http://www.gautammalkani.com/about_londonstani.htm (accessed June 5, 2014).

Figure 11.1.   Almost Native
Computer Image, art by John Jennings

11

✛

"A True and Faithful Account of Mr. Ota Benga the Pygmy, written by M. Berman, Zookeeper"

Adam Mansbach

I am Mordecai Berman, a zookeeper. Morty, they call me at the zoo. Also shit-shoveler. Of the two, shit-shoveler I prefer. I have been keeping clean the Primates House eight years now, and though I have no fancy education to prove it, I know more about the animals than probably anyone. Simply from spending time. What else I got to do? Sit in my cold-water flat, smelled up the same way every night from the wilted carrots and chicken fat of my neighbors? Chase after dames, on a crap-carrier's salary? Maybe sit in synagogue? To this I say: ha ha, good one my friend.[1]

I bought tonight this notebook, and in it will keep record of what is to begin tomorrow at the zoo: a very curious affair. Who knows, perhaps I sell my story, if I make one, to the New York Times. Probably not, I think—already I am babbling on a like a babushka, saying nothing.

So: tomorrow arrives at the Bronx Zoological Park Mr. Ota Benga the Pygmy, the great success (I wonder whether he would say so) of last year's World's Fair in St. Louis. He is brought by the great explorer Samuel Verner, the same man who took Mr. Benga from his home in the Belgian Congo together with some others of the Pygmy's tribe. As reported by the NYT—which is daffy for both Benga and Verner, so you see my plan is not entirely absurd—Mr. Benga returned from the successful hunting of an elephant to find his whole village destroyed, including sad to say his wife and child. Thus was he agreeable to Mr. Verner's entreaties to board the great ship. Just how the village was destroyed, and what form of entreaty was employed by the Man of Science, the NYT leaves to the imagination of the reader.

In St. Louis, Mr. Benga was displayed in the Fair's Anthropology Department, as part of the Exhibition of Savages. Those who believe like Mr. Darwin that we come of the monkeys have lately decided that the different races of man derive from different races of monkey. They hold the Negro to be of the Gorilla, an animal considered strong of body but weak of mind. The Oriental, they have paired with the Orangutan, and the White with the cleverest of apes, the Chimpanzee. They further believe that under Mr. Darwin's idea of Evolution man's inferior species will die off, and in particular the Negro. When slavery ended, they were certain this would right away begin. I do not know how they square the fact that it has not with the continuation of the theory, but then true Men of Science are in many ways a mystery.

I will now put aside Mr. Benga for only a moment to record my own lowly opinion of these ideas: it is clear to me that the men behind them have never been to a zoo. If they had, they would not be so eager either to compare themselves to Chimps, or Negroes to Gorillas. The Gorilla, you see, is the most lovely of all Apes. He is quiet, thoughtful, he takes care of his babies and his fellows. His eyes, when you look into them, you see yourself there. The Gorilla knows sadness. He knows he is a prisoner, and yet does not hate his jailer. Perhaps you cannot know what I mean if you have only, like most people, been to the zoo for an afternoon's fun with your girl or children.

The Chimpanzee, meanwhile, is by nature an asshole. He throws his feces by the handful—does not pluck them from the ground, mind you, but defecates directly into his palm for this purpose and no other. He attacks his cohort without reason, quarrels with him all the day. Alone among apes, he has been known even to murder.

Sometimes, it is true, he seems the most human to me, but only on days when my landlord has threatened to shut off my heat, or a pretty girl, when I smile at her on the subway she turns away, or prankster kids break into the zoo's sanitation room and knock over my shitcans.

To resume: in St. Louis Mr. Benga was tested in his intelligence, to see how he rated against defective Whites. He was tested also for the speed of his reaction to pain, and for his athletic ability, which was found to be in severe lack. Of this last I remember reading with some confusion, for the Pygmies were made to compete in games we here have made up: the shot-put, the javelin, and other such contests of Track and Field. How a man who has killed an elephant could be in so bad a shape, I cannot fathom. But I imagine Honus Wagner might fare just as badly if he were stripped naked, dropped into the middle of the jungle, and told to kill himself some dinner.

"A True and Faithful Account of Mr. Ota Benga the Pygmy" 171

When Mr. Benga was not being tested, he sat in a mud-field, outside a shack constructed for him. Occasionally the Anthropologists arranged between the Pygmies a mud fight for the enjoyment of the Public. Of this, the NYT gave a picture. Verner was quoted in the report that followed, wondering whether the Pygmy was highest ape or lowest man. He then suggested that the Bushmen of Africa be collected into reservations and the continent colonized and run by Whites, as the Bushmen have no religion, no tradition, and can neither remember the past nor contemplate the future. He was described in the report as an exceedingly Christian person, a lover of all creatures and one of the few men who can accept the ideas of Mr. Darwin and of Scripture both, no problem. He will make a speech tomorrow, I am sure. A man like Verner, that is what he does. I expect I may meet him, as Mr. Benga is to make his home in the Primate House.

* * *

The Pygmy is four feet eleven inches tall, twenty-three years of age, and weighs one hundred and three pounds. He was presented today by Verner to our Director Hornaday; the word around the zoo is that the explorer has fallen on hard times, and lacks the money to keep Mr. Benga himself. To this, at least, I can relate.

The crowd was the biggest we have ever drawn, I am sure in great part because of today's NYT headline, "Bushman shares a cage with the Bronx Park apes." Verner I did not meet, though I did shake the hand of Mr. Henry Fairfield Osborn, an Evolutionist who made some opening remarks. I have copied into my notebook one of his statements. Through Mr. Benga, he said, Modern Man will have "access to the wild in order to recharge itself." This I liked, as I have often felt recharged through visiting with the Apes and other Animals. Then Mr. Osborn declared that "The great race"—he means the White—"needs a place to turn to now and then where, rifle in hand, it can hone its instincts."

I myself understand this to be merely a lofty way of speaking, but still its effect on me was discomforting. I do not hope to see rifles in the hands of any visitors to the Bronx Zoo, and I'm sure even Mr. Hornaday, although he nodded his head all throughout the speech, would agree.

My own first glimpse of Mr. Benga came together with the crowd's. He was brought forward by Mr. Verner, and at a signal from the explorer, the Pygmy opened wide his mouth so as to show off to the crowd his teeth, which are filed down into sharp points. This the crowd seemed to relish, for Mr. Benga's teeth were met with loud applause.

Mr. Benga's contact with Whites has contaminated him in the eyes of his people, Mr. Verner said, for when he brought the Pygmy home from St. Louis, his tribesmen would not speak to him. They believe he stands with the race of white warlocks who separate men's voices from their souls. This is what Edison cylinder-phonographs mean to them: that the body sits and listens to the soul speak.

Mr. Benga watched the explorer closely as he held forth, and if I had not known different, I would have sworn he understood the words, and pitied himself. He is to me a strange looking fellow, the darkest and tiniest I have ever seen, with hairless skin and an odd sense of balance about him, as if he is leaning always forward into a strong wind. But I do not look at Mr. Benga and wonder what he is, for that is clear. He is a man. A man who is in a very bad way.

* * *

It was not until this morning at seven a.m. that I was able to make the acquaintance of the Pygmy. He has been provided, as companions, with an African parrot and an Orangutan named Dohong, the both of them also donated by Verner. I found all three asleep when I arrived, each in a separate corner of the cage. It is furnished lightly, and contains a sleeping pallet, a blanket, and some bales of hay.

Mr. Benga did not stir as I went about my morning duties, no doubt worn down by yesterday's crowds, which stayed on well after the zoo would normally have closed. Verner, Osborn, and Hornaday set out to lead him on a tour of the grounds when the speech-making was concluded, and the visitors swarmed around them in such a density that the trip took hours. Great laughter boomed forth often, at what I do not know. Today Mr. Benga is to be kept locked up, and if he seems able to handle it, he may be walked again in the afternoon, accompanied by several keepers.

But when I entered his cage, the Pygmy was immediately to his feet, and the Orangutan as well—both of them regarding me with no small fear. Mr. Benga's hands stayed to his sides, an odd thing for a man if he feels threatened. Unless he has learned that raising them will make the danger worse.

"I mean no harm," I said, and found myself bending at the knees, in the manner almost of a lady's curtsy, to speak to him. "It is an honor to meet you, Mr. Benga."

I do not know what response I expected. The Pygmy looked to the Orangutan, the Orangutan to the Pygmy. First the one, and then the other, bared his teeth. On the Orangutan, I have seen the gesture many times and know it to be harmless. On the man, I decided to believe it was a smile.

"I am Mr. Berman," I told him, and reached out my hand. He took a step back, and so did I. In a cage, there is only so much room. "I am a Jew," was my next remark. I cannot say why these words leaped out of me.

Mr. Benga made some response in his own language. The effect of my presence had diminished, for his body seemed to loosen, to relax. The Orangutan Dohong, at this point, swung himself over and wrapped his arms around my legs. I scratched his head, as this the Orangutans enjoy.

Mr. Benga watched, and again his lips peeled back and the teeth came into view. This time, I was sure it was a smile.

"Are you cold?" I asked, for Mr. Benga had when I entered been wrapped in his blanket, and now the cold air of the morning was causing him to shiver.

I read back my account and realize I have failed to discuss Mr. Benga's attire: he is clad only in a sort of loincloth, to which has been added a canvas vest and a straw hat. It is a wholly insufficient costume, and the vest and hat are badly oversized, and make Mr. Benga appear even smaller. Whoever gave these items to him, Verner I suppose, gave little care to the matter, or else little care to the Pygmy's comfort.

"I will get you some better clothes," I told him. "They will be too large, but better than what you have got." With that, I disentangled myself from the Orangutan and repaired to the sanitation room, where I fetched for Mr. Benga a spare uniform. It is a one-piece, such as I wear, due for the laundry but not badly soiled.

I returned to the cage and presented him with it, but Mr. Benga could not be convinced to put it on. It took me the better part of an hour to demonstrate to him just how stepping into the suit might be accomplished. I do not know whether his reluctance was due to mistrust. Perhaps he simply found the garment confining and prefers to be cold. In any event, no sooner did he have the thing on than I was called away, to attend to shit-related matters in the smaller primate cages. When I returned to Mr. Benga, another keeper, a man called Stanton, was in the cage, yanking roughly the Pygmy's limbs from the jumper.

"What's the big idea," I called. "Hey, Stanton! What gives?"

Stanton looked up. He is a big, red-faced man, a drinker. "This your idea of a joke, Morty?" he replied. "I been trying to get him undressed fifteen minutes already."

"He's cold," I said.

"The people don't wanna see him dressed up like a zookeep!" Stanton shouted. "Hornaday's fit to be tied. You might as well start puttin' dinner jackets on the Chimps."

It was at this moment that Mr. Benga, having reached his limit after a morning—a life!—of being pulled and prodded about, managed to free his arm from the suit, and swinging it clumsily through the air, elbow Stanton squarely in the eye. I do not think it was deliberate, but Mr. Benga, seeing what he had done, scampered away and, grinning mightily, hid behind Dohong across the cage. He then removed the suit himself.

"Jesus Christ," said Stanton, holding a palm over the eye. "That nigger bastard hit me."

It was at this moment that the gates opened and the crowds began to stream in. Shouts of "Where's the Pygmy," and "In the monkey house," filled up the air. Stanton ducked out of the cage, and behind me surged a mass of eager visitors. Mr. Benga peered out at them and then, to my surprise, he emerged from his cover and walked straight to the front bars of the cage.

"The Pygmy!" And up went a cheer. A hand grabbed at his leg, and Mr. Benga pulled back, though he did not retreat. Soon hands were poking through the bars all over. Someone threw inside a shoe, and Mr. Benga picked it up and sat upon the floor, turning it over in his hands with fascination. This prompted sustained laughter, and soon more objects were being tossed between the bars for his consideration: compact-mirrors, handkerchiefs, even an empty billfold. Mr. Benga's every action produced great response, and this frantic attention continued, without pause, throughout the day.

* * *

Things at the zoo are taking a sinister turn. Today's NYT reported on the objections of two parties to the exhibition of Mr. Benga: one is a delegation of Colored Ministers. Their leader is a Reverend Gordon, who told the NYT, "our race is depressed enough without exhibiting one of us with the apes. We think we are worthy of being considered human beings, with souls." They have asked Director Hornaday to call off the exhibit, and he has put them off, saying that the Zoological Society supports his efforts. They have requested also to meet with Mayor McClellan, and he has responded that he is too busy. Meanwhile, a separate body of White Clergy has also taken exception, on the grounds that the exhibit of Mr. Benga promotes Evolution at the expense of their Christian beliefs. Director Hornaday will meet with them tonight.

It may be, though, that the exhibit comes to an end for reasons distinct from all of the above. This morning Hornaday gave Mr. Benga a crudely fashioned bow and arrow, and encouraged the Pygmy to shoot it at a target set up in his cage, for the enjoyment of the tourists. This in addition to the rubber balls, mouth organs, and other toys now piled in Mr. Benga's cage, gifts from zoo and visitors alike.

Can Hornaday truly be so doltish? It was no great surprise to me that Mr. Benga, by afternoon, had begun to use the bow to fire arrows at the most obnoxious of the visitors standing before his cage, molesting him and making him the butt of jokes at every turn. He is an excellent shot, and clever enough to stand at the back of his cage when he shoots so that the missiles have some time to build up speed before they meet their targets.

A great outcry has gone up, and though no one was seriously injured, the bow and arrow have been seized. Many take the Pygmy's aggression to be proof of his savagery, but to me it is something quite different: proof against those who hold that Mr. Benga is mentally deficient, that he cannot learn. He is learning very well. He is learning to hate them.

* * *

Hornaday today gave in somewhat to the pressures of the ministers, both White and Colored, and allowed Mr. Benga to spend much of the day out of his cage. He was this afternoon dressed in a white suit and taken for a walk. Myself, Stanton, and two other keepers were responsible for holding back from him the crowd that followed. Mr. Benga was brought first to the Elephant House, and there photographed for the newspapers with a newly born Pachyderm. We then proceeded to the house of the lesser primates, where Mr. Benga, with evident joy, helped us to feed the small monkeys. He also took the chance to feed himself, to the crowd's great jeering delight, though it was only some vegetables such as any one of them might himself eat for dinner.

Managing the crowd was a job more suited to police than shit-shovelers. The tourists poke relentlessly at Mr. Benga, try to trip him up when he walks. Some gather pebbles from the pathways and pelt him. Others simply want to touch his skin or rub his woolly head, which is level with most men's chests and thus difficult for him to protect.

At the Primate House, Mr. Benga grabbed off of a table a small knife, and with it in hand dashed out of doors. The crowds fell back as he swung the blade before him in great arcs. It is a dull thing, used by us for cutting through twine rope and such, but still the spectators fled in panic. Mr. Benga ran aimlessly about the grounds for thirty minutes, as keepers and crowd followed. Finally, seeing him desperate, I walked slowly up to Mr. Benga and removed the instrument from his hand. He gave it willingly, as if thankful to be relieved of a burden, and collapsed to the ground at my feet. This earned me great praise, and a fellow from the NYT asked me my name and position. Which is a considerable thing, but little did I enjoy it.

I imagine as I write this the fuss tomorrow's newspaper will make over the incident, and fully expect to wake up to a headline of the order of "Bushman Tries to Kill." When the truth is that the only person Mr. Benga would have hurt, had we let him keep his weapon, is himself. It is now morning. The exhibit is to be shut down, and Mr. Benga will this evening be turned over to the custody of the Howard Colored Orphan

Asylum in Brooklyn. My name appears twice in the NYT, and I am identified as "courageous."

* * *

It is one-and-a-half months since Mr. Benga left the zoo, and today I had my first news of him, courtesy the NYT in a short account some pages removed from any position of prominence, "Ota Benga Now a Real Colored Gentleman; Little African Pygmy Being Taught Ways of Civilization."

He is said to be learning English, slowly but with promise, and to have taken up Christianity. His teeth, a dentist has capped.

It is my intention to visit him tomorrow. I hope he will remember me, and not too harshly.

* * *

Mr. Benga received me in the sitting room of the Howard Asylum, a well-appointed brownstone located in the neighborhood of Fort Greene. He greeted me attired in a shirt and a short necktie of the type worn commonly by young boys. His hair has been shorn close to the scalp, and his first words, upon recognizing me, were "Friend. God bless you." I shook his small hand, which he surrendered calmly to the purpose, and we sat down to tea served by the house Matron, a handsome colored woman by the name of Robinson.

"Friend," Mr. Benga said again, smiling. The difference affected by the tooth-capping was striking and agreeable.

"Yes," I said. "I am your friend."

Mr. Benga nodded, then shook his head from side to side. "Zoo," he said. "No God bless zoo. No God bless."

"I'm sorry," I said. "You should not have been there, Mr. Benga."

"No God bless."

"No," I said. "I suppose not."

We sipped our tea, Mr. Benga using both hands to bring the cup to his mouth.

"Tea God bless," he said. I nodded.

"Ota go home," he said after a moment. "My home God bless."

"Your home is beautiful, I am sure."

"Yes," said Mr. Benga. "Friend."

"A True and Faithful Account of Mr. Ota Benga the Pygmy"   177

We sat together one hour, me asking Mr. Benga various small questions and the Pygmy answering with different combinations of the words he knew: zoo, home, God bless, no, yes, Bible, please, thank you, friend, and so forth. The bar of chocolate I had brought him he had no use for, but after I removed it from my coat pocket, he embarked on a thorough investigation of my person, and was happy to find a package of the cheap cigarettes I am accustomed to puffing at.

"You smoke?" I asked him.

"Smoke," the Pygmy agreed. He reached into the pack and extracted a cigarette with a nimbleness to his fingers that was quite impressive, and we sat smoking. Mr. Benga held his fag with all five fingers, blowing into the end as often as he inhaled from it and taking much interest in the clouds we two created. I blew a smoke ring and he leaped up from the couch, delighted. I tried to teach him the trick, with little luck. His laughter made me laugh, and mine him, and so smoke and laughter replaced conversation until Matron Robinson reappeared to escort Mr. Benga to his next engagement. A Colored minister had arrived, and was waiting to see him in the study.

* * *

Mr. Benga was taken last week to Lynchburg, Virginia, there to work at a tobacco factory and be further tutored in religion and the English tongue at a local seminary. His departure was sudden, so sudden that I learned of it from Matron Robinson upon arriving at the Howard Asylum to call on my friend—in advance even of the NYT, which only yesterday published an account.

There had been an incident, Matron Robinson informed me, involving another of the Howard charges. Creola, the young lady is called. She and Mr. Benga had become close friends—here Matron Robinson gave me a queer sideways look, to be sure I understood what she meant by friends. The only thing for it was to remove one of the parties, before the two parties became three. Mr. Benga, it was decided, would benefit greatly from the open air and natural beauty of the South.

* * *

I have spent all day attempting to locate this notebook, and finally unearthed it from a steamer trunk in the basement of the house in which I now keep an apartment, in return for my services as superintendent to this and other properties. I have written nothing here for some nine years, as there has been little in that time to report of the life of Mr. Ota Benga the Pygmy. It is my sad duty to say, that is no longer the case. Today, at an age of thirty-three, my friend ended his life.

By all accounts, Mr. Benga's mood had for some months been quite black. He had learned to read and write, and had taken up research on the cost of a steamship ticket to Africa, finally concluding that he would never be able to afford one. He could not speak of this without beginning to cry.

This despite the fact that the Colored community of Lynchburg had accepted Mr. Benga as one of their own. He was often entrusted to look after their children, and enjoyed leading groups of young people on forest expeditions. He was a great favorite of theirs, although the children considered him over-protective when it came to shepherding them through the wild.

The moments preceding his death, the NYT describes as follows: Mr. Benga, after an excursion, refused the urging of his small companions to take them back into the woods, and instead sent them away. When the children were out of sight, he removed the caps from his teeth, brought to his chest a revolver borrowed from a neighbor woman, and sent a bullet straight into his heart.

The article concludes with a quote from Director Hornaday, who remains in place as the top man at the esteemed Bronx Zoological Park. It is a shame, Hornaday says, that the Pygmy would rather die than work for a living.

NOTE

1. Reprint from Adam Mansbach, "A True and Faithful Account of Mr. Ota Benga the Pygmy," written by M. Berman, Zookeeper, http://adammansbach.com/other/otabenga.html (accessed April 22, 2014).

IV

CULTURE OF PERSONALITY

Part IV features several academic essays and one keynote speech/talk. Each selection explores how the projection of artistic personas, especially the constructions of racial identity that inform these projections, contributes to the popular appeal of these figures across mainstream media platforms. Sean Springer's insightful exploration of "Richard Pryor's Pain" reveals the subtle comedic strategies that framed Pryor's craft in ways that were both explicit in a racial sense but palatable and accessible across racial boundaries. Springer interprets part of Pryor's genius as his unique ability to articulate the existential pain that is a consequence of white supremacy for black folk, in ways that at once make that pain undeniable and real for all audiences of American popular culture. Wilfredo Gomez's paper on Jay-Z's major television interviews/appearances serves as a discourse analysis that unpacks the rapper's "cool pose," especially as it applies to his public presentations of himself at the height of his artistic career. For Gomez, Jay-Z's cool pose on television is a complex negotiation of where he has come from—that is, the Marcy Housing Projects in Brooklyn, New York— and where he has arrived as a transcendent Hip Hop figure in American popular culture. Carrie Walker's essay on Janelle Monae's *Metropolis* is an in-depth examination of how Monae deploys the concepts of the cyborg, Afrofuturism, and the form of the neo-slave narrative to critique the limitations designed for black women artists. Walker's reading, viewing, and listening of/to *Metropolis* puts into bold relief the "matrix" of race, gender, and popular culture and the significance of black women's artistic genealogy in the discourses on identity politics. Finally, Michael Eric Dyson's speech, "Dreams of the Drum," brilliantly teases out the metaphorical expansiveness of the drum as black art—in all of its manifestations: rapping, preaching, painting, politicking, and singing. According to Dyson, the tensions between popular black art and issues of representation are at the very heart of the African American experience.

Figure 12.1. Tears of a Clown
Computer Image, art by John Jennings

12

✢

Richard Pryor's Pain
From Stand-Up Comedy to Hollywood Film

Sean Springer

Critics and biographers tend to divide the career path of American actor-comedian Richard Pryor (1940–2005) into three stages: (1) his start in the early 1960s as a stand-up who performed the stereotypical Negro character on nationally televised variety shows; (2) his reinvention, beginning in the late 1960s, as a racially conscious comedian who, despite his aggressively political routines, gained a mass following among diverse audiences; and (3) his undistinguished film career in which he starred in a string of popular yet critical flops. Regarding his success as a stand-up, critics are unanimously gushing—Comedy Central placed Pryor at number one on their list of the top one hundred comedians of all time. As for his film career, the general consensus is that Pryor compromised his integrity. "He certainly didn't work hard to make us believe that he was anyone other than himself as he walked through shameful duds like *Adios Amigo*," Hilton Als writes in the *New Yorker*. "On the other hand, his fans paid all the love and all the money in the world to see him be himself: they fed his vanity, and his vanity kept him from being a great actor."[1] Whoopi Goldberg explains in the BBC documentary *Life of Pryor* that "if he had had more control over himself, [his film career] might have gone in a different direction. And the movies that he chose, and the way that he went about them, and the discipline that he didn't have, made it a little harder to watch on occasion."[2] Among his "motivations" to accept a demeaning role in *The Toy* (1982), scholar Bambi Haggins assumes, was "a salary that would continue to support his self-destructive lifestyle."[3]

Comedian Paul Mooney, Pryor's long-time friend and collaborator, calls Pryor "the funniest man America has ever seen," and adds, "But I know he is a junkie first, and a genius second."[4] Pryor himself in his autobiography claims that a four million dollar return, "more than any black actor had ever been paid,"[5] persuaded him to appear in a film he felt was "a piece of shit," *Superman III* (1983).

Such claims, however accurate they may or may not be, nevertheless divert attention away from the racism Pryor endured throughout his career. As such, in this chapter I want to move away from blaming Pryor to focus on how the respective conventions of stand-up comedy, celebrity journalism, and Hollywood film affected Pryor's public image. Pryor performed stand-up for three decades; however, I will limit my analysis to those stand-up albums and concert films from the mid-1970s to the early-1980s that represent his career's peak: the albums *That Nigger's Crazy* (1974), *Is It Something I Said?* (1975), and *Bicentennial Nigger* (1976); and the concert films *Richard Pryor: Live in Concert* (1979) and *Richard Pryor: Live on the Sunset Strip* (1982). During this same era, Pryor starred in more than a dozen films, two of which went on to become huge box-office successes: *Silver Streak* (1976) and *Stir Crazy* (1980), the latter the third-highest grossing film of 1980. Although Pryor did star in the more racially conscious comedy *Which Way Is Up?* (1977) and the drama *Blue Collar* (1978), Pryor's performances in *Silver Streak* and *Stir Crazy* became the model for the undistinguished film roles in the 1980s for which he is now largely remembered.[6] I will therefore restrict my focus of his screen persona to these two films.

In opposition to Als, who claims that Pryor "didn't work hard to make us believe that [in certain film roles] he was anyone other than himself," I argue that certain racist social conventions enabled the film audience to construct a simplified version of Pryor's "self" far removed from any "real" Richard Pryor. Pryor did portray richly nuanced characters, not only in *Which Way Is Up?* and *Blue Collar* but also in the Billie Holiday biopic *Lady Sings the Blues* (1972) and the loosely autobiographical *Jo Jo Dancer, Your Life Is Calling* (1986), but if box office returns are any indication, audiences far preferred Pryor in roles that fulfilled racial stereotypes. Arguably, the flat characters in the relatively successful *Silver Streak* and *Stir Crazy* are not indicative of Pryor's "self," but rather of a depoliticized screen persona that appealed to a mass audience. This persona differs radically from the "self" that emerges from an analysis of his stand-up career, in which Pryor described the pain he experienced as a result of racial oppression. Pryor's dichotomous career paths reinforced Walter Benjamin's thesis that "the place of the intellectual in the class struggle can only be determined, or better still chosen, on the basis of his position within the production process."[7] When Pryor retained control over his public image, as he did in his stand-up comedy, he convinced audiences to take his pain seriously—to see it as a product of his oppressed social position. But when his public image fell into the hands of the press and the film industry, we see not Benjamin's intellectual artistry but instead what Max Horkheimer and Theodor W. Adorno deemed the culture industry's prime output: "pseudoindividuality" in the service of "detoxifying tragedy."[8] When framed by press coverage and stereotyping film roles, Pryor's public image detoxified the tragedy of racism by reinforcing the hegemonic belief that an African American man has no right to indict underlying societal pressures and inequalities. As Richard Delgado explains to his professor in *The Rodrigo Chronicles: Conversations about America and Race*, this belief stems from the illusion of racial equality which "prevents white folks from seeing how their own system advantages them, indeed it enables their more aggressive elements to blame minorities for their plight."[9] Hollywood catered to this belief by casting Pryor in biracial buddy films (four with Gene Wilder) where Pryor's pain is not only a product of his own purportedly self-destructive behavior, but he is also deemed unworthy or unwilling to feel this pain as deeply as his white counterpart. This narrative pattern enabled audiences to live vicariously through Pryor's exoticized body before going on to dismiss him as an undisciplined African American male who had only his own apparent shortcomings to blame for any suffering he may have endured.

What follows is a three-part analysis of Pryor's career, focusing on his stand-up performances, press coverage, and film roles. Pryor worked simultaneously as a stand-up comedian and a Hollywood film actor for most of his career, but in order to differentiate between the impact each had on his public image, I begin by addressing separately the political content of Pryor's stand-up comedy before moving on to deal with its depoliticization in the press and on film.

PRYOR'S PAIN STANDS UP

A key distinction between Pryor's stage and screen personas is how each grapples with the pain resulting from racial oppression. On stage, Pryor consistently references pain inflicted by white supremacist ideology. As dozens of examples from his act demonstrate, Pryor clearly served as an exception to bell hooks's observation that

> Black males are unable to fully articulate and acknowledge the pain in their lives. They do not have a public discourse or audience within racist society that enables them to give their pain a hearing. Sadly, black men often evoke racist rhetoric that identifies the black male as animal, speaking of them-

selves as "endangered species," as "primitive," in their bid to gain recognition of their suffering.[10]

We see a stark counterexample in *Live on the Sunset Strip*, in which Pryor tells the audience that

> Racism is a bitch. You know, I mean, white people, it fucks you up, but what it does to black people is a bitch, because no matter—it's hard enough being a human being. It's really fuckin' hard enough just to be that. Right, just to go through everyday life without murdering a motherfucker. It's hard enough just to walk through life . . . decent . . . as a person. But here, there's another element added to it when you're black. The mothers've got that little edge on us—*it's enough to make ya crazy*. It's if you're in an argument with another man and he may be white, but it's man on man, and for a minute the shit get rough, and he ends up calling you "nigger!" You gotta go, "Aw shit. Fuck. Now I ain't no man no more, *nigger*, now I got to argue with that shit. Throw my balance all off." But you know, it's an ugly thing. I hope someday they give it up.[11]

As this example shows, Pryor did not reduce his pain to a punchline. Functioning as a coping mechanism, the humor arose instead from highlighting the absurdity of racism—by taking the banality of hatred and making it funny. For example, on *That Nigger's Crazy*, he says,

> Cops put a hurtin' on your ass. They really degrade you. White folks don't believe that shit though. Don't believe the cops degrade—"Oh, come on, those beatings? Those people were resisting arrest! I'm tired of this harassment of police officers." Cause the police live in your neighborhood! See? And you be knowing them as "Officer Timson. Hello, Officer Timson, going bowling tonight? Yes, ah, nice pinto you have. Ha-ha-ha." Niggers don't know 'em like that. See white folks get a ticket, they pull over, they're like, "Oh, hi officer. Yes! Glad to be of help." Nigger got to be talking about "I-AM-REACHING-INTO-MY-POCKET-FOR-MY-LICENSE! . . . Cause I don't want to be no motherfucking accident."[12]

Routines like this one helped Pryor earn a reputation, as *Rolling Stone* journalist David Felton noted in 1974, "as a rare and serious innovator, a perfectionist in the arts of comedy, mime, drama and, as the students at San Jose State College recently put it, in awarding him an honorary PhD, 'black street history.'"[13] By the early-1970s, Pryor had already revolutionized stand-up, having become the first black performer not only to appeal to white audiences (as had Dick Gregory, Redd Foxx, Flip Wilson, and Bill Cosby), but also to do so in an unwavering political manner. Pryor's achievements are well-documented by Mel Watkins and Bambi Haggins in their respective histories of African American humor, also by the authors who contributed to *Richard Pryor: The Life and Legacy of a "Crazy"*

Black Man, a collection of scholarly essays which celebrates Pryor as a champion of black liberation, a social critic, a folklorist of African American culture, a philosopher, and a foul-mouthed poet.[14]

While no one has explored whether stand-up comedy is a more inherently political art form than, say, Hollywood film, a slowly growing body of academic writing suggests that stand-up may have offered Pryor a powerful vehicle for dissent. In one of the first scholarly essays on stand-up, Lawrence Mintz praised the generic stand-up comedian for his "role as our comic spokesperson, as a mediator, an 'articulator' of our culture, and as our contemporary *anthropologist*."[15] Since then, many have paid homage to the transgressive performances of Lenny Bruce,[16] George Carlin,[17] and Bill Hicks,[18] among others. Although Philip Auslander did condemn mainstream stand-up for its endorsement of "conservative and conformist values,"[19] it is not hard to see that stand-up has provided individual performers like Pryor the kind of creative autonomy they would never see on a Hollywood film set. Relatively free from the economic pressures, ideological conventions, and professional hierarchies that restrict any enterprising film performer, the stand-up has much more opportunity for critical self-expression.

Regarding stand-up's formal properties, the quality of liveness may have catalyzed Pryor's rhetorical success insofar as the intimate and transient relationship a performer has with a live audience makes it harder for the audience to identify the performer with a stereotype and thus makes it easier for the performer to present him or herself as a uniquely political subject. As Peggy Phelan argues, live performance "in a strict ontological sense is nonreproductive"[20] and thus gives the performer the opportunity to frame his or her body as unique and irreducible to "a vertical hierarchy of value."[21] Although Pryor's performances *were* reproduced through albums and concert films, the audience heard laughing would have influenced audiences listening and watching at home (much in the way a laugh track would) to see Pryor as a politicized subject. As opposed to Hollywood film, which cannot mediate an intimate performance between a performer and a specific audience, stand-up comedy allows performers to drop the fourth wall and interact as a subject (not an object) with the audience. By conveying his feelings of exasperation, Pryor used the intimate relationship comics have with their audiences to develop a political subjectivity. These include his exasperation with respect to a range of issues. Concerning the lack of African American characters in Hollywood, Pryor concludes, after seeing no African Americans in the futuristic drama, *Logan's Run*, that there are no plans for black people to exist in the future. With respect to racial injustice in the south, Pryor joked that the criminal justice system gives out time, that is, jail sentences, as if they were giving out lunch. And in comedic narratives related to the censorship of sexual discourse, Pryor argued that you would be chastised for talking about "fucking" but if you talked about violence or killing, that was acceptable in terms of American censorship. In each example, by framing his pain within a political context, Pryor discouraged the audience from indulging their tendency to reduce African American performers to stereotypes.

In his history of stand-up in the 1970s, Richard Zoglin breaks down Pryor's rhetorical effectiveness. He writes, "The black comics who reached out to white audiences before [Pryor] tried to foster racial understanding by stressing how much alike we are. Pryor rubbed our noses in the differences—and made us feel their universality."[22] By "[rubbing] our noses in the differences" between people, Pryor was depriving certain groups of people of their dignity. In fact, his unique approach to comedy lay partially in that he deprived *everybody* of dignity. He contrasted the social realities of racism with his own idealized perspective, in which people are not only created equal, they are all equally base. Viewed side-by-side, Pryor's character sketches constituted an appealing utopia where every conceivable object was equally oblivious to its apparent baseness. Moreover, as he described this utopia, Pryor never privileged one object over another—in his view, they were all equally base. This is a key point made by John Limon in *Stand-up Comedy in Theory, or, Abjection in America*, in which Limon observes that during *Richard Pryor: Live in Concert*, "Whites and blacks laugh together and they laugh for the same duration."[23] Limon refers to the opening minutes when Pryor "divides" the audience by distinguishing between the black and white members:

> Who is at risk? First, the blacks: "You niggers takin' a chance in Long Beach, Jack." But no—a Richard Pryor concert is not white country, even at the Long Beach venue. "This is the fun part for me when the white people coming back after the intermission and find that niggers stole their seats. [One of Pryor's white voices, nasal:] 'Weren't we sitting there, dear?' [Black gangster voice:] 'Well, you ain't sittin' here now, motherfucker.'"[24]

Pryor invokes "a cliché of black lawlessness and vulgarity"[25] but also announces that the white members are returning not just from any old place—they're apparently coming back from "the bathroom." By associating the black members with a base stereotype and the white members with a base activity, Pryor equalizes them.[26]

Homi Bhabha's writings on the stereotype help to clarify Zoglin's reference to the "universality" of our differences. "[T]he stereotype," Bhabha explains, "is a form of knowledge and identification that vacillates between what is always 'in place,' already known, and something that must be anxiously repeated."[27] In contrast to the minstrel show's static stereotype, Pryor's routine consisted of dozens upon dozens of impersonations, the majority of which were based on his experiences growing up as a member of the African American working class. His range of characters—which include the junkie, the wino, the storyteller, the minister, the prostitute, the mother, the father, the lousy fighter, among many, many others—subverted the minstrel show's cruel stereotype by supplanting what Bhabha might call its "fixity." By moving rapidly from one character impression to the next, Pryor turned his performance into a site where notions of an African American identity could not be reduced to a singular, "fixed" concept. And by stressing the irreducible differences between each character, Pryor participated in the kind of discourse Bhabha himself encourages:

> What is denied the colonial subject, both as colonizer and colonized, is that form of negation which gives access to the recognition of difference. It is the possibility of difference and circulation which would liberate the signifier of *skin/culture* from the fixations of racial typology, the analytics of blood, ideologies of racial and cultural dominance or degeneration.[28]

As Pryor offered impersonations of the racist hillbilly and the anal-retentive white guy, he characterized the differences between white and African American lifestyles; however, he did so outside a racist ideology that privileges one racial group's experiences over another's. For example, on the differences between the mourning rituals of white and black people, he says, "White people love their dearly departed, but their funerals be different. They don't give it up easy. They hold that shit in until they get home. Then they cry softly.... But black people let it hang out ... Then they fall on your ass ... You have to carry them to the car."[29]

The reproduction of racist African American stereotypes, such as the Donald Bogle, *Toms, Coons, Mulattoes, Mammies, and Bucks*,[30] implies a normative whiteness,[31] whereas Pryor's routines consistently stressed the irreducible differences between whites and African Americans, between African Americans of different class backgrounds, and between himself and other African Americans. His impersonations created a nonhierarchical plane of identifiable African American typologies, each performed with a unique voice and set of bodily gestures. On *Bicentennial Nigger*, Mudbone, the teller of tall tales and Pryor's most famous character, says that after World War I he moved to California

> 'cause I gonna get in the motion picture business. Come out here 'cause in the paper it said "we want stars." Well, shit, I knowed I was a star. Natural-born, see, cause I couldn't do nothin'. So I'd come out here and went for this audition. Motherfucker said it was for King Kong. Gave me the script, and I didn't know what the story was. I said, "King Kong?" I said, "I don't mind being a king, but shit, that's a pretty good part—change that motherfucker's last name to William or something."[32]

Pryor mocks Mudbone; however, he does not contrast Mudbone with an invisible white norm. As we see in a bit from *That Nigger's Crazy*, Pryor constantly sought to deprive whiteness of its status as the invisible norm:

> White folks do things a lot different than niggers do. They eat quiet and shit. "Pass the potatoes... Thank you darling... Could I have a bit of that sauce? ... How are the kids coming along with their studies? ... Think we'll be having sexual intercourse this evening? ... We're not? ... Well, what the heck?"[33]

Pryor did not invent the anal-retentive white-guy impression, but as John Strausbaugh points out in *Black Like You: Insult and Imitation in American Popular Culture*, he did make it public: "it started with a routine that Richard Pryor later legitimized in the 1960s but that had been a perennial joke within the black community from the beginning—mimicking the constipated gait of stiff-butt white folks."[34]

Pryor "legitimized" these routines in part because he represented whites and blacks nonhierarchically: although every single one of Pryor's characters was absurd, they were all equally absurd. By refusing to frame race relations within morally judgmental language, Pryor allowed white audience members to feel less defensive, which put them in a better position to empathize with Pryor's experiences. He received empathy from white audiences by showing empathy towards them: much in the way Pryor situated the behaviors of black people within a political context, Pryor suggested that the behaviors of white people, while problematic, were at least in part socially constructed as well. These behaviors found expression whenever Pryor stiffened his butt, popped out his eyeballs, and dropped into a nasal voice. They appear in the opening minutes of *Richard Pryor: Live in Concert*, when he pokes fun at white liberal guilt without judgment. He says, "You ever notice how nice white people get when there's a bunch of niggers around? Right, they get outside, they talk to everybody. They say, 'Hi! How ya doing? I don't know you, but here's my wife! Hello!'"[35] In this sense, Pryor served as an exception to another observation made by bell hooks in *Black Looks*:

> Collectively black people remain rather silent about representations of whiteness in the black imagination. As in the old days of racial segregation where black folks learned to "wear the mask," many of us pretend to be comfortable in the face of whiteness only to turn our backs and give expression to intense levels of discomfort.[36]

Although Pryor did not "wear the mask," he nevertheless did appeal to white audiences. Felton attended the performance where *Live in Concert* was filmed and estimated that the audience "was seventy-percent white." He added,

I think what happens is you come to the show with all these fears inside you—racial, cultural, sexual—and Pryor assaults you with them right off the bat. But now you experience these fears under the warm shelter of mass laughter. It puts you at ease, with yourself and the people around you. And it puts you at ease with Pryor.[37]

As he impersonated an ignorant "redneck"— "You know this country is a god damn good place to live? Fuckin' A, better believe it, buddy. When our forefathers come over, there wasn't shit here!"—Pryor did not imply that whites are mindless objects who exist solely for the sake of the audience's pleasure; instead, he implied that both whites and African Americans often fail to behave rationally. As with African Americans, whites were funny due to their obliviousness to their own irrational behavior. Pryor put the audience "at ease with" him because his comedy criticized racial hierarchies for their harmful effect on everyone.

Pryor characterized both whites and African Americans as products of a white supremacist society, but in several ways—especially in his use of the n-word—he neither equated his own experiences with a white person's nor made apologies for whites. Although comedic performances can and often do trivialize racism, Pryor's artistic use of the n-word resignified its meaning in a manner later theorized by Judith Butler. In *Excitable Speech: A Politics of the Performative*, Butler does not mention Pryor specifically, but she does argue that state regulation of hate speech has the potential to censor such resignifying practices as Pryor's. Regarding an artist's use of injurious words, Butler writes,

> [I]t may be that an aesthetic reenactment *uses* [an injurious word], but also *displays* it, points to it, outlines it as the arbitrary material instance of language that is exploited to produce certain kinds of effects. In this sense, the word as a material signifier is foregrounded as semantically empty in itself, but as that empty moment in language that can become the site of semantically compounded legacy and effect. This is not to say that the word loses its power to injure, but that we are given the word in such a way that we can begin to ask: how does a word become the site for the power to injure?[38]

When Pryor used the n-word, the word of course retained the power to injure, but his use of irony prompted audiences at least to ask how the word—and more generally, the racism it connoted—has injured Pryor. The irony exhibited on the title track from Pryor's 1976 album *Bicentennial Nigger* leads the listener to consider "how black humor started" as a kind of gallows humor:

> You all know how black humor started? It started in slave ships. You know, cat was on his way over here rowin', and dude said, "What you laughing about?" He said, "Yesterday, I was a king." They're havin' a bicentennial—200 years!

They're gonna have a bicentennial nigger. They will. They'll have some nigger 200 years old in blackface. With stars and stripes on his forehead. With eyes and lips just all shiny—and he'll have that lovely white-folks expression on his face. But he's happy. [*Drops into a minstrel voice.*] He happy 'cause he been here 200 years: "I'm just so thrilled to be here! Over here in America! . . . I'm just so pleased America's gon' last. They brought me over in a boat—there was 400 of us come over here. [*Laughs*] 360 of us died on the way over here. [*Laughs*] I loved that! [*Laughs*] That just thrilled me so! I don't know, you white folks are just so good to us! [*Laughs*] Got over here—another 20 of us died from disease. [*Laughs*] Ah, but you didn't have no doctors to take care of us. I'm so sorry you didn't. Upset you all some too, didn't it? [*Laughs*] Then they split us all up, yes-siree: took my mama over that way, took my wife that way, took my kids over yonder. [*Laughs*] I'm just so happy. [*Laughs*] I don't know what to do! I don't know what to do if I don't get 200 more years of this! Lord have mercy, yes-siree—I don't know where my own mama is now! She up yonder with the big white folks in the sky! Y'all probably done forgot about it . . . But I ain't gonna never forget it."[39]

With the accompanying satire, the n-word does not lose its derogatory meaning, but the listener should gain an appreciation for how the word affects a black man who's spent the past 200 years in America.

The word's legacy was not lost on white talk show host Dinah Shore who struggled during a 1975 interview with Pryor to describe her feelings toward the n-word.

SHORE: I don't know how you feel about the title of your album, but I find it difficult to say.

PRYOR: You do? Most white people—it's hard to say "crazy." [*Everyone laughs.*]

SHORE: You tell them the title of the album, I can't say that.

PRYOR: The title of the album is *That Nigger's Crazy*, and don't that nigger look crazy? [*Shows the audience the album cover.*]

SHORE: See, you can just say that! If I said that, wouldn't you get mad?

PRYOR: I'd punch you out! [*Everyone laughs.*]

SHORE: Of course! I knew it! [*Starts to mumble.*]

PRYOR: See, niggers can say nigger with different feelings. "Hey nigga, what's happening? Nigga! My nigga!" But white people say, "Hey nig-ger." [*Drops into a southern, hillbilly accent.*] "C'mon nigger, I'm gonna tell you something. See that tree? Go hang yourself on it."[40]

What does Shore mean when she says, "I knew it"? Arguably, she catches on to the subtext of Pryor's use of the n-word, which invokes the white supremacist context in which Pryor performed. She senses that her use of the word would inflict pain on Pryor, who resignifies *That Nigger's Crazy* as a metaphor for "That Oppressed Person Is Traumatized." Using the word to demonstrate the painful impact it has had on him, Pryor evidently succeeds given that in their interaction Shore begins to reflect upon how the n-word has "become the site for the power to injure." In order to further emphasize the word's injurious role, Pryor impersonates a white southerner who uses the word to persuade an African American into hanging himself. That said, the word's rhetorical limits are evident: his use of the word is open to misinterpretation, considering that Pryor needs to clarify it.[41] Explaining his decision to avoid the n-word in his act, Pryor wrote that "Its connotations weren't funny, even when people laughed. I felt its lameness. It was misunderstood by people. They didn't get what I was talking about. Neither did I."[42]

THE PRESS' PREJUDICED PERCEPTION OF PRYOR'S PAIN

Although he does get Shore to reflect upon the n-word's injurious effects, in a 1977 *New York Times* interview Pryor noted the disparity between his desire to give his pain a hearing and a talk show host's desire to present Pryor as evidence that in the post–civil rights era, African Americans have no right to protest racist, dehumanizing conditions:

> There comes a time in your life. . . . when the host on the talk show turns to you and says "Isn't America great, Richard?" and you're supposed to say "It sure is," and then he says, "See, guys, *he* did it—what's the matter with the rest of you?" I've gone along with that in the past, but no more.[43]

In order to become a star, Pryor nevertheless continued to adapt his humor to film and television productions. And yet, no matter how inclusive his humor, the masses resisted his politics (even though they had embraced it when expressed in the form of a stand-up comedy act). When Pryor was awarded his own television variety show on NBC, his political humor did not attract a wide audience, in spite of the success his rhetoric had found with racially mixed crowds in comedy clubs. Although *The Richard Pryor Show* (1977) was burdened by a poor time slot, meddling network censors, and Pryor's escalating drug habit, the show's poor ratings arguably fell out in part from the relative lack of intimacy between the televised performer and the audience. Whereas his stand-up comedy albums had garnered acclaim for their antiracist messages, his short-lived sketch comedy show from 1977 received reviews such as the following from the *New York Times*:

On several levels, despite the humorous surfaces, the material is both bitter and militant, delivering the message that "black is beautiful." Even an impersonation of Uganda's Idi Amin, hardly a figure to inspire lighthearted fun, gets in some simple-minded swipes at whites. This is Mr. Pryor at his most confused and objectionable.[44]

In a televised form, Pryor's political humor takes on an apparent negative connotation, appearing "bitter and militant." As for "simple-minded swipes at whites," perhaps the critic feels that the cold-blooded Ugandan President is in no place to mock American racism and should not have said that "Americans don't want the black man to know nothing. Don't even want the black man to go to Africa to fight. You know why? Because nobody there call them nigger."[45] Although this line is political, it pales in comparison to the politics of Pryor's stand-up routines. (The fact that Amin is both morally bankrupt and morally superior to racist Americans is exactly the point.) Unable to give intimate performances, in which he juxtaposes his impersonations with a narrative voice that conveys his exasperations, on television Pryor becomes stereotyped as a "militant" black man.

As Pryor's stardom continued to rise, thanks in part to his charismatic performance in *Silver Streak*, he lost control over his ability to convince audiences to see his pain within a political context. The public's notion of Pryor's "self" was increasingly mediated through the press, which sought to distinguish between the "real" Richard Pryor and the apparently contrived, political Pryor. In a clear example of the press' desire to look beyond Pryor's performance in order to discover a flawed self, TV critic Kay Gardella dismissed Pryor's 1979 interview with Barbara Walters as a failed attempt to indict a racist society:

> The unpredictable comic, whose hostility to whites is expressed in cruel but brilliant humor, feels he will never achieve recognition. He wants people to look at him with their hearts, he tells Barbara. "Whatever you feel about me when you see me right now is the truth and don't ever forget it," he says . . .
> Either I was missing a few pieces of the Pryor puzzle or Barbara knows something she did not see fit to share with her viewers. It's an effort to gloss over a subject, to help him present the image he prefers, but one the facts contradict.[46]

Such facts include Pryor's drug habit and domestic disputes, neither of which "contradict" his politics, but which do divert attention away from it. Nevertheless, the press sought to draw attention to stories about the supposed "real" Pryor. For example, in 1978, *Parade* magazine published and responded to a letter from a reader who questioned whether the painful stories he told about growing up in his grandmother's brothel were at all factual:

> Q: Richard Pryor, the black comedian from Peoria, has been married how many times? Have all of his wives been black? Was he really raised in his grandmother's bordello, or is that just publicity to make him glamorous?—B. R., Decatur, Ill.
>
> A: To date Richard Pryor, 37, has been married five times—twice to white women, three times to black. He claims to have been reared in his grandmother's brothel, and there is no reason to doubt him.[47]

(Note that his grandmother owned three brothels, not one, and that at this point in his life Pryor had actually been married three times, not five.) Why might a reader care whether Pryor had ever been married to a white woman, and why would *Parade* publish and respond to this inquiry (without fact-checking)? Pryor described his feelings without describing himself as flawed or as abnormal whereas certain others did the opposite; in this case, gossiping about interracial marriage (a taboo subject) amounted to a conspiracy to frame Pryor as deviant. Similarly, Pryor's director in *Blue Collar*, Paul Schrader, told *Newsweek* that Pryor's success depended on how well he could discipline himself: "Richard will be the biggest black star in history if he can keep the reins on himself or bite his tongue."[48]

In general, the press tried to pathologize Pryor's anger while at the same time sweep aside his politics. A *Playboy* profile of Pryor from 1979 does both when it implies that Pryor has no right to express his pain because, apparently, racism has been to his *benefit* and not to his detriment:

> It's difficult to describe this schizophrenic, torn, often unfunny funnyman. A former close friend, a witness to his blinding changes of temperament, probably comes closest: "He is, I think, a black, berserk angel."
>
> He may complain, as he did to Barbara Walters, that racism prevents him from being the biggest comedian in the business. But the obvious reply is that were it not for racism, he wouldn't be a big comedian today.[49]

The author's second paragraph reflects the audience's desires to frame Pryor as someone suffering from his own demons. This desire mirrored an absurd yet widespread suspicion among white Americans that in the post–civil rights era, black Americans had pressed for enough change, that America had moved into a post-racial era, and that the country had solved racial inequality. In other words, if African Americans were struggling, they had only themselves to blame.

PRYOR'S PAIN ON FILM: DEPOLITICIZED, DIMINISHED, AND DISPLACED

Even though Pryor's stand-up routine successfully invited audiences to acknowledge racial inequality, Hollywood cast Pryor in roles that catered to desires to regard Pryor's pleas for empathy as a scam carried out by an African American man who refused to take responsibility for himself. In *Silver Streak*, Pryor plays Grover Muldoon, a happy-go-lucky thief who through a series of wacky mishaps winds up helping a white man named George Caldwell (Gene Wilder) rescue his love interest (Jill Clayburgh) from the clutches of Devereau, a white, smarmy, upper-class criminal (Patrick McGoohan). *Silver Streak*'s theatrical trailer closes with a clip where Pryor is obviously faking his trauma in an apparent effort to gain sympathy. "This has been a nerve-shattering experience for me, sir!" he says to someone off-camera.[50]

On two occasions, a white character calls Grover "nigger." The Pryor from his stand-up routines would not have let the moment pass without stressing the word's injurious effects, whereas in the film Grover responds differently. The first instance occurs when a night watchman (Raymond Guth) catches Grover trying to steal a car off the watchman's lot. He points a shotgun at Grover and says, "Hold it right there, nigger." Feigning ignorance, Grover perks up and immediately tries to divert the night watchman's attention away from the fact that he is trying to steal the car. After George saves Grover by jumping the watchman from behind, Grover laughs heartily and the pair speed away. The second instance occurs when Grover, pretending to be a porter so as to infiltrate Devereau's scheme, intentionally spills coffee on Devereau, who exclaims, "You ignorant nigger!" This time, Pryor pulls out a gun and shouts back, "Say man, who you calling nigger, huh? You don't know me well enough to call me no nigger." In the first instance, the film frames Grover as a subtle version of the Uncle Remus stereotype whose "mirth . . . has always been used to indicate the black man's satisfaction with the system and his place in it."[51] In the second instance, Grover engages in male posturing, behaving like the stereotypical buck, "the white man's notion of the all-powerful brutal black man."[52] And in neither instance do we sense that Grover has suffered. Moreover, instead of indicting white supremacist ideology, the film attributes racism to a couple of bad apples.

Even though Pryor does appear to experience real suffering in *Stir Crazy* (he's "stir crazy," after all), the film depoliticizes his pain as a product of his own idiosyncrasies, diminishes his pain to an emotional state shared with his white buddy, and finally displaces his pain entirely onto the buddy for whom Pryor must care. In the second of Pryor's four films with Gene Wilder, Pryor plays actor Harry Monroe who along with Skip Donahue (Wilder) lands in jail after the pair are framed for armed robbery. Most of Harry's comical moments feature him screaming hysterically as his situation goes from bad to worse, but in each—for example, Harry having a nervous breakdown as he's marched into his cell for the first time—Harry comes off as someone suffering from his own demons. To further demonstrate that Harry's hysteria has nothing to do with racism, the film pairs him with the even more hysterical Skip. Equating the black man's experiences with the white man's is a trope of the biracial buddy film, which as Cynthia J. Fuchs explains serves as historical revisionism by erasing racial differences.[53] "[A] narrative of shared victimization," bell hooks notes, "not only acts to recenter whites, it risks obscuring the particular ways racist domination impacts on the lives of marginalized groups."[54] In fact, by the end, Harry's pain is not merely shared but displaced entirely onto Skip, who is clearly the "crazier" of the two and who constantly requires Harry's guidance. In *Stir Crazy*, Harry's role is largely to give Skip a dose of reality, to help him escape from prison, and to ensure that in the end he gets the girl. Such films perpetuate the racist myth that an African American's duty is to care for his white masters.[55]

The films' most famous scenes are also their most racially problematic. In *Silver Streak*, Grover helps George slip past the police by smearing shoe polish on George's face and showing him how to act "black." In *Stir Crazy*, Harry shows Skip how to "act bad"—code for "acting black"—because "if you don't act bad [in jail], you're gonna get fucked." By suggesting that "blackness" is a contrived facade, each scene reinforces the myth that an African American's presentation of self—including their request for empathy—is simply a pleasurable performance that should be treated frivolously. That the performance seems pleasurable—as he acts "black," dancing and shouting "outta sight," George finally appears to be loosening up—reflects what bell hooks describes as "[t]he desire to make contact with bodies deemed Other," which "establishes a contemporary narrative where the suffering imposed by structures of domination on those designated Other is deflected by an emphasis on seduction and longing where the desire is not to make the Other over in one's image but to become the Other."[56] In Pryor's case, his antiracist discourse is buried beneath the white audience's desire to emulate his performance.

Ironically, the apparent authenticity of Pryor's star image, which had emerged out of a candidly political stand-up comedy act, worked to legitimize the scene's racist subtext. In his essay on the biracial buddy film formula, Ed Guerrero notes that "one could not imagine either of these scenes surviving without protest if it were not for Pryor's star power or negotiating presence in them."[57] And as Pryor himself tells the *New York Times* in an interview from 1976, "Gene does a scene in black face, and they felt that having a real black actor in the movie would sort of make it all right. So I'm the token black, a modern Willie Best. It was a career move, and I'm not sorry I did it. But I'll be glad when the movie is out and over with."[58] (Willie Best was an African American actor who, in Hollywood films from the 1930s and 1940s, played the stereotypical lazy, unintelligent, and servile black man.) Pryor described himself as "a *real* black actor"; perhaps what he meant is that his political, antiracist star persona helped to legitimize Wilder's blackface. The two scenes co-opt the apparently authentic impersonation of a black male that Pryor had developed in his stand-up act. Pryor's intent had been to demonstrate the irreducibility of blackness to whiteness, whereas the white audience presumably sought to live vicariously through Pryor in order to repress "the fear that one must always conform to the norm in order to remain 'safe.'"[59] In general, through such films, Pryor's image was altered, from that of a black male asking America to acknowledge racism's painful effects on African Americans, to an idiosyncratic African American who exists for the audience's amusement. This alteration has, consequently, all but erased Richard Pryor's political legacy from the nation's collective memory.

NOTES

1. Hilton Als, "A Pryor Love: The Life and Times of America's Comic Prophet of Race," *New Yorker* (September 13, 1999): 76.
2. *Life of Pryor: The Richard Pryor Story,* documentary, first broadcast October 14, 2006 by the BBC, hosted by Lenny Henry and produced by Mobashir Dar.
3. Bambi Haggins, *Laughing Mad: The Black Comic Persona in Post-Soul America* (Piscataway, NJ: Rutgers University Press, 2009), 65.
4. Paul Mooney, *Black Is the New White: A Memoir* (New York: Simon Spotlight Entertainment, 2009), 92.
5. Richard Pryor and Todd Gold, *Pryor Convictions, and Other Life Sentences* (New York: Pantheon, 1995), 205.
6. Ed Guerrero, "The Black Image in Protective Custody," in *Black American Cinema,* ed. Manthia Diawara (New York: Routledge, 1993), 241.
7. Walter Benjamin, "The Author as Producer," *Understanding Brecht,* trans. Anna Bostock (London: Verso, 1998), 93.
8. Max Horkheimer and Theodor W. Adorno, *Dialectic of Enlightenment,* trans. Edmund Jephcott (Stanford, CA: Stanford University Press, 1992), 125.
9. Richard Delgado, *The Rodrigo Chronicles: Conversations About America and Race* (New York: New York University Press, 1995), 78.
10. bell hooks, *Black Looks: Race and Representation* (Boston: South End Press, 1992), 34.
11. Quoted in Eddie Tafoya, *The Legacy of the Wisecrack: Stand-up Comedy as the Great American Literary Form* (Boca Raton: BrownWalker, 2009), 192–193.

12. Quoted in Bob Avakian, *Reflections, Sketches, and Provocations: Essays and Commentary, 1981–1987* (Chicago: RCP Publications, 1990), 3–4.

13. David Felton, "Jive Times: Richard Pryor, Lily Tomlin, and the Theater of the Routine," *Rolling Stone*, no. 171 (October 10, 1974): 42.

14. *Richard Pryor: The Life and Legacy of a "Crazy" Black Man*, ed. Audrey T McCluskey (Bloomington: Indiana University Press, 2008).

15. Lawrence Mintz, "Standup Comedy as Social and Cultural Mediation," *American Quarterly* 37, no. 1 (Spring 1985): 75.

16. Edward Azlant, "Lenny Bruce Again: 'Gestapo? You Asshole, I'm the Mailman!'" *Studies in American Humor* NS3, no. 15 (2006): 75–99; Ronald K. L. Collins and David M. Skover, *The Trials of Lenny Bruce: The Fall and Rise of an American Icon* (Naperville, IL: Sourcebooks MediaFusion, 2002); Ioan Davies, "Lenny Bruce: Hyperrealism and the Death of Jewish Tragic Humor," *Social Text* 22 (Spring 1989): 92–114.

17. Glenn C. Altschuler and Patrick M. Burns, "Snarlin' Carlin: The Odyssey of a Libertarian," *Studies in American Humor* NS3, no. 20 (2009): 42–57; Christine A. Corcos, "George Carlin, Constitutional Law Scholar," *Stetson Law Review* 37 (July 21, 2008): 899–940.

18. Paul McDonald, "Stand-Up Comedy as Poetry: Transcendentalism and Romantic Anti-Capitalism in the Work of Bill Hicks," *Journal of Ecocriticism* 1, no. 2 (July 2009): 104–113, http://ojs.unbc.ca/index.php/joe/article/viewFile/118/225 (accessed April 12, 2014).

19. Philip Auslander, "Comedy About the Failure of Comedy: Stand-up Comedy and Postmodernism," in *Critical Theory and Performance*, ed. Janelle G. Reinelt and Joseph R. Roach (Ann Arbor: University of Michigan Press, 1992), 201.

20. Peggy Phelan, *Unmarked: The Politics of Performance* (New York: Routledge, 1993), 148.

21. Ibid., 150.

22. Richard Zoglin, *Comedy at the Edge: How Stand-up in the 1970s Changed America* (New York: Bloomsbury USA, 2008), 63.

23. John Limon, *Stand-up Comedy in Theory, or, Abjection in America* (Durham, NC: Duke University Press, 2000), 85.

24. Ibid., 83–84.

25. Ibid., 84.

26. Ibid., 85.

27. Homi K. Bhabha, *The Location of Culture*, 2nd ed. (New York: Routledge, 2004), 94–95.

28. Ibid., 108.

29. Quoted in Richard Pryor and Gold, *Pryor Convictions*, 104.

30. Donald Bogle, *Toms, Coons, Mulattoes, Mammies, and Bucks: An Interpretive History of Blacks in American Films*, 4th ed. (New York: Continuum International Publishing Group, 2001).

31. Phelan, *Unmarked*, 47.

32. Richard Pryor, *Bicentennial Nigger*, Warner Bros. Records, BS 2960, LP, 1976.

33. Richard Pryor, *That Nigger's Crazy*, Partee Records, PBS-2404, 1974.

34. John Strausbaugh, *Black Like You: Blackface, Whiteface, Insult & Imitation in American Popular Culture* (New York: Jeremy P. Tarcher, 2007), 337.

35. *Richard Pryor: Live in Concert*, directed by Jeff Margolis (Burbank, CA: Elkins Entertainment, 1979).
36. hooks, *Black Looks*, 169.
37. David Felton, "Richard Pryor's Life in Concert," *Rolling Stone* (May 3, 1979): 52.
38. Judith Butler, *Excitable Speech: A Politics of the Performative* (New York: Routledge, 1997), 100.
39. Quoted in Laurajane Smith, *Representing Enslavement and Abolition in Museums: Ambiguous Engagements* (New York: Routledge, 2011), 224–225.
40. Interview by Dinah Shore with Richard Pryor on the BBC's *Life of Pryor: The Richard Pryor Story*.
41. The similarities between Pryor's dilemma and that of comedian Dave Chappelle's have been explored in Glenda R. Carpio, "The Conjurer Recoils: Slavery in Richard Pryor's Performances and *Chappelle's Show*," in *Laughing Fit to Kill: Black Humor in the Fictions of Slavery* (New York: Oxford University Press, 2008), 72–117; and Kimberley A. Yates, "When 'Keeping It Real' Goes Right," in *The Comedy of Dave Chappelle: Critical Essays*, ed. K. A. Wisniewski (Jefferson, NC: McFarland & Co., 2009), 139–55.
42. Pryor and Gold, *Pryor Convictions*, 175. Although more than thirty years have passed since Pryor's trip to Africa, which he claims led him to renounce the n-word in his act, the word remains as polarizing as ever. For a close analysis of Pryor's use of the term, see Jacquelyn Rahman, "The N Word: Its History and Use in the English Language," *Journal of English Linguistics* (July 31, 2011): 1–35, accessed February 15, 2011, doi:10.1177/0075424211414807.
43. Joyce Maynard, "Richard Pryor, King of the Scene-Stealers," *New York Times*, January 9, 1977, sec. 2, 11.
44. John J. O'Connor, "TV: Pryor and Chase Take Their Pot Shots," *New York Times*, May 5, 1977, C27.
45. *The Richard Pryor Show*, (1977; Chatsworth, CA: Image Entertainment, 2004), DVD.
46. Kay Gardella, "Barbara Walters' Big Trap," *New York Daily News*, May 29, 1979.
47. *Parade*, Letter to the Editor, April 23, 1978, Billy Rose Collection, New York Public Library.
48. Maureen Orth, "The Perils of Pryor," *Newsweek* (October 3, 1977): 60–63.
49. William Brashler, "Berserk Angel," *Playboy* 26, no. 12 (December 1979): 243–48, 292–96.
50. "Silver Streak, Movie trailer" [n.d.]. www.Youtube.com, 0.29, posted by Brian Durham, March 25, 2008. http://www.youtube.com/watch?v=NXwMClqVPhs (accessed February 15, 2012).
51. Bogle, *Toms*, 8.
52. Ibid., 242.
53. Cynthia J. Fuchs, "The Buddy Politic," in *Screening the Male: Exploring Masculinities in Hollywood Cinema*, ed. Steven Cohan and Ina Rae Park (London and New York: Routledge, 1993), 202–6.

54. hooks, *Black Looks*, 13.
55. Melvin Burke Donalson, *Masculinity in the Interracial Buddy Film* (Jefferson, NC: McFarland, 2006), 9.
56. hooks, *Black Looks*, 25.
57. Guerrero, "Black Image," 241.
58. Guy Flatley, "At the Movies," *New York Times*, August 6, 1976, Weekend, C4.
59. hooks, *Black Looks*, 22.

13

✢

You Are Now Tuned Into the . . . Greatest

Jay-Z and the Spectacle of the Cool

Wilfredo Gomez

Hip Hop is aging. It is a genre of music whose commercial introduction to the world came via the release of 1979's "Rappers Delight" recorded by the Sugar Hill Gang. Since that time, Hip Hop has had its fair share of stars, emcees (MCs) who have risen to a level of notoriety well above that of their peers, further cementing the claim that it is the emcee that reigns supreme in Hip Hop culture over the other elements of deejaying, breaking (dancing), and graffiti writing. In a culture gone global, the role of the MC resonates with fans, especially the message(s), lyrical dexterity, flow, and the requisite ability to move the crowd. While fans, scholars, and journalists alike may quibble amongst themselves over their respective top ten MCs/rappers, some choices are obvious and perhaps unanimously included on these lists. Jay-Z is one such choice.

In an attempt to establish some context for the concept of cool as it relates to the discussion of Jay-Z in this chapter, I turn to the work of Herman Gray who critically engages the relationship between American culture and black youth culture. Gray suggests that the sphere of popular culture is the primary space through which we understand, come in contact with, and consume notions of what becomes multicultural and cool, noting that:

> In the case of popular music, sports, and fashion, black style and youth culture are at the center of representations of American popular culture. Video images . . . and cinematic images of black hip-hop artists . . . dominate commercial

culture. As cultural signifiers of urban lifestyles and identities, representations of black youth culture are major conduits through which the commodification of multiculturalism—sexuality, youth, race, and gender—proceeds.[1]

Corporate entities such as Anheuser-Busch, Heineken, Reebok, Turner Network Television (TNT), HP computers, the NBA, Samsung, and (candidate) Barack Obama invoke (and signify upon) Jay-Z's commercial appeal beyond the realm of Hip Hop culture. As a result of this exceptional popularity and fame, many television viewers, critics, and consumers believe that the spectacle of Jay-Z emerged almost overnight.[2] The foundations of Jay-Z's meteoric rise to success in the corporate world is rooted in the lived experiences and (lyrical) savvy of a drug-dealing hustler who became a successful rapper, moving beyond the confines of Marcy Projects in Brooklyn, New York's Bedford-Stuyvesant section, to selling out shows in mere seconds at the famed Madison Square Garden in Midtown Manhattan. This public and paradigmatic shift from "Marcy to Hollywood and back again"[3] is carefully rooted in what I am referring to as the *Spectacle of the Cool*, manifested in Jay-Z's public personae, especially in his popularly televised interviews.[4] The spectacle of the cool has its foundations in the creative, real, and imagined synthesis of the working class roots of the hustler and the middle class sensibilities and aspirations of the corporate executive. Jay-Z's artistic spectacle is a symbiotic creative and commercial relationship mediated through the framework of the cool pose. Thus the narrative surrounding Jay-Z's origins and his humble beginnings in Brooklyn as a former hustler or drug dealer afford him a certain level of social, cultural, and human capital to which corporate America and media outlets ascribe their own commercial capital. The wedding of these seemingly diametrically opposed images, deconstructs, exposes, and ultimately exploits what would seem to be a dialogical relationship between a corporate hustler or go-getter as understood in the popular media (with positive connotations) and the street-bred hustler whose urban sensibilities and backstory may be seen as threatening to a broader audience. In the following pages, I will argue that this spectacle of the cool, as it pertains to Jay-Z, is what creates the space for him to operate as a representative and domestic ambassador of Hip Hop within the broader context of the United States. This representative status is reflected in his August 28, 2009 appearance on HBO's *Real Time with Bill Maher*, as well as his September 24, 2009 appearance on the *Oprah Winfrey Show*.

My analysis of these shows as critical written and visual texts will further enhance claims that "media spectacle is indeed a culture of celebrity which provides dominant role models and icons of fashion, look, and personality. In the world of spectacle, celebrity encompasses every major social domain from entertainment to politics to sports to business."[5]

I also contend that in terms of television, what ethnomusicologist Guthrie Ramsey refers to as public "community theaters"[6] are shaped, molded, and modified by Jay-Z, Oprah Winfrey, Bill Maher, and their respective audiences into community spectacles, whereby specters of discontent and the (un)mediated role(s) of spectators are thrown into flux. Community theaters function as sites of cultural memory "not limited to cinema, family narratives and histories, the church, the social dance, the nightclub, the skating rink, and even literature, or the 'theater of the literary.'" They "combine to form living photographs, rich pools of experiences, and a cultural poetics upon which theoretical and analytical principles can be based."[7] Community spectacles build on this model by encompassing contested and contorted sites of knowledge (re)production and induction. In the example of Jay-Z's appearance on *Oprah*, there is an explicit social and (un)conscious adherence to a racial contract in the performance of leftist politics appealing in the broadest sense possible to greater ideals of democratic inclusion. Furthermore, this example suggests a convergence between actual and imagined corporeal realities distinguishing the public and private sphere(s) betwixt and between generations and consequently allowing the cool pose to function and manifest itself in ways that are authentic to Jay-Z's target audience as well as Oprah Winfrey and Bill Maher's audiences. What can and does become authentic in terms of popular culture is the public discourse of Hip Hop's acceptance amongst mainstream television audiences including the live show and the televisual experience at home.

In a rare media decision, Jay-Z sat down to join comedian and political satirist, Bill Maher, for an interview on August 28, 2009. Immediately after being introduced as the man to "beat" in Hip Hop culture, Bill Maher begins his conversation with Jay-Z by suggesting that he has a loyal fan base that loves and adores him, despite all the misogynistic language present in his music. Jay-Z proceeds to downplay his conscious participation in delivering such lyrics, suggesting that there is a distance between the personal message of the lyrics and the incentive and/or inclination to entertain. Such a response, while clearly meant to divert any kind of personal accountability in perpetuating the use of gender-biased language successfully shifts the conversation from the topic of personal accountability in Hip Hop to holding the media accountable for fanning the flames of a musical rivalry that ultimately resulted in the "East Coast–West Coast" debates ("beef") that claimed the lives of the Notorious B.I.G. and Tupac Shakur. The conversation begins as one that attempts to confront artistry and personal accountability, but quickly shifts as the interview fails to garner much of a response from Jay-Z on the opening questions about misogynistic language. After a short introduction that situates Jay-Z as a musical mogul and corporate brand, Bill Maher suggests that audiences (specifically women) all over continue to support Jay-Z's brand and image in spite of all the hurtful and demeaning comments he has directed at them. Jay-Z sidesteps these questions offering little substantive responses when pressed to be accountable or self-reflexive about his artistic output. The exchange, hashed out in the mode of playful banter is moved along after Jay-Z suggests that his music, or perhaps music more generally is multilayered and complex. Those complexities and blurred boundaries are only further obscured when the expectations, frame of reference, and critical lens of audience members and consumers intersect and interact with the artistic product as something that is both a manifestation of expressive and corporate culture(s).[8]

Eventually, Bill Maher questions his attempt at being a transcendent pop cultural figure who has achieved exceptional access to wealth, and thereby has been exposed more and more in the public eye. In this exchange Maher implicitly alludes to the Jay-Z song "PSA" (Public Service Announcement) where Jay-Z explicitly alludes to being like revolutionary, Che Guevara, "with Bling On."[9] This seemingly oxymoronic lyric may suggest that there is a personal sacrifice involved in betraying one's class-consciousness to fight for exceptional or transcendent success. It also suggests some level of self-reflection through which Jay-Z is aware of how material success confounds one's progressive origins. Jay-Z insists that he is someone who has tapped into the real emotions of memory and remembering that are at once tangible, readily identifiable, and easily recalled. Through this process he transcends racial identity and the policing of racialized boundaries (space, place), age, and genre specificity in American popular culture. Here Jay-Z applies a "pseudoethnographic lens"[10] to himself and thereby "establishes the contingency of the subject as agent and the agent as subject."[11] This filter is present in his television appearances that tend to function as a site through which he can confront and engage the subject of his agency with respect to the impact and potential of his music. While Jay-Z readily dismisses the characterization that his intentions are to inspire, invite aspiration, and/or inform his audience, that is, he does not consider himself to be a progressive role model; he subtly suggests that he is accountable to Hip Hop culture.

Jay-Z's music enjoys broad commercial appeal in popular culture. The creative processes surrounding his initial recording projects were specific to place, space, culture, and community. These early projects were coded in a particular language specific to self and others that were intimate in their descriptions of urban existence because they were mediated through the lens of Jay-Z the hustler from Marcy Projects. Jay-Z's attempts at lyrical ethnography are specific to his growing and evolving interests and broadened experiences. Thus, these days his lyrics are mediated through the lens of Jay-Z the successful business mogul who happens to be married to one of the greatest pop cultural figures on the planet. Bryant Keith Alexander's work on "autoethnography" is useful here. Alexander claims that he writes "about cultural performance through autoethnography because of autoethnography's peculiar ability to be both specific to individual experience and to implicate others in the act of telling."[12] Alexander's approach helps to contextualize the subtleties of Jay-Z's television appearances (body language, pauses, hesitation based on self-reflection) as well as the allusions to the songs, experiences, and figures that have fundamentally shaped Jay-Z's lyrical personae; his commitment to perfecting his craft and the enhancement of his popular appeal and commercial empire. The concept of an "autoethnography" also helps to analyze the potential impact and layered meanings behind Jay-Z's claim to search for and successfully identify a "true emotion" or "real emotion" that resonates with his own experiences as well as the experiences of others.[13] Those who hear Jay-Z's music as aspirational are the cultural "others" he identifies in responding to Bill Maher's questions. Since Jay-Z repeatedly states that he speaks to true emotion (grounded presumably in universal truths), there is an attempt on his part to have these cultural others engage in the process of autoethnography as well.

As the interview progresses, Bill Maher gets Jay-Z to open up about the details of "Song Cry," as they discuss several lines from Jay-Z's extensive music catalogue. Jay-Z's "Song Cry" claims that he cannot cry; thus he must make the song cry in order to reflect his innermost emotions.[14] The song explores the themes of distance in masculine emotion and in Jay's discussion of it his concept of "true emotion" is contained by the song's premise which is something to the effect of: "I can't cry because that's not manly, but because I have mastered the art of rapping, I can make the song cry for me."[15] The construction of subjects (in this case a song that can cry) is critical to Jay-Z's creative process. He suggests to Maher that he takes all of these matters into consideration to enhance the listening experience had by consumers of his music. Then the exchange, an extension of a dialogue about Jay-Z's creative process, shifts from the power and thought that goes into lyrical content towards one centering on the lyrical oeuvre and his longevity as an artist. These are subjects that are currently debatable given the contemporary landscape of Hip Hop. An excerpt of the exchange between Maher and Jay-Z reflects on the tentative nature of Jay-Z's success and how he focuses on full-length projects as opposed to popular singles. Maher begins the exchange by expressing a curiosity over Jay-Z having had success with numerous number one albums, without releasing a number one single. Maher goes on to note that the discrepancy between singles and album sales may be indicative of a fan base that appreciates Jay-Z's collective body of work. Jay-Z responds by suggesting that he had yet to release a single that captivated audiences with universal appeal. When pressed to elaborate and further own up to his thought process, Jay-Z reiterates a commitment to craft, consistency, and an overall listening experience. Being cognizant of the eclectic music interests of audiences and the changing landscape of the music industry, Jay-Z reaffirms his commitment to deep listening, a substance-driven body of work that focuses its attention on tempo, emotion, and affect. Ultimately, Jay-Z's creative process values the importance of patience and his music's timelessness.[16]

At the outset of the interview with Maher, Jay-Z suggests that his speech patterns and lyrical delivery were denser on his debut album *Reasonable Doubt* because he had much to say and did not intend to continue recording any more music. He was in it for the "hustle." He goes on to further suggest that the first album was coded in a street "language" (African American Vernacular English) that was specific to space, place, and time; it was music meant to be consumed, listened to, and engaged by a select group of people who presumably were in his inner circle. He claims that the album was recorded to make an impression on his friends. As Jay-Z has grown older, more established, and more famous, his experiences have broadened and his autoethnographic responses have likewise expanded to accommodate how he discusses and figures his life and body of work. Gone are his (illegal) hustler ways in search of "Dead Presidents,"[17] and in its place are lyrics about the MOMA, or how old, "blueblood"[18] money looks at him disdainfully. But while his autoethnographic lens may have changed, the condition of the poor and dispossessed people who live in the Marcy Projects in Brooklyn has not.

Jay-Z draws a distinction between listeners who find his music to be aspirational and those who find it to be an honest, tangible, and vividly lived experience. These tensions are represented visually when Oprah began her televised interview with Jay-Z by showing clips of the two-and-a-half hours that they spent at Marcy Projects and at his grandmother's house talking about a wide range of experiences—including, but not limited to drugs and spirituality. In his attempt to set a backdrop for those tensions between where he is and where he is from, Jay-Z opts for a sense of the panoptic perspective that begins and ends at the Marcy Projects. With Oprah and at the site where Jay-Z's artistic persona was honed, Jay seems to be more reflective. In the Oprah interview, he speaks from and with the voice of Marcy Projects, giving voice to the marginal, invisible, and voiceless. When asked about his credibility among young people, Jay-Z responded, "My responsibility is to the culture. You know my job is to show it a great light so I guess I'm a role model in that way, but as far as the way I live my life, I'm a human being."[19] Again Jay-Z is reluctant in his televised self-reflections to concede that he is a role model for Hip

Hop and popular audiences—audiences beyond his inner circle and the hustlers for whom he recorded his first album.

These tensions also take shape and reflective articulation on Music Television (MTV) in three high profile music videos filmed in the vicinity of Marcy Projects. These three songs, "Where I'm From," "Hard Knock Life," and "Anything,"[20] further illustrate the points of convergence between autoethnography in visual form and those in lyrical form. In the song "Where I'm From" on *In My Lifetime, Vol. 1*, his sophomore release, Jay-Z describes his neighborhood as one where gunshots ring out constantly and where news cameras never venture.[21] Jay's Brooklyn neighborhood is a place where gunshots are heard with such frequency that it has become a part of everyday life. So much so that even though news coverage would be appropriate, news corporations do not bother to report the continuous violence. As the verse continues, Jay-Z makes it clear that he is from a place where one's everyday experiences are confined to the realm of the ghetto; where's one's speech is authentic in the sense that nothing can be fabricated—one must live the experiences about which he or she speaks. He is from a place where cars are pulled over to engage in debates about which rappers appear to have the most skill and talent, the same locations where the drug kingpins' faces are constantly changing, and many more aspire to these tenuous positions. He's from a place where people are frequently found and sentenced to jail. Jay-Z is from a place that births raps stars—those born and raised in the Marcy Projects. In one verse he craftily informs his listeners of all of this and more.

Songs such as "Where I'm From" recount popular Hip Hop narratives where unchecked crime, illegal activities, criminals, and everyday folks all coexist. Songs with these themes reflect important attributes of contemporary popular culture. They become "ghetto anthems," that is, songs that celebrate and honor the experiences of places and people who reside in communities similar to Marcy Projects in Brooklyn. While Jay-Z offers other songs that espouse similar narratives, the descriptive substance or pseudoethnographic notes in "Where I'm From" tell multiple stories, many of which might be otherwise untold. Perhaps because of these narratives and the personal memories that accompany them Jay-Z is delighted to have someone like Oprah Winfrey bring cameras into the Brooklyn community. Winfrey opens her interview with a visual montage of Jay-Z, offering up his magazine spreads, clips from concerts, his marriage to global pop star Beyoncé, in addition to mentioning his record label and clothing line (which Bill Maher does as well when he introduces Jay-Z). Although Oprah has been known to be an ardent anti–Hop Hop spokesperson (which she acknowledges during the show in front of Jay-Z), she sets the stage of the spectacle by saying that regardless of what one's beliefs are about Hip Hop or Jay-Z, the parents in her audience should be well aware that their children have Jay-Z on their iPods. Furthermore audience members, both at home and in the studio, are invited to be impressed by Jay-Z and to know that he is a "sweet guy."[22] Jay-Z's appearance on the *Oprah Winfrey Show* recreates a spectacle of him in his "cool pose." For Jay-Z, this exposure, centered on his artistic merits, is also an opportunity to expose and shed light on a particular reality shared by many. His social and cultural capital exposes him to the mainstream in the form of Oprah's audience, while Oprah's audience is exposed to a visual image and narrative that expands the sense/perception of a pop cultural figure to include his emergence from the projects.[23]

In the respective interviews conducted by both Bill Maher and Oprah Winfrey, artistic practice and the place of origin/"Where I'm From" theme present themselves as significant aspects of the discourse. Herman Gray's insights on these matters are worth reviewing at length. According to Gray:

> practices, representations, and meanings, at the sites of the popular, are very much the subjects and objects of struggles across and within difference. Commercial culture is increasingly the central place where various memories, myths, histories, traditions, and practices circulate. At the site of commercial culture these practices and identifications are constantly assembled, torn apart, reassembled, and torn apart yet again by critics, viewers, and television makers such that they find discursive order resonance in everyday life.[24]

For Gray there is a multifaceted rubric that defines the site of the popular. Additionally, there is a set of contested expectations as to what symbols define the popular and its significance in the public and private spheres. Social and cultural capital is ascribed to popular culture; the inherent meanings of these ascriptions are debated across cultural, racial, gender, geographic, and generational lines. Increasingly, the realm of contemporary commercial culture is the site where competing narratives: memory, myth, history, traditions, and cultural practices vie for popular attention in the mainstream. Many of these debates are cyclical in nature and continue to shape the patterns of discourse in the collective public psyche, implicating both everyday observers and astute cultural critics. The boundaries of such discourse over what is acceptable in commercial culture are constantly negotiated and themselves are performances, much like what constitutes the commercial product being dissected. Bryant Keith Alexander corroborates this claim noting that: "Cultural performances are framed events; they are also important dramatizations of the codes and ethics of living in specific cultural communities."[25] Cultural performances are offered as scripted events, palatable accounts of the moral and ethical standards that provide context to the behaviors that govern interaction within cultural communities. A platform—in this instance, a set of television interviews—serves as a lens though which to articulate and write self and community into existence, offering nuance and critical substance to the experiences of everyday living that may otherwise appear black and white to the outsider. The behaviors that establish the rules of a given cultural community, it's "do's" and "don'ts" are explained and coded in a language that is accessible to cultural "others." While many who critique cultural performance tend to focus on rituals of representation (that is, performing rap music), moments of self-reflection vis-à-vis those performances (that is, an in-studio interview about the craft and art of one's performing Hip Hop music) offer similar opportunities to critically engage the social constructions of markers, space, place, and gender that determine appropriate responses to cultural realities.

The respective work of Alexander and Herman Gray establish important theoretical grounds for some of what is being staged via interviews with Jay-Z on *Real Time with Bill Maher* and the *Oprah Winfrey Show*. An application of these discourses helps to shed light on the structure and responses offered (both verbal and nonverbal) in the exchanges between hosts and Jay-Z on each respective show.[26] Commercial media outlets such as Bill Maher's *Real Time* and the *Oprah Winfrey Show* allow a figure like Jay-Z the opportunity to explain his rise from street hustler to rapper to corporate mogul. Jay-Z is in fact a figure that has transcended the realm of popular culture, at least as it pertains to the expressive culture of Hip Hop music. Beyond the actual act of performing his music, Jay-Z the talk show guest has an opportunity to offer clarity, moments of self-reflection, and ultimately an opportunity to counter, challenge, and represent a culture that he is very much a part of—a culture, that facilitated his emergence as the transcendent pop cultural figure that he has become.

One contributing factor to what makes Jay-Z Jay-Z, is his "cool pose" and how it is communicated in an audiovisual format. Richard Majors and Janet Mancini Billson argue that the cool pose is rooted in the construction of a cool masculinity that seeks to undermine and deconstruct dominant archetypes of masculine identity and behaviors: "Some African American males have channeled their creative energies into the construction of a symbolic universe. Denied access to mainstream avenues of success, they have created their own voice. Unique patterns of speech, walk, and demeanor express the cool pose. This strategic style allows the Black male to tip society's imbalanced scales in his favor. Coolness means poise under pressure and the ability to maintain detachment, even during tense encounters."[27] Coolness, for Jay-Z, includes a knack for dismissing questions that categorize him in unpopular ways by deflecting them to topics and/or issues with which he is comfortable. This is readily apparent when Bill Maher questions Jay-Z's ability to remain progressive (socioeconomically) when he has security and has amassed a significant amount of wealth. Jay-Z dismisses Maher's "Captain Save-a-Ho"[28] comment suggesting that his lyrics touch on universally understood emotions about the ups and downs, and anxieties associated with a desire to be successful. Jay-Z answers this question with a pause and a well-thought-out response, suggesting that he is neither rattled nor intimidated by Maher's challenge. Right after a series of questions dealing with the height of the East Coast–West Coast feud that claimed the lives of Hip Hop luminaries the Notorious B.I.G. and Tupac Shakur, Maher poses a question that exposes some inherent contradictions. Maher inquires into whether someone can claim to be a revolutionary figure when they are surrounded by great material wealth and security. Not only does Jay-Z dismiss the question, he reinforces the posturing of hypermasculine behavior expected of Hip Hop when suggesting that he would win a one-on-one fight against most rappers. While Maher attempts to use satire to extrapolate a critique of gendered relationships in Hip Hop, Jay-Z proceeds to gloss over any responsibility to be held accountable to his lyrical content. His retort is one that attempts to reframe the conversation without elaborating on the substance of that topic.[29]

When Maher asks about one of his favorite Jay-Z lyrics—lines that claim that Jay-Z did not cross over to the mainstream of popular culture, but instead brought the mainstream to the 'hood[30]—Jay-Z, offers a simple "yea," in response, as if to brush off the accomplishment or say "so what." The lyrics Maher was referencing came from a song entitled "Renegade" from Jay-Z's album *The Blueprint*. In answering Maher's question, Jay-Z alludes to the countless young men for whom his songs are empowering and aspirational. He understands that while they may not have gone through his exact experiences, the tone, delivery, and message of his story all resonate with them. Maher also outs Jay-Z as a friend of president Barack Obama. Jay-Z casually brushes the comment aside but Maher proceeds to show Jay-Z a clip. The clip is short, but it gets the point across. Jay-Z's video "Dirt Off Your Shoulder" plays and Jay-Z is seen brushing the dirt off his shoulders. The next clip shows Barack Obama engaging in the same act of brushing the dirt off of his shoulders; in this case showing a signifying response to his opponent's attack during the 2008 campaign. Through the artistic signification of Jay-Z, Obama performs a "cool pose." This a remarkable gesture in popular culture, especially given that President Obama's gesture is explicitly connected to Jay-Z by mainstream media commentators. Jay-Z's response to the juxtaposition of his music video and Obama's gesture is simply: "Wow."

I have very briefly here attempted to make sense of commercial television's fascination with Hip Hop mogul, Jay-Z, and his rise from hustling in

Brooklyn, New York to hustling in the boardrooms of corporate America. I have focused my attention on his appearances on *Real Time with Bill Maher* and the *Oprah Winfrey Show* respectively. Through a brief reading of these televised interviews, Jay-Z's carefully crafted image, merging his personal narrative from the streets of Brooklyn with his current status as a pop star, is unveiled as a spectacle of cool. This merger of seemingly opposed realities rests on Jay-Z's ability to project his "cool pose," all the while providing figures such as Bill Maher and Oprah Winfrey the opportunity to engage him in conversation about controversial and sometimes illegal topics. Ultimately the hosts and their audiences feel more enlightened about who Jay-Z is, who he claims to be, and how he represents Hip Hop culture in the popular public sphere. When thinking about the cool pose embodied by Jay-Z at the intersections of television, music, and popular culture, there has to be an acknowledgement of Shawn Carter the person and Jay-Z, the creative artistic persona, particularly when Shawn Carter/Jay-Z offers a nuanced and self-reflexive analysis of living and survival that confronts and attempts to unpack rigid notions of popular culture as being about certain narratives, places, and/or people. In these ways, on these respective outlets, Jay-Z offers insightful wisdom that seeks to redefine the parameters and contours of culture. Jay-Z's many insights and ability to diplomatically negotiate the contemporary terrain of multiple media outlets and public spheres is a testament to the fact that his genius is his cool pose, even as his cool pose is central to his artistic genius.

NOTES

1. Herman Gray, *Watching Race: Television and the Struggle for "Blackness"* (Minneapolis: University of Minnesota Press, 1995; repr. 2004).

2. Such thinking seems accurate to those outside of Hip Hop culture, but it is rather presumptuous given that this hustler-turned-rapper-turned-corporate mogul has navigated (and survived) the so-called urban concrete jungle, and only subsequently moved into the plush leather seats of corporate executive suites and corner offices. Gone are the Mitchell & Ness authentic throwback athletic jerseys, the baggy jeans, and the sneakers. This urban chic apparel is now replaced by custom-made tailored suits, Ralph Lauren clothing line ambitions, and lyrical punch lines about good credit particularly reflected in allusions to the American Express Black Card.

3. The paradigmatic shift alluded to in "Marcy to Hollywood & back again" is a line taken from the song "Marcy to Hollywood." Jay-Z featuring Memphis Bleek and Sauce Money, "Marcy to Hollywood," *The Players Club (Music From and Inspired by the Motion Picture)*, A&M Records, 1998.

4. I have argued elsewhere that Jay-Z suffers from a lyrical existentialism—pitting Shawn Corey Carter against his rap alter ego Jay-Z (as manifested in the

songs "Dead Presidents" and other songs on his debut album *Reasonable Doubt*, Roc-A-Fella Records, June 25, 1996 (compact disc).

5. Douglas Kellner, *Media Spectacle* (New York: Routledge, 2003), 5.

6. Guthrie P. Ramsey, Jr., *Race Music: Black Cultures from Bebop to Hip-Hop* (Berkeley: University of California Press, 2003), p. 4.

7. Ibid., 4.

8. Jay-Z, interview with Bill Maher on HBO's *Real Time*.

9. The "bling" cited in the song is an allusion to the ways in which jewelry shines when hit by light. The reference to bling vis-à-vis a historical figure like Che Guevara suggests that Jay-Z can simultaneously occupy the position of revolutionary figure and cultural icon, while being adorned by opulent symbols of wealth and capitalism. For Jay-Z, such a juxtaposition is without contradiction, perhaps an allusion of sorts to the complexities of music and creative expression. Jay-Z, "PSA," *The Black Album*, Roc-A-Fella Records, 2003.

10. In this context I am in conversation in Vershawn Ashanti Young and his text *Your Average Nigga: Performing Race, Literacy, and Masculinity* (Detroit: Wayne State University Press, 2007). In his visit back home to Chicago, Young self-reflects about the untapped potential for greatness present in his former neighborhood. He states:

> I don't want to think about how academically competitive they were in elementary school. How skilled they were in science and math, the arts, and sports. I don't want to get a headache from wondering whether they could just as easily be professors—or doing something even better. I want to be intellectual in my remembering—objective—as I turn a pseudoethnographic lens on my childhood community. (p. 21)

11. Bryant Keith Alexander, *Performing Black Masculinity: Race, Culture, and Queer Identity* (New York: AltaMira Press, 2006), xvi.

12. Ibid., 10.

13. This may be because those "others" share the same experiences and feel that Jay-Z authentically represents their plight or, because the narrative of the hustler or person making his way through society is somehow aspirational and perhaps in some way universal, as America seems to have a fascination with the reformed hustler.

14. Jay-Z, "Song Cry," *The Black Album*, Roc-A-Fella Records, 2003 (compact disc).

15. This reflects my analytical engagement and reading of Jay-Z's "Song Cry" which appears on *The Black Album* released by Roc-A-Fella Records in 2003.

16. "Empire State of Mind" discussed by Professor Imani Perry in chapter 1 was Jay-Z's first number one single. His response to Maher's line of questioning might further allude to an aural ethnographic experience had by the fan and/or listener, as they are given the agency and flexibility to tap into the raw emotions they take away from any his music. As Jay-Z continues to grow older as an artist, his fan base may continue to grow, but his position of self vis-à-vis his recorded music will remain the same.

17. Jay-Z, "Dead Presidents," *Reasonable Doubt*, Roc-A-Fella Records, 1996 (cassette).

18. These references to high culture and subsequently high culture's disdain of Jay-Z appears on songs such as "Somewhere in America," *MagnaCarta HolyGrail*, Roc Nation, 2013.

19. Jay-Z, interview with Oprah Winfrey on *The Oprah Winfrey Show*.

20. Songs such as "Hard Knock Life" and "Anything" appeared on the followup to *In My Lifetime, Vol.1*, entitled *Vol. 2 . . . Hard Knock Life*, Roc-A-Fella Records, 1998 (cassette).

21. Jay-Z, "Where I'm From," *In My Lifetime, Vol. 1*, Roc-A-Fella Records, 1997 (compact disc).

22. Jay-Z, interview with Oprah Winfrey on *The Oprah Winfrey Show*.

23. These mutual experiences of greater exposure illuminate deliberate interventions aligned with Alexander's argument that voice, place, and increasingly race and gender (in this case the male voice and perspective of Jay-Z) are central to shaping the images and experiences that alter the spectator's memory through which they understand self and construct their operational framework of "others."

24. H. Gray, *Watching Race*, 4.

25. B. K. Alexander, *Performing Black Masculinity*, 73.

26. Herman Gray's work on commercial culture suggests that the images, representation, and the messaging that accompany a popular medium such as Hip Hop are contested on a daily basis, including but not limited to, the public and private conversations happening in urban and middle America. With the increasingly global popularity of a commercial culture such as Hip Hop, we have a cultural space that conveys images of urban America, African American identity, black expressive culture, language (African American Vernacular English), and styles of authentic behaviors (think: Hip Hop moniker of "keeping it real"); all of which are packaged and marketed in a global economy, often without reason, rationale, or anticipation of how these images and rituals are being understood and appropriated in cultural specifically arenas. What results is a clash of cultures, whereby these practices and markers of identity are in constant conversation. A reinvention or representation of culture emerges that is perhaps a hybrid of traditional culture and commercial culture. These hybridized manifestations of culture then become part of the fabric of everyday life (*Watching Race*).

27. Richard Majors and Janet Mancini Billson, *Cool Pose: The Dilemmas of Black Manhood in America* (New York: Touchstone Books, 1992), 2.

28. This was something uttered by Bill Maher during a line of questioning directed at Jay-Z, interview with Bill Maher on HBO's *Real Time*.

29. Jay-Z, interview with Bill Maher on HBO's *Real Time*.

30. Jay-Z, "Renegade," *The Blueprint 2: The Gift & the Curse*, Roc-A-Fella/Island Def Jam, November 12, 2002 (compact disc).

Figure 14.1. Metropolis Reduxxed
Computer Image, art by John Jennings

14

✛

Disassembling the "Matrix of Domination"
Janelle Monáe's Transformative Vision
Carrie Walker

The cover of Janelle Monáe's album *Metropolis: The Chase Suite* (2008) indicates a story already set in motion. It features the mutilated bust and head of a young, attractive adult female against the backdrop of a theatrical standard: a red stage curtain. Her expression is intelligent but wary, lips slightly parted and her eyes averted. Her hair is styled in a Mohawk-bouffant hybrid, and missing flesh near her ear reveals an electronic interior below her porcelain skin. Loose wires, an open circuit board, and the number 57821 further testify that the woman is a droid who has been the target of intense violence. Though the woman is intact from the neck up, her torso is missing and her arms have been dismembered.[1] Through this image, Monáe introduces her cybernetic alter ego, Cindi Mayweather, and prepares her audience to enter the Metropolis, the decadent society where Mayweather's chronicle unravels through song. Monáe's audience is introduced to specific details regarding Mayweather's personal history through the album liner notes that introduce *Metropolis*. These notes explain that Mayweather—an organic cyborg—has a charmed life in the post-war 2719. Unlike other cyborgs in the Metropolis, Mayweather is equipped with a "rock star proficiency package and a working soul."[2] Other details elucidate the background of the amputated figure of Mayweather on the album cover and explain that Mayweather's stars are crossed. Though she had risen to become the figurehead of the Metropolis' cybersoul movement, Mayweather is now a fugitive. She has fallen in love with Anthony Greendown, a human, which is an action that is illegal in the Metropolis. Due to her transgression, Mayweather has fled to the Wonderground in order to avoid disassembly by the Druid Control, a mercenary force hired by the Metropolis' elites to enforce the law.

By inventing Mayweather and the Metropolis, Monáe crafts a dystopic future to guide audiences to reflect upon social inequities of the American present while also paying tribute to historical memory. Her work leads audiences to consider how hegemonic ideologies, stemming from the Enlightenment, continue to inflict injustices on citizens of the twenty-first century. Monáe's performances challenge the continued dissemination of Cartesian mind/body dichotomies by contemporary media—particularly its limited representation of black women. She critiques the way that popular culture and the music industry perpetuate epistemic violence. Despite the fact that developments in media technologies can enhance connectivity between people, Monáe's work suggests that humans have become enslaved by commercialism and disconnected from their organic selves. She exposes media failures, yet works within the system to rehabilitate it. She argues for a greater equilibrium between the human and the machine, the modern and the folk. Performing as a cyborg, an entity that is both human and machine, Monáe eludes categorization, operating in a liminal space that resists clearly defined categories. As Mayweather, it is difficult to circumscribe Monáe within the common stereotypes imposed upon black women performers: queen, "around-the-way girl," bitch, or whore.[3] Thus, Monáe's status as an entertainer provides her a platform to reinscribe the image of women in contemporary media and to encourage audiences to revolt against what Patricia Hill Collins calls the "matrix of domination." In its place, she offers listeners a transformative vision.[4]

The Metropolis, Mayweather's home, is a contested space.[5] The liner notes explain that the Metropolis is "one last great city," an urban center that has become a haven from the ecological devastation wrought by five World Wars. It is "known for its partying robo-zillionaires, riotous ethnic, race and class conflicts and petty holocausts."[6] This description signals that the Metropolis reproduces "the matrix of domination" described in Collins' book *Black Feminist Thought*. Collins uses this term to identify the structures through which the intersecting oppressions of race, class, gender, sexuality, and nation function in American culture.[7] She highlights several ways in which domination depends on constructions of black women's sexuality and cites the "capitalist commodity relations that sell Black women's bodies on the open market" as one example.[8] In this chapter I argue that Monáe's work critiques the conditions that allow for such "relations" and through her artistry she aims to inspire a more sustainable, equitable society.

Any attempt to describe Monáe's body of work through conventional musical categories can easily fail to honor her singular aesthetic. Monáe's fluid performances pull from genres and traditions inherited from or established by earlier artists, including blues singers, soul divas, musical theater performers, rock n' roll icons, and rappers.[9] On her website, Monáe's voice is compared to Shirley Bassey, and her partner, Wonder, states that working with her is "like having Judy Garland and Lauryn Hill team up on a record."[10] Her video "Many Moons" integrates concepts from Fritz Lang's 1927 film *Metropolis* and Ridley Scott's *Blade Runner* (1982). In addition, Monáe's dance performance in the "Many Moons" video replicates James Brown's footwork, reproduces Michael Jackson's "moonwalk," and evokes the stage presences of Grace Jones, Gwen Stefani, and Andre 3000.[11] By emulating the vocals of Garland and Bassey as well as invoking other iconic performances and productions, Monáe taps into the energy of the images and styles valued by American consumers of popular culture. Thus, her hybrid sound blurs the boundaries between the present and the past as well as the borders between various musical genres. Because Monáe's music is energetic, provocative, and timeless, critics commend her work but also struggle to describe her music.

In response to critics and interviewers who categorize her music as "Hip Hop," Monáe explains: "I don't really categorize anything that I do or say at all—you know, this is the genre that I'm trying to go into. And, you know, still to this day, I don't have a name for necessarily what I call my sound or what it is that we're doing . . . I don't force anything. And by nature, I think that I've always been drawn to women like Judy Garland, who always kept a very classic and timeless voice even Anita Baker at times. I love her voice, as well. So, you know, taking those out would just be taking a part of me away."[12] Though it is incorrect to formally label Monáe's work as Hip Hop, her genre-blending style honors the ethos of Old School era Hip Hop and the work of politically conscious artists who have followed this tradition. Like many Hip Hop artists, her performances employ a playful aesthetic to represent and challenge serious social inequalities. Her songs also include record scratching, sampling, breaks, and rapping, and they exhibit the bricolage that defined Hip Hop music before it became standardized via the influence of the recording industry and the marketplace. Monáe's work fulfills what Paul Gilroy deems the three strands of Hip Hop in *The Black Atlantic*—pedagogy, affirmation, and play—yet her performance should not be read through these elements alone.[13] Her multifaceted methods are also representative of what Gilroy labels a "changing" same, for they illustrate "the breaks and interruptions which suggest that the invocation of tradition may itself be a distinct, though covert, response to the destabilizing flux of the post-contemporary world."[14] By responding to contemporary social forces in a way that celebrates fluidity, Monáe appropriates and expands the elements of various genres that appeal to her and rejects content and attitudes inconsistent with her egalitarian values. One distinct element of popular culture—and American culture in general—that Monáe rejects are the "narrow spaces" available to black women performers.[15] In opposition to current commercial popular culture and videos that valorize patriarchal pornographic fantasies, Monáe's performances promote female subjectivity and affirm women's participation in contemporary music culture. In doing so, Monáe's work contributes to an increasing body of art that promotes a post–Hip Hop aesthetic. In "We Are the Post Hip-Hop Generation," M. K. Asante Jr. defines the term "post hip-hop" as:

> a period of time—now—of great transition for a new generation of black youths in search of a deeper understanding of themselves in a context outside of the hip-hop monopoly. Post hip-hop is an assertion that encapsulates my generation's broad range of abilities and ideas and incorporates recent social advances (i.e., the women's movement, gay rights) that hip-hop has refused to acknowledge or respect.[16]

Because Monáe's performances cross the boundaries of diverse musical genres and narrative traditions, addressing social justice issues often ignored by mainstream media sources, they are emblematic of the post–Hip Hop aesthetic that Asante describes. This label eschews limitations in a manner consistent with Monáe's adaptation of various performance strategies, and it also encompasses the post-urban and feminist sensibilities promoted throughout *Metropolis*.

The inclusive nature of Asante's "post hip-hop" label suits Monáe's cyborg persona as well as the neo-slave narrative approach she adopts. Ashraf H. A. Rushdy defines neo-slave narratives as "contemporary novels that assume the form, adopt the conventions, and take the first person voice of the antebellum slave narrative." In addition, he argues that authors of neo-slave narratives are conscious of the way they borrow from the past.[17] Evidence that Monáe is evoking historical memory can be found throughout *Metropolis*; connections between the fictional details of Mayweather's flight and the material realities of enslaved people under the institution of American slavery and Jim Crow are evident in many of her songs. For instance, like most enslaved people, Mayweather is not permitted to choose her own mate. When she falls in love with Greendown, she is forced into exile and, as shown in the song "Violet Stars Happy Hunting," she uses the stars as a map to guide her escape.[18] As such, Monáe's lyrics allude to the song "Follow the Drinking Gourd" which is popularly understood as a slavery-era spiritual that details an escape route to freedom in the North.[19] Thus, Monáe's lyrics convey the same desire for autonomy sought by enslaved people who fled persecution by way of the Underground Railroad. Rushdy also asserts that authors use the neo-slave narrative form to critique contemporary culture.[20] As will be demonstrated later in this chapter, Monáe utilizes the conventions of slave narratives to critique various forms of modern economic exploitation and to comment on the ways in which contemporary artists can be enslaved by the strictures that govern commercialism and fame in American popular culture.

In addition to engaging the neo-slave narrative structure, Monáe draws on early figures of resistance, both historical and literary, whose actions disrupted the white supremacist and patriarchal notions that African American people were disposable and less than human. Precursors for Monáe include historical figures like Harriet Tubman, Sojourner Truth, and Harriet Jacobs; each of these women is renowned for her flight from slavery as well as her contributions to the abolitionist movement. Mayweather also bears similarities to fictional characters such as Pauline Hopkins' Dianthe in *Of One Blood* (1903), Octavia Butler's Lilith in *Dawn* (1987), Toni Morrison's Sethe in *Beloved* (1987), and Nalo Hopkinson's Mi-Jeanne in *Brown Girl in the Ring* (1998). However, unlike Sethe who kills her daughter in order to save her from future suffering, Lilith, who remains enslaved, and Dianthe and Mi-Jeanne who are killed by their victimizers, Mayweather's fate is unknown. In an interview with Leital Molad on *Studio 360*, Monáe explains "I want to change history with this story."[21] With this statement in mind, audiences can hope that Mayweather will be safe from the violent outcomes that threatened other characters in her literary genealogy.

Like Hopkins, Butler, Morrison, and Hopkinson, Monáe draws upon speculative fiction themes. The time travel motif present in Monáe's performances also link her work to the musical performances of Sun Ra, George Clinton, Lee "Scratch" Perry, and DJ Spooky, artists whose works represent the tenets of Afrofuturism. In his essay "Black to the Future," Mark Dery defines Afrofuturism as "African American signification that appropriates images of technology and a prosthetically enhanced future," and he explains that it represents "past abduction, displacement and alien-nation" in order to challenge the status quo.[22] J. Griffith Rollefson extends the definition of Afrofuturism with his "Robot Voodoo Power" thesis, arguing that Afrofuturism is itself a mode of meaning-making and historical production that navigates, counters, and ultimately transcends the history of African American oppression while retaining a critical blackness. While Afrofuturist dialects recognize myths and collapse ossified binaries into dynamic unities, the episteme is grounded in its materialist opposition to white racist universalism. By stepping outside of the white liberal tradition and rewriting blackness in all its complexity,

Afrofuturism offers a novel form of revolution that is rooted in a long history of black opposition.[23]

Monáe's work exemplifies Afrofuturist challenges to Western racist universalism, and her performances promote a complex vision of blackness. Because she critiques misogyny using speculative fiction tropes, Monáe's music also expands the parameters of Afrofuturism—a traditionally masculine domain. Though there are several music videos in which female performers use futuristic elements to contest the subjugation of black women's bodies, including TLC's "No Scrubs" (1999), Lil' Kim's "How Many Licks" (2000), Missy Elliot's "Lose Control" (2005), and MC Lyte's "Lyte As A Rock" (1998) and "I Can't Make A Mistake" (2007), no other female performer emphasizes futuristic themes—or challenges the parameters of black female performance using Afrofuturism—as explicitly as Monáe.

In the tradition of Afrofuturist performance style, Monáe fuses samples into a synergistic aesthetic that contributes to an enhanced sensory experience. By doing so, she uses music as an interface between technology and the body to deconstruct the mind/body dichotomy and, in its place, enacts what Kodwo Eshun calls "rhythmic intelligence." In "Abducted by Radio," Eshun writes:

> Rhythm isn't really about notes or beats, it's about intensities, it's about crossing a series of thresholds across your body. Sound doesn't need any discourse of representations, it doesn't need any idea of discourse or the signifier; you can use sound as an immediate material intensity that grabs you ... Sound moves faster than your head, sound moves faster than your body ... sound is literally articulating you as a kind of exo-skeleton. It's almost like your feet are gaining an intelligence at the expense of your head ... Anywhere you have a sense of tension, that's the beginning, that's the signs of bodily intelligence switching itself on.[24]

Similar to the process that Eshun describes, Monáe's music "abducts" listeners with its intense rhythms, inviting them to "switch on" and to participate in a dialogue—consciously or unconsciously—about the modern world. Further, by doing so, Monáe subverts the pattern of the slave narrative; though her Mayweather character is a victim of domination, Monáe refuses to be subordinated. Instead, she manipulates the emotions of her listeners so that they become more conscious of the effects of rhythmic intelligence—a state in which the mind, body, and sonic technologies are fused, rendering all hegemonic structures useless.

An examination of the musical components of Monáe's song "Many Moons" demonstrates this phenomenon in three distinct movements. In the first segment of the song, a VOX Continental organ drives the tempo with a fervent drumbeat and, as Monáe sings in fluctuating pitches and measures, her vocals are framed and echoed by a harmonizing chorus. Together, these effects create a rising tension that, regardless of the meaning of the lyrics, causes the listener an increasing feeling of angst. Three minutes into the song, Monáe's vocals shift from a classic lyrical delivery into a slow, clear rap and the instrumentals drop in intensity. Behind the main vocalization, the chorus continues to sing "na-na-na" in the backdrop and an electronic guitar begins to add interference. By reducing the pace, Monáe gives listeners the opportunity to absorb the anxiety that the music generates. When the rap ends, Monáe's primary voice is silent and the final minute of the song consists of a dreamy guitar and ethereal voices, creating an ambient sound that gradually fades to silence. This finale leaves listeners with a sense of weightlessness, as though time has been suspended. However, this sequence also leaves listeners confused, without a sense of resolution or pointed idea as to how to interpret the "rhythmic intelligence" just experienced.[25] Ultimately, Monáe denies her listeners aural catharsis, guiding them to contemplate the ambiguity of their auditory abduction and to reflect on their sonic journey outside of the matrix of domination.

Because the cyborg occupies a liminal space, Monáe's Mayweather persona further challenges the mind/body dichotomy as well as the hegemonic notions that accompany it. According to Donna Haraway in "A Manifesto for Cyborgs," liminality, or an ontological space between binary categories such as male/female, human/machine, primitive/civilized, mind/body, is a position of power.[26] For this reason, Mayweather's liminality offers Monáe the ability to create meaningful dialogue about gender, and it offers an alternative model of consciousness. As Mayweather, Monáe escapes the limitations of socially constructed categories like race, gender, class, and sexuality described by Haraway.[27] Haraway writes, "cyborg imagery can suggest a way out of the maze of dualisms in which we have explained our bodies and our tools to ourselves. This is a dream not of a common language, but of powerful infidel heteroglossia."[28] Haraway contends that, under this "infidel heteroglossia," resistance to systematic oppression is possible. In addition, she states, the "cyborg myth is about transgressed boundaries, potent fusions, and dangerous possibilities which progressive people might explore as one part of needed political work."[29] An examination of Monáe's work reveals that she explores these same boundaries, fusions, and policies.

Monáe's social critique is predicated on Mayweather's cybernetic status. In light of Haraway's observations about the role of the cyborg, Monáe's choice to perform as a human/machine hybrid should be read as a challenge to those who supply and demand images that purport women to be little more than a body (or booty) to be consumed. Through her cyborg persona, Monáe disrupts the stereotypes imposed upon black female performers.[30] Thus, using this technological ruse to create what does not yet exist in market realities, Monáe protests the continued methods by which women continue to be objectified. Monáe's choice to adopt a cybernetic alter ego disrupts these harmful hierarchies and urges that women should be represented with dignity rather than being reduced to their female anatomy. Her oeuvre directs audiences to reimagine society in more humane, less exploitative ways in order to prevent the dystopian nightmare of the Metropolis from coming to fruition. The image of Mayweather's dismembered body from the *Metropolis* album cover stresses the urgency of this message.

Monáe's lyrics in "Violet Stars Happy Hunting" foster a cyber-feminist sensibility that continues throughout the album. In this song, Monáe juxtaposes a critique of the objectification of women with a depiction of how the public sphere infringes upon interpersonal relationships. This song begins with an ironic assertion of selfhood; she identifies herself as a cybernetic female alien who is lacking a face, heart, and brain. By characterizing Mayweather as lacking the organs and features necessary for life, Monáe signifies on rap videos and other media that objectify women—particularly black women—by portraying them as gyrating eye candy and "tip drills" rather than thinking, feeling human beings.[31] In this sense, Monáe's lyrics echo the sentiments of Audre Lorde, who describes the pornographic as "sensation without feeling," and the song exposes how misogyny alienates women from their erotic power.[32]

In addition, "Violet Stars Happy Hunting" details the reason why Mayweather absconds from the Metropolis; the song explains that Mayweather is being hunted by the droid control because, as a cyborg, she has broken the law by falling in love with a human. Though the consequences Greendown faces are unknown, lyrics identify that Mayweather's life is in peril. Mayweather's predicament recalls instances in American history when the state unjustly intervened in citizens' interpersonal relationships. Her reference to the genocidal mercenaries alludes to institutionalized efforts to control black women's sexuality through forced contraception and sterilization.[33] In addition, these lyrics evoke an era in American history before the 1967 court case *Loving v. Virginia* overturned laws prohibiting interracial marriage. By pairing examples of racist public policies with misogynist media representations, Monáe's lyrics calls attention to the means by which capitalist, patriarchal technologies of control criminalize women's sexuality in order to maintain power.[34]

Mayweather's description of herself as raceless slave in "Violet Stars Happy Hunting" further positions her work as a neo-slave narrative, and it contributes to contemporary debates regarding race and gender in a globalized society. These lyrics also direct listeners to, at least momentarily, consider Monáe's work as a resistance to the objectification of women on a transnational scale. In *Black Feminist Thought*, Collins cites Pearl Cleage's definition of feminism as "the belief that women are full human beings capable of participation and leadership in the full range of human activities—intellectual, political, social, sexual, spiritual, and economic." Collins continues, "in its broadest sense, feminism constitutes both an ideology and a global political movement that confronts sexism, a social relationship in which males as a group have authority over females as a group."[35] By performing as a raceless slave who is on the lam, Monáe joins the "global political movement" named by Collins, and she draws attention to the "absence of choices" faced by women around the world. Her work honors those women and their advocates who, like Mayweather, breech unjust laws in the pursuit of equal rights on behalf of women everywhere.[36]

On the other hand, Mayweather's racelessness, as identified in "Violet Star Happy Hunting" lyrics, may cause audience members reason for concern because, in some ways, it reflects a liberal subjectivity that claims that race does not matter in contemporary American society. While Monáe may be expressing a yearning for a time when the social constructions of race will no longer be used as a divisive strategy to maintain systems of white supremacy, this post-race notion works against the larger trajectory of her work which otherwise contests marginalization generally and subordination of black women specifically. In addition, this lyric separates Monáe's work from the collective metaphor of Afro-alienation experienced by African Americans who are "descendants of alien abductees."[37] This moment of racial erasure also connects to concerns regarding the "blanching of the future" that occurs throughout speculative fiction.[38] In following these ideas, Monáe's words, too, can be critiqued because they step away from the task of repairing the "digital divide" to which the rest of her work gestures.[39] Furthermore, this notion indicates that the erasure of differences would be preferable to a future in which racial, ethnic, sexual, socioeconomic, and/or gender differences are equally valued or expressed.

Like her song lyrics, Monáe's stage performances are tailored to resist sexual objectification and they, too, explore the intersections between beauty and exploitation. Although Monáe could allure admirers with her physical attractiveness, she chooses instead to engage her audiences' intellectual and aesthetic sensibilities in an unconventional manner. Monáe consistently performs in a tuxedo, saddle shoes, and a Mohawk hairdo, a hybrid combination unlike any other artist. Although absent from the art in Monáe's liner notes, Monáe routinely wears this uniform during concerts, photo shoots, and in her short film "Many Moons." Except for two deliberate scenes in the video, Monáe, performing as Mayweather, is clothed from head to foot, a strategy that limits viewers' ability to visually consume her body. By dressing androgynously, Monáe separates herself from the stereotype of a hypersexualized artist typically depicted in music videos, and, by doing so, she establishes a model of subjectivity. Further, unlike female artists whose eyes engage the viewers' gaze as either a means of seduction or as a challenge to domination, in "Many Moons," Mayweather rarely maintains consistent eye contact with the camera/viewer.[40] Instead, her eyes move rapidly, mechanically. Such disengagement highlights Mayweather's cybernetic nature; as a nonhuman, she refuses to participate in the economy of the gaze, neither challenging nor endorsing it.[41]

The "Many Moons" video is a sci-fi trip doubling as a neo-slave narrative, and it offers a further critique of the contemporary society. Though the setting is futuristic, Monáe compares the production of contemporary music performances and fashion shows with the characteristics of a slave trade. The video begins *in medias res* with respect to Mayweather's story—captions identify Lady Maxxa, the hostess of the Annual Android Auction, as the woman who appears on the stage. In her welcome speech, Maxxa indoctrinates Monáe's audience with the values of the Metropolis, asking the auction attendees, "Who built ya' body? Angels or demons? God or a computer? It's a simply question really. But, who cares? As long as it's beautiful."[42] With this declaration, Maxxa turns her body and sways her curvy backside, eliciting laughter from the crowd. Through Maxxa's induction, Monáe's viewers learn that, in the Metropolis, beauty—genuine or artificial—reigns supreme. The material realities of these ideals are inconsequential. Maxxa's gesture also shows Monáe's viewers that the same market "principles" that led to the exploitation of Saartjie Baartman (the "Hottentot" Venus) in the nineteenth century continue to flourish in 2719. During Maxxa's prologue, the camera pans the audience and captions identify the notable participants in the crowd.[43] The blithe atmosphere indicates patrons' complicity with the commoditization and/or fetishization of female bodies, whether for profit or individual gratification.

Next, Maxxa introduces Mayweather as the Alpha Platinum 9000 prototype and, when Monáe rushes onto the runway stage, a scene eliciting historical memory unfolds. Mayweather begins to sing, and the chic droid models—all played by Monáe—are auctioned off to the elites in the crowd. As replica models sashay down the runway, an analogy between past and present oppressions ossifies; the platform is a modern-day auction block. This parallel is emphasized when a wealthy redheaded white woman leans over to the tuxedoed man sitting beside her and whispers "I want one" in a manner reminiscent of a time many white women enthusiastically endorsed slavery.[44,45] While it is unlikely that Monáe is suggesting that viewers feel an equal level of sympathy for fashion models and actual enslaved people, her performance critiques industries that profit from the objectification of women. Meanwhile, the bidding continues and cheering fans clap along to the beat. The fervor of the crowd is a reminder that people of all demographic backgrounds—not just the affluent bidders—collaborate in the matrix of domination that sanctions female subjugation.

Analyzed in conjunction with the video, the lyrics of "Many Moons" underscore the Metropolis's failure to ensure the liberties of its citizens. Monáe's words suggest that, while residents seemingly dance freely in underground spaces, they are really imprisoned in a place where speech, sunshine, safety, and dreams are deferred.[46] In these lyrics, Monáe draws attention to the fact that no individual is truly liberated while living in a system that silences its citizens. Her words indicate that, since freedom continues to be denied for many people, the principles on which the Metropolis was founded remain unfulfilled. She suggests that while many individuals may dance freely, doing so does not represent real liberty when various forms of epistemic violence persist. Not only does Monáe critique the state in this passage, but also those individuals who disengage from the world, choosing complicity instead of taking action against injustice. In addition, these lyrics evoke historical memories of "sundown towns," American towns, mostly in the Midwest, where people of color were not allowed to be in public spaces after sundown due to legal restrictions or threat of violence.[47] Thus, again, Monáe draws attention to the intersections between past, present, and future injustice. Furthermore, Monáe's attention to a dearth of sunshine throughout these lyrics speaks to environmental quality concerns that connect to the nuclear devastation that has given rise to the Metropolis. These lyrics suggest that, without natural light, crime and violence persist. As such, Monáe's words indicate a longing for a more spacious, organic existence rather than continuing to live in a stifled, underground hideout.

In the chorus of "Many Moons," Monáe draws upon vernacular language and more imagery from the natural world to protest the Metropolis' corrupt principles. Through her direction to "make it rain," Monáe utilizes a folk expression that calls for social action.[48] And, though a silver bullet traditionally symbolizes a technological cure for social ills, here, the silver bullet—a natural element reshaped by human technology—also stands for "Truth." In this case, Monáe argues that truth and love are the artillery needed to equip the revolution that her lyrics implore. In addition, her panther allusion pays tribute to the Black Panthers, a Black Nationalist organization founded in 1962, reminding listeners of historical precedents for social justice campaigns like the Black Power movement. Her use of the word panther also solicits the image of the large black predatory cat, which, though revered for its stealth and power, is nearing extinction. Thus, this image symbolizes the imperative to protect human society and the natural world from the destructive side effects of technology. Collectively, these lyrics suggest that, by balancing the organic with the machine, harmful ideological dualisms can be replaced with a more sustainable, equitable system. Monáe tells listeners that they possess the solution to the social and ecological hazards that threaten to destroy them, and that by choosing love, citizens of the twenty-first century can use technology to actualize their liberatory potential.

Monáe's use of natural imagery and vernacular language in the lyrics of "Many Moons" and throughout *Metropolis* work to draw her audiences' awareness to the ways in which the issues of gender, race, class, and the environment overlap. In *Converging Stories: Race, Ecology, and Environmental Justice in American Literature*, Jeffrey Myers argues that the very existence of the Euroamerican subject depends on imagining not only the racial Other, but a priori on imagining the essential "otherness" of the physical world—of the human body, the bodies of plants and animals, and the body of the earth itself.[49] Monáe's work signals that just as American slavery and the commodification of women's bodies by the entertainment industry has depended on the "otherness" of human beings so, too, has ecological exploitation relied upon an artificial divide between humans and the natural world. Monáe's regular references to natural imagery and use of names like Mayweather, Greendown, and Deep Cotton for her characters shows that she rejects Enlightenment-based notions that subjugate the "primitive" natural world. Rather than reiterating divisive rhetoric, she constructs a technologically infused spirituality where "green" is "down" and Mayweather's "cyber*soul*" integrates scientific innovation, humaneness, and popular culture.[50] This gesture toward ecological consciousness reminds listeners that simply working to eradicate one form of oppression—such as racism or sexism—would be ineffective when the matrix of domination is fueled by multiple forms of injustice. Monáe's lyrics urge that all forms of oppression—racial, socioeconomic, gender, environmental, etc.—must be eliminated for the sake of social progress and prosperity.

"Many Moons" not only challenges the ways in which women's bodies are commodified by the mainstream media, but it also parodies the method by which artificial, pornographic fantasies are "pieced together."[51] In one scene, Monáe links oppressive beauty standards from the past with current practices when one of Mayweather's replicas is laced into a white corset—a classic signifier of patriarchal beauty ideals and means to control female sexuality. As Mayweather is literally tied up by her white male stylist, the droid mouths the words "your freedom's in a bind" and looks to the viewer with a dejected expression. Meanwhile, another shot shows a different replica whose long, sleek extensions are being combed, this time by a white woman, drawing attention to the ways in which many black women deviate from natural hair styles in order to fit Western beauty ideals.[52] In between these scenes, Mayweather continues her performance, and the robotic precision of her dance moves further signifies on videos that portray women as automatons.

During the "Many Moons" video, Monáe acknowledges that the political nature of her performance forces her to make aesthetic sacrifices. While dancing the "Funky Chicken," a dance popularized by James Brown, Mayweather tells her audience that despite the strength she has show throughout her career, all she really wants to do is sing.[53] This moment of frustration highlights the laborious nature of inciting revolution, and it suggests that, perhaps, Monáe would rather produce art for its own sake rather than using it as a medium to deliver a sociopolitical message regarding inequality in the modern world. Moreover, in voicing Mayweather's wish to sing, Monáe protests the silencing that occurs under racist, capitalist, patriarchal hegemony. To drive home this point, Mayweather raises a clenched fist, a Black Power salute that suggests the power of solidarity, while, again, singing the word "freedom" to underscore her rebellious message. Immediately after this gesture, viewers' attention is drawn to the issues of police corruption and criminality among the auction attendees when a bidding war erupts over a droid named Charlotte Dedeaux. The police captain 61X Savage arrests Chung Knox, a snarling character, for outbidding him. This disturbance does not disrupt the auction; instead, the wealthy attendees continue to buy cyborg models and Mayweather's fans cheer her on in traditional rock-concert fashion. The lack of reaction among the crowd signals the general apathy of citizens who endorse corruption by way of their complicity rather than breaking from the revelry to fight against it.

After this scene, Mayweather segues into a "cybernetic chantdown" that augments her message regarding social injustice in the Metropolis.[54] Monáe's rap functions as verbal collage, bombarding listeners with word associations that deconstruct the realities of the underclass and expose the contradictions of present day society. While the lyrics of "Many Moons" are seemingly random, patterns are recognizable. For example, her focus on racialized features relates to the earlier discussion of the imposition of Western beauty standards on black women. With these images, Monáe calls into question discriminatory attitudes and social constructions of beauty that alienate women and girls who do not fit conventional prototypes. Also, the phrases juxtaposing creativity and love with stupidity and erasure tie back to the recording industry strictures that deter innovation. These phrases remind listeners that, though creativity and love are theoretically valued by many consumers, performances that perpetuate stereotypes, especially violent ones, are more highly rewarded in commercial markets.[55] These lyrics also articulate the anxiety an artist can experience when breaking free from the conventional modes of cultural production, an idea that is further explored in the video's conclusion.

During Mayweather's chantdown, the camera alternates between Mayweather, her audience, droid models, and the vintage film clips projected against the backdrop of the stage. The montage includes footage from Civil Rights marches, Andy Warhol's art, marching soldiers, Amelia Earhart, and an atomic bomb explosion. Monáe's fans scream in Beatlemania fashion while, in step with Mayweather's rhythm, droid models dressed as Earhart march across the stage. The khaki-clad replicas pay tribute to Earhart since, as a female pilot, she transgressed traditional gender roles but also because Earhart was a successful clothing designer and an editor of a column for *Cosmopolitan* magazine.[56] By invoking Earhart, Monáe provides a historical example of how the beauty industry can merge with technology to promote an uplifting image of women. At the same time, however, this perspective on Earhart is complicated by a caption which names one of the droids Emily Empire, indicting the American military industrial complex of which Earhart, an aviation pioneer, played a role. The droids' uniforms can also be read as an allusion to the Tuskegee Airmen, World War II pilots who, despite their patriotism and training, were barred from combat due to segregation laws. By invoking the memories of Earhart and the Tuskegee Airmen, Monáe draws attention to historical attempts made by the power structure to maintain dominance using objectification and alienation based on artificial categories of gender and race. These multiple readings of the droids' uniforms reflect the paradoxes of modernity highlighted in the images projected on the screen. By pairing these images, Monáe exposes the contradictions underlying technological progress, especially its Janus-like ability to uplift and degrade humanity.

During the remaining portion of Mayweather's rap in "Many Moons," cheering fans transform into swaying zombies, indicating the collusion of everyday people in the status quo. The confluence of iconography— particularly the mushroom cloud that concludes the series—further challenges the complacency of everyday citizens and adds a new layer of urgency to the chorus. With these film clips, Monáe reminds viewers that, as shown throughout history, individuals can use technology to fight on behalf of oppressed people or they can stand by while leaders gamble with the fate of humanity. By ending the montage with a nuclear explosion, Monáe leads viewers to contemplate the role of nuclear technology in world history and to reconsider fundamental notions of freedom during an era when many governments possess the tools to annihilate entire nations with ease. Since Mayweather is a messenger from a post-nuclear state, the urgency underlying her message is heightened; her presence reminds listeners of their own tenuous existence and begs them to safeguard their humanity from the hazards of modern technology.

After the nuclear bomb detonates on the screen, Mayweather becomes overwhelmed and, dancing into a frenzy, she rises into the air where she is zapped by an electrical field. The onlookers are speechless—some horrified and others mesmerized—as they watch her suspended body. In the air, Mayweather's body doubles into two versions itself, enacting both Dubois' notion of double consciousness and the "flying African" motif foreshadowed by the Earhart/Tuskegee uniforms.[57] Though folklore surrounding the flying African maintained that, during American slavery, slaves could sprout wings to fly back to Africa when facing death, Mayweather's transcendence should not be read as a yearning to escape suffering and fly to freedom.[58] Instead, she remains committed to the present. Her actions echo the words of Ralph Ellison's character, Todd, who, in "Flying Home" states that he wants to fly because "it's as good a way to fight and die as I know."[59] At this point in the video, another droid named Lady Maestra, Master of the Show Droids, appears on horseback and sings the final lyrics with her group of green-eyed bride droids. Slowly, an unconscious Mayweather descends to the floor where Maestra's "mechanical brides"—figures who symbolize the perilous aspects of the marriage between human and machine—encircle her.[60] While, lyrically, Lady Maestra and the brides offer listeners the option to retreat to Shangri-La, no such solace is extended to Mayweather. The ethereal lullaby Maestra sings reveals her Revolutionary War garb to be a facade. Maestra and her brides are not part of Mayweather's progressive movement; instead, they aim to deter social transformation by manipulating the audience to forget the trauma that unfolded before them. Mayweather has the final word, however. When the scene fades to black, a quote appears, stating, "I imagined many moons in the sky lighting the way to freedom—Cindi Mayweather."[61] This conclusion leaves viewers without a resolution; the only certainty is that Mayweather is in jeopardy.

By ending the film ambiguously, Monáe forces her audiences to imagine their own conclusion. Because the video picks up Mayweather's story before she falls in love with Greendown, it is possible that her collapse is the beginning of her displacement from the Metropolis. In addition to being a possible plot device in Mayweather's larger story, the finale of "Many Moons" protests the continued existence of misogyny, economic inequality, and capitalist exploitation that persists in contemporary media despite other cultural and technological advances by resisting a happy ending when, in reality, social ills continue to thrive. Furthermore, the conclusion suggests that, under current conditions, no plausible space exists for a female artist who wants to be recognized for her talent rather than sexual desirability. As such, Mayweather's breakdown may reflect Monáe's anxiety regarding her own marketability in an anti-intellectual climate that discourages innovative musical contributions.

In addition, the video's unresolved conclusion is a part of the strategy through which Monáe dares her audience to rise up and become part of the revolution that she implores. In *Blues Legacies and Black Feminisms*, Angela Davis argues that:

> Art may encourage a critical attitude and urge its audience to challenge social conditions, but it cannot establish the terrain of protest by itself. In the absence of popular mass movement, it can only encourage a critical attitude. When the blues "name" the problems community wants to overcome, they help create the emotional conditions for protest but do not and could not, of themselves, constitute social protest.[62]

Consistent with Davis' ideas regarding the intersection of art and political protest, the finale of the "Many Moons" video proposes that each audience member examine his or her own participation in the matrix of domination. Monáe's conclusion implies that, from this point, individuals will either choose to change their behaviors or remain captives of an escapist fantasy. Considering Monáe's work in its entirety, readers can presume that she hopes to motivate the former action rather than the latter. Through Mayweather, her cyborg delegate, Monáe suggests that social action is not the responsibility of any single person but a global community of dedicated citizens.

This argument is more explicit in the song "Sincerely Jane," which builds upon the sociopolitical commentary Monáe constructs in "Many Moons." In "Sincerely Jane," a song inspired by a letter from her mother, Monáe calls specifically for community involvement. This song begins by listing contemporary social problems that plague many communities: youth violence, high school dropouts, teen pregnancy, illiteracy, premature death, drug abuse, depression, complacency, lost dreams, and abandonment of hope. The orchestrations and record scratching which accompany these lyrics heighten the urgency of Monáe's call to address these problems directly. In the chorus, Monáe questions listeners whether they are alive or merely soulless zombies. Monáe's distress regarding the status quo is evident, and she beseeches listeners to awaken their consciousness and transform society by way of active engagement. Her lyrics also grieve the unfulfilled promises of past social movements that have yet to come to fruition. While the events to which Monáe refers remain unidentified, listeners can look to the unfinished work of Emancipation, the Suffrage Movement, the Civil Rights Movement, colonial independence movements, and the counter-cultural revolutions of the latter half of the twentieth century, since these campaigns critique the same problems Monáe highlights.

Through the lyrics in "Sincerely Jane," Monáe highlights the crucial role that adults play in young people's development, and she reminds listeners that, without the presence of teachers and other positive role models, the media can negatively influence young women's decision-making ability.[63] Rather than criticizing these women for their choice to participate in the matrix of domination, Monáe portrays them as confused individuals who have fallen victim to the superficial lures offered by the music industry. "Sincerely Jane" reminds listeners—including consumers, producers, and performers involved in music industry—of the inherent value of women and seeks to unify citizens through an ethos of shared responsibility.

On her website, Janelle Monáe identifies the space she strives to occupy in the music industry. Monáe states:

I want to be looked at as a leader and a businesswoman . . .
I really feel that music and artists have a huge influence in the way we think. My goal is to help bring as many people as I possibly can together with my music . . . With regards to the way that I dress, to the things that come out of my mouth, I'm really trying to give a different perspective.

After a moment of consideration, she adds,
and I think there are a lot of young girls out there who are like me.[64]

Her goals demonstrate that, unlike members of the unconscious masses she attempts to rouse by her performances, Monáe actively promotes positive images for young girls to emulate. Monáe's statement indicates she believes that there are many people, young girls in particular, who desire images that provide an alternative to the denigrating depictions of women promoted by mainstream media and American culture. As discussed throughout this chapter, Monáe's performances refuse conventionality and expand the boundaries of contemporary musical aesthetics. As such, Monáe succeeds in her attempt to create a new outlook and inspires her readers to suspend their own collusion with the matrix of domination.

During a lecture at the Inaugural Conference for the Hip Hop Archival Collection at Cornell University, Tricia Rose discussed the need to create a safer space for women in the male-dominated Hip Hop sphere. She called for efforts to build consciousness and to transform expectations in order to achieve "love, dignity, and possibility."[65] I argue that Janelle Monáe's performances embody these goals. Responding to the narrow roles available to women artists, Monáe employs cyber-feminism to promote a broader, more egalitarian representation of women in contemporary society. Monáe's *Metropolis* creates a new interface where technology is used to affirm women's bodies rather than perpetuate epistemic violence and dehumanization. Her work disassembles binary categorizations and exposes social problems in a manner that avoids reproducing the symptoms of the matrix of domination. Monáe's performances draw on a folk aesthetic to urge engaged citizenship and, through her art, she encourages dignity and respect. Witness to the philosophy that Monáe promotes in her music, audiences experience a transformational vision, one in which freedom and love are not just cyborg fantasies but real possibilities.[66]

NOTES

1. The illustrations for *Metropolis* were created by Chad Weatherford.
2. Janelle Monáe, liner notes to *Metropolis: The Chase Suite*, Bad Boy Records 511234-1, 2007 (compact disc).
3. These stereotypes are often imposed upon black female performers. In *Black Looks: Race and Representation* (Boston: South End Press, 1992; repr. New York: 1999), bell hooks argues, "contemporary films continue to place black women in two categories, mammy or slut, and occasionally a combination of the two" (74). The terms included above are based on stereotypes of black women that have existed for centuries, including mammy (an asexual, full bodied matriarch), jezebel (a sexual temptress), and sapphire (an emasculating spitfire). The "around-the-way girl"—most famously characterized by LL Cool J's 1990 song by the same title—is a more recent, less violent stereotype. The "around-the-way girl" is a generally respected "girl-next-door" figure, yet she is also put on a pedestal and often an object of male conquest because of her confidence and attractiveness.
4. This application of Collins term the "matrix of domination" will be followed by a discussion of what Donna Jean Haraway calls the "informatics of domination." In many ways, these terms have overlapping meaning yet are distinct to specific conversations. Here, I draw upon Collins' term "matrix of domination" as it applies specifically to my discussion of Monáe's work as challenging the exploitation of black women's bodies in general. Later, when Monáe's cyborg status is discussed specifically, I will examine her work through Haraway's discussion of the "informatics of domination" as "scary new networks" that are based on the former "comfortable old hierarchal dominations." Using this term, Haraway examines the dualisms that have persisted in Western ideologies of domination (including self/other, mind/body, culture/nature, male/female, civilized/primitive, reality/appearance, whole/parts, etc.). ("A Manifesto for Cyborgs: Science, Technology, and Socialist Feminism," in *The Haraway Reader* [New York: Routledge, 2004], 1–45.)
5. The fact that Mayweather has been forced to leave her home in order to preserve her life dovetails with ideas raised by Carole Boyce Davies' in *Black Women, Writing, and Identity: Migrations of the Subject* regarding the nature of "home" and "nation." Boyce Davies writes that home is contradictory, contested space, a locus for misrecognition and *alienation*"(my italics). Boyce Davies explains that Afro-Caribbean women's writing in the United States "doubly disrupts the seamless narrative of home and so of nation. Further, her location in a variety of social and political contexts allows internal critiques of new inscriptions of coloniality and imperialism ([London and New York: Routledge, 1994], 113)." While Mayweather

is not an Afro-Caribbean woman, her status as a fugitive from the Metropolis—a colony of sorts—positions her in a similar position. As will be demonstrated throughout this paper, Monáe's work also offers "internal critiques" and disrupts the narrative of contemporary America as a state which prioritizes the freedom and safety of some citizens over others/Others.

6. Janelle Monáe, liner notes to *Metropolis: The Chase Suite*, Bad Boy Records 511234-1, 2007 (compact disc).

7. Patricia Hill Collins, *Black Feminist Thought: Knowledge, Consciousness, and the Politics of Empowerment*, 2nd ed. (New York: Routledge, 2009), 21.

8. Ibid., 218.

9. Rap music, which evolved from MC-ing (a term originally used to describe the "master of ceremonies" or person who provided lyrics to DJ's backbeats and announcement at parties), has become the most prominent feature of Hip Hop music. According to Tricia Rose in *Black Noise: Rap Music and Black Culture in Contemporary America* (Middletown, CT: Wesleyan University Press, 1994), "Rap music is a black cultural expression that prioritizes black voices from the margins of urban America" and a "form of rhymed storytelling accompanied by highly rhythmic, electronically based music" which began in the Bronx in the 1970s (2). In the twenty-first century, rap music is not only one of the most vibrant cultural movements in the United States but it is a global phenomena.

10. Janelle Monáe, "Biography," contactmusic.com, http://www.contactmusic.com/info/janelle_monae (accessed April 12, 2014).

11. Janelle Monáe, "Many Moons," *Metropolis: Suite I (The Chase)*, August 2008, directed by Alan Ferguson and The Wondaland Arts Society, http://www.youtube.com/user/janellemonae (accessed April 23, 2014).

12. Janelle Monáe, interview by Terry Gross," *Fresh Air*, National Public Radio, June 17, 2009, http://www.npr.org/templates/transcript/transcript.php?storyId=105491960 (accessed April 12, 2014).

13. Paul Gilroy, *The Black Atlantic: Modernity and Double Consciousness* (Cambridge, MA: Harvard University Press, 1993), 85.

14. Ibid., 101.

15. In an interview with Farai Chideya called "Rapping, Woman to Woman," rapper Monie Love laments the "narrow spaces" available to women in commercial Hip Hop markets (*Hip Hop: The Past, Present & Future*, NPR Music, "Hip-Hop's Herstory," June 11, 2007, http://www.npr.org/templates/story/story.php?storyId=10948089 [accessed April 12, 2014]).

16. M. K. Asante, Jr. "We are the Post Hip-Hop Generation." *San Francisco Gate*, February 7, 2006, http://www.sfgate.com/opinion/openforum/article/We-are-the-post-hip-hop-generation-2504977.php (accessed April 11, 2014).

17. Ashraf H. A. Rushdy, *Neo-Slave Narratives: Studies in the Social Logic of a Literary Form* (New York: Oxford University Press, 1999), 3.

18. During slavery, slaves who sought to escape to the free states used the North Star as a means to navigate their journey northward. The "North Star" became an emblem of freedom and Frederick Douglass adopted this term for his abolitionist paper, *The North Star*. For more information on these topics, see Eber Pettit's "Fugitives Follow the North Star (1879)," in *Slavery in the United States: A Social, Political, and Historical Encyclopedia*, ed. Junius P. Rodriguez (Santa Barbara,

CA: ABC-CLIO, 2007), 572; and Douglass, *The Narrative of the Life of Frederick Douglass: An American Slave, Written by Himself* (1845), ed. David Blight, 2nd ed. (Boston: Bedford/St. Martin's, 2003).

19. Whether or not the historical reality of "Follow the Drinking Gourd" matches the folklore that surrounds it has come under scrutiny. See Joel Bressler's website "Follow the Drinking Gourd: A Cultural History," 2008–2012, http://followthedrinkinggourd.org/ (accessed May 31, 2014) and James B. Kelley's "Song, Story, or History: Resisting Claims of a Coded Message in the African American Spiritual 'Follow the Drinking Gourd,'" *The Journal of Popular Culture* 41, no. 2 (2008) for more information about the representation of this song in American popular culture.

20. Rushdy, *Neo-Slave Narratives*.

21. Janelle Monáe, interview by Leital Molad, *Studio 360*, March 27, 2009, http://www.studio360.org/episodes/2009/03/27/segments/127229 (accessed April 14, 2014).

22. Mark Dery, ed., "Black to the Future: Interviews with Samuel R. Delany, Greg Tate, and Tricia Rose," in *Flame Wars: The Discourse of Cyberculture* (London and Durham, NC: Duke University Press, 1994), 179–222. Originally published *South Atlantic Quarterly* 92, no. 4 (1993): 735–36.

23. J. Griffith Rollefson, "The 'Robot Voodoo Power' Thesis: Afrofuturism and Anti-Anti-Essentialism from Sun Ra to Kool Keith," *Black Music Research Journal* 28, no 1 (Spring 2008): 108.

24. Kodwo Eshun, "Abducted by Audio," *Abstract Culture*, http://afrofuturism.net/literature/ (accessed April 12, 2014).

25. Ibid.

26. Haraway, "A Manifesto for Cyborgs," 35.

27. Later in this paper, I problematize the ways in which one of Monáe's lyrics, like Haraway's cyber-theories, gestures at the idea that escape from these categories should/can be sought. The "elimination" of race in the future is a major concern for those who fear that ethnic or racial differences may be "whitewashed."

28. Haraway, "A Manifesto for Cyborgs," 39.

29. Ibid., 12.

30. Though, here, I argue that Monáe's power lies in her liminal cyborg identity, it is important to address that many black female artists reinscribe stereotypes as powerful creative sites. For example, in "Empowering Self, Making Choices, Creating Spaces: Black Female Identity via Rap Music Performance," Cheryl L. Keyes explores four categorizations imposed on women rappers including "Queen Mother," "Fly Girl," "Sista with Attitude," and "Lesbian" and argues how various emcees revolutionize these stereotypes to promote female agency (*Journal of American Folklore* 113, no. 449 [2000], 256).

31. The term "tip drill," used to describe a woman with a "hot" body who has an "ugly" face and who should be "fucked" from behind, was the basis for a 2003 song by the rapper Nelly (Nelly, "Tip Drill" *Da Derrty Versions: The Reinvention*, UMVD Labels, 2003). The video is controversial due to its misogynistic lyrics. The video also features Nelly and his cohorts throwing money at scantily clad dancers and Nelly running a "credit card swipe" through buttocks of one of his dancers. The video became the basis for a 2004 protest at Spelman College when

Nelly attempted to host a "Jes Us 4 Jackie" bone marrow drive on the campus. As part of the protest, members of Spelman's Feminist Majority Leadership Alliance students demanded Nelly participate in a forum about the song. He refused and the drive was cancelled by his foundation. See Byron Hurt's *Hip Hop: Beyond Beats and Rhymes* DVD (Lugano: Independent Lens, 2007); and Moya Bailey's blog post "Dilemma: Students at Spelman College Protest Nelly's video, "Tip Drill," May 23, 2004, at http://www.alternet.org/story/18760/ (accessed April 23, 2014), for more information about the protest.

32. In *Sister Outsider,* Lorde defines the erotic as "the measure between the beginnings of our sense of self and the chaos of our strongest feelings. It is an internal sense of satisfaction to which, once we have experienced it, we know we can aspire. For having experienced the fullness of this depth of feeling and recognizing its power, in honor and self-respect we can require no less of ourselves," p.54.

33. See Dorothy Roberts' *Killing the Black Body: Race, Representation, and the Meaning of Liberty* (New York: Vintage, 1998), for a thorough exploration of the continued struggle of African American women to gain full control of their reproductive choices.

34. U.S. Supreme Court, *Loving v. Virginia,* June 12, 1967, Records of the Supreme Court of the United States, Record Group 338, Washington, DC: Archives, 1967.

35. Pearl Cleage's definition of feminism quoted in Patricia Hill Collins, "What's in a Name? Womanism, Black Feminism, and Beyond," *Black Scholar* 26, no. 1 (Winter/Spring 1996): 12. It is important to note that, after Collins discusses feminism as a global movement in this essay, she focuses on the distinct nature of black feminism in particular, the ways in which it disrupts assumptions of a "universal" feminism, and the challenges which arise when discussing black feminism.

36. The phrase "absence of choices" is used by bell hooks to define the state of "being oppressed" in bell hooks' *Feminist Theory: from Margin to Center,* 2nd ed. (Cambridge, MA: South End Press, 2000), 5.

In "Letter from Birmingham Jail," Martin Luther King, Jr. draws upon St. Aquinas' differentiation between just laws and unjust laws in order to argue the false logic underlying American segregationist policies. King paraphrases Aquinas, stating "An unjust law is a human law that is not rooted in eternal law and natural law. Any law that uplifts human personality is just. Any law that degrades human personality is unjust" (Martin Luther King, Jr., "Letter From Birmingham Jail," *A Testament of Hope: The Essential Writings and Speeches of Martin Luther King, Jr.* [New York: Harper Collins, 1986], 293). This definition of what constitutes justice informs my analysis of Monáe, "Violet Stars Happy Hunting."

37. Mark Dery, "Black to the Future: Interviews with Samuel R. Delany, Greg Tate, and Tricia Rose," in "Flame Wars: The Discourse of Cyberculture," *South Atlantic Quarterly* 94, no. (1993), 736.

38. In the essay "Futuristic Fiction & Fantasy: The Racial Establishment," Gregory E. Rutledge uses the term "blanching of the future" to problematize the ways in which race has been deemphasized throughout speculative fiction (*Callaloo* 24, no. 1 [2001]: 239). Citing Sandra Govern, he argues, "since futurist fiction writers reinscribe into their futures quotidian vices such as greed, classism, and theft, then surely racism would be present, too" (*Callaloo* 24, no. 1 [2001]:239).

39. Alondra Nelson defines the "digital divide" in her article "Introduction: Future Texts," *Social Text* 20, no. 1 (Spring 2002): 1. She explains, "most notably, the digital divide, a phrase that has been used to describe gaps in technological access that fall along lines of race, gender, region, and ability but has mostly become a code word for the tech inequities that exist between blacks and whites . . . Blackness gets constructed as always oppositional to technologically driven chronicles of progress."

40. Imani Perry, *Prophets of the Hood: Politics and Poetics in Hip Hop* (Durham, NC: Duke University Press, 2004), 176.

41. For more on the subject of feminism and the "economy of the gaze" see Laura Mulvey's *Fetishism and Curiosity* (Bloomington: Indiana University Press, 1998).

42. Janelle Monáe, "Many Moons [Official Short Film]," Bad Boy Records, 2008, online music video, 5:27, https://www.youtube.com/watch?v=LHgbzNHVg0c&feature=kp.

43. Examples include Mousey (Neon Valley Crime Lord), Chung Knox (Tech Daddy), Sir Lucious Leftfoot (Auctioneer Extraordinaire), 61X Savage (Captain of Metropolis Polis), Deep Cotton (the Punk Prophets), and Lady Maestra (Master of the Show Droids). As will be described, several of these characters play a role in the video while others play minor characters in Monáe, "Many Moons" (suggesting they may play a more significant role in Monáe's forthcoming performances as Mayweather).

44. Janelle Monáe, "Many Moons [Official Short Film]," Bad Boy Records, 2008, online music video, 5:27, https://www.youtube.com/watch?v=LHgbzNHVg0c&feature=kp.

45. In *Ain't I a Woman? Black Women and Feminism*, bell hooks explores the relationship between black and white women during slavery, arguing that due to the patriarchal Victorian social conventions of the time, white women often benefitted from the oppression of female slaves ([Boston and Cambridge, MA: South End Press, 1981], 36). Here, viewers are left to interpret this woman's enthusiasm for the droid in a similar light and to consider how the droid will be used after the auction.

46. Monáe, "Many Moons."

47. James Loewen, in his book *Sundown Towns: A Hidden Dimension of American Racism*, identifies sundown towns as municipalities ranging from places that have historically posted signs that say "Nigger, Don't Let the Sun Go Down on You in _____" to other areas which are exclusionary through and/or intentional and defacto segregation (New York: Touchstone, 2006), 3–4.

48. The colloquial rap definition of "make it rain" identifies the act of throwing money up in the air at strip clubs or "making it rain" dollar bills. This concept informs Little Joe's song "Make It Rain" (2006), and his video features scantily-clad women gyrating while dollar bills fall to the ground around them. Usher's "Make It Rain" (2008) and Twista's "Wetter" (2009) also elaborate on this definition. Here, by calling audiences to "make it rain," Monáe reclaims the older vernacular definition that calls for action against situations involving injustice. In doing so, she revises the misogynistic behaviors portrayed by male rappers and restores the meaning that urges social change.

49. Jeffrey Myers, *Converging Stories: Race, Ecology, and Environmental Justice in American Literature* (Athens: University of Georgia Press, 2005), 16.

50. Here, I stress Monáe's vernacular usage in which "green" is synonymous with ecological awareness and being "down" means in the know, cool, or agreeable to something. Further, Mayweather's "cybersoul," (Janelle Monáe, liner notes to *Metropolis: The Chase Suites*, Bad Boy Records, 2008), regardless of its oxymoronic twist, alludes to soul music, an American form popularized in the 1950s and 1960s which drew upon gospel, jazz, and rhythm and blues. These terms highlight Monáe's ecoconscious lyrics and underscore the assemblage of Monáe's influences.

51. In *Prophets of the Hood: Politics and Poetics in Hip Hop*, Imani Perry critiques the beauty standards promoted in rap videos, describing music video actresses as "fantasy elements pieced together in bodies." ([Durham, NC: Duke University Press, 2004], 176).

Perry elaborates that "the women are often presented as vacuous, doing nothing in the videos but swaying around seductively" indicating that, essentially, these women are acting like robots (177). In addition, Perry discusses both the physical unrealities of both hair and body features, considers the effect these images have on women's (particularly girls') self-esteem, and explores the ways in which female performers such as India Arie, Lauryn Hill, and Erykah Badu have responded to such imagery.

52. For more information regarding the aesthetics of black women's hairstyles, see Perry, *Prophets of the Hood*, 177; Dery, *Flame Wars*, 170, 182; T. Denean Sharpley-Whiting, *Pimps Up, Ho's Down: Hip Hop's Hold on Young Black Women* (New York: New York University Press, 2007), 27; Tracey Owens Patton's article "Hey Girl, Am I More than My Hair?: African American Women and Their Struggles with Beauty, Body Image, and Hair," *NWSA Journal* 18, no. 2 (Summer 2006): 24–51; Noliwe M. Rooks' *Hair Raising: Beauty, Culture, and African American Women* (New Brunswick, NJ: Rutgers University Press, 1996); and Ayana Byrd's *Hair Story: Untangling the Roots of Black Hair in America* (New York: St. Martin's Press, 2001).

53. Monáe, "Many Moons."

54. Janelle Monáe, liner notes to *Metropolis: The Chase Suite*, Bad Boy Records 511234-1, compact disc, 2007.

55. In the documentary *Hip Hop*, Hurt explores the issue of masculine performance in Hip Hop. Throughout the film, Hurt interviews young men who rap about violence. When pressed as to why the content of their songs is so violent, one young man offers a rhyme about all the professional choices he could have pursued, but then explains "no one wants to hear that."

56. See Susan Butler, *East to the Dawn: The Life of Amelia Earhart* (De Capo Press, 2009) for more information on Earhart's contributions to the fashion world.

57. W. E. B. Du Bois, *Souls of Black Folks*, coined the phrase double consciousness, using the term to describe the "two-ness" felt by African Americans who experience conflict between their social identities as Americans and African Americans—"an American, a Negro; two souls, two thoughts, two unreconciled strivings." Du Bois' description of "the sense of always looking at one's self through the eyes of others, of measuring one's soul by the tape of a world that looks on in amused contempt and pity" serves as an apt metaphor for Monáe's

struggle to carve a space as an artist in an industry that devalues women (W. E. B. Du Bois, "Of Our Spiritual Strivings," *The Oxford W.E.B. Dubois Reader*," ed. Eric J. Sundquist [Oxford: Oxford University Press, 1996], 101).

58. Stories of flying Africans reoccur throughout African American folklore. For more information, see the Georgia Writers Project, *Drums and Shadows: Survival Studies Among the Georgia Coastal Negroes* (Savannah: University of Georgia Press, 1986); and La Vinia Delois Jennings, "Kanda: Living elders, the ancestral presence, and the ancestor as foundation," in *Toni Morrison and the Idea of Africa* (Cambridge: Cambridge University Press, 2008), 81–136.

59. Ralph Ellison, *Flying Home: And Other Stories*, ed. John F. Callahan (New York: Vintage, 1998).

60. Lady Maestra's brides personify Marshal McLuhan's *Mechanical Bride: Folklore of Industrial Man* (Berkley, CA: Gingko Press, 2002); they intend to stifle Monáe's revolutionary message just as the advertising industry that McLuhan critiques manipulates consumer culture.

61. Janelle Monáe, "Many Moons [Official Short Film]," Bad Boy Records, 2008, online music video, 5:27, https://www.youtube.com/watch?v=LHgbzNHVg0c&feature=kp.

62. Angela Y. Davis, *Blues Legacies and Black Feminisms: Gertrude "Ma" Rainey, Bessie Smith, and Billie Holiday* (New York: Vintage, 1999), 113.

63. Sharpley-Whiting's *Pimps Up, Ho's Down: Hip Hop's Hold on Young Black Women* explores the multilayered relationship between young black women and Hip Hop culture through her discussion of video vixens, beauty culture, sexual violence, "groupies," and the adult entertainment industry. Sharpley-Whiting argues that the commercial success of Hip Hop is "heavily dependent" on young black women even as it exacerbates the challenges faced by black women in patriarchal American culture, particularly sexual violence, color prejudice, homophobia, objectification, and economic exploitation (T. Denean Sharpley-Whiting, *Pimps Up, Ho's Down* [New York: New York University Press, 2008], 11). Whereas Sharpley-Whiting's work examines reasons why women participate in misogynistic practices associated with Hip Hop culture, Monáe's performances create an alternative space for women to avoid the pitfalls to which Sharpley-Whiting refers.

64. Janelle Monáe, "Biography," contactmusic.com http://www.contactmusic.com/info/janelle_monae (accessed April 12, 2014).

65. Tricia Rose, "Hip Hop Futures: A Lecture and Discussion," presentation, Inaugural Conference, Statler Auditorium, November 2, 2008, Cornell University Hip Hop Collection (Ithaca, NY: Cornell University, 2008).

66. In the conclusion of her book *The Hip Hop Wars: What We Talk About When We Talk About Hip Hop—and Why It Matters*, Tricia Rose draws on theologian William F. May's discussion of affirmational and transformational love. Rose distinguishes between the two by identifying that affirmational love provides unconditional support while transformational love provides boundaries and criticisms to ensure the well-being of the individuals involved. While Rose uses these terms to explore the relationship between the supporters and opponents of Hip Hop, Rose's discussion also clarifies Monáe's project. While Monáe works within the strictures of contemporary media demands, she also critiques the system from within and, as such, her work embodies "transformational love." ([New York: Basic Civitas Books, 2008], 270–73).

15

✣

"Dreams of the Drum"
A Keynote Address
Michael Eric Dyson

Tonight, I want to talk about "Dreams of the Drum" and speak to the importance of black arts.[1] Since this black arts festival is occurring here at this remarkable university, it is important to reflect upon the critical acumen that has often been associated with the best artists in American society and among the most noteworthy artists in American society (who also happen to be people of color). In this case, I am especially thinking of black artists. This topic suggests an outline to think about the powerful consideration of black arts and the degree to which the black arts have been influential in American society. But for me, "Dreams of the Drum" immediately conjures *Dreams from My Father*. It is not that Mr. Obama has overtaken Langston Hughes in terms of the black dream discourse. But in the recent collective imagination of America, dreams of black people have become intimately webbed with the dreams of this African son, who is now the President of the United States of America. I still have to pinch myself each time I say it. Sometimes I think it is like a hoax. It might be just a dream. I wake up sometimes and say, "Boy, I just had the craziest dream. I had a dream that America actually elected a black man as president." So this is my first thought—my first association when I think about dreams of the drum, dreams from the drum, or dreams associated with the drum. When we consider the impact of the black arts in American history, we think about the drum as a central metaphor for how black arts have had to exist often in veiled and signified relationships to and within hegemonic societies. It could also be argued that the drum exists within the context of multiple and simultaneous African and African American cultures as well. By saying veiled and signified I am actually being repetitive and redundant because signifying is the way in which veiled meanings are communicated in ways that exempt the signifier from moral and social suspicion because they have covered their language and intention in such a way as to misdirect. The "Dream of the Drum" is to veil the meaning, hide the meaning, make the meaning implicit, or imply the meaning, rather than explicitly saying it. An explicit expression has often meant the destruction or the interruption of black community, and in some cases, the destruction of black art itself.

Constituents of African and African American cultures have learned to manipulate signifying, the veiled communication of moral intention, because to say it plainly and explicitly could incur the wrath of those who could interrupt the process either of black survival or the communication of critical messages from one black person to another or one black community to another. Signifying became a practice that was deliberately refined. Misdirecting communication is not the only source or the (only) findable and traceable origin for signifying practices, but it is one of the most remarkable ones, and one of the most useful ones because black folks as minorities didn't have the opportunities sometimes just to tell the truth that they were thinking. Let me give you an example of what happens when you don't signify and you just say it straight up.

Kanye West. He went up on the stage at the MTV Awards and snatched the microphone. There was no signifying going on there. Although, ultimately it can be argued that the moment was rife with significance and certain signifying elements, he was (in that moment) rather direct. Like a blunt instrument, he literally snatched the means of amplification away from a talented young artist who happened to be a young white woman, Taylor Swift, a country musician. She is as sweet and innocent as she can be. She was stunned as were the rest of us sitting there. I was with several MTV executives. You know they were not too happy. Kanye West went up and snatched the microphone and said: "Excuse me, but everybody knows that the best video was really Beyoncé." Now, that wasn't no signifying. There wasn't any implication. There was no misdirection. There was no suggestion; no shackle of potential meaning that could be, what the philosophers call, multi-evidential. That was just straight up breaking and entering into the public space of Taylor Swift.

Now, I don't want to assign any value or moral interpretation to this. There is a way of signifying and getting communal affirmation. I think that even though it was rude, crude, bombastic, and typically Kanye Westian—he has a big ego—but it is more than that, isn't it? Kanye West snatched a microphone, a means of amplification, what he thought was the amplification of an untruth. He had this weird idea that people should get awards that they deserve. Who is he to be the arbiter of who deserves an award? People voted after all. But historically, award shows have been problematic for black folk because when we knew certain black artists deserved an award and they did not receive recognition, they didn't have a means to amplify their disgruntlement. Mr. West, in an act of cultural condensation—please note that he didn't intend this. I don't want you to think I am inventing his consciousness. I'm not suggesting that Kanye West consciously had this in mind, but he didn't have to. That's my job to determine the significance and his job to speak a truth. He did something serious in this moment. He says look, everybody knows that the moon man, the award that is given to those who win MTV honors, should have gone to Beyoncé. Though Taylor Swift is a very talented woman, even roaches and rats were singing "All the Single Ladies." Everybody was singing that song and there's a video that has been remade/remixed in some of the most pervasive small 'd' democratic ways. I thought to myself that Chuck Berry probably wished Kanye West had been around when they were giving the award he deserved to Elvis. Maybe Little Richard was so satisfied that finally after fifty years, some black person had the position, the assertiveness, the ego, the self-centeredness, and also the courage to step up and say, "Damn it, stop giving away what belongs to black people to somebody else. Give me my record. Shut up. Woo!" [in Little Richard voice]

I am not suggesting that Kanye West was a part of a soul patrol that was policing the boundaries of appropriate awarding of artistic merits for black artists. After all, Beyoncé isn't exactly without awards. The point is that Mr. West bluntly bludgeoned the moment—he beat the drum—and as a result, he felt the bloodcurdling response from the American audience. They punished him. They had to stop his tour. He had to go on Jay Leno's program. For him to break down publically as Mr. Leno asked him about his mama and what she would feel, that was awful. It was horrible. Then on the other hand, Ms. Swift was awarded every award under the sun. I think she is set to receive a Nobel Prize, and maybe male artist of the year the year after that. You get my point. The overwhelming sense of protection for this laudable young white girl in light of this black man having unfairly accosted her denied the legitimate undergirding principles, principles that were lost in the exchange, the brutally rude exchange, between Mr. West and the audience and Ms. Swift by extension. When you don't signify and you are blunt and brutal, there are consequences that are fierce. That is why people rely upon inferential, implicatory, suggestive, and signifying languages, so you can survive your own communication. Kanye enjoys his own privilege as a rich pop star. Of course there have been many millions of young people of color and white people for that matter who have been "Taylor Swifted" everyday, who never get a chance to recover the means of amplification as did Ms. Swift. That day, that night on that program, she was handed the microphone by a member of the tribe that had offended her—by Beyoncé—by the same person on whose behalf Mr. West ostensibly acted. That was an act of poetic and rhetorical justice that is often denied to others.

Now, you might say why do I start here. I start here to show why it is critical, crucial, and central to the black arts traditions that they have more or less dealt with the implied and inferred, the signified aspects of black identity—usually it is humor or veiled critique through humor, often using music to veil critiques of American society. Even Sam Cooke singing "Any Day Now," not the later song made famous by another artist, but a two-minute and nearly 50-second song that was imagining the prospects for heaven, but was really a veiled critique of the lack of heaven here on earth. Black artists, from the very beginning, and the drum speaks directly to this, have engaged in signifying practices that veiled their critique of the dominant and mainstream society so that they could exist long enough to create a livelihood out of that art; so that they could use that art to revisit the scene of the injury to black identity for which black art was called into existence. It was not exclusively, not necessarily or even primarily so, but it was central. And so, the drum is a metaphor for that veiled activity in the way that the drum in the Congo Square in New Orleans was a means by which black people communicated to each other. They could communicate explicitly and speak widely even though they had different languages and were from different tribes and different cultures. They also had suspicions and skepticisms about each other. Imagine a bunch of Americans taken from every stage and thrown together into slavery. They might speak the same language, not in the case of Africans, but they might be from the South versus the North, different sensibilities, different traditions or some could have even spoken different languages. Some are primarily Spanish-speaking versus those who were primarily English-speaking. They had different regions and geographies and cultures and expectations all seen as American, not Arkansan.

So imagine the eradication of all that complexity and cultural diversity in Africa, subject to the brutal weight of the Middle Passage and slavery. Individuals thrown together, deliberately taken out of their element so that they could not communicate. What happens of course is that the drum maintained itself as a signifying device to communicate where the voice had failed. The voice was interrupted. The voice was muffled. The mouths of slaves were muffled. There was a systemic refusal to prevent black people from communicating for fear that they would somehow undermine the dominant culture that had enslaved them.

So black art, at least in this country, black art at least since 1619, black art in the context of slavery and Reconstruction and legalized segregation and Jim Crow, and then on into the late part of the twentieth century and then into the twenty-first century, had its origins in the determination of black people to preserve their humanity and to communicate with each other in a hostile environment that denied the legitimacy of their humanity. Black artists had a moral purpose thrust upon them from the very beginning without being asked why or if they were okay with the fact that they were suffused with such unintended, but necessary meaning. The signifying conditions in which they engaged always had implications beyond themselves or their own families or communities, but they had implications for the broader community.

When we argue now about the meaning of black art and whether a rapper should pay attention to why his or her words might have an impact on young people, or why an artist who is a visual artist should pay attention to why the stereotypes for which she experiments may have particular meaning for those who understand the stereotypes and a different one for those who don't, the question of moral utility and social function attach rather immediately to the prospects of black art. Black art never existed in isolation from either the moral or the social consequences on black American communities. The drum was the signifier of that. The drum—literally the percussive tonality and texture of black artistic expression, the very means by which we beat it, the means by which we percussively express the tones and temper of black existence, the very character of black artistic imagination—beats itself out on surfaces that were stretched taut between holes of denial and opportunity. As a result of that, the drum became a signifying and symbolizing measure of black humanity and black artistic expression. The drum itself became eventually outlawed because people figured out that black folk were communicating even through the drums. They couldn't talk. They couldn't speak, but they could beat out the meaning.

Eventually they had to stop beating the drums, but the drum continues to signify the best of the black arts; it becomes a metaphor handed down from one generation of black people to another. The drum is a signifying condition. The drum contains implicit meaning. The drum is the signified meaning. The drum is the meaning that might be veiled for/from people to catch on, if not for the literal Kanye West—like in-your-face meaning, although some black art certainly does that as well. But black art works along the edges of traditions, through implied and inferred response, working in a medium that has as its rich reward in the ability of black people to hibernate inside that drum from where the very rhythms of lived experience are emanating. Generated at the very base of that drum, these rhythms allowed them to amplify their deepest and most refined aspirations without being caught. That is why black language has a kind of percussive, throbbing, and rhythmic tonality. That is why there is a profound difference between George Bush and Barack Obama. It is in the way they talk—the way that they walk. I don't want to make any other claims, but the most significant point of Obama being in the White House may not be his color. You can hear and feel the difference when Obama is speaking and talking: "yes we can, yes we can." There is a rhythm that he gets from the black church. The black church affords its ministers a platform to speak out rhythms in their own speech. Listen to the best rhythmic intensity and poetic agitation that is mediated through the artistic expression of preaching. I know that preachers are usually thrown into black arts, but tell me what is more poetic and artistic than a real black preacher who knows what he or she is doing? There is all kinds of black preaching. Martin Luther King, Jr. is one variety. There is the Al Sharpton variety, and the Jesse Jackson variety is more well-known. But even with King, you can chart the beautiful rhythmic intensities. King's voice was like a trumpet, not a drum. "I may not get there with you, but I want you to know tonight, we as a people, will get to the Promised Land." Isn't that beautiful? Or when he delivered the "I Have a Dream" speech: "five score years ago . . . The emancipation proclamation. . . ." You can say it another way. The trademark of black dialect in the rhythmic tonality and the rhythmic intensity. And the drum-like tonality of black speech is the common character—that black vernacular force found in the voices of the best black preachers. Some of them nearly sing their meaning.

Catholic priests may say the same thing, but there is a rhythm to black speech, and that rhythm is from the drum. The drum is from the same location. The beats per minute articulated, you can hear it even in the artistry of black speech. "It's not God bless America, God damn America." Now, I know that many people miss the rhythmic intensity and the well-formed oratorical conventions in their efforts to grasp the literal interpretation of what Reverend Wright was saying, even though I have taken him out of context here. Many white brothers and sisters were appalled at Reverend Wright's comments. I am still talking about black art, the pounding on a drum, the rhythmic intensity. I'm talking about black preaching as one of the very elements of black art. Reverend Wright was beating the drum. White folk thought: "my God, I thought you people went to church and talked about Jesus. How dare you speak about AIDS and white supremacy and who runs America and the like?" Well, in black churches, that is the kind of stuff that we talk about and we will talk about these matters in a certain way.

Some black folk think that Jesus is about speaking in tongues and wearing the right dress and the right makeup and the like, just like some in the white conservative fundamentalist churches. But then there is the rhythmic intensity of black preaching. The preaching itself becomes the articulable sound of black survival. Black preaching becomes the way in which the interpreter of the Word speaks to the lived experiences of black folk. The Word. The Word was seminal. It gave voice and birth. It gave birth to the voice and voice to the birth. The Word was seminal and it had a tremendous amount of possibility wrapped up in it. The Word itself gave birth to new vision, new imagination, new ways of organizing life. The black preacher was central to the artistic expression of black euphony, black sounding. The drum, the syncopation of the sound, the tonality, the rhythmic intensity, all of that stuff from Congo Square got compressed and some would say instilled in the vocal cords of the black preacher. How they talk is just as important as what they say. A lot of people give that a twist and they think that black people just sound stylish, but they aren't saying a damn thing.

Some people think that black rhetorical performances have no meaning and significance, that they have no logic because they are passionate, so they have no reason. America is skeptical, especially white America; they are very skeptical of emotional expression. You have to be tight, straightforward. There is something beautiful about that to, and it has its purposes. You don't want a person with her hand on the button acting the fool. There's something to be said for calm and reasoned articulation, which is of course central to many African and African American traditions. But there is skepticism about emotion and passion. It is as if when you say something like you mean it, you therefore cannot be saying much of substance. But black people and their use of black artistic expression are fusing style and substance. Just because LeBron James looks fierce when he is dunking doesn't mean that he ain't scoring two points. Just because Kobe Bryant led the league in scoring, the youngest to do so at twenty-one years of age, averaging a little bit over 30 points a game, just because he has style and he looks a different way than Larry Bird, it doesn't mean that what he is doing is not efficacious and effective, that it is not literally substantive.

Black preaching invites the discussion of our tendency to bifurcate passion and intellectual respectability. If you don't say it with a kind of calm, cool, distance, clinical dispassion, then somehow you lack the substance upon which any coherent expression of truth rests. Black art through black preaching, black art from the drum of Congo Square, and also through black comedy. You can hear it in a Chris Rock. You can hear it in a Bill Cosby. You can hear it in a Richard Pryor. They deploy a wide range of expressions and sometimes, explicit expressions. Here is where my argument about veiled expression and that signifying is an inferential means of black identity—is to be reasonably challenged. Of course, in search of black comedy, there is the more explicit expression, but even that explicit expression is a signification upon both our needs within the context of black culture, as well as signifying our needs beyond black culture.

Some people like Bill Cosby are bridge figures. "And the people said that Jell-O is the pudding pop." Mr. Cosby is one of the original geniuses. Mark Twain meets Nancy Russell. If you ever see Mr. Cosby in 1984's "Cosby Himself," you will see him working an extraordinary genius. You will see a man with a microphone get up and share on a stage, entertaining Americans for nearly an hour and a half with unstinting genius. He is able to weave narratives into narrative and make that patchwork of extraordinary humor and completed meaning. And then use that to force Americans to reflect in a nonracially specific fashion upon the context of their common existence. Bill Cosby's rhetorical genius was never explicit about race, though subsequently his social critique has been almost exclusively about race. Thus, his genius of signifying in nonracial terms has been compromised when it makes the transition from the stage to the podium. He didn't have that much practice at the value of interpretation within social critique. As a result, he is rather flat. I think he is ineffectual in the resident position of critic that has been practiced by people far more astute with legitimate furor and fury and desire.

Richard Pryor after him was a man in full anger about the limits imposed on him because of race. Now the drum becomes articulate. Richard Pryor used his talent as an incredibly powerful drum, wielding it in defense of poor and vulnerable black people in a way that Mr. Cosby could not. Mr. Pryor told of the angry passions that occupy the breasts of common, ordinary black folk. He told stories about black folk life. He told stories about people who are character types that we didn't often see on the American stage. He brought them into full view. The power of speech, that drum radiating out, beating the story, not simply of signifying, but of explicit expression. He told numerous stories that try to reveal the heart of American darkness. Joseph Conrad was a black eye. [Many of us would have liked to have given Mister Conrad a black eye]. But when Richard Pryor gave him a black tongue, the heart of African darkness, he turned it in on itself, so to speak. He showed the light deep in the heart of the African American struggle, striving for existence and subsistence. The interesting thing is that Mr. Pryor is taking the drum in a different direction. He is trying to articulate subversive meanings that have been submerged. That is what Richard Pryor was. He wasn't just Joseph Conrad. He was *the savage* with a microphone on stage, telling jokes.

Richard Pryor did it to himself: strung himself up, strung himself out on drugs, freebasing, but he simultaneously exposed the interior struggles of black people trying to make sense of the world. What is more absurd than living in a country that tells you you can't be seen as equal because of your skin color even as it exploited your genius to build the nation? What's more absurd than Americans calling black folk lazy when they worked for 350 plus years for free? What's more absurd than putting forth the notion of white supremacy when white brothers and sisters knew it was a lie to begin with? They knew about their cousins and uncles who were attracted to even the so-called worst black person. It was the dirty light of whiteness that we didn't want washing up in our racially bifurcated reality. Richard Pryor's voice became the archiving of the attempt to overcome white supremacy and to expose the lunacy of the mythologies of whiteness, often burning himself along his path towards clarity. In the light of his own self-destruction, he illuminated the context of black mythology and the pathology that made blackness a sin. So the drum kept beating. It beats now in Martin Lawrence and Chris Rock too, and Mo'Nique. She was vicious in *Precious*—anything but precious. A lot of black people are mad. This is what black art does. It often exposes the fault lines of black identity that white folk don't know about.

Obviously, there are many arguments about the film *Precious*. Why do we have nothing depicted in film aside from pathological characterizations? Black people acting crazy; white folk love that. When I went to see *Precious* I was maybe one of four black people in the theater that is double the size of this hall. White brothers and sisters and I said this one is going to be a hit. I knew it was going to be a hit because white people were coming out to see a black film. Are white folk attracted to the stories of black pathologies? Or is it that white brothers and sisters don't see genius beyond black pathology? Is it that white brothers and sisters would rather give Denzel an Oscar for *Training Day* and not for *Malcolm X*? Black folk were pissed about that too. They were pissed. But I love Denzel in *Training Day*. He was evil and I was tired of him playing the good Negro. I loved that luminous darkness. People are mad, but he should have won it for *Malcolm X*. The drum beats in all kinds of explicit ways in black cinema because in black cinema, the drumbeat commands much more money. The percussive tones are sometimes stretched out, maybe even more percussive on some surfaces, and sometimes muffled on others. With *Precious*, the argument was why do black people have to be pathological for white people to come see us? Why can't we just be good and positive? Why does Denzel have to win for *Training Day*, not for *Malcolm X* and he was brilliant in *Malcolm X*. As brilliant as he was in *Training Day*, he was brilliant in *Malcolm X*.

The question of black art, the moral status, the burden of representation, this is where the drum gets even louder. Are black arts responsible for black people? Does it represent positive aspects of black existence? Do white folk even care about that? Is Tom Cruise obsessed with representing whiteness positively? And Tom is my man, Scientology and all. But for the most part, if Tom goes down, he has Brad, Ashton Kutcher, and on, and on, and on, and on ... If Denzel goes down, you have Lawrence Fishburne, about a couple other brothers, maybe Terence Howard, and that's about it. So the dearth, the paucity, the lack of depth and density of black representation of authority places undue burdens on the backs of black artists and freights black art with even more meaning and menace. This is where the drum begins to beat most loudly and you see it amplified through varieties of microphones. What is a black artist to do? Is the first obligation of black art to the black convention? Black art can't really do that because art sometimes is used to challenge people and get in their faces. It can't just represent your positive character because sometimes what you think is positive rests upon the broken dreams of people whose voices you've muffled. It doesn't mean that we are not obsessed with the negative because we know many people are. That's the Catch-22 that we are in. In a sense, on the one hand, we don't have enough art out there from black people to balance and counterbalance some of the negative stuff that we see. There may be Guru and 50 Cent but 50 Cent is the one on the poster with the money. 50 Cent is the one people respond to. All of the so-called negative forces, which have legitimate right to exist, are exaggerated and seen as representative. That is part of the problem. The problem is the so-called negative, the so-called dark, the so-called subversive is seen as the utterly authentic expression of blackness. So we get trapped in that box, and so people think that pathology is the norm. Yet at the same time, people have every right to explore pathology or what you think is pathology and to raise questions about what it truly means.

Black art does that. It makes us uncomfortable. When Kara Walker does her cutouts right there in Austin, Texas and people consider her brilliant visual play on black and white—and the human body, she forces people to think, and rethink their own understandings of what the stereotypes are. What is a stereotype but a shortcut that is made lucid in the minds of thinking people? Stereotype is a lazy person's way of negotiating difference. How do we continue to explore the biases that require stereotypes? How do we play with that? Some subversive art does just that. Some gangsta rap art really is funny even though it is vicious and powerful and pathological and dark and brilliant all at the same time. Some of the stuff that I listen to from Snoop is just sheer genius. Some of it makes my toes curl. Sometimes it's at the same time, on the same record. Do we get rid of Snoop? Hell no. Snoop Dogg now is making commercials with Lee Iacocca. He is a GPS system. He's mainstream. Snoop Dizzle, fo shizzle ma nizzle. So the drum beats. It continues to grow louder. It's this drumbeat that demands responsibility of artists. And in their hands it makes us believe that everything they do doesn't imply something, that unavoidable representationality of black art that cannot be helped. Whether it wants to or not, it becomes representative. The significance of blackness literally is inscribed into the black body. My point simply is to propose that a lot of these young people say things in their Hip Hop music and do things that are worthy of studying. If we do not acknowledge this fact, we will miss in our own culture the evidence that it is part of the black arts tradition, part of the drum, speaking, preaching, and informing the percussive tonality of black rhetoric.

NOTE

1. This is a transcription of a speech given by Michael Eric Dyson, "Dreams of the Drum: Fulfilling the Dream through the Arts," keynote address, Black Arts Festival, Bucknell University, Lewisburg, Pennsylvania, April 23, 2010.

Bibliography

Audiovisual references are listed under the heading of *Sound Recordings* in this bibliography.

Adams, Dart. "Black Like Me: The History of Comic Book Heroes Through The Ages, Part One 1900–1968 (Re Up)." *Poisonous Paragraphs* (blog), February 21, 2008. http://poisonousparagraphs.blogspot.com/2008/02/dart-adams-presents-black-like-me.html.
Ahmad, Aijaz. *In Theory: Classes, Nations, Literatures*. London: Verso, 1993.
Ahmed, Sara. *The Cultural Politics of Emotion*. New York: Routledge, 2004.
———. *Queer Phenomenology: Orientations, Objects, Others*. Durham, NC: Duke University Press, 2006.
Alexander, Bryant Keith. *Performing Black Masculinity: Race, Culture, and Queer Identity*. New York: AltaMira Press, 2006.
Alexander, Elizabeth. "'Can You Be BLACK and Look at This?': Reading the Rodney King Video(s)." In *Black Male: Representations of Masculinity in Contemporary American Art*, edited by Thelma Golden, 91–110. New York: Whitney Museum of American Art, 1994.
Alim, H. Samy. *Roc the Mic Right: The Language of Hip Hop Culture*. New York: Routledge, 2006.
Alloway, Lawrence. "The Arts and the Mass Media." In *Art In Theory, 1900–2000: An Anthology of Changing Ideas*, edited by Charles Harrison and Paul Wood, 716. Maiden: Blackwell Publishing, 1992.
Als, Hilton. "A Pryor Love: The Life and Times of America's Comic Prophet of Race." *New Yorker*, September 13, 1999, 68–81.
Alsford, Mike. *Heroes and Villains*. Waco, TX: Baylor University Press, 2006.

Altschuler, Glenn C., and Patrick M. Burns. "Snarlin' Carlin: The Odyssey of a Libertarian." *Studies in American Humor*, n.s. 3, no. 20 (2009): 42–57.
The American Heritage College Dictionary. 4th ed. New York: Houghton Mifflin, 2002.
Anderson, Benedict. *Imagined Communities: Reflections on the Origin and Spread of Nationalism*. London and New York: Verso, 1983.
Asante, M. K., Jr. "We are the Post Hip-hop Generation." *San Francisco Gate*, February 7, 2006. http://www.sfgate.com/opinion/openforum/article/We-are-the-post-hip-hop-generation-2504977.php (accessed April 11, 2014).
Auslander, Philip. "Comedy About the Failure of Comedy: Stand-up Comedy and Postmodernism." In *Critical Theory and Performance*, edited by Janelle G. Reinelt and Joseph R. Roach, 196–207. Ann Arbor: University of Michigan Press, 1992.
Avakian, Bob. *Reflections, Sketches, and Provocations: Essays and Commentary, 1981–1987*. Chicago: RCP Publications, 1990.
Ayres, Ian. *Pervasive Prejudice?: Unconventional Evidence of Race and Gender Discrimination*. Chicago: University of Chicago Press, 2001.
Ayres, Ian, Fredrick E. Vars, and Nasser Zakariya. "To Insure Prejudice: Racial Disparities in Taxicab Tipping." Yale Law School, Public Law Working Paper 50; and Yale Law & Economics Research Paper 276, May 3, 2005. http://islandia.law.yale.edu/ayres/toinsureprejudice.pdf (accessed April 15,2014).
Azlant, Edward. "Lenny Bruce Again: 'Gestapo? You Asshole, I'm the Mailman!'" *Studies in American Humor* n.s. 3, no. 15 (2006): 75–99.
Bailey, Julius, ed. *Jay-Z: Essays on Hip Hop's Philosopher King*. Jefferson, NC: McFarland, 2011.
Bailey, Moya. "Dilemma: Students at Spelman College Protest Nelly's video 'Tip Drill.'" *Alternet: Wiretap* (blog), May 23, 2004. http://www.alternet.org/story/18760/ (accessed April 23, 2014),
Baldwin, Davarian. "Black Empires, White Desires: The Spatial Politics of Identity in the Age of Hip Hop." In *That's the Joint!: The Hip-Hop Studies Reader*, edited by Murray Forman and Mark Anthony Neal, 159–76. New York: Routledge, 2004.
Baldwin, James A. *Notes of a Native Son*. Boston: Beacon Press, 1955. Reprint 1984.
———. "The Negro Child—His Self-Image." *Saturday Review*, December 21, 1963; Reprint.
———. *The Price of the Ticket, Collected Non-Fiction 1948–1985*. New York: St. Martin's, 1985.
Barker, Martin. *Comics: Ideology, Power, and the Critics*. New York: St. Martin's Press, 1989.
Bass, Patrik Henry. *Like a Mighty Stream: The March on Washington, August 28, 1963*. Philadelphia: Running Press, 2002.
Bazin, Andre, trans. Hugh Gray. "The Ontology of the Photographic Image." *Film Quarterly* 13, no. 4 (Summer 1960): 4–9.
Bederman, Gail. *Manliness and Civilization: A Cultural History of Gender and Race in the United States, 1880–1917*. Chicago: University of Chicago Press, 1995.
Bell, Derrick A., Jr. "Racial Realism." In *Critical Race Theory: The Key Writings that Formed the Movement*, edited by Kimberlé Crenshaw, et al., 302–12. New York: New Press, 1995.

Benjamin, Walter. "The Author as Producer." In *Understanding Brecht*, translated by Anna Bostock, 85–103. London: Verso, 1998.
Berger, John. *Ways of Seeing*. London: BBC, 1972.
Berger, Maurice. "A Momentous Day Driven by Ordinary People." *New York Times*, LENS (blog). http://lens.blogs.nytimes.com/2013/08/22/a-momentous-day-driven-by-ordinary-people/?_php=true&_type=blogs&_r=0 (accessed April 17, 2014).
Berlant, Lauren. *The Female Complaint: The Unfinished Business of Sentimentality in American Culture*. Durham, NC: Duke University Press, 2008.
Bhabha, Homi K. *The Location of Culture*. 2nd ed. New York: Routledge, 2004.
Blair, Irene V., Charles M. Judd, and Kristine M. Chapleau. "The Influence of Afrocentric Facial Features in Criminal Sentencing." *Psychological Science* 15, no. 10 (October 2004): 674–79.
Blair, Irene V., Charles M. Judd, and Jennifer L. Fallman. "Attitudes and Social Cognition: The Automaticity of Race and Afrocentric Facial Features in Social Judgments." *Journal of Personality and Social Psychology* 87, no. 6 (December 2004): 763–78.
Bogle, Donald. *Toms, Coons, Mulattoes, Mammies, and Bucks: An Interpretive History of Blacks in American Films*. 4th ed. New York: Continuum International Publishing Group, 2001.
Bolter, Jay David, and Richard Grusin. *Remediation: Understanding New Media*. London and Cambridge, MA: MIT Press, 2001.
Boyce Davies, Carole. *Black Women, Writing, and Identity: Migrations of the Subject*. London and New York: Routledge, 1994.
Bradley, Adam. *Book of Rhymes: The Poetics of Hip Hop*. New York: Basic Civitas Books, 2009.
Brashler, William. "Berserk Angel." *Playboy* 26, no. 12 (December 1979): 243–48, 292–96.
Bressler, Joel. "Follow the Drinking Gourd: A Cultural History." http://followthedrinkinggourd.org/, 2008–2012, (accessed May 31, 2014).
Brown, Jeffrey A. *Black Superheroes, Milestone Comics, and Their Fans*. Jackson: University Press of Mississippi, 2000.
———. "Comic Book Masculinity and the New Black Superhero." *African American Review* 33, no. 1 (Spring 1999): 25–42.
Brown, Mary Ellen, and Bruce A. Rosenberg, eds. *Encyclopedia of Folklore and Literature*. Oxford and Santa Barbara, CA: ABC-CLIO, 1998.
Brummett, Barry. *Rhetoric in Popular Culture*. New York: St. Martin's Press, 1994.
Bryson, Norman. "The Natural Attitude. In *Visual Culture: The Reader*, edited by Jessica Evans and Stuart Hall, 23–32. London, New Delhi, and Thousand Oaks, CA: Sage Publications, 1999.
Bullard, Robert D., Paul Mohai, Robin Saha, and Beverly Wright. "Toxic Wastes and Race at Twenty: 1987–2007: Grassroots Struggles to Dismantle Environmental Racism in the United States." In *A Report Prepared for the United Church of Christ Justice and Witness Ministries*. Cleveland, OH: United Church of Christ, 2007. http://www.ucc.org/assets/pdfs/toxic20.pdf (accessed April 14, 2014).

Burrelli, David F. "Don't Ask, Don't Tell:" Military Policy and the Law on Same-Sex Behavior. CRS Report R40782. Washington, DC: Congressional Research Service, 2010.
Butler, Judith. Bodies That Matter: On the Discursive Limits of "Sex." New York: Routledge, 1993.
———. Excitable Speech: A Politics of the Performative. New York: Routledge, 1997.
———. "Status, Conduct, Word, and Deed: A Response to Janet Halley." GLQ 3, nos. 2–3 (1996): 253–80.
Butler, Susan. East to the Dawn: The Life of Amelia Earhart. De Capo Press, 2009.
Byrd, Ayana. Hair Story: Untangling the Roots of Black Hair in America. New York: St. Martin's Press, 2001.
Carnes, Valerie. "Icons of Popular Fashion." In Icons of America, edited by Ray B. Browne and Marshall Fishwick, 228–40. Bowling Green, OH: Popular Press, 1978.
Carpio, Glenda R. "The Conjurer Recoils: Slavery in Richard Pryor's Performances and Chappelle's Show." In Laughing Fit to Kill: Black Humor in the Fictions of Slavery, 72–117. New York: Oxford University Press, 2008.
Cham, Mbye Baboucar. "Art and Ideology in the Work of Sembene Ousmane and Haile Gerima." Presence Africaine: Revue Culturelle du Monde Noir [Cultural Review of the Negro World] 129, no. 1 (1984): 79–91.
Chang, Jeff. Can't Stop Won't Stop: A History of the Hip-Hop Generation. New York: St Martin's Press, 2005.
Cheney, Charise L. Brothers Gonna Work It Out: Sexual Politics in the Golden Age of Rap Nationalism. New York: New York University Press, 2005.
Chin, Daryl. "From Popular to Pop. The Arts in/of Commerce: Mass Media and the New Imagery." Performing Arts Journal 13, no. 1. (January 1991): 5–20.
Cleaver, Eldridge. "Notes on a Native Son." In Soul on Ice, 122–37. New York: McGraw-Hill, 1999.
Coates, Ta-Nehisi. "The Mask of DOOM: A Nonconformist Rapper's Second Act." New Yorker, September 21, 2009, 52–57.
Cobb, William Jelani. To the Break of Dawn: A Freestyle on the Hip Hop Aesthetic. New York: New York University Press, 2007.
Cole, David. No Equal Justice: Race and Class in the American Criminal Justice System, 16–62. New York: New Press, 2000.
Collins, Patricia Hill. Black Feminist Thought: Knowledge, Consciousness, and the Politics of Empowerment. 2nd ed. New York: Routledge, 2000. Reprint. 2009.
———. "What's in a Name? Womanism, Black Feminism, and Beyond." Black Scholar 26, no. 1 (Winter/Spring 1996): 9–17.
Collins, Ronald K. L., and David M. Skover. The Trials of Lenny Bruce: The Fall and Rise of an American Icon. Naperville, IL: Sourcebooks MediaFusion, 2002.
Commonweal. Review of "Men and Angels." March 9, 1990, 150.
Coogan, Peter. The Superhero: The Secret Origin of a Genre. Austin, TX; Monkey Brains Books, 2006.
———. "The Definition of the Superhero." In Super/Heroes: From Hercules to Superman, edited by Wendy Haslem, Angela Ndalianis, and Chris Mackie, 21–36. Washington, DC: New Academia, 2007.
Conley, Dalton. Being Black, Living in the Red: Race, Wealth and Social Policy in America. Berkeley: University of California Press, 1999.

Connor, Marlene Kim. *What is Cool? Understanding Black Manhood in America*. Chicago: Agate Press, 2003.
Corcos, Christina A. "George Carlin, Constitutional Law Scholar." *Stetson Law Review* 37 (July 21, 2008): 899–940.
Corrigan, Timothy. "Literature on Screen, A History: In The Gap." In *The Cambridge Companion to Literature on Screen*, edited by Deborah Cartmell and Imelda Whelehan, 29–44. Cambridge: Cambridge University Press, 2007.
Cowie, Elizabeth. "Fantasia." In *Visual Culture: The Reader*, edited by Jessica Evans and Stuart Hall, 356–69. London, New Delhi, and Thousand Oaks, CA: Sage Publications, 1999.
Crosley, Hillary. "Ready for Duty: Online Fame Leads Soulja Boy to Radio, Interscope." *Billboard* 119, no. 38 (September 22, 2007): 70–71. http://books.google.com/books?id=hQ4EAAAAMBAJ (accessed April 11, 2014).
———. "Song and Dance Routine: Labels Work to Turn Teen Dance Crazes Into Hits." *Billboard* 119, no. 43 (October 27, 2007), 14–15. http://books.google.com/books?id=rw4EAAAAMBAJ (accessed April 11, 2014).
Cruse, Harold. *The Crisis of the Negro Intellectual: A Historical Analysis of the Failure of Black Leadership*. New York: Quill, 1984.
Davies, Ioan. "Lenny Bruce: Hyperrealism and the Death of Jewish Tragic Humor." *Social Text* 22 (Spring 1989): 92–114.
Davis, Angela Y. *Blues Legacies and Black Feminisms: Gertrude "Ma" Rainey, Bessie Smith, and Billie Holiday*. New York: Vintage, 1999.
Dayan, Daniel, and Elihu Katz. *Media Events: The Live Broadcasting of History*. Cambridge, MA: Harvard University Press, 1992.
Debord, Guy. *The Society of the Spectacle*. Translated by Donald Nicholson-Smith. New York: Zone Books, 2005.
Delgado, Richard. *The Rodrigo Chronicles: Conversations about America and Race*. New York: New York University Press, 1995.
D'Emilio, John. *Sexual Politics, Sexual Communities: The Making of a Homosexual Minority in the United States, 1940–1970*. Chicago: University of Chicago Press, 1983.
Denver, Nate. "Down and Out." *Vibe*, July 2005, 46.
Dery, Mark, ed. "Black to the Future: Interviews with Samuel R. Delany, Greg Tate, and Tricia Rose." In *Flame Wars: The Discourse of Cyberculture*, 179–222. London and Durham, NC: Duke University Press, 1994. Originally published *South Atlantic Quarterly* 92, no. 4 (1993).
Diawara, Manthia. "Afro-Kitsch." In *Black Popular Culture*, A Project by Michele Wallace, edited by Gina Dent, 285–91. New York: Bay Press, 1983.
DiMarco, Danette. "Rehistoricizing the Past Through Film: Considering the Possibilities of Haile Gerima's *Sankofa*." *EAPSU Online: A Journal of Critical and Creative Work* 1 (2004): 11–22. http://media.tripod.lycos.com/2845573/1478334.pdf (accessed April 12, 2014).
Dimitriadis, Greg. *Performing Identity/Performing Culture: Hip Hop as Text, Pedagogy, and Lived Practice*. New York: Peter Lang, 2001. Rev. ed. 2009.
Dolan, Jill. *Utopia in Performance: Finding Hope at the Theater*. Ann Arbor: University of Michigan Press, 2005.
Donalson, Melvin Burke. *Masculinity in the Interracial Buddy Film*. Jefferson, NC: McFarland, 2006.

Dougall, Alastair, et al., eds. *The Marvel Comics Encyclopedia: The Complete Guide to the Characters of the Marvel Universe.* New York and London: DK Publishing, 2008.

Douglass, Frederick. *Narrative of the Life of Frederick Douglass, An American Slave, Written by Himself* (1845). Cambridge, MA Belnap Press, 1960. Reprint (1845), edited by David Blight. 2nd ed. Boston: Bedford/St. Martin's, 2003.

Dream Defenders. "#Our March" (blog). http://dreamdefenders.org/ourmarch/ (accessed October 1, 2013).

Dreisinger, Baz. "You'll Never Rap Alone." *Los Angeles Times*, May 25, 2003, Special to the *Times*.

Drumming, Neil. "The Nerd Behind the Mask" *Village Voice*, August 7, 2001. http://www.villagevoice.com/2001-08-07/music/the-nerd-behind-the-mask (accessed April 12, 2014).

Du Bois, W. E. B. *The Souls of Black Folk.* In *Three Negro Classics*, introduction by John Hope Franklin, 207–390. New York: Avon Books, 1965.

———. *The Souls of Black Folk.* New York: Penguin, 1996.

———. "Of Our Spiritual Strivings," *The Oxford W. E. B. Du Bois Reader*," Ed. Eric J. Sundquist. Oxford: Oxford University Press, 1996.

Duggan, Lisa. *The Twilight of Equality? Neoliberalism, Cultural Politics, and the Attack on Democracy.* Boston: Beacon Press, 2003.

Dunbar, Erica Armstrong. *A Fragile Freedom: African American Women and Emancipation in the Antebellum City.* London and New Haven, CT: Yale University Press, 2008.

Dunbar, Paul Laurence. "We Wear the Mask." In *Lyrics of Lowly Life*, 167. New York: Dodd Mead, 1896.

Ellison, Ralph. *Flying Home: And Other Stories.* Edited by John F. Callahan. New York: Vintage, 1998.

Eshun, Kodwo. "Abucted by Radio." *Abstract Culture*, http://afrofuturism.net/literature/ (accessed April 12, 2014).

Euchner, Charles C. *Nobody Turn Me Around: A People's History of the 1963 March on Washington.* Boston: Beacon Press, 2010.

Farber, Paul M. "The Last Rites of D'Angelo Barksdale: The Life and Afterlife of Photography in The Wire." *Criticism* 52, nos. 3–4 (2010): 413–39.

Feagin, Susan L., and Patrick Maynard, eds. *Aesthetics.* New York: Oxford Press, 1997.

Fellner, Jamie, and Marc Mauer. *Losing the Vote: The Impact of Felony Disenfranchisement Laws in the United States.* Washington, DC: Human Rights Watch, Sentencing Project, 1998.

Felton, David. "Jive Times: Richard Pryor, Lily Tomlin, and the Theater of the Routine." *Rolling Stone*, no. 171, October 10, 1974, 42.

———. "Richard Pryor's Life in Concert," *Rolling Stone*, May 3, 1979, 52.

Ferguson, Roderick A. "Race-ing Homonormativity: Citizenship, Sociology, and Gay Identity." In *Black Queer Studies*, edited by E. Patrick Johnson and Mae G. Henderson, 52–67. Durham: Duke University Press, 2005.

FHM, "100 Sexiest Women in the World 2011," *FHM: Good News for Men*, May 5, 2011.

———. "Andrej Pejić Apology," *FHM: It's Great to Be a Man*, May 30, 2011, http://www.fhm.com/upgrade/fhm-andrej-pejic-apology-81335 (accessed April 19, 2014).
Figart, Deborah M. "Pay Equity and Race/Ethnicity: An Annotated Bibliography." Hyattsville, MD: National Committee on Pay Equity, October 2001.
Fingeroth, Danny. *Superman on the Couch: What Superheroes Really Tell Us about Ourselves and Our Society*. New York: Continuum International Publishing, 2007.
Fiske, John. *Understanding Popular Culture*. Boston: Unwin Hyman, 1989.
Fisseha, Kedamai, and Nicholas Yannuzzi. "Linguistic Profiling: Pilot Studies on Restaurants, Car Dealerships, and Apartment Rentals." Unpublished article, January 12, 2007.
Flatley, Guy. "At the Movies," *New York Times*, August 6, 1976, Weekend, C4.
"Food Insecurity and Race." Share Our Strength for Multicultural Foodservice & Hospitality Alliance (MFHA). Symposium. 2005.
Forman, Murray. *The Hood Comes First: Race, Space, and Place in Rap and Hip-Hop*. Hanover, NJ: Wesleyan University Press, 2002.
———. "'Keeping It Real'? African Youth Identities and Hip-Hop." In *Critical Studies: Music Popular Culture Identities* 19, edited by Richard A. Young, 101–32. New York: Rodopi, 2002.
Freccero, Carla. *Popular Culture: An Introduction*. New York: New York University Press, 1999.
Freed, Leonard, Julian Bond, Michael Eric Dyson, and Paul M. Farber. *This is The Day: The March on Washington*. Los Angeles: J. Paul Getty Museum, 2013.
Fuchs, Cynthia J. "The Buddy Politic." In *Screening the Male: Exploring Masculinities in Hollywood Cinema*, edited by Steven Cohan and Ina Rae Park, 194–210. London and New York: Routledge, 1993.
Gabbin, Joanne. "A Laying On of Hands: Black Women Writers Exploring the Roots of Their Folk and Cultural Tradition." In *Wild Women in the Whirlwind: Afra-American Culture and the Contemporary Literary Renaissance*, edited by Joanne M. Braxton and Andrée Nicola McLaughlin, 246–82. New Brunswick, NJ: Rutgers University Press, 1990.
Gardella, Kay. "Barbara Walters' Big Trap." *New York Daily News*, May 29, 1979.
Gates, Henry Louis, Jr. *The Signifying Monkey: A Theory of African-American Literary Criticism*. New York: Oxford University Press, 1988.
———. *Figures in Black: Words, Signs, and the "Racial" Self*. New York: Oxford University Press, 1987.
"Gay Sex Decriminalised in India." *BBC News*. July 2, 2009, http://news.bbc.co.uk/2/hi/8129836.stm (accessed April 22, 2014).
George, Nelson. *Hip Hop America*. New York: Penguin, 1998.
Georgia Writers' Project. *Drums and Shadows: Survival Studies Among the Georgia Coastal Negroes*. Savannah: University of Georgia Press, 1986.
Gilbert, James B. "Popular Culture." *American Quarterly* 35, no. 1/2, Special Issue: Contemporary America. (Spring-Summer 1983): 141–54.
Gilroy, Paul. *Against Race: Imagining Political Culture Beyond the Color Line*. Cambridge, MA: Harvard University Press, 2000.

———. *The Black Atlantic: Modernity and Double Consciousness*. Cambridge, MA: Harvard University Press, 1993.
———. *Postcolonial Melancholia*. New York: Columbia University Press, 2005.
———. *There Ain't No Black in the Union Jack: The Cultural Politics of Race and Nation*. Chicago: University of Chicago Press, 1991.
———. "'. . . to be real': The Dissident Forms of Black Expressive Culture." In *Let's Get It On: The Politics of Black Performance*, edited by Catherine Ugwu, 12–33. Seattle, WA: Bay Press, 1995.
Goethals, Gregor. "Sacred-Secular Icons." In *Icons of America*, edited by Ray B. Browne and Marshall Fishwick, 24–34. Bowling Green, OH: Popular Press, 1978.
Golianopoulos, Thomas. "KING Legacy: Nasir Jones." *King Magazine*, April 29, 2008, http://www.king-mag.com/online/?p=5304 (accessed April 12, 2014).
Goulart, Ron. *Comic Book Culture: An Illustrated History*. Portland, OR: Collectors Press, 2000.
Gray, Herman. *Watching Race: Television and the Struggle for "Blackness."* Minneapolis: University of Minnesota Press, 1995. Reprint 2004.
Gray, Richard J., and Betty Kaklamanidou. *The 21st Century Superhero: Essays on Gender, Genre and Globalization in Film*, Jefferson, NC: McFarland, 2011.
Grayson, Sandra M. "'Spirits of Asona Ancestors Come': Reading Asante Signs in Haile Gerima's *Sankofa*." *CLA Journal* 42, no. 2 (1998): 212–27.
Gregory, Derek, Ron Johnston, Geraldine Pratt, Michael J. Watts, and Sarah Whatmore, eds. *The Dictionary of Human Geography*. 5th ed. Malden, MA: Wiley-Blackwell, 2009.
Griffin, Farah Jasmine. *Who Set You Flowin? The African-American Migration Narrative*. Oxford and New York: Oxford University Press, 1995.
Guerrero, Ed. "The Black Image in Protective Custody." In *Black American Cinema*, edited by Manthia Diawara, 237–46. AFI Film Readers. New York: Routledge, 1993.
Haggins, Bambi. *Laughing Mad: The Black Comic Persona in Post-soul America*. Piscataway, NJ: Rutgers University Press, 2009.
Haile Gerima. "Haile Gerima." November 10, 2009. http://www.sankofa.com/haile_gerima.html.
Halberstam, Judith. *Female Masculinity*. Durham, NC: Duke University Press, 1998.
———. *Skin Shows: Gothic Horror and the Technology of Monsters*. Durham, NC: Duke University Press, 1995.
Halley, Janet E. *Don't: A Reader's Guide to the Military's Anti-Gay Policy*. Durham, NC: Duke University Press, 1999.
Halliburton II, J. V. "Who Was the First Black Superhero?" *Yahoo Contributor Network*. May 18, 2009. http://voices.yahoo.com/who-was-first-black-superhero-3327260.html (accessed April 12, 2014).
Hammad, Suheir. "Jabaliya," in *Born Palestinian Born Black and the Gaza Suite*, New York: UpSet Press, 2010: 89.
———. "Mic Check: Can You Hear Me?" In *ZaatarDiva*. New York: Cypher Books, 2005: 62–63.
———. "mahmoud darwish."
———. "new orleans."

———. "A Prayer Band."
———. "rafah." In *Born Palestinian Born Black and the Gaza Suite*. New York: UpSet Press, 2010: 90.
Haraway, Donna Jeanne. "A Manifesto for Cyborgs: Science, Technology, and Socialist Feminism in the 1980s." In *The Haraway Reader*, 1–45. New York: Routledge, 2004.
Hariman, Robert, and John Luis Lucaites, *No Caption Needed: Iconic Photographs, Public Culture, and Liberal Democracy*. Chicago: University of Chicago Press, 2007.
Harper, Phillip Brian. "Marlon Riggs: The Subjective Position of Documentary Video." *Art Journal* 54, no. 4 (Winter 1995): 69–72.
Harris, Anne-Marie G. "Shopping While Black: Applying 42 U.S.C. § 1981 to Cases of Consumer Racial Profiling." *Boston College Third World Law Journal* 23, no. 1 (Winter 2003): 1–56.
Harris-Lacewell [Harris-Perry], Melissa Victoria. *Barbershops, Bibles, and BET: Everyday Talk and Black Political Thought*. Oxford and Princeton, NJ: Princeton University Press, 2004.
Haslem, Wendy, Angela Ndalianis, and Chris J. Mackie. *Super/Heroes: From Hercules to Superman*, Washington DC: New Academia, 2007.
Hebdige, Dick. "Digging for Britain: An Excavation in Seven Parts." In *Black British Cultural Studies: A Reader*, edited by Houston A. Baker Jr., Manthia Diawara, and Ruth H. Lindeborg, 120–62. London and Chicago: University of Chicago Press, 1996.
Hegel, Georg Wilhelm Friedrich. *The Philosophy of History*. Trans. J. Sibree. Ontario, CA: Batoche Books, 2001.
Hess, Mickey, ed. *Icons of Hip Hop: An Encyclopedia of the Movement, Music, and Culture*. Westport, CT: Greenwood Press, 2007.
Heyd, Thomas, and John Clegg, eds. *Aesthetics and Rock Art*, Farnham: Ashgate 2005.
Hill Collins, Patricia. *Black Sexual Politics: African Americans, Gender, and the New Racism*. New York: Routledge, 2004.
———. *From Black Power to Hip-Hop: Racism, Nationalism, and Feminism*. Philadelphia: Temple University Press, 2006.
Hochschild, Jennifer. "When Do People Not Protest Unfairness? The Case of Skin Color Discrimination." *Social Research* 73, no. 3 (Summer 2006): 473–98, 736
Holloway, Karla F. C. *Moorings & Metaphors: Figures of Culture and Gender in Black Women's Literature*. New Brunswick, NJ: Rutgers University Press, 1992.
hooks, bell. *Ain't I a Woman?: Black Women and Feminism*. Boston and Cambridge, MA: South End Press, 1981.
———. *Black Looks: Race and Representation*. Boston: South End Press, 1992. Reprint. New York: 1999.
———. *Feminist Theory: From Margin to Center*. 2nd ed. Cambridge, MA: South End Press, 2000.
Horkheimer, Max, and Theodor W. Adorno. *Dialectic of Enlightenment*. Translated by Edmund Jephcott. Stanford, CA: Stanford University Press, 1992.
Huggins, Nathan. *Harlem Renaissance*. New York: Oxford University Press, 1971.
Hughes, Langston. "The Negro Artist and the Racial Mountain." In *The Heath Anthology of American Literature*, edited by Paul Lauter, vol. 2, 2nd ed. Lexington, MA: D. C. Heath and Company, 1994.

Hurston, Zora Neale. "Characteristics of Negro Expression (1934)." In *African American Literary Expression: A Reader*, edited by Winston Napier, 31–44. New York: New York University Press, 2000.

Hutchinson, Earl Ofari. *The Assassination of the Black Male Image*. New York: Simon & Schuster, 1996.

Imogen, Tyler. "'Chav Mum, Chav Scum': Class Disgust in Contemporary Britain." *Feminist Media Studies* 8.1 (2008): 23.

Inge, M. Thomas. *Comics as Culture*. Jackson: University Press of Mississippi, 1990.

Instagram, "Marking 50 Years Since MLK's March on Washington," (blog). http://blog.instagram.com/post/59618165996/mow50, (accessed October 1, 2013).

Iton, Richard. *In Search of the Black Fantastic: Politics and Popular Culture in the Post–Civil Rights Era*. Oxford: Oxford University Press, 2008.

James, Joy. "Radicalizing Feminism." In *The Black Feminist Reader*, edited by Joy James and T. Denean Sharpley-Whiting, 239–60. Malden, MA: Blackwell, 2000.

Jenkins, Sacha, Elliott Wilson, Chairman Mao, Gabriel Alvarez, and Brent Rollins. *Ego Trip's Book of Rap Lists*. New York: St. Martin's Press, 1999.

Jennings, La Vinia Delois. "Kanda: Living Elders, the Ancestral Presence, and the Ancestor as Foundation." In *Toni Morrison and the Idea of Africa*, 81–136. Cambridge: Cambridge University Press, 2008.

Johnson, James Weldon. *The Autobiography of an Ex-Colored Man*. In *Three Negro Classics*, introduction by John Hope Franklin, 391–511. New York: Avon Books, 1965.

Jones, William Powell. *The March on Washington: Jobs, Freedom, and the Forgotten History of Civil Rights*. New York: W. W. Norton, 2013.

Jong, Irene J. F. de. "In Media Res." In *Routledge Encyclopedia of Narrative Theory*, ed. David Herman, Manfred Jahn, and Marie-Laure Ryan, 242. New York: Routledge, 2005.

Joselit, David. "The Video Public Sphere." *Art Journal* 59, no. 2 (Summer 2002): 46–53.

Kafewo, Samuel Ayedime. "Exploring Narratives of the Trans-Atlantic Slave Trade in *Amistad* and *Sankofa*." In *Africa and Trans-Atlantic Memories: Literary and Aesthetic Manifestations of Diaspora and History*, edited by Naana Opoku-Agyemang, Paul E. Lovejoy, and David V. Trotman, 147–59. Trenton, NJ: Africa World, 2008.

Kandé, Sylvie. "Look Homeward, Angel: Maroons and Mulattos in Haile Gerima's *Sankofa*." *Research in African Literatures* 29, no. 2 (Summer 1998): 128–46.

Katznelson, Ira. *When Affirmative Action was White: An Untold History of Racial Inequality in Twentieth-Century America*. New York: W. W. Norton, 2005.

Keehm, Anne. "Walk this Way." *Source* 222 (June 2008): 52.

Kelley, James B. "Song, Story, or History: Resisting Claims of a Coded Message in the African American Spiritual "Follow the Drinking Gourd." *The Journal of Popular Culture* 41, no. 2 (2008).

Kelley, Robin D. G. *Race Rebels: Culture, Politics, and the Black Working Class*. New York: Free Press, 1994.

———. *Yo' Mama's DisFunktional: Fighting the Culture Wars in Urban America*. Boston and New York: Beacon Press, 1997.

Kellner, Douglas. *Media Spectacle*. New York: Routledge, 2003.

———. *Media Spectacle and the Crisis of Democracy: Terrorism, War, and Election Battles*. Boulder, CO: Paradigm Publishers, 2005.

Keyes, Cheryl L. "Empowering Self, Making Choices, Creating Spaces: Black Female Identity via Rap Music Performance." In *That's the Joint!: The Hip Hop Studies Reader*, edited by Murray Forman and Mark Anthony Neal, 265–75. New York: Routledge, 2004.

———. "Empowering Self, Making Choices, Creating Spaces: Black Female Identity via Rap Music Performance," *Journal of American Folklore* 113, no. 449 (Summer 2000): 255–69.

Kilbourne, Barbara, Paula England, and Kurt Beron. "Effects of Individual, Occupational, and Industrial Characteristics on Earnings: Intersections of Race and Gender." *Social Forces* 72, no. 4 (June 1994): 1149–76.

King, Martin Luther, Jr. "I Have A Dream," NPR, " DR. MARTIN LUTHER KING JR. AND THE PUBLIC IMAGINATION." January 18, 2013. http://www.onthemedia.org/story/263577-dr-martin-luther-king-jr-and-public-imagination/ (accessed April 18, 2014).

———. "Letter from Birmingham Jail," *A Testament of Hope: The Essential Writings and Speeches of Martin Luther King, Jr.* New York: Harper Collins, 1986.

King, Ryan S. *Disparity by Geography: The War on Drugs in America's Cities*. Washington, DC: Sentencing Project, 2008. http://www.sentencingproject.org/doc/publications/dp_drugarrestreport.pdf (accessed April 15, 2014).

Kitwana, Bakari. *The Hip Hop Generation: Young Blacks and the Crisis in African American Culture*. New York: Basic Civitas, 2002.

Knight, La'Jaunda, and Devin the Dude. "Devin the Dude: More to Know." Allhiphop.com., Features, February 21, 2008. http://allhiphop.com/stories/features/archive/2008/02/21/19322374.aspx (accessed April 12, 2014).

Kno. "An Open Letter To MF DOOM." *QN5Music* (blog), posted August 13, 2008. http://www.qn5.com/blog/entry/an-open-letter-to-mf-doom/ (accessed November 9, 2009).

Krasner, David. *Resistance, Parody, and Double Consciousness in African American Theatre, 1895–1910*. New York: St. Martin's Press, 1997.

Kweli, Talib. "Rising Down." The Roots. *Two.One.Five Magazine* 1, no. 2, 2008.

Landsman, Julie. "Confronting the Racism of Low Expectations: Subtle or Blatant, Racist Attitudes Poison Life at School." *Educational Leadership* 62, no. 3 (November 2004): 28–32.

Lane, Alycee J. "Black Bodies/Gay Bodies: The Politics of Race in the Gay/Military Battle." *Callaloo* 17, no. 4 (Fall 1994): 1074–88.

Levinas, Emmanuel. *Dialogues With Contemporary Continental Thinkers: The Phenomenological Heritage*, edited by Richard Kearney, 62. Manchester: Manchester University Press, 1984.

Levine, Lawrence W. *Black Culture and Black Consciousness: Afro-American Folk Thought from Slavery to Freedom*. Oxford and New York: Oxford University Press, 1997.

Lewis, George H. "Taste Cultures and Culture Classes in Mass Society: Shifting Patterns in American Popular Music." *International Review of the Aesthetics and Sociology of Music* 8, no. 1 (June 1977): 39–48.

Limon, John. *Stand-up Comedy in Theory, or, Abjection in America*. Durham, NC: Duke University Press, 2000.

Lipsitz, George. "Race and Racism." In *Modern American Culture: An Introduction*, edited by Mick Gidley, 120–41. London: Longman, 1993.

Lock, Graham. *Blutopia: Visions of the Future and Revisions of the Past in the Work of Sun Ra, Duke Ellington, and Anthony Braxton*. Durham, NC: Duke University Press, 1999.

Lorde, Audre. *Sister Outsider: Essays and Speeches*. Berkley, CA and Trumansburg, NY: Crossing Press, 1984.

Lott, Tommy L. "A No-Theory Theory of Black Cinema." In *Representing Blackness: Issues in Film and Video*, edited by Valerie Smith, 83–96. New Brunswick, NJ: Rutgers University Press, 2003.

Love, Monie, Queen Latifah, and Tricia Rose. "Rapping, Woman to Woman," interview by Farai Chideya." *Hip Hop: The Past, Present & Future*, NPR Music, Hip-Hop's Herstory, June 11, 2007. http://www.npr.org/templates/story/story.php?storyId=10948089 (accessed April 12, 2014).

Lynn, Michael, Michael Sturman, Christie Ganley, Elizabeth Adams, Mathew Douglas, and Jessica McNeal. "Consumer Racial Discrimination in Tipping: A Replication and Extension." *Journal of Applied Social Psychology* 38, no. 4 (April 2008): 1045–60.

Majors, Richard, and Janet Mancini Billson. *Cool Pose: The Dilemmas of Black Manhood in America*. New York: Touchstone Books, 1992.

Malkani, Gautam. *Londonstani*. New York: Penguin Press, 2006.

———. "Londonstani Style Guide." http://www.gautammalkani.com/style_guide.pdf (accessed April 23, 2014).

Mallozzi, Vincent M. *Asphalt Gods: An Oral History of the Rucker Tournament*. New York: Doubleday, 2003.

Manza, Jeff, and Christopher Uggen. *Locked Out: Felon Disenfranchisement and American Democracy*. New York: Oxford University Press, 2006.

Markman, Rob [a.k.a. BK Cyph]. "Ride for My . . ." *Don Diva: The Original Street Bible*, 8th Anniversary, no. 32, August/2008, 65–67.

Marx, Sherry. *Revealing the Invisible: Confronting Passing Racism in Teacher Education*. New York: Routledge, 2006.

Maultsby, Portia, K. "Africanisms in African-American Music." In *Africanisms in American Culture*, edited by Joseph E. Holloway, 185–210. Bloomington: Indiana University Press, 1990.

Maume, David J., Jr. "Glass Ceilings and Glass Escalators: Occupational Segregation and Race and Sex Differences in Managerial Promotions." *Work and Occupations* 26, no. 4 (November 1999): 483–509.

Maynard, Joyce. "Richard Pryor, King of the Scene-Stealers," *New York Times*, January 9, 1977, sec. 2, 11.

McCluskey, Audrey T., ed. *Richard Pryor: The Life and Legacy of a "Crazy" Black Man*. Bloomington: Indiana University Press, 2008.

McDonald, Paul. "Stand-Up Comedy as Poetry: Transcendentalism and Romantic Anti-Capitalism in the Work of Bill Hicks." *Journal of Ecocriticism* 1, no. 2 (July 2009): 104–13. http://ojs.unbc.ca/index.php/joe/article/viewFile/118/225 (accessed April 12, 2014).

McLeod, Ken. "Space Oddities: Aliens, Futurism and Meaning in Popular Music." *Popular Music* 22, no. 3 (October 2003): 337–55.

McLuhan, Marshall. *The Mechanical Bride: Folklore of Industrial Man*. Berkeley, CA: Gingko Press, 2002.

Micallef, Ken. "Earth, Sun, Moon." *Remix* 10, no. 3 (March 2008): 30–36.

Michigan Court of Appeals. *People v. Schmitz*. 586 NW2d 766, 678 (1998).

Mintz, Lawrence. "Standup Comedy as Social and Cultural Mediation," *American Quarterly* 37, no. 1 (Spring 1985): 71–80.

Mittell, Jason. *Genre and Television: From Cop Shows to Cartoons in American Culture*. New York: Routledge, 2004.

Mooney, Paul. *Black Is the New White: A Memoir*. New York: Simon Spotlight Entertainment, 2009.

Monáe, Janelle. "Bio: Janelle Monae A Girl from Another Planet." http://www.jmonae.com/bio.

———. "Janelle Monáe, interview by Leital Molad." *Studio 360*, March 27, 2009, http://www.studio360.org/episodes/2009/03/27/segments/127229 (accessed April 14, 2014).

———. "Janelle Monáe's Funky Otherworldly Sounds, interview by Terry Gross." *Fresh Air*. National Public Radio. June 17, 2009. http://www.npr.org/templates/transcript/transcript.php?storyId=105491960 (accessed April 12, 2014).

———. "Many Moons." *Metropolis: Suite I (The Chase)*. August 2008, directed by Alan Ferguson and The Wondaland Arts Society. http://www.youtube.com/user/janellemonae (accessed April 23, 2014).

———. "Sincerely Jane." *Metropolis: The Chase Suite*. August 2007. Purple Ribbon Entertainment. Compact disc.

———. Liner notes to *Metropolis: The Chase Suite*. 2007. Bad Boy Records 511234-1. Compact disc.

———. "Violet Stars Happy Hunting." *Metropolis: The Chase Suite*. August 2007. Purple Ribbon Entertainment. Compact disc.

Morgan, Marcyliena H. *The Real Hip Hop: Battling for Knowledge, Power, and Respect in the LA Underground*. Durham, NC: Duke University Press, 2009.

Morley, David and Kuan-Hsing Chen, ed. *Stuart Hall: Critical Dialogues in Cultural Studies*, New York: Routledge, 1996.

Morrison, Toni. *Song of Solomon*. New York: Vintage, 1977.

Moss, Philip, and Chris Tilly. *Stories Employers Tell: Race, Skill, and Hiring in America*. New York: Russell Sage Foundation, 2001.

Muhammad, Lyle. "SANKOFA FIRE! Arson Fire Destroys over 10,000 Copies of Landmark Film." November 5, 2009. http://afgen.com/sankofa.html.

Mulvey, Laura. *Fetishism and Curiosity*. Bloomington: Indiana University Press, 1998.

Myers, Jeffrey. *Converging Stories: Race, Ecology, and Environmental Justice in American Literature*. Athens: University of Georgia Press, 2005.

National Park Service. "We Are Still Marching." *March On Washington*. http://www.wearestillmarching.com (accessed October 1, 2013).

Nauman, Bruce. "Interview with Michele De Angelus." In *Art In Theory, 1900–2000: An Anthology of Changing Ideas*, edited by Charles Harrison and Paul Wood, 910. Maiden: Blackwell Publishing, 1992.

Neal, Mark Anthony. *What the Music Said: Black Popular Music and Black Public Culture.* London: Routledge, 1999.
Nelson, Alondra. "Introduction: Future Texts." *Social Text* 20, no. 1 (Spring 2002): 1–14.
New York Times. "Witnesses to History, 50 Years Later." U.S. (online). http://www.nytimes.com/interactive/2013/08/23/us/march-on-washington-anniversary-memories.html?_r=0 (accessed October 1, 2013).
Nye, David E. "Industrialization, Business, and Consumerism." *Modern American Culture: An Introduction,* edited by Mick Gidley, 166–88. London: Longman, 1993.
O'Connor, John J. "TV: Pryor and Chase Take Their Pot Shots." *New York Times,* May 5, 1977, C27.
Ogbar, Jeffrey O. G. *Hip-Hop Revolution: The Culture and Politics of Rap.* Lawrence: University Press of Kansas, 2007.
O'Malley Greenburg, Zack. *Empire State of Mind: How Jay-Z Went from Street Corner to Corner Office.* New York: Portfolio/Penguin, 2011.
O'Meally, Robert G. *The Jazz Cadence of American Culture.* New York: Columbia University Press, 1998.
The Original Hip Hop-Lyrics Archive. http://ohhla.com (accessed April 12, 2014).
Orr, David Gerald. "The Icon in the Time Tunnel." In *Icons of America,* edited by Ray B. Browne and Marshall Fishwick, 13–23. Bowling Green, OH: Popular Press, 1978.
Orth, Maureen. "The Perils of Pryor." *Newsweek,* October 3, 1977, 60–63.
Osayande, Ewuare X. *Misogyny and the Emcee: Sex, Race, and Hip Hop.* Philadelphia: Machete Media, 2008.
Otter, Nancy. "*Sankofa* vs. *Beloved.*" October 30, 2009. *African Diaspora* 6, no. 4 (Fall 1999). Africa Update Archives, http://www.ccsu.edu/afstudy/updvol64.htm#642 (accessed April 12, 2014).
Parade. Letter to the Editor. April 23, 1978. Billy Rose Collection, New York Public Library.
Patton, Tracey Owens. "Hey Girl, Am I More than My Hair?: African American Women and Their Struggles with Beauty, Body Image, and Hair." *NWSA Journal* 18, no. 2 (Summer 2006): 24–51.
Perry, Imani. *More Beautiful and More Terrible: The Embrace and Transcendence of Racial Inequality in the United States.* New York: New York University Press, 2011.
———. *Prophets of the Hood: Politics and Poetics in Hip Hop.* Durham, NC: Duke University Press, 2004.
Pettit, Eber. "Fugitives Follow the North Star (1879)." In *Slavery in the United States: A Social, Political, and Historical Encyclopedia,* edited by Junius P. Rodriguez, 572. Santa Barbara, CA: ABC-CLIO, 2007.
Phelan, Peggy. *Unmarked: The Politics of Performance.* New York: Routledge, 1993.
Potter, Russell A. *Spectacular Vernaculars: Hip-Hop and the Politics of Postmodernism.* Albany: State University of New York Press, 1995.
Pough, Gwendolyn D. "Hip-Hop Soul Divas and Rap Music: Critiquing the Love That Hate Produced." In *Black Women and Music: More Than the Blues,* edited by Eileen M. Hayes and Linda F. Williams, 23–50. Urbana: University of Illinois Press, 2007.

Pryor, Richard, and Todd Gold, *Pryor Convictions, and Other Life Sentences*. New York: Pantheon Books, 1995.

Puar, Jasbir K. *Terrorist Assemblages: Homonationalism in Queer Times*. Durham, NC: Duke University Press, 2007.

Public Enemy, with Chuck D. "Righstarter (Message to a Black Man)." *Yo! Bumrush the Show*. April 1987. Def Jam Recordings. http://www.publicenemy.com/album/5/13/righstarter-message-to-a-black-man.html (accessed April 15, 2014).

Quinn, Eithne. *Nuthin' But a "G" Thang: The Culture and Commerce of Gangsta Rap*. New York: Columbia University Press, 2005.

Raboteau, Albert J. *Slave Religion: The "Invisible Institution" in the Antebellum South*. Oxford: Oxford University Press, 1980.

Ragone, August. *Eiji Tsuburaya: Master of Monsters: Defending the Earth with Ultraman, Godzilla, and Friends in the Golden Age of Japanese Science Fiction Film*. San Francisco: Chronicle Books, 2011.

Rahman, Jacquelyn. "The N Word: Its History and Use in the English Language." *Journal of English Linguistics* (July 31, 2011): 1-35. Accessed February 15, 2011, doi:10.1177/0075424211414807. Reprint. "The N Word: Its History and Use in the African American Community." *Journal of English Linguistics* 40, no. 2 (June 2012): 137–71.

Ramsey, Guthrie, Jr. *Race Music: Black Cultures from Bebop to Hip-Hop*. Berkeley: University of California Press, 2003; Chicago: Center for Black Music Research, 2004.

Raw, Laurence. "Mapping Adaptation Studies." Review of *The Literature-Film Reader: Issues of Adaptation*, by James M. Welsh and Peter Lev; and *Cambridge Companion to Literature on Screen*, by Deborah Cartmell and Imelda Whelehan. *Literature Film Quarterly* 36, no. 3 (2008): 233–37.

Rawlston, Valerie A., and William E. Spriggs. "Pay Equity 2000: Are We There Yet?" Washington, DC: National Urban League Institute for Opportunity and Equality, SRR-02-2001, April 2001.

Reid, Shaheem. "Jay-Z: Hip Hop Has Done More Than Any Politician To Improve Race Relations." *MTV News*. March 20, 2009. http://www.mtv.com/news/articles/1607418/jay-z-hip-hop-has-done-more-than-any-politician-improve-race-relations.jhtml (accessed April 15, 2014).

Reynolds, Richard. *Super Heroes: A Modern Mythology*. Jackson: University Press of Mississippi, 1992.

Richardson, Elaine B. *Hiphop Literacies*. New York: Routledge, 2008.

Richardson, Jeanita W., and Kim A. Scott. "Rap Music and Its Violent Progeny: America's Culture of Violence in Context." *Journal of Negro Education* 71, no. 3 (Summer 2002): 175–92.

Robbins, Richard H. *Global Problems and the Culture of Capitalism*. New York: Pearson, 2004.

Roberts, Dorothy. *Killing the Black Body: Race, Reproduction, and the Meaning of Liberty*. New York: Vintage, 1998.

———. *Shattered Bonds: The Color of Child Welfare*. New York: Basic Books, 2002.

Rollefson, J. Griffith. "The 'Robot Voodoo Power' Thesis: Afrofuturism and Anti-Anti-Essentialism from Sun Ra to Kool Keith." *Black Music Research Journal* 28, no. 1 (Spring 2008): 83–109.
Rooks, Noliwe M. *Hair Raising: Beauty, Culture, and African American Women*. New Brunswick, NJ: Rutgers University Press, 1996.
Rose, Tricia. *Black Noise: Rap Music and Black Culture in Contemporary America*. Middletown, CT: Wesleyan University Press, 1994.
———. *Hip Hop Futures: A Lecture and Discussion*. Presentation, Inaugural Conference, Statler Auditorium, November 2, 2008. Cornell University Hip Hop Collection. Ithaca, NY: Cornell University, 2008.
———. *The Hip Hop Wars: What We Talk About When We Talk About Hip Hop—and Why It Matters*. New York: Basic Civitas Books, 2008.
Rushdy, Ashraf H. A. *Neo-Slave Narratives: Studies in the Social Logic of a Literary Form*. New York: Oxford University Presses, 1999.
Rutledge, Gregory. "Futuristic Fiction and Fantasy: The *Racial* Establishment." *Callaloo* 24, no. 1 (2001): 236–52.
Said, Edward. "Opponents, Audiences, Constituencies, and Community." In *Art In Theory, 1900–2000: An Anthology of Changing Ideas*, edited by Charles Harrison and Paul Wood, 1058. Maiden: Blackwell Publishing, 1992.
Shabazz, Ilyasah, with Kim McLarin. *Growing Up X*. New York: One World, 2002.
Shakespeare, William. *Hamlet*. In *The Norton Shakespeare*, edited by Stephen Greenblatt, et al. New York: W. W. Norton, 1997.
Sharpley-Whiting, T. Denean. *Pimps Up, Ho's Down: Hip Hop's Hold on Young Black Women*. New York: New York University Press, 2007.
Sherman, Natalie. "Group Alleges Racial Disparities in Bank of America Practices at Foreclosed Baltimore Homes." *Baltimore Sun*, November 15, 2013. http://articles.baltimoresun.com/2013-11-15/business/bs-bz-boa-suit-20131115_1_nfha-minority-areas-complaint (accessed April 17, 2014).
Shifman, Limor. *Memes in Digital Culture*. Cambridge, MA: MIT Press, 2014.
Simmons, Russell, with Nelson George. *Life and Def: Sex, Drugs, Money, and God*. New York: Three Rivers Press, 2001.
Singer, Marc. "'Black Skins' and White Masks: Comic Books and the Secret of Race." *African American Review* 36, no. 1 (Spring, 2002): 107–19.
Smedley, Brian D., Adrienne Y. Stith, and Alan R. Nelson. *Unequal Treatment: Confronting Racial and Ethnic Disparities in Health Care*. Washington, DC: National Academy Press, 2003.
Smith, Laurajane. *Representing Enslavement and Abolition in Museums: Ambiguous Engagements*. New York: Routledge, 2011.
Smith, Valerie, ed. *Representing Blackness: Issues in Film and Video*. New Brunswick, NJ: Rutgers University Press, 2003.
Smithsonian National Museum of American History. "Changing America: The Emancipation Proclamation, 1863 and the March on Washington, 1963." http://americanhistory.si.edu/exhibitions/changing-america (Accessed October 1, 2013; Library of Congress, "A Day Like No Other," http://www.loc.gov/exhibits/march-on-washington/ (accessed October 1, 2013).
Spillers, Hortense J. "Mama's Baby, Papa's Maybe: An American Grammar Book." *Diacritics: A Review of Contemporary Criticism* 17 no. 2 (Summer 1987): 65–81.

Starr, Larry, and Christopher Alan Waterman. *American Popular Music: From Minstrelsy to MTV*. New York and Oxford: Oxford University Press, 2003.

Stewart, Jimmy. "Music: Introduction to Black Aesthetics in Music." In *The Black Aesthetic*, edited by Addison Gayle, 81–96. Garden City, NY: Doubleday & Company, 1971.

Stolberg, Sheryl Gay. "Obama Pledges Again to End 'Don't Ask, Don't Tell.'" *New York Times*, October 10, 2009, A24. http://www.nytimes.com/2009/10/11/us/politics/11speech.html (accessed December 20, 2009).

Stoute, Steve. *The Tanning of America: How Hip Hop Created a Culture That Rewrote the Rules of the New Economy*. New York: Gotham Books, 2011.

Strausbaugh, John. *Black Like You: Blackface, Whiteface, Insult & Imitation in American Popular Culture*. New York: Jeremy P. Tarcher/Penguin, 2006. Reprint 2007.

Suffredini, Kara S. "Pride and Prejudice: The Homosexual Panic Defense." *Boston College Third World Law Journal* 21, no. 2 (May 2001): 279–314.

Swindell, Warren. "Aesthetics and African American Musical Expression." In *The African Aesthetic: Keeper of the Traditions*, edited by Kariamu Welsh-Asante, 175–94. Westport, CT: Greenwood Publishing Group, 1993.

Tafoya, Eddie. *The Legacy of the Wisecrack: Stand-up Comedy as the Great American Literary Form*. Boca Raton: BrownWalker, 2009.

Telotte, J. P. "Heinlein, Verhoeven, and the Problem of the Real *Starship Troopers*." In *The Literature/Film Reader: Issues of Adaptation*, edited by James M. Welsh and Peter Lev, 187–97. Lanham, MD: Scarecrow Press, 2007.

Tillet, Salamishah. *Sites of Slavery: Citizenship and Racial Democracy in the Post–Civil Rights Imagination*. Durham, NC: Duke University Press, 2012.

Time Magazine. "One Man. One March. One Speech. One Dream." #ONEDREAM. http://content.time.com/time/onedream/ (accessed April 17, 2014).

Tomkins, Silvan S. "Shame-Humiliation and Contempt-Disgust." In *Shame and its Sisters: A Silvan Tomkins Reader*, edited by Eve Kosofsky Sedgwick, Adam Frank, and Irving E. Alexander; 133–78. Durham, NC: Duke University Press, 1995.

Tyrangiel, Josh. "The Un-Retirement of Jay-Z." *Time*, November 24, 2006. http://www.time.com/time/arts/article/0,8599,1562881,00.html (accessed April 13, 2014).

Uhlmann, Eric, Nilanjana Dasgupta, Angelica Elgueta, Anthony G. Greenwald, and Jane Swanson. "Subgroup Prejudice Based on Skin Color Among Hispanics in the United States and Latin America." *Social Cognition* 20, no. 3 (2002): 198–226.

Ukpokodu, I. Peter. "African Heritage from the Lenses of African-American Theatre and Film." *Journal of Dramatic Theory and Criticism* 16, no. 2 (Spring 2002): 69–94.

U.S. Department of the Interior. Remarks by the President and Vice President at Signing of the *Don't Ask, Don't Tell Repeal Act of 2010*. December 22, 2010, http://www.whitehouse.gov/the-press-office/2010/12/22/remarks-president-and-vice-president-signing-dont-ask-dont-tell-repeal-a (accessed April 22, 2014).

U.S. Department of Labor. "Judge Orders Bank of America to Pay Almost $2.2 Million for Racial Discrimination Against More Than 1,100 African-American Job Seekers." News Release, no. 13-1967-NAT. http://www.dol.gov/opa/media/press/ofccp/OFCCP20131967.htm (accessed April 17, 2014).

U.S. House. *Don't Ask, Don't Tell Repeal Act of 2010*. Public Law 111–321. 111th Cong. (December 22, 2010). Repeal 10 U.S.C. § 654 (1994).

———. *National Defense Authorization Act for Fiscal Year 1994*, 10 U.S.C. § 654 (1994).

U.S. Postal Service. New Release, "Postal Service Issues March on Washington Stamp." August 23, 2013, no. 13-067. http://about.usps.com/news/national-releases/2013/pr13_067.htm (accessed April 17, 2014).

U.S. Supreme Court. *Brown v. Board of Education of Topeka*. May 17, 1954. Records of the Supreme Court of the United States. Record Group 267. Washington, DC: Archives, 1954.

———. *Loving v. Virginia*. June 12, 1967. Records of the Supreme Court of the United States. Record Group 338. Washington, DC: Archives, 1967.

Van Straten, Roelof. *An Introduction to Iconography*. Langhorne, PA: Gordon and Breach, 1994.

Vasey, Ruth. "The Media." In *Modern American Culture: An Introduction*, edited by Mick Gidley, 213–38. London and New York: Longman, 1993.

Vaughn, Viktor. "Doctor Doom (Victor Von Doom)" *Marvel Universe*, http://marvel.com/universe/Doctor_Doom_(Victor_von_Doom) (accessed February 19, 2010).

Walton, Kendall L. *The Dictionary of Art*. Edited by Jane Turner. 34 vols. New York: Macmillan, 1996.

Warner, Michael. *Publics and Counterpublics*. New York: Zone Books, 2005.

Warner, William. "The Resistance Popular Culture." *American Literary History* 2, no. 4 (Winter 1990): 726–42.

Watkins, Mel. *On the Real Side: Laughing, Lying, and Signifying—The Underground Tradition of African-American Humor That Transformed American Culture, from Slavery to Richard Pryor*. New York: Simon & Schuster, 1994.

Watkins, S. Craig. *Hip Hop Matters: Politics, Pop Culture, and the Struggle for the Soul of a Movement*. Boston: Beacon Press, 2005.

Weheliye, Alexander G. "'Feenin': Posthuman Voices in Contemporary Black Popular Music." *Social Text* 20, no. 2 (Summer 2002): 21–47.

———. *Phonographies: Grooves in Sonic Afro-Modernity*. Durham, NC: Duke University Press, 2005.

Weinstein, Rhona S. *Reaching Higher: The Power of Expectations in Schooling*. Cambridge, MA: Harvard University Press, 2004.

Wells, Ida B. *Southern Horrors: Lynch Law in All Its Phases*. New York: New York Age Print, 1892.

Westhoff, Ben. "Private Enemy: Two New York Rappers Dreamed of Stardom. MF Doom Got It. MF Grimm Didn't." *Villagevoice.com*, October 31, 2006. http://www.villagevoice.com/2006-10-31/music/private-enemy (accessed April 13, 2014).

Wheeler, Elizabeth A. "'Most of My Heroes Don't Appear on No Stamps': The Dialogics of Rap Music." *Black Music Research Journal* 11, no. 2 (Autumn 1991): 193–216.

White, Hayden. "Historical Text as Literary Artifact," In *The History and Narrative Reader*, edited by Geoffrey Roberts, 221–36. New York and London: Routledge, 2001.

Williams, Linda. *Playing the Race Card: Melodramas in Black and White from Uncle Tom to O. J. Simpson*. Princeton, NJ: Princeton University Press, 2001.

Winning, Brolin. "Redman: Still Smokin," March 14, 2007. http://www.mp3.com/features/stories/9042.html.
Wood, Andy. "'Original London Style': London Posse and the Birth of British Hip Hop." *Atlantic Studies* 6, no. 2 (August 2009): 175–90.
Woolford, Pamela. "Filming Slavery: A Conversation with Haile Gerima." *Transition* 64 (1994): 90–104.
Yates, Kimberley A. "When 'Keeping It Real' Goes Right." In *The Comedy of Dave Chappelle: Critical Essays*, edited by K. A. Wisniewski, 139–55. Jefferson, NC: McFarland & Co., 2009.
Yinger, John M. [McHenry]. *Closed Doors, Opportunities Lost: The Continuing Costs of Housing Discrimination*. New York: Russell Sage, 1995.
Yoshino, Kenji. *Covering: The Hidden Assault on Our Civil Rights*. New York: Random House, 2006.
Young, Vershawn Ashanti. *Your Average Nigga: Performing Race, Literacy, and Masculinity*. Detroit: Wayne State University Press, 2007.
Zittoun, Tania. Ed. *Transitions: Development through Symbolic Resources*. Charlotte, NC: Information Age Publishing, 2006.
Zoglin, Richard. *Comedy at the Edge: How Stand-up in the 1970s Changed America*. New York: Bloomsbury USA, 2008.

SOUND RECORDINGS

Listing by Artist and Composition and Video Titles

50 Cent. "What Up Gangsta." *Get Rich or Die Tryin*. February 6, 2003. Interscope Records (2 compact discs).
———. "In Da Club." *Get Rich or Die Tryin*. February 6, 2003. Interscope Records (2 compact discs).
Ahearn, Charlie. *Wild Style*. November 23, 1983. New York: First Run Features, 1983.
Alton, Peter, and Peter Spirer. *Beef*. Music by J-Force, QD3 [Quincy Jones III], and Femi Ojetunde. DVD. Directed by Peter Spirer. Chatsworth, CA: Image Entertainment, 2003.
Big Punisher. *Capital Punishment*. August 24, 1999. Relativity (compact disc).
Black Star. *Mos Def & Talib Kweli are Black Star*. August 18, 1998. Rawkus/UMDG (compact disc).
Boogie Down Productions (Scott La Rock, KRS-One, and Ced-Gee). *Criminal Minded*. March 3, 1987. B-Boy Records (compact disc).
Buchanan, Pat. *Hardball with Chris Matthews*. MSNBC. Quoted by Mamta Trivedi. First broadcast February 23, 2011.
Dyson, Michael, and Jay-Z. "Michael Eric Dyson and Jay-Z, Part 1 of 3." YouTube video, 6:00, from a three-part interview scheduled to air on November 18, 2010 on The Michael Dyson Show. www.dysonshow.org, posted November 17, 2010. http://www.youtube.com/watch?v=z-QTyamJcoE (accessed December 13, 2011).
———. "Michael Eric Dyson and Jay-Z, Part 2 of 3." YouTube video, 6:00, from a three-part interview scheduled to air on November 18, 2010 on The Michael

Dyson Show. www.dysonshow.org, posted November 17, 2010. http://www.youtube.com/watch?v=z-QTyamJcoE (accessed December 13, 2011).
George Holliday's video of the Rodney King beating. Collection: Copyright Collection (© registration no. PA 518-451). Call number: VAB 4242. Library of Congress control number (LCCN): 91789926.
Gerima, Haile. *Sankofa.* DVD. Directed and screenplay by Haile Gerima. Washington, DC: Mypheduh Films Inc., 1993.
Grae, Jean. *Jeanius.* July 8, 2008. Blacksmith Music (compact disc).
———. *The Evil Jeanius.* September 30, 2008. Babygrande Records (compact disc).
Hill, Lauryn. *The Miseducation of Lauryn Hill.* August 25, 1998. Sony Records (compact disc).
Hitchens vs Mos Def. 2009. http://www.youtube.com/watch?v=-Ew9CngVeFA (accessed December 15, 2009).
Hurt, Byron. *Hip Hop: Beyond Beats and Rhymes,* DVD. Lugano: Independent Lens, 2007.
Jay-Z. "30 Something." and "Kingdom Come." *Kingdom Come.* 2003. Roc-A-Fella Records (compact disc).
———. "Anything." YouTube video, 4.20, posted JayZVEVO, June 16, 2009. Roc-A-Fella Records, LLC. http://www.youtube.com/watch?v=odThhIA2gUM (accessed December 15, 2009).
———. *Black Album.* November 25, 2003. Roc-A-Fella (compact disc).
———. "Dead Presidents." *Reasonable Doubt.* June 25, 1996. Roc-A-Fella (compact disc.)
———. "Hard Knock Life." YouTube video, 4.15, posted by monkk, March 1, 2007, owned by UMG. http://www.youtube.com/watch?v=zxtn6-XQupM (accessed December 15, 2009).
———. "Hovi Baby." and " Renegades." *The Blueprint 2: The Gist & the Curse.* November 12, 2002. Roc-A-Fella/Island Def. (compact disc).
———. "Interview with Howard Stern Full Video, parts 4 of 4." November 15, 2010. KillerHipHop.com, posted maladapt, November 21, 2010. http://www.killerhiphop.com/jay-z-interview-howard-stern-video (accessed December 13, 2011).
———. "Interview with Bill Maher on HBO's *Real Time.*" Youraudiofix.com video, 14.31, 2009. http://www.republicaupdate.com/2009/09/jayzs-interview-with-bill-maher-on-hbos-real-time.html (accessed December 15, 2009).
———. "Interview with *Real Time with Bill Maher,* part 2." DimeWars video, 14.31, posted 2009. http://dimewars.com/Video/Jay-Z-On-Real-Time-With-Bill-Maher-Part-2--Bill-Maher-Asks-About-Some-Of-His-Favorite-Jay-Lyrics-.aspx?bcmediaid=a782aec9-06bd-42d9-8b63-6dd5b5e4d2b5&activetab=1 (accessed December 15, 2009).
———. "PSA." *Black Album.* November 25, 2003. Roc-A-Fella (compact disc).
———. "Where I'm From?" YouTube video, 2.01, posted by BoomBap90s, March 24, 2008. http://www.youtube.com/watch?v=1X46RsCxgqE (accessed December 15, 2009).
Jeru the Damaja. *The Sun Rises in the East.* May 24, 1994. Fontana Island (compact disc).
Kool Keith, *First Come, First Served.* May 4, 1999. Funky Ass Records.

Life of Pryor: The Richard Pryor Story. Hosted by Lenny Henry, produced by Mobashir Dar. Documentary first broadcast October 14, 2006 by the BBC.

Lil Wayne. "Banned From TV." *No Ceilings.* October 31, 2009. Young Money, Cash Money, Universal Motown (mixtape).

———. "Drop the World, featuring Eminem" *Rebirth.* December 22, 2009. Young Money, Cash Money, Universal Motown.

MF DOOM. *Operation Doomsday.* April 20, 1999. Fondle 'Em Records, Sub Verse Music (compact disc).

———. *Madvillain.* March 23, 2004. Stones Throw (compact disc).

———. *MF. Food.* November 16, 2004. Rhymesayers Entertainment (compact disc).

Monáe, Janelle. "Many Moons." *Metropolis: Suite I (The Chase).* August 2008. Alan Ferguson and The Wondaland Arts Society. Bad Boy Records. http://www.youtube.com/user/janellemonae (accessed April 23, 2014).

———. *Metropolis: Suite I (The Chase).* August 2008. Atlantic Records (compact disc).

———. "Biography." Contactmusic.com. http://www.contactmusic.com/info/janelle_monae (accessed April 12, 2014).

———. Interview with Terry Gross," *Fresh Air,* National Public Radio, June 17, 2009. http://www.npr.org/templates/transcript/transcript.php?storyId=105491960 (accessed April 12, 2014).

Mos Def. "UMI Says." *Black on Both Sides.* June 4, 2002. Rawkus/UMDG.

Nelly. "Tip Drill." *Da Derrty Versions: The Reinvention.* UMVD Labels, 2003.

Notorious B. I. G. Biggie, featuring Method Man. "The What." *Ready to Die.* 1993–1994. Bad Boy Records (compact disc).

NPR. "DR. MARTIN LUTHER KING JR. AND THE PUBLIC IMAGINATION." January 18, 2013. http://www.onthemedia.org/story/263577-dr-martin-luther-king-jr-and-public-imagination/ (accessed October 1, 2013).

N.W.A. *N.W.A. and the Posse.* November 6, 1987; reissue November 13, 1989. Priority/Ruthless Records (compact disc).

oj1-oj4. YouTube video, removed Harpo, Inc. http://www.youtube.com/watch?v=t5ZGxwZSXlI&feature=related (accessed December 15, 2009).

Redman. *Whut? Thee Album.* September 22, 1992. Def Jam (compact disc).

Richard Pryor. *Bicentennial Nigger.* Warner Bros. BS 2960, LP, 1976.

Richard Pryor: Live in Concert. Directed by Jeff Margolis. Burbank, CA: Elkins Entertainment, 1979.

The Richard Pryor Show. 1977. Chatsworth, CA: Image Entertainment, 2004.

"Silver Streak, Movie trailer" [n.d.]. www.Youtube.com, 0.29, posted by Brian Durham, March 25, 2008. http://www.youtube.com/watch?v=NXwMClqVPhs (accessed February 15, 2012).

"Skin Deep." *House, M.D.* Directed by James Hayman. Los Angeles: NBC Universal Television, 2006.

Sorkin, Aaron. *A Few Good Men.* DVD. Directed by Rob Reiner. Culver City, CA: Sony Pictures, 1992; 2001.

———. "Take Out the Trash Day." *The West Wing: The Complete First Season.* DVD. Directed by Thomas Schlamme, et al. (January 26, 2000). Burbank, CA: Warner Home Video, 2003.

Soulja Boy. *Soulja Boy Tell 'Em.* October 2, 2007. Collipark Music (compact disc).

Index

50 Cent, 59–61, 69n72, 70n83, 248

ABC News, 79, 81
"Abducted by Radio" (Eshun), 220
activists, 82, 83, 111–12
adolescence. *See* youth
aesthetics, 60–61, 64n2; Mafioso-style, 52, 53, 59; of Monáe, 223–24; superhero, 10, 49–56, 63, 64; supervillain, 58–59
African Americans. *See* blacks
Africans, 22–23, 129, 229, 238n58
aggression, 174–75
Agnew, Phillip, 82–83
Ahmad, Aijaz, 24
Ahmed, Sara, 89, 90, 91
AIDS, 29, 98
AIS. *See* androgen insensitivity syndrome
Alexander, Bryant Keith, 205, 208–9, 213n23
Alexander, Elizabeth, 29–30
alienation, 223, 228
"Almost Native," *168*
Als, Hilton, 181, 182

alter egos, 56–57, 58, 215
ambiguity, 95, 97
Amedure, Scott, 97
ancestry, 126, 128, 129. *See also* mediation, ancestral
Anderson, Benedict, 22–23, 24
Andrade, Allen, 97
androgen insensitivity syndrome (AIS), 92–93
anti-gay policy, 104–5, 109, 114n13
apes, 169, 171. *See also specific types*
appeal, commercial, 202, 210–11
Arab Americans, 113n10
archetypes, 30, 50, 59, 60, 62, 63, 65n8, 144, 153, 209
art, 81–82, 179, 185, 239–40, 242–43, 247–49
artist, 23, 39, 41, 82, 179, 224, 239. *See also* black artists
Asian Britons. *See* British Asians
audiences, 191, 241–42; Jay-Z and, 203–4, 206–7; online, 79–80; Pryor and, 181–86, 188–89, 196; white, 186, 188, 195, 196
authenticity, 155–56

273

autoethnography, 205, 206
awards, 240–41

badman, 51, 54, 55–56, 59, 61–63, 70n81, 70n92, 144, 153–54
Baldwin, James, 15, 17
Bank of America, 80, 84n12
Bannerman, Helen, 35, 41, 45n2
Batman, 69n77, 70n89
beatings, 133–34, 139, 140n18. *See also* police brutality
beauty, 95, 226–28, 237n51
behavior, 40, 62, 96, 183, 189, 210
Benga, Ota, 118, 169–78
Benjamin, Walter, 182–83
Berger, John, 23
Berger, Maurice, 77, 78
Berman, Mordecai, 169–78
Beyoncé, 207, 240, 241, 242
Bhabha, Homi, 186–87
Bicentennial Nigger, 182, 187, 189–90
Biden, Joe, 112
bigotry, 14–15, 17, 105
Big Punisher (Big Pun), 52, 53, 62–63, 70nn90–93
biracial buddy film, 195
birth, 245
black art, 21, 43, 44, 179, 239–40, 242–43, 244, 245, 247–49
black artists, 240–41, 242, 243, 247–48
Black Culture and Black Consciousness: Afro-American Folk Thought from Slavery to Freedom (Levine), 50
blackface, 39–40, 145, 195–96
Black Feminist Thought (Collins), 216, 223
Black Like You: Insult and Imitation in America Popular Culture (Strausbaugh), 39, 188
Black Looks: Race and Representation (hooks), 188, 232n3
Black Nationalism, 21–22, 53, 56, 225–26
blackness, 40, 46n26, 155, 165n40, 195, 219–20, 247, 248–49
Black Panthers, 225–26

Black Power movement, 56, 225–26, 227
Black Prophet (Jeru's alter ego), 56–57
blacks, 40, 104–5, 152, 183–85, 223; mainstream America and, 37–38; state violence against, 27–28; stereotypes of, 186–87, 195–96, 216, 232n3
"Black to the Future," 219–20
Bl_ck B_st_rds, 35–36, 41–42
Bloods and Crips, 69n74. *See also* East Coast-West Coast debates
Blues Legacies and Black Feminisms (Davis), 230
body, 98, 136, 235n33; black, 134, 135; image, 152; mannerisms and, 152–53; maternal, 134–35; mind and, 220–21; perverse, 94–95; sculpting of, 151; technology and, 220; women and, 93, 94, 117, 135, 137, 221–22, 226
Bollywood, 145, 148, 154
Boone, Will, 5, 10, 49–64
boundaries, 87–88, 91–92, 204, 218
British Asians (Asian Britons), 155–56
Britishness, 154, 155, 157, 162, 164n3
Bronx Zoological Park, 169, 171
Brooklyn, New York, 202, 206, 207, 210–11
brothel, 192–93
Brown v. Board of Education (1954), 16
Bushmen, 171
Butler, Octavia, 219

cancer, 92, 98
"Can't we all just get along?," 29
capital, 202, 208
"Capital Punishment," 62–63
car, luxury, 150–51, 159
Cartoon Network, 36
The Catherine Tate Show, 161
censorship, 35, 36, 41, 185–86, 189
the chav, 144–45, 158, 161–62
child removal policies, 12
chimpanzee, 170, 173
church, black, 33n31, 244–45

Churilla, Emily, 5, 71, 87–99
cities, 17
civil rights, 29, 37, 105, 111
Civil Rights Movement, 12, 81, 82, 230
Clinton, Bill, 101, 102, 110–11
Cobb, William Jelani, 61
codenames, 58
Code Red, 102–3, 108–9
collective, 89–90, 93, 208
Collins, Patricia Hill, 216, 223, 232n4
"Colonel Jessup," 6, 102–11, 115
comedy: black, 245; political, 195; racially conscious, 182; sketch, 161, 191–92; stand-up, 182–92, 195
Comedy Central, 181
comic books, 66n17. *See also* Marvel Comics; superheroes
commemorations, 73–75, 78–81
commercialism, 216, 219
commodification, 3, 226
the communal womb, 117, 126, 128, 130, 138–39
communication, 242–43
community, 1, 3, 203; black, 15–16, 126–27; gay, 112n4; Latino, 14; media interaction and, 87. *See also* slave community
conformity, 37, 41
Congo Square, 242, 245
Conrad, Joseph, 246
conspiracy, 109, 193
consumerism, 57, 162
Converging Stories: Race, Ecology, and Environmental Justice in American Literature (Myers), 226
Coogan, Peter, 51–52
coolness, 209–10
cool pose, 151–152, 179, 202, 203, 208, 209, 210, 211
"Cop Killer," 28
cops, 184. *See also* police brutality
Cosby, Bill, 245–46
Covering: The Hidden Assault on our Civil Rights (Yoshino), 37
"Crank That (Soulja Boy)," 49–50, 64n5, 66n23

creative process, 205–6
crime, 13, 62, 225; hate, 97, 106–7, 114n13; organized, 159–60
criminal system, United States, 9
critique, 1, 127, 208
Crow, Jim, 218, 243
crowdsourcing, 74
Cruise, Tom, 102–4, 247–48. *See also* "Lieutenant Kaffee"
crying, 205
cultural commodity, 3–4
cultural hybrid, 155–56
cultural influence, 154–56
cultural-nationalist, 25, 30n3
cultural norm, 15, 154
The Cultural Politics of Emotion (Ahmed), 89
cultural resources, 3–4
culture, 24, 37, 161; African, 138, 139; African American, 46n26, 50–51, 59, 63, 154–55; commercial, 208, 213n26; contemporary, 76, 217–19, 244; globalized, 6; identity and, 145–46, 152, 157, 160; memes and, 81–82, 85n16; South Asian, 154–55, 158; youth, 162, 201–2. *See also* Hip Hop culture; popular culture
culture, contemporary, 76, 217–19, 224
cyborgs, 7, 215–18, 221–22, 227, 230, 232n4

Darwin, Charles, 170, 171
Davis, Angela, 230
death, 106, 121, 123, 136
decontextualization, 104–5
dehumanization, 97–98, 127, 129, 231
demoralization, 134–35
Dery, Mark, 219–20
the desi, 144–45, 153–54
desire, 89
deviancy, 92, 93, 95, 96, 98
differences, 186–87
digital divide, 236n39
digital realm, 74–77
dignity, 186, 232
Dimitriadis, Greg, 59

discrimination, 12, 14; Bank of America and, 80, 84n12; in education, 16; by employers, 13, 19n26, 84n12; historic, 17; in housing, 15–16; language based, 19n26; racial, 13, 84n12
diversity, 3–4
DJ turntables, 147
domination, 231, 232n4
"Don't Ask, Don't Tell," 6, 71, 101–102, 110–12, 112n4, 113nn5–6
DOOMposters, 43–44
double-consciousness, 10, 37–39
doubt, 95
Dr. Doom, 42
#*DreamDay*, 79–80
Dream Defenders, 82, 83
dreams, 239–40
"Dreams of the Drum" (Dyson), 7, 179
dressing, androgynous, 224
drive-bys, audio, 150–51
drug dealer, 153, 202
Du Bois, W.E.B., 37–38, 39, 40, 237n57
Dumile, Daniel, 42–45. *See also* MF DOOM
Dunbar, Paul, 38–39, 54
the dungeon, 128–29
Dyson, Michael Eric, 7, 179

Earhart, Amelia, 228, 229, 237
East Coast-West Coast debates, 203, 210
economy, 24–25; gray, 12; self-interest and, 115n25; struggles in, 56
editing, 9, 25–26, 29–30
education, 2, 14, 16
ego, 89, 222
Elektra Records, 35, 41, 42
Ellington, Duke, 23
Elmina Castle, 128–29, 132, 139
emotions, 55, 62, 88, 129, 134, 151, 194–95, 204, 205, 210, 220, 245
empire state of mind, 11–12, 17
"Empire State of Mind," 3, 5, 9, 57, 212n16
employers, 13, 19n26, 84n12

empowerment, 154
epics, 2
equality, 112n4, 183
Eshun, Kodwo, 220
ethical dilemma, 109
European enslavers, 22–23
Evil Jeanius, 54
Evolution, 169, 174

"faggoty white uniform," 104, 108, 109, 111
Fair Housing Act, 16
faith. *See* prayer and faith
Farber, Paul, 5
fashion icon, 202
fashion models, 224–25, 228
father, 92, 93–94
fear, 95, 106
Federal Housing Administration (FHA), 15–16
femininity, 95
feminism, 32n8, 53, 115n25, 218, 223, 231–32, 235n35
Ferguson, Roderick, 113n10
A Few Good Men, 3, 5–6, 71, 101–11, 114n13
FHA. *See* Federal Housing Administration
FHM, 97–98
fiction, futuristic, 235n38
film, 24, 31n4, 194–96
Fiske, John, 3
flesh. *See* body
folk heroes, 65n8
folklore, 234n19; African American, 62–63, 65n8, 229, 238n58; modern, 76–77; slavery and, 229
foreclosure, 13, 84n12
freedom, 125, 225, 226, 233n18
"Fuck the Police," 28
funerals, 187
futuristic themes, 219–20

gangsta culture, 53, 57–62, 69nn65–66, 144–45, 149, 153
Garland, Judy, 217
Gates, Henry Louis, Jr., 38, 40

gays and lesbians, 112n4, 113n10; bashing of, 153; civil rights and, 105, 111; fears about, 106; marriage and, 87–88; military and, 102, 104–8, 110–11, 114n13. *See also* anti-gay policy; Lesbian, Gay, Bisexual, Transgendered, Queer
gender, 5, 8, 99; alienation and, 228; ambiguity, 95, 97; biological sex and, 93; dialogue, 221; Hip Hop culture and, 53, 210; identity and, 71, 92; limitations and, 221; nonnormative, 96, 97; normative, 90, 93; sexuality and, 102, 105. *See also* transgendered
gender roles, 96, 109–10, 133, 161, 228
genealogy, artistic, 179, 219
genius, 179, 182, 211, 246, 247
Gerima, Haile, 125–26, 128, 138
Get Rich or Die Tryin, 60
Ghostface Killah, 36–37, 52
Gilliam, Tanji, 5, 6–7, 9
Gilroy, Paul, 39, 143, 217–18
The Godfather, 59, 69nn65–66
Goldberg, Whoopi, 181
Gomez, Wilfredo, 7, 179, 201–11
gorilla, 170
Grae, Jean, 52, 54–55, 58, 67n33
grammar. *See* language
graphic design, 81–82
grassroots history, 75, 78, 80, 84n3
Gray, Herman, 201–2, 208, 209, 213n26
the Great Depression, 15–16
The Guardian, 97
Gulf War, 28

Haggins, Bambi, 181, 184–85
hair, 19n26, 151
Halberstam, Judith, 91, 95–96
Hall, Stuart, 3
Halley, Janet, 106–7, 110
Hamlet (character), 91
Hammad, Suheir, 6, 117, 119–24
Haraway, Donna, 221, 232n4
Hariman, Robert, 75, 76
Harlem, 147
hashtags, 79–80

hate, 25–26, 174–75
hate crimes, 97, 106–7, 114n13
hazing, 102–3, 106–7. *See also* Code Red
health care, 14
herbs, 133, 134
heritage, 117–18, 129–30
heroes, 65n8, 69nn65–66. *See also* superheroes
heterosexuality, 104, 108, 152, 165n35
hierarchies, 187, 189, 222
high schools, public, 16
Hill, Lauryn, 53, 217
Hip Hop culture, 23, 42, 45n1, 66n26, 160; British, 156–57, 163n1; as commercial culture, 213n26; creativity in, 65n15; economies in, 24–25; gender and, 53, 210; history and, 21–22; identity and, 6, 10; linguistic mannerisms in, 147–50, 157–58; male-dominated, 231; media and, 30, 36; Old School, 217; on police in media, 28; popular culture and, 9, 10, 36; superhero aesthetics in, 10, 49–56, 63, 64; superhuman abilities within, 57; super-villains in, 58–59; women and, 53–54, 233n15, 238n63. *See also* gangsta culture; Hip Hop music
Hip Hop generation, 7, 9, 24, 25, 29, 40, 44–45, 46n19, 117
Hip Hop music, 7, 11–12, 42, 201; Hip Hop generation and, 44–45; independent, 35, 43
Hip Hop nation, 29–30
hiring practices, 80
history, 38, 89; African, 127; African American, 7, 126; black arts in, 239–40; grassroots, 75, 78, 84n3; Hip Hop culture and, 21–22; of oppression, 3–4; of slavery, 137; woman in, 126
Holliday, George, 25–30
Holloway, Karla, 126, 128
Hollywood, 185–86
homeownership, 13, 15–16
homonormativity, 113n10

homophobia, 68n48, 103, 104, 107, 153, 165n35, 165n40
homosexuality, 97, 115n26, 115n28; masculinity and, 152–53, 165n35; nationalism and, 108; soldiers and, 102, 104, 105, 106, 108, 110–11. *See also* gays and lesbians
hooks, bell, 188, 195, 232n3, 235n36
hope, 121
Hopkins, Pauline, 219
horror, 91–92, 95, 96, 97
House M.D., 5, 71, 88, 92–99
housing. *See* real estate industry
Howard Colored Orphan Asylum, 175–76, 177
"How Deep? Skin Deep?" (Churilla), 5, 71, 87–99
Huffington Post, 97
Huggins, Nathan, 38
humanity, black, 243
human rights, 29
humiliation, 97, 132, 134–35
humor, 184–85, 189–93, 242. *See also* comedy
hunger, 120–21
Hurricane Katrina, 98, 120–22
Hush mode, 166n56
hustler, 202, 204, 206, 211n2, 212n13
hypermasculinity, 51, 54, 57, 61, 117–18, 143–45
hysteria. *See* nervous breakdown

Ice Cube, 25, 32n25
iconic imagery, 75–78, 81–83
iconography: African American, 65n8; Black Nationalists, 53; gangsta, 53, 58–62; of identity, 50; King, Martin Luther Jr., and, 76; Kung Fu cinema, 57, 68n52; March on Washington and, 76; superhero, 50, 52, 55–56, 58, 60, 70n84
icons, 50–51, 202
idealism, 29
identity, 4, 129–30, 167n77; African American, 37–38, 187, 213n26; artistic, 10, 39, 52–53, 179; authentic, 155–56; black, 242, 245; conformity and, 41; construction of, 44, 58; crisis, 157; cultural, 145–46, 152, 157, 160; cyborg, 234n27; gender, 71, 92; Hip Hop culture and, 6, 10; hypermasculinity and, 57; iconography of, 50; LGBTQ, 71; markers of, 213n26; masculine, 143–45, 160, 209; the mask and, 39, 41; national, 9, 89; politics, 71, 179; popular culture and, 71, 117; public and, 99n7; raceless, 222–23; racial, 6, 144, 145–46, 204; removal of, 137; self, 9, 21; sexual, 95, 97, 115n20, 153; slavery and, 129; social, 237n57; South Asian, 154; superhero, 52–53, 56, 58; as victim, 131; whites and, 187; women and, 135, 157
ignorance, 15, 149
"I Have a Meme," 72
illness, 13
imagery, 5, 7, 213n23; digitized, 77; iconic, 75–78, 81–83; March on Washington and, 77–78, 80–81; memetic, 77; rap, 159; Rodney King tape and, 26–29. *See also* photography
immigrants, 16, 113n10, 167n77
inaction, 90
Inaugural Conference for the Hip Hop Archival Collection, 231
incest, 92–94, 96, 99
inclusion, 87, 113n10
"In Da Club," 60
inequality, 4–5, 14, 17, 183, 229
in medias res, 2, 4
interactivity, 11, 78–79, 81, 87
interpretation, moral, 240–41

Jabaliya (Hammad), 123
Jackson, Curtis (Curtis "50 Cent" Jackson), 60
Jackson, Jesse, 244
James, Nicholas, 5, 9–10
"Jas," 143–44, 146–47, 152–53, 158–59, 161–63
Jay-Z, 3–5, 7, 9, 11–12, 201; audience of, 203–4, 206–7; creative process

of, 205–6; Maher and, 203–6, 208, 209–10, 211, 212n16; Marcy Projects and, 206–7; Obama and, 210; Oprah and, 203, 206–9, 211; retirement and, 57–58; as role model, 202, 204; on television, 179, 210–11
Jennings, John, 7
Jenny Jones Show, 97
Jeru, 56–57, 68n52
Jesus, 70n93, 244–45
justice system, 30; civil, US, 9; criminal, 26, 28

Keys, Alicia, 4
King, Martin Luther Jr., 75–76, 78–82, 235n36, 244
King, Rodney, 3, 9, 25–29, 33n28. *See also* Rodney King tape
"Kingdom Come," 57–58
KKK, 69n62
KMD, 35–36, 41, 42
Kno, 43–44
Krasner, David, 37–38, 40
"Kuta," 127, 130–37, 139–40

Lady Maxxa, 224
Lane, Alycee, 104–5
language, 19n26, 166n58, 167n77, 206, 209, 213n26, 242; black, 243–44; Hip Hop culture and, 147–50, 157–58; misogynistic, 203–4, 234n31; vernacular, 226. *See also* speech patterns
LAPD, 25–26, 27, 28
Latinos, 14
Lawrence, Martin, 247
lectures, 2
lending practices, 80
Lesbian, Gay, Bisexual, Transgendered, Queer (LGBTQ), 71, 87–88
lesbians. *See* gays and lesbians
Levine, Lawrence, 50
LGBTQ. *See* Lesbian, Gay, Bisexual, Transgendered, Queer
Library of Congress, 25, 33n26
"Lieutenant Commander Galloway," 102–3, 113n9

"Lieutenant Kaffee," 102–5, 107–11, 113n9, 115nn25–26
Life of Pryor, 181
limitations, 221
linguistic idioms, 150, 157–58
listeners, 220, 221, 226, 230–31
literature, 2, 126
Little Black Sambo (Bannerman), 35, 41, 45n2
Little Britain, 161
Little Richard, 241
Logan's Run, 185
Londonstani (Malkani), 6, 143–46, 150–52, 157
Los Angeles, 25, 29
Lott, Tommy, 31n4
love, 238n66
Loving v. Virginia (1967), 222
Lucaites, John Luis, 75, 76
Lynchburg, Virginia, 177, 178
lynching, 28, 42
lyrics, 203–5, 210, 222–23, 225–26, 234n27, 234n31, 237n50

Maher, Bill, 203–6, 208, 209–10, 211, 212n16. *See also Real Time with Bill Maher*
mahmoud darwish (Hammad), 122–23
mainstream America: blacks and, 37–38; media in, 30, 87, 226; whites and, 37. *See also* popular culture
Malcom X, 247
males, 27, 183–84, 231
Malkani, Guatam, 6, 143–44, 150–52, 157, 162
"A Manifesto for Cyborgs" (Haraway), 221
mannerisms, 144, 146, 151, 154; body and, 152–53; linguistic, 147–50, 157–58
Mansbach, Adam, 6, 117, 118, 169–78
"Many Moons," 217, 220–21, 223–30
March on Washington for Jobs and Freedom, 73, 76; fiftieth anniversary of, 80, 82–83; imagery and, 77–78, 80–81; photography of, 74–75, 77–79
Marcy Projects, 202, 204, 206–7

marines, 102–3, 106–7
marriage, 87–88, 222
Martin, Kelvin (Kelvin "50 Cent" Martin), 59–60, 70n83
Martin, Trayvon, 82
Marvel Comics, 42, 54
masculinity, 6, 95, 146; black, 66n16, 151–52; gangsta rap and, 153; homosexuality and, 152–53, 165n35; identity and, 143–45, 160, 209; South Asian, 165n21. *See also* hypermasculinity
the mask, 38, 54; blackface, 39–40; identity and, artistic, 39, 41; MF DOOM and, 9–10, 36–37, 39–44; minstrel shows and, 39–40; Pryor and, 188; racial segregation and, 188; of rappers, 36–37; whites and, 188
maternity, 134–36
Mayweather, Cindi, 215–16, 218–23, 226–29
McCluskey, Audrey, 184–85
media, 5, 8, 191–93, 229; community interaction and, 87; Hip Hop culture and, 30, 36; mainstream, 30, 87, 226; misogyny in, 222; police in, 28; social, 82; video, 22–24; women and, 226, 231
mediation, ancestral, 126–27, 128, 138
melancholia, 143
memes, 76–77, 81–83, 85n16
memory, 30, 74, 75, 77, 80–83, 126, 128, 139
Metal Face Records, 36
Metropolis, 216, 222, 224, 225
"Metropolis Reduxxed," 214
Metropolis: The Chase Suite, 179, 215, 218, 226, 231–32
metrosexuality, 151
MF DOOM, 5, 52, 62; identity and, 44; James on, 9–10; Kno and, 43–44; mask of, 9–10, 36–37, 39–44
"Mic Check" (Hammad), 6
military, United States, 112n3, 113n7, 113n10; anti-gay policy, 104–5, 109, 114n13; gays and lesbians and, 102, 104–8, 110–11, 114n13; race in, 104. *See also* soldiers
military reform, 101. *See also* Don't Ask, Don't Tell
mind/body dichotomy, 220–21
minstrel shows, 39–40, 186–87
misogyny, 68n48, 103, 220, 229; image and, 153; language and, 203–4, 234n31; in media, 222
Mitchell, Tony, 156–57
Modood, Tariq, 155–56
molestation. *See* sexual abuse
Monáe, Janelle, 7, 179, 215, 231–32; aesthetics of, 223–24; Afrofuturism and, 219–20; boundaries and, 218; lyrics of, 222–23, 225–26, 234n27, 237n50; style of, 217; vocals of, 221. *See also* Mayweather, Cindi
"Mona/Shola," 127–32, 137–39
Mo'Nique, 247
monkey. *See* apes
monster, 95–96, 97
Moore, Demi, 102, 103. *See also* "Lieutenant Commander Galloway"
More Beautiful and More Terrible: The Embrace and Transcendence of Racial Inequality in the United States (Perry), 11, 18n1
Morrison, Toni, 219
mortgages, 15–16
motherhood, 134–36
MSNBC, 79
MTV. *See* Music Television
Mudbone, 187–88
multiculturalism, 161–62, 202
murder, 97, 131, 132, 139
muscles, 152
music, 203–4, 203–5, 237n50; contemporary, 217–18, 224; conventional, 217; genres of, 218; loud, 150–51; rap, 42, 233n9; slavery era, 218–19; spiritual, 218–19. *See also* Hip Hop music; Music Television
music industry, 216, 231
Music Television (MTV), 207, 240, 241

music videos, 225
Myers, Jeffrey, 226
mythical ideal, 90–91, 98

national collective, 89–90
national identity, 9, 89
nationalism, 22–23, 24, 108. *See also* Black Nationalism
nationalist agenda, 22
National Mall, 73, 74, 76, 82–83
national order, 96
National Park Service, 78
NBC, 79–80, 81
Negro, 37–38, 169
Nelly, 234n31
neoliberal movement, 3–4
neo-slave narratives, 218–19, 224
nervous breakdown, 195
New Orleans, 98, 120–22, 242
new orleans (Hammad), 120–22
news, 25–26, 30, 75. *See also* ABC News
New York Times, 78, 191–92, 195–96
Nicholson, Jack, 5–6, 102–3, 110. *See also* "Colonel Jessup"
nigger, 184, 194. *See also* the n-word
"Noble Ali," 134–35, 136
norm, cultural, 15
normalcy, 91, 99n7
normativity, 89–90, 93, 115n23
North Star, 233n18
Notorious B.I.G, 53, 203, 210
nuclear bomb, 229
"NuNu," 127–28, 130–39
N.W.A, 28, 52–53, 58–59, 61, 66n22
the n-word, 189–91, 198n42

Obama, Barack, 101–2, 239, 244; "Don't Ask, Don't Tell" Repeal Act and, 111–12, 112n4, 113nn5–6; Jay-Z and, 210; memes and, 81–82
objectification, 150, 222–25, 228, 237n51
"An Open Letter to MF DOOM" (Kno), 43–44
Ophelia (character), 91
oppression, 138, 191, 224, 235n36; elimination of, 226; history of, 3–4; racial, 183–84, 226; sexism and, 226

The Oprah Winfrey Show, 7, 202–3, 208, 209, 211
oral sex, 103
orangutan, 169, 172–73

pain, 179; emotional, 194–95; prejudice perceptions of, 191–93; of Pryor, 183; words and, 191, 194
painting, 23
panic, 97
Parade magazine, 192–93
patriotism, 108
peace, 122
Pejić, Andrej, 97–98
perceptions: of gender, 92; prejudice, 191–93; racial, 11
performance, 224, 245
performers, 2, 40, 237n51; stereotypes of, 185, 216, 232n3; women as, 218
Performing Identity/Performing Culture (Dimitriadis), 59
perjury, 109
Perry, Imani, 4–5, 9, 11, 18n1, 57
persona. *See* identity
perverseness, 94–95, 96
Phillips, Delores, 6, 117
Phoenix force, 54
photography, 5, 80, 81; iconic, 75, 83; of the March on Washington, 74–75, 77–79; political, 75, 78–79
poems, 119–24
the poet, 122
police brutality, 25, 26–28, 29; Rodney King tape and, 30, 32n25; silenced response to, 30
political expression, 22
politics, 195; Black Power, 56; of gender and sexuality, 102, 105; identity and, 71, 179; photography and, 75, 78–79; of Pryor, 191–93; of race, 105
poncey gora, 155–56, 157, 166n47
popular culture, 3–5, 8, 37, 208; bodies of color in, 117–18; Hip Hop culture and, 9, 10, 36; identity in, 71, 117; minstrel shows and, 39–40; racism and, 39–40; Rodney King tape and,

29; video and, 25; women in, 216, 218
positive action, 90
possession, 129–30, 140n13
post-racial movement, 4–5, 14
Post-Traumatic Stress Disorder (PTSD), 92
postures. *See* mannerisms
poverty, 12–13, 14, 120–21
power, 149
power dynamic, 94
prayer and faith, 131
A Prayer Band (Hammad), 119–20
preaching, 244–45, 249
Precious, 247
preening, 151
prejudice perceptions, 191–93
press. *See* media
pride, 88
Primates House, 169, 171
"Private Santiago," 104, 106–7
privilege, 105, 149, 153, 156, 157
programming, 1, 2, 4
Pryor, Richard, 179, 190, 198n41, 245–47; achievements of, 184–85; audience and, 181–86, 188–89, 196; demeaning roles of, 181–82; film and, 194–96; grandmother's brothel and, 192–93; the mask and, 188; media and, 191–93; n-word and, 198n42; political humor of, 191–93; public image of, 182–83; racism and, 182, 184, 192–93, 194; stand-up and, 194; stereotypes and, 192; on television, 191–92; whites and, 186–89, 192
pseudohermaphroditism, 92, 96
Psychopathology (Schmitz), 97, 98
PTSD. *See* Post-Traumatic Stress Disorder
Puar, Jabir, 106, 108
public, 99n8; identity and, 99n7; image, 182–83; integration into, 87; nation as, 89; normative building process of, 87–88; threat to, 96
public collective, 208
Publics and Counterpublics (Warner), 89

the Punisher, 70n89
punishment, 107
the Pygmy, 169–78. *See also* Benga, Ota

Queer Phenomenology: Orientations, Objects, Others (Ahmed), 90

race, 4–6, 10, 12–14, 17, 113n10, 169; alienation and, 228; elimination of, 234n27; ethnicity, 146; gay issues and, 105; identity and, 222–23; in military, 104; narrative on, 8; politics of, 105
race relations, 9, 11
racial profiling, 33n30
racism, 4, 9, 76, 186, 189, 226; end of, 105; Hip Hop music and, 11; intentional, 14–15; minstrel shows, blackface, 39–40; mocked, 192; popular culture and, 39–40; prejudice views of, 193; Pryor and, 182, 184, 192–93, 194; tragedy of, 183
racist universalism, 220
radicalism, 32n8
rafah (Hammad), 124
Ragone, August, 67n38
Raiders, 66n22
rap, 5, 35–37, 154, 159, 211n2; gangsta, 58–59, 153; music, 42, 233n9
rape, 29, 94, 96, 99, 130–32, 139
reaction, 99
real estate industry, 15–16
realism, 24, 53, 56, 69n73
Real Time with Bill Maher, 7, 202–3, 209, 211
rebellion, 125, 130, 153–54; slavery and, 133, 138; women and, 128, 137
recording industry, 24–25. *See also* Elektra Records; Metal Face Records
redlining, 16, 17
Redman, 52, 53, 55–56, 67n38, 69n77
reform, progressive, 110–11. *See also* Don't Ask, Don't Tell
refugee camp, 123

Reiner, Rob, 101, 102. *See also A Few Good Men*
remorse, 96
"Renegade," 210
representations, 40, 179, 222, 247–48
repression, 118
resistance, 117, 125, 127, 130–33, 137, 138, 219
Resistance, Parody, and Double-Consciousness in African American Theater, 1895–1910 (Krasner), 37–38
respect, 232
restrictive covenants, racially, 15–16, 17
"Reverend Wright," 244
rhythm, 243–44
The Richard Pryor Show, 191–92
"Richard Pryor's Pain" (Springer), 6–7, 179
Richard Pryor: The Life and Legacy of a "Crazy" Black Man (McCluskey), 184–85
riots, 29
Rock, Chris, 245, 247
Rodney King tape, 3, 5, 9, 22, 25–30, 32n25, 33n26
role models, 202, 204, 231
Rolex, 81
Rose, Tricia, 54, 231, 238n66
Rucker Park, 147, 164n9
rudeboy, 144–46

safe nation, 108–9
safety, 108–9, 110, 112, 115n20, 231
Sankofa, 6, 125–28, 133, 137, 139
satire, 38, 190, 210
Schifman, Limor, 76–77
Schmitz, Jonathan, 97, 98
security, national, 112
seducing, 94
segregation, 188, 242–43
self, ideal, 98
self-esteem, 162–63
sensuality, 131
sentiments, public, 87
sex, 103. *See also* gender
sexism, 54, 223, 226

sexual abuse, 92, 93, 130–32
sexual exploitation, 129, 131
sexual identity, 95, 97, 115n20, 153
sexuality, 94, 101, 104, 115n26, 135, 151; gender and, 102, 105; of women, black, 216, 222. *See also* heterosexuality; homosexuality
Shakur, Tupac, 61, 203, 210
shame, 87, 88–93, 96, 97, 98. *See also* humiliation
shaming, 71, 87, 89
Sharpton, Al, 244
"Shola." *See* "Mona/Shola"
Shore, Dinah, 190–91
Silver Streak, 182, 192, 194, 195
"Sincerely Jane," 230–31
Singer, Melanie, 28
skepticism, 245
skin, 91–92
skin color, 12–13, 144
"Skin Deep," 71, 88, 92–99
Skin Shows: Gothic Horror and the Technology of Monsters (Halberstam), 91
slave community, 134–35, 138, 139
slavery, 125, 130, 136, 169, 218, 226; folklore and, 229; history of, 137; identity and, 129; motherhood in, 134; music and, 218–19; rebellion in, 133, 138; resistance in, 127, 138; women and, 6, 127, 132–33, 137–39, 219, 224–25, 237n45
slaves, 22–23, 129, 138, 233n18; owners of, 136–37; realities of, 218; voice of, 242
slave trade, 117, 224
slum clearance, 16
Snoop Dogg, 11, 159, 248
social cognition, 15
social justice, 25, 82, 106, 218, 225
social welfare system, 12
soldiers, 113n10; Clinton and, 101, 102, 110–11; homosexual, 102, 104, 105, 106, 108, 110–11; sexual orientation of, 101
"Song Cry," 205
"Sooperman Lover," 56, 68n48

the South, 37
South Asian culture, 154–55, 158
speakers, 1, 2
specimen, 95, 96
speech patterns, 13, 179, 206, 209, 243–44
Spider-Man, 69n77
spiritual health, 127
sponsorship, 80, 81
Springer, Sean, 6–7, 179
stamp, commemorative, 73–74, 75
stereotypes, 15, 23–24, 146, 161, 234n30, 248; in America, 46n26; black art and, 243; of blacks, 186–87, 195–96, 216, 232n3; chav, 144–45; in comic books, 66n17; degrading, 39–40; desi, 144–45; equalization with, 186–87; gangsta, 144–45; of hypersexualized artist, 224; of performers, 185, 216, 232n3; Pryor and, 192; racial, 39–40, 46n26, 182; rudeboy, 144–45; white America and, 39–40, 187–88; of whites, 186–87; of women, 150, 216, 232n3
sterilization, 222
Stir Crazy, 182, 194–95
Stoute, Steve, 55
St. Pierre, Scott, 5–6, 71
Strausbaugh, John, 39, 188
strength, 108–9, 110, 112
students, 1, 2, 3–4
style, 217, 245. *See also* aesthetics
suburbs, 17
sundown towns, 225, 237n47
"Super G," *48*
superhero conventions, 5, 51, 53–55, 58, 63–64
superheroes, 54, 61, 66n16; aesthetics and, 10, 49–56, 63, 64; black, 51; iconography and, 50, 52, 55–56, 58, 60, 70n84; identity and, 52–53, 56, 58
superheroine, 54
Superhero: The Secret Origin of a Genre (Coogan), 51–52
Superman, 57, 58, 60
superpowers, 57, 65n14
super-villains, 58–63, 64, 70n89

Supreme Court, 16
Swift, Taylor, 240, 241–42

The Tanning of America: How Hip Hop Created A Culture That Wrote the Rules of the New Economy (Stoute), 55
"Tears of a Clown," *180*
technology, 31n6, 220, 225–26, 228–29, 236n39
television, 31n4, 31n6, 77; audiences, 79, 191; interviews, 208–9; Japanese, 67n38; Jay-Z and, 179, 210–11; Pryor on, 191–92. *See also* Music Television
terrorism, 115n28
That Nigger's Crazy, 182, 184, 187–88, 190–91
theater, 39–40, 203
theft, 120
Tillet, Salamishah, 77, 81, 82, 83
Time Magazine, 80–81
time travel, 219
tipping, 19n25
token black, 196
To the Break of Dawn: A Freestyle on the Hip Hop Aesthetic (Cobb), 61
The Toy, 181
Training Day, 247
transatlantic slave trade, 117
transgendered, 97
transgressions, cultural, 154
trauma, 96
the trickster, 61
"A True and Faithful Account of Mr. Ota Benga the Pygmy, written by M. Berman, Zookeeper" (Mansbach), 6, 169–78
Truth, Sojourner, 219
Tsuburaya, Noboru, 67n38
Tubman, Harriet, 219
Tuskegee Airmen, 228, 229
Tyson, Mike, 29, 33n35

Understanding Popular Culture (Fiske), 3
unemployment, 13, 56
United Postal Service (USPS), 73

universities, 1–4
urban renewal, 16
USPS. *See* United Postal Service

Verner, Samuel, 169–73
victimization, 27–29, 131
victims, 95, 96, 137
video, 22–25, 31n6
videographer, 23
violence, 76, 132, 135, 225; acts of, 98; music industry and, 216; state, against blacks, 27–28; women and, 215, 216
"Violet Stars Happy Hunting," 218, 222–23
vocals, 221
voice, 33n31, 217, 242–45. *See also* speech patterns
vote, right to, 13

Walker, Carrie, 7, 179
Waller-Peterson, Belinda Monique, 6, 117
Walters, Barbara, 192, 193
wannabes, 159, 162
Warner, Michael, 89–90, 91
Washington, Denzel, 247
Watkins, Mel, 184–85
Ways of Seeing, 23
weakness, 109–10
West, Kanye, 240–43
The West Wing, 114n13
"We Wear the Mask" (Dunbar), 38–39, 54
"Where I'm From," 207
whiteness, 164n3, 247–48; as invisible norm, 187–88; of Jas, 146, 147, 152–53, 158
white privilege, 105
whites, 169, 171–72; mainstream culture of, 37; Pryor and, 186–89, 192; stereotypes of, 186–87
white supremacy ideology, 179, 183–84, 189, 194, 223, 247

Wilder, Gene, 194–96
Willie Best, 196
Winfrey, Oprah, 203, 206–9, 211. *See also The Oprah Winfrey Show*
wives, 192–93
womb, 126, 128–29, 130, 131, 134, 138–39. *See also* the communal womb
wom(b)anism, 126, 132–33, 138, 140n5
women, 124; African, 131, 235n33; Afro-Caribbean, 232n5; artistic genealogy of, 179; body and, 93, 94, 117, 135, 137, 221–22, 226; hierarchies and, 222; Hip Hop culture and, 53–54, 233n15, 238n63; identity of, 135, 157; media and, 226, 231; men and, 92, 94–95; objectification of, 150, 222–23, 224–25, 237n51; as performers, 218; in popular culture, 216, 218; rebellion and, 128, 137; safety of, 231; sexual exploitation of, 129, 131; sexuality of, 216, 222; slavery and, 6, 127, 132–33, 137–39, 219, 224–25, 237n45; stereotypes of, 216, 232n3; as victims, 137; violence and, 215, 216; voice of, 33n31; white, 224–25, 237n45; young, 227, 231, 238n63
the Word, 245
words, 190–91, 194. *See also* the n-word
World War II, 113n10
writing, 232n5

yardi, 149, 165n21
Yoshino, Kenji, 37, 41, 42
youth, 144, 163n1; activists, 82; black, 56, 201–2, 218; black art and, 243; culture, 162, 201–2; education for, 16; programs, decline of, 56

Zapata, Angie, 97
Zev Love X, 35–36, 41, 42
Zimmerman, George, 82
Zoglin, Richard, 186–87

About the Contributors

William Boone is an associate professor of English and foreign languages at Winston-Salem State University. Boone received his PhD in African American studies from Temple University. His dissertation, "The Beautiful Struggle: An Analysis of Hip Hop Icons, Archetypes, and Aesthetics," explores the influence of African American icons on Hip Hop cultural expressions. Professor Boone has taught courses on Hip Hop at Temple University and Winston-Salem State University. He is the founder of Afro Blew Media, Inc. He has facilitated numerous workshops on Hip Hop and African American culture/history. His research interests include music and literary criticism, cultural history, popular culture, American iconography, and African American images in media and sports culture.

Emily Churilla is a PhD candidate at Stony Brook University in English and cultural studies. Her research interests are in American society and critical race and gender theory; more specifically her dissertation focuses on geek culture, virtual subjectivity, and questions of digital life.

Michael Eric Dyson is a professor of sociology at Georgetown University. Dr. Dyson's pioneering scholarship has had a profound effect on American ideas. His first book, 1993's *Reflecting Black: African-American Cultural Criticism*, helped establish the field of black American cultural studies. His next book, 1994's *Making Malcolm: The Myth and Meaning of Malcolm X*, was named one of the most important African American books of the twentieth century. Dr. Dyson's first book on Martin Luther King, 2000's *I May Not Get There with You: The True Martin Luther King, Jr.*, made a significant contribution to King scholarship by recovering the radical legacy of the slain civil rights leader. According to book industry bible *Publisher's Weekly*, his 2001 book, *Holler if You Hear Me: Searching for Tupac Shakur*, helped to make books on Hip Hop commercially viable. His 2006 book *Come Hell or High Water: Hurricane Katrina and the Color of Disaster* was the first major book on Katrina and probed the racial and class fallout from the storm. Dr. Dyson's 2005 *New York Times* bestseller, *Is Bill Cosby Right? Or Has the Black Middle Class Lost Its Mind?*, helped to jumpstart a national conversation on the black poor that has been called the most important debate in black America since the historic debate between Booker T. Washington and W. E. B. Du Bois. His book, The *New York Times* bestselling *April 4, 1968: Martin Luther King Jr.'s Death and How It Changed America*, has been hailed by the *Washington Post* as "an excellent sociological primer on institutionalized racism in America." His most recent book, *Can You Hear Me Now? The Inspiration, Wisdom, and Insight of Michael Eric Dyson*, offers a sampling of his sharp wit, profound thought, and edifying eloquence on the enduring problems of humanity, from love to justice, and the latest topics of the day, including race and the presidency.

Paul M. Farber is a postdoctoral writing fellow at Haverford College. He is a scholar of American and urban studies. He has a PhD in American culture from the University of Michigan. His current book project is a study of representations of the Berlin Wall in American art, literature, and popular culture from 1961 to the present. He is also curating the exhibition, *The Wall in Our Heads: American Artists and the Berlin Wall* for the Goethe-Institut Washington, DC, in Fall 2014, and is co-curator of the Pew Center for Arts & Heritage–funded public history project, *Monument Lab: Creative Speculations for Philadelphia* in Spring 2015. He has contributed essays and helped produce several photography books including *This Is the Day: The March on Washington* (Getty Publications, 2013); a new critical edition of *Made in Germany* with the booklet *Re-Made: Reading Leonard Freed* (Steidl Verlag, 2013); and *Kodachrome Memory: American Pictures 1972–1990* (powerHouse, 2013). He is also the co-editor of a special issue of the journal *Criticism* on HBO's series, *The Wire* (2010).

Tanji Gilliam, PhD/MFA is the director of community revitalization for the Trenton Housing Authority. She is also founder and principal of Oil House Productions, a multimedia design firm. She is the recipient of numerous awards from the Social Science Research Council. She was the Hip Hop and media researcher on the Black Youth Project contributing to successful grant proposals for the Ford Foundation and Robert Wood

Johnson Foundation. In 2010, she received the Art and Change Grant from the Leeway Foundation for her work on domestic violence. Gilliam received her PhD in 2009 in history of culture from the University of Chicago. She also received her MFA in film, video and new media from the School of the Art Institute of Chicago in 2006. In 2002, she graduated cum laude from the University of Pennsylvania where she received her BA in Afro-American studies and English.

Wilfredo Gomez is a cultural critic who has masters degrees in literature from Bucknell University and in Africana studies from the University of Pennsylvania. He is currently pursuing a PhD in the Cultural Foundations of Education program at Syracuse University.

Suheir Hammad is a Palestinian-American poet, author, and political activist. She was born in Amman, Jordan. Her parents were Palestinian refugees who immigrated along with their daughter to Brooklyn, New York City when she was five years old. As an adolescent, Hammad was heavily influenced by Brooklyn's vibrant Hip Hop scene. She had also absorbed the stories her parents and grandparents had told her of life in their hometown of Lydda, before the 1948 Palestinian exodus, and the suffering they endured afterward, first in the Gaza Strip and then in Jordan. Hammad has written several volumes of poetry and/or prose including: *Drops of This Story* (1996), *ZaatarDiva* (2008), *Breaking Poems* (2008), and *Born Palestinian, Born Black & The Gaza Suite* (2010).

Nicholas James is a writer, teacher of English, and dean of middle school at Friends Select School in Philadelphia, Pennsylvania. He is also a founding consultant for Hip Hop Scholars, Inc. Nic has developed curriculum and consulted with schools, educators, and students in an effort to engage the educational potential of Hip Hop and youth culture. Nic will be writing a chapter called "The Treatment of the Educated Negro in *Invisible Man* and *The Chaneysville Incident*" for the upcoming anthology *Only a Grave: The Hip-Hop Generation Revisits The Chaneysville Incident*. He is also currently at work with film director Andre Robert Lee on a book titled *The Prep School Negro: A Look at the Black Experience in Private School* and on a literary memoir titled *Speaking for Me: My Life with Ralph Ellison's Invisible Man*.

John Jennings is an associate professor in the Department of Art at SUNY, Buffalo. His research and teaching focus on the analysis, explication, and disruption of African American stereotypes in popular visual media. His research is concerned with the topics of representation and authenticity, visual culture, visual literacy, social justice, and design pedagogy. He is an accomplished designer, curator, illustrator, cartoonist, and award-winning graphic novelist. His work overlaps into various disciplines including American studies, African American studies, design history, media studies, sociology, women and gender studies, and literature.

Adam Mansbach is the author of the #1 *New York Times* Best Seller *Go the Fuck to Sleep*, which has been translated into forty languages, is forthcoming as a feature film from Fox 2000, and was *Time Magazine*'s 2011 "Thing of the Year." His latest novel, *Rage is Back*, was named a Best Book of 2013 by NPR and the *San Francisco Chronicle* and is currently being adapted for the stage; his previous novels include the California Book Award–winning *The End of the Jews* and the cult classic *Angry Black White Boy*, taught at more than eighty schools. Mansbach is the recipient of a Reed Award, a Webby Award, and a Gold Pollie from the American Association of Political Consultants for his 2012 campaign video "Wake The Fuck Up," starring Samuel L. Jackson. He was the 2009–2011 New Voices Professor of Fiction at Rutgers University, a 2012 Sundance Screenwriting Lab Fellow, and a 2013 Berkeley Repertory Theater Writing Fellow, and will be a 2015 Artist in Residence at Stanford University's Institute for Diversity in the Arts. His work has appeared in *The New Yorker, New York Times Book Review, Esquire, The Believer*, and on National Public Radio's *All Things Considered*.

Imani Perry is an interdisciplinary scholar who studies race and African American culture using the tools provided by various disciplines including: law, literary and cultural studies, music, and the social sciences. She has published numerous articles in the areas of law, cultural studies, and African American studies, many of which are available for download at: imaniperry.typepad.com. She also wrote the notes and introduction to the Barnes and Nobles Classics edition of the *Narrative of Sojourner Truth*. Professor Perry teaches interdisciplinary courses that train students to use multiple methodologies to investigate African American experience and culture. She is the author of two books: *More Beautiful and More Terrible: The Embrace and Transcendence of Racial Inequality in the United States* (New York: New York University Press, 2011) and *Prophets of the Hood: Politics and Poetics in Hip Hop* (Duke University Press, 2004).

James Braxton Peterson is the director of Africana studies and associate professor of English at Lehigh University. His first book, *The Hip Hop Underground and African American Culture* was published on Palgrave Macmillan Press (2014). Peterson is a regular blogger for the Huffington Post, a contributor to TheGrio.com, and he has written opinion pieces for OkayAfrica.com, BET.com, and *The Daily Beast*. He is currently an

MSNBC contributor and has appeared on MSNBC, Al-Jazeera, CNN, HLN, Fox News, and other networks as an expert on race, politics, and popular culture.

Delores B. Phillips currently serves as an assistant professor in the Department of English at Old Dominion University where she teaches and conducts research in postcolonial theory and literature. Her work focuses on the affective connections that people build in culinary writing and uses literature written in Anglophone diasporas to expose the limitations of the strategies that people undertake to address conditions of loss and displacement.

Sean Springer, a doctoral candidate in cultural studies at Stony Brook University, recently completed a dissertation on the history of "filthy" stand-up comedians. As he prepares for his defense, he continues to teach courses in popular culture at Ryerson University.

Scott St. Pierre is visiting assistant professor of English and gender & women's studies at Oklahoma State University where he teaches courses in literature, theory, writing, and masculinity studies. His essays have appeared or are forthcoming in the journals *Criticism, Disability Studies Quarterly, GLQ, The Henry James Review,* and *Textual Practice.* He is currently at work on his first book, entitled *Abnormal Tongues: Style and Sexuality in Modern Literature and Culture.*

Carrie J. Walker is an associate professor of English at Concordia University. She has a PhD in English from the University of Nebraska and a master's degree from Bucknell University. Her research interests include women's literature, Africana literature, and letter writing as a social practice. She is currently working on her book *Epistolary Interventions,* which examines the resurgence of the epistolary novel among women writers across the Black Atlantic and focuses on how authors use this form to intervene in public debates on women's human rights.

Belinda Monique Waller-Peterson is a PhD candidate in English literature at Lehigh University. She is also a licensed registered nurse who specializes in labor and delivery. In her academic work she focuses on women's health issues in literature. She is currently working on her dissertation tentatively titled: "Are You Sure, Sweetheart, That You Want to be Well?": Desire and Wellness in Black Women's Literature.

5